Time Out

Lisbon

timeout.com/Lisbon

Published by Time Out Guides Ltd, a wholly owned subsidiary of Time Out Group Ltd.
Time Out and the Time Out logo are trademarks of Time Out Group Ltd.

Previous editions 1999, 2001, 2004.

10 9 8 7 6 5 4 3 2

This edition first published in Great Britain in 2007 by Ebury Publishing
Ebury Publishing is a division of The Random House Group Ltd,
20 Vauxhall Bridge Road, London SW1V 2SA

Random House Australia Pty Limited 20 Alfred Street, Milsons Point, Sydney, New South Wales 2061, Australia
Random House New Zealand Limited 18 Poland Road, Glenfield, Auckland 10, New Zealand
Random House South Africa (Pty) Limited Isle of Houghton, Corner Boundary Road & Carse O'Gowrie, Houghton 2198, South Africa

Random House UK Limited Reg. No. 954009

Distributed in USA by Publishers Group West
1700 Fourth Street, Berkeley, California 94710

Distributed in Canada by Publishers Group Canada
250A Carlton Street, Toronto, Ontario M5A 2L1

For further distribution details, see www.timeout.com

ISBN 10: 1-84670-009-4
ISBN 13: 9781846700095

A CIP catalogue record for this book is available from the British Library

Printed and bound by Firmengruppe APPL, aprinta druck, Wemding, Germany

Papers used by Ebury Publishing are natural, recyclable products made from wood grown in sustainable forests.

Time Out Guides Limited
Universal House
251 Tottenham Court Road
London W1T 7AB
Tel + 44 (0)20 7813 3000
Fax + 44 (0)20 7813 6001
Email guides@timeout.com
www.timeout.com

Editorial
Editor Alison Roberts
Deputy Editor Edoardo Albert
Listings Editor Alexandre Bezerra
Proofreader Patrick Mulkern
Indexer Anna Norman

Managing Director Peter Fiennes
Financial Director Gareth Garner
Editorial Director Ruth Jarvis
Deputy Series Editor Dominic Earle
Editorial Manager Holly Pick

Design
Art Director Scott Moore
Art Editor Pinelope Kourmouzoglou
Senior Designer Josephine Spencer
Graphic Designer Henry Elphick
Junior Graphic Designer Kei Ishimaru
Digital Imaging Simon Foster
Ad Make-up Jenni Prichard

Picture Desk
Picture Editor Jael Marschner
Deputy Picture Editor Tracey Kerrigan
Picture Researcher Helen McFarland

Advertising
Sales Director Mark Phillips
International Sales Manager Fred Durman
International Sales Executive Simon Davies
International Sales Consultant Ross Canadé
Advertising Assistant Kate Staddon

Marketing
Group Marketing Director John Luck
Marketing Manager Yvonne Poon
Marketing & Publicity Manager, US Rosella Albanese

Production
Group Production Director Mark Lamond
Production Manager Brendan McKeown
Production Coordinator Caroline Bradford

Time Out Group
Chairman Tony Elliott
Financial Director Richard Waterlow
Time Out Magazine Ltd MD David Pepper
Group General Manager/Director Nichola Coulthard
Time Out Communications Ltd MD David Pepper
Time Out International MD Cathy Runciman
Group Art Director John Oakey
Group IT Director Simon Chappell

Contributors
Introduction Alison Roberts **History** Brad Cherry, Alison Roberts **Lisbon Today** Alison Roberts **Architecture** Dave Rimmer, Alison Roberts **Where to Stay** Alexandre Bezerra, Rupert Eden **Sightseeing** Brad Cherry, Alison Roberts (*Walking Lisbon* Peter Wise) **Restaurants** Alison Roberts **Cafés** Alison Roberts **Shops & Services** Alison Roberts, Thomas Tranaeus **Festivals & Events** Alison Roberts **Children** Barry Hatton, Alison Roberts **Film** Martin Dale, Gareth Evans, Alison Roberts **Galleries** Ruth Rosengarten, Alison Roberts **Gay & Lesbian** Simon Gillibrand, John Owens **Music: Classical & Opera** Alison Roberts, Ivan Moody **Music: Fado** Alison Roberts, Thomas Tranaeus **Music: Rock, Roots & Jazz** Alison Roberts, Peter Wise **Nightlife** Alison Roberts, Alexandre Bezerra, Jared Hawkey (*Cherry aid* Dave Rimmer) **Performing Arts** Alison Roberts **Sport & Fitness** Alison Roberts, Sam Le Quesne **Trips Out of Town** Alison Roberts **Directory** Alexandre Bezerra

Maps john@jsgraphics.co.uk.

Photography by Lydia Evans, except: page 12 Museu Nacional de Arte Antigua, Lisbon, Portugal/ The Bridgeman Art Library; page 15 Service Historique de la Marine, Vincennes, France, Lauros/ Giraudon/ The Bridgeman Art Library; pages 16, 21 Bettmann/ Corbis; page 18 Private Collection/ The Stapleton Collection/ The Bridgeman Art Library; page 24 Henri Bureau/ Sygma/ Corbis; pages 110, 117 Andrés Lejona; page 152 AFP/ Getty; page 159 Nextmoov/ DKprod/ Sygma/ Corbis; page 168 British Council Lisbon/ Palacio Nacional de Mafra; page 170 Instituto de Turismo de Portugal; page 196 Jorge Gonçalves; page 197 Instituto de Turismo de Portugal.

The following images were provided by the featured establishments/ artists: pages 162, 196.
The Editor would like to thank Edoardo Albert, Alexandre Bezerra, Mafalda Enes Dias, Bruna Oliveira, Dave Rimmer, Paula Sá Pereira, Helena Santana, João Seixas, Tony Smith and all contributors to previous editions of *Time Out Lisbon*, whose work forms the basis for parts of this book.

Contents

Introduction

Lisbon's situation does more to define its nature than anything else. The city perches on hills and slumbers in valleys on a bend in the river Tagus at a point where it widens out into a vast expanse. While the estuary reflects the southern light onto the gleaming white and pastel surfaces of older buildings, its up-and-down layout provides myriad viewpoints or *miradouros* that make the city at times 'almost narcissistic', in the words of writer Paul Buck. As he notes, visitors should not feel they are doing something especially touristy by whiling away an entire afternoon on one of these esplanades – lisboetas do it too.

If you want to enjoy Lisbon to the full, the best thing to do is to fall into its rhythm. Don't be fooled by all the construction sites and the frenetic rush hour traffic. The bleary eyes you see on their way from the commuter ferry or Metro station belong to the same people who take time out mid-morning to nip out for a coffee with colleagues in one of Lisbon's countless cafés, or make sure to eat a hearty lunch in an unmarked first-floor *tasca* in the Baixa.

The Portuguese work long hours (among the longest in the EU) but at night you can find many of them in bars, some of which don't just close late but have no particular closing hours at all. Lisbon's laidback nightlife – much of it outdoors in summer – is one of its most engaging attractions for visitors. And for many, its beaches are the biggest surprise.

Don't make the mistake, though, of expecting Portugal to be Brazil in Europe, or like another region of Spain. The Portuguese are more reserved than either Brazilians or most Spaniards: this is not a Latin American country nor even a Mediterranean one – despite centuries of influences from that region that go back to Phoenician times. A glance at the atlas gives the clue: Portugal is an Atlantic country, its southern warmth tempered and dampened by ocean winds.

And, unless you're Spanish yourself, tackle locals with English or French or even a few words of Portuguese, if you can manage them – but not Castillian. The Portuguese are proud of having the longest established (some 800 years) national border in the world, and it is from Spain that they are divided.

The two nations have much in common, of course, but the Portuguese are extremely proud of their heritage and language, and the unique role their country played in world history – effectively launching the process that we today call globalisation. That has now rebounded on Portugal with a vengeance, of course, bringing McDonald's and Zara, though not Starbucks – the native café culture would be hard to uproot.

Some lament and some embrace such changes. Others just carry on as normal. The Church remains a symbol of continuity: approximately 92 per cent of the population (the highest in western Europe) describe themselves as Catholic and while only about one third attend mass regularly you'll find downtown churches bustling with people dropping in to light a candle or say a prayer. Many old widows still wear black and whole families will visit their loved ones' graves on All Saint's Day. People of all ages listen to fado music, which is currently thriving. And all Lisbon turns out for June's Festas Populares. You could do a lot worse than join them.

ABOUT TIME OUT CITY GUIDES

This is the fourth edition of *Time Out Lisbon*, one of an expanding series of Time Out guides produced by the people behind the successful listings magazines in London, New York and Chicago. Our guides are all written by resident experts who have striven to provide you with all the most up-to-date information you'll need to explore the city or read up on its background, whether you're a local or a first-time visitor.

THE LIE OF THE LAND

We have divided Lisbon by area, covering the places that are likely to be of most interest to visitors. Our Sightseeing chapters, which begin on page 59, cover central Lisbon, the areas east and west of Baixa, the city's waterfront including Belém, São Bento and beyond, northern Lisbon and south of the river Tagus. Throughout the guide we also give as part of the address the area of Lisbon in which that particular establishment is to be found. But bear in mind that some shops, restaurants, theatres, bars, clubs or cafés may lie outside the specific zones that are covered in the sightseeing chapters. For each entry that is covered by our maps, which begin on page 241, we have given a map reference indicating the page and square on which the address will be found.

ESSENTIAL INFORMATION

For all the practical information you might need for visiting the area – including visa and customs information, details of local transport, a listing of emergency numbers, information on local weather, a guide to Portuguese vocabulary and just what you need to do to get your mobile to work – turn to the Directory at the back of this guide. It begins on page 219.

THE LOWDOWN ON THE LISTINGS

We have tried to make this book as easy to use as possible. Addresses, phone numbers, bus information, opening times and admission prices are all included in the listings. However, businesses can change their arrangements at any time. Before you go out of your way, we'd strongly advise you to phone ahead to check opening times and other particulars. While every effort and care has been made to ensure the accuracy of the information contained in this guide, the publishers cannot accept responsibility for any errors it may contain.

PRICES AND PAYMENT

We have noted where venues such as shops, hotels, restaurants and theatres accept the following credit cards: American Express (AmEx), Diners Club (DC), Discover (Disc), MasterCard (MC) and Visa (V). Many will also accept travellers' cheques, and/or other cards such as Carte Blanche.

The prices we've listed in this guide should be treated as guidelines, not gospel. If prices vary wildly from those we've quoted, ask whether there's a good reason. If not, go elsewhere. Then please let us know. We aim to give the best and most up-to-date advice, so we want to know if you've been badly treated or overcharged.

TELEPHONE NUMBERS

Lisbon numbers all start with 21, but this forms part of the number so you do need to dial it. We've included it throughout the guide. For more on telephones and codes, *see p232*.

MAPS

The map section at the back of this book includes the area around Lisbon, a map of Greater Lisbon, street maps and a larger scale representation of the centre of the city. The maps start on page 241, and they now also pinpoint the specific locations of hotels (❶), restaurants (❶) and cafés (❶).

LET US KNOW WHAT YOU THINK

We hope you enjoy *Time Out Lisbon*, and we'd like to know what you think of it. We welcome tips for places that you consider we should include in future editions and take note of your criticism of our choices. You can email us at guides@timeout.com.

Advertisers

We would like to stress that no establishment has been included in this guide because it has advertised in any of our publications and no payment of any kind has influenced any review. The opinions given in this book are those of Time Out writers and entirely independent.

There is an online version of this book, along with guides to over 100 international cities, at **www.timeout.com**.

Time Out
Miami
Milan
Mumbai & Goa
Naples
New Orleans
New York
Paris
Patagonia
Prague
Rome
San Francisco
Seville & Andalucía
Shanghai
Singapore
South of France
Stockholm
Sydney
Tokyo 東京
Turin
Venice
Vienna
Washington, DC
Amsterdam
Athens
Bangkok
Barcelona
Beijing
Boston
Brussels
Budapest
Buenos Aires
California
Cape Town
Chicago
Copenhagen
Croatia
Dublin
Edinburgh
Florence
Havana
Hong Kong
Istanbul
Las Vegas
Lisbon
London
Madrid
Mallorca
Marrakech
Miami
Milan
Mumbai & Goa
Naples
New Orleans
New York
Patagonia
Prague
Rio de Janeiro
Rome
San Francisco
Seville & Andalucía
Shanghai
Singapore
South of France
Sydney
Tokyo 東京
Toronto
Turin
Venice
Vienna
Washington, DC
Amsterdam
Athens
Barcelona
Beijing
Berlin
Boston
Brussels
Budapest
Buenos Aires
California
Cape Town
Copenhagen
Croatia
Dubai
Dublin
Edinburgh
Florence
Havana
Hong Kong
Istanbul

PORTUGAL BIKE
CYCLING HOLIDAYS IN PORTUGAL
HYBRID TOURS
MTB TOURS
BEGINNER TOURS
SENIOR TOURS
VISIT
WWW.PORTUGALBIKE.COM

CRUZEIROS NO TEJO
LISBOA VISTA DO RIO
1 de Abril a 31 de Outubro
Partida diária do Terreiro do Paço · 15h00
LISBON SEEN FROM THE RIVER
From April 1st to October 31st
Daily departure from Terreiro do Paço · 3 p.m.
www.transtejo.pt

In Context

Features

Praça do Comércio. *See p62.*

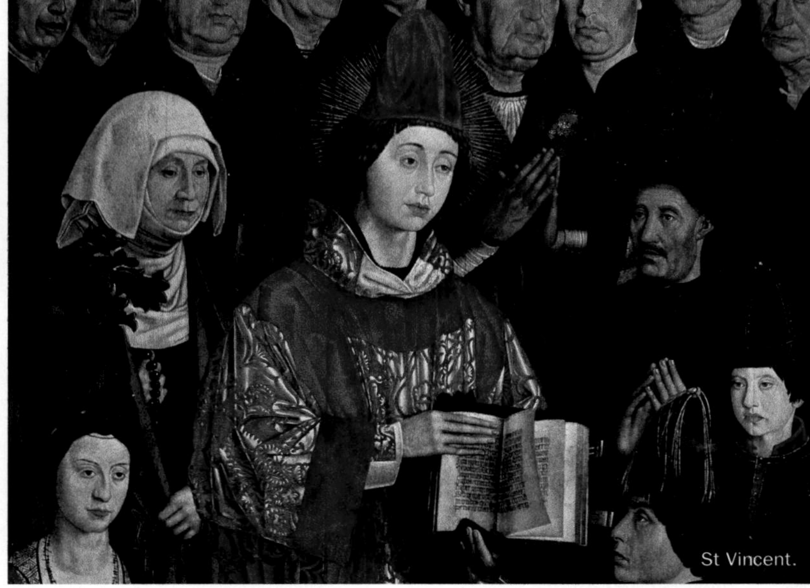
St Vincent.

History

From Phoenician outpost to the European mainstream.

Before reaching Lisbon, the River Tagus broadens into one of the world's largest natural harbours, before narrowing again and emptying into the Atlantic. On its northern bank freshwater streams flow in from surrounding hills. The south bank is flatter, with inlets famed for millennia for rich oyster beds and fisheries; salt pans still exist around Alcochete and Montijo. Lisbon grew up on the north bank's most prominent hill, near where the current runs fastest and deepest. It owes its eminence partly to the river, the longest in the Iberian peninsula, whose basin stretches beyond Madrid.

One tradition has it that Ulysses founded the city and that its name is a corruption of his, but more credible is the story that Phoenician mariners who ventured this far dubbed the place 'Alis Ubbo' – 'peaceful harbour' – which mutated to Olisipo, then Lisbon. In any case, the region has been populated for millennia. Nomadic hunting societies left their mark, while later agricultural populations settled on small tributaries of the Tagus, and the estuary harboured primitive shell-gathering cultures. The area was a crossroads of late Bronze Age trade, and from the eighth to the sixth centuries BC the Phoenicians extended their trade up from Cádiz to the Tagus estuary, where they established an entrepôt for tin coming from Cornwall. Lisbon was a Mediterranean port many centuries before it became the first Atlantic one.

ROMAN PROVINCE

The Roman presence in Iberia dates to the Second Punic War in the late third century BC, which ended half a century of Carthaginian domination. Putting down restive locals proved more difficult, and it took two centuries to establish the Pax Romana all the way across the peninsula. One local chieftain – Viriatus – gained renown as a resistance leader between 147 and 139 BC, harrying Roman legions from his base in the Serra da Estrela. His Lusitani tribe gave its name to the Roman province of Lusitania, which encompassed most of present-day Portugal. (The prefix 'Luso' is still used to mean 'Portuguese'.)

Lisbon fell in 138 BC and was occupied by the governor Decimus Junius Brutus. He fortified the emergent city, though it's not clear where he built his walls. Lisbon became a district capital under the provincial capital Mérida in what is now Spain. By 30 BC the city was renamed Felicitas Julia Olisipo after Julius Caesar, then a peninsula commander. The city spread down from today's Castelo de São Jorge (*see p72*) to the Tagus and westwards towards what is now Rossio – then a hippodrome. The main exports via its port were the fish paste known as garum, salt and local horses; Pliny the Elder described mares from the Tagus as 'fine, docile and impregnated by the west wind, (which) brought forth offspring of surprising fleetness'.

The principal Roman remains in Lisbon are the Teatro Romano (*see p71*), an amphitheatre built under Emperor Augustus that is only part-excavated. The Forum was probably near an arch that stood by today's Largo da Madalena. In the middle of Rua da Conceição is the entrance to vaulted cellars – probably the foundations of a waterfront temple or similar building, not fish-conserving tanks as once thought.

For four centuries Olisipo prospered, ruling a district that extended northwards towards present-day Torres Vedras and Alenquer. Rich farmland was dotted with estates known as *villae*; remains have been found near the airport and around Cascais. Waterfront activity centred on salting fish and maritime commerce.

Christianity was established by the middle of the fourth century. There is a persistent legend of three Christians – Verissimus, Maximus and Julia – martyred during the persecution by Emperor Diocletian on a river beach later named Santos. (Portugal's first king much later was to address his prayers to them before conquering Lisbon.) The city's first bishop was later canonised as St Gens.

Roman rule in Iberia crashed in 409 when hordes of Suevi, Alans and Vandals swept over the Pyrenees. The Suevi swung north; one group of Vandals headed up to Galicia and the other south, and the Alans settled between the Douro and the Tagus. Lisbon fell to this Iranian people who left few traces. In 418 the Romans called in the Visigoths to kick out the other tribes. The Alans joined with the Vandals in the south (in Vandalusia, later Andalucía), before all retreated to North Africa. The Visigoths, based in Toledo, soon dominated the peninsula, taking over Olisipo in 469.

MOORISH INVASION

In 711 Muslim armies hit southern Spain and within five years conquered most of the peninsula, with Lisbon – now much reduced in size after three centuries of sacking and pillaging – falling in 714. Iberian Christendom regrouped in northern Spain and began the Reconquista. By the mid 800s northern Portugal was Christian again. The area around Oporto was called Portucale, the 'gateway to Cale'.

Although forays were made as far as the Tagus, Lisbon remained in Muslim hands for three centuries. Moorish traveller Al-Idrisi wrote of the city then called al-Ushbuna: 'This lovely city is defended by a ring of walls and a powerful castle'. The castle was built over the earlier Roman fortification where the Castelo now stands. The Moorish siege walls – Cerca Moura – enclosed about 15 hectares (37 acres), from the Castelo to the present-day Portas do Sol, where one tower houses the Cerca Moura café (*see p126*). From there the line can be traced through Alfama, or over to Largo da Madalena where the Roman arch was now the city gate.

Much of the city stood outside the walls, including most of Alfama. Its name (Al-Hama, 'springs') refers to the abundance of water – later medieval fountains on Largo do Chafariz de Dentro and Chafariz d'el Rei are still extant.

Moorish Lisbon at its ninth-century height was a major city of Al-Andalus, with 30,000 residents. Immigrants, from Yemenis to newly converted Moroccan Berbers, flooded in and Arabic predominated. Christians (known as *moçárabes*) and Jews could practise their religions, within the strict limits prescribed by their rulers.

BIRTH OF A NATION

In 1128 Afonso Henriques wrested control of Portucale from his mother Teresa after the death of his father, Henrique. In 1139 he trounced the Moors at Ourique and a year later proclaimed himself king of Portugal. The pope approved the new nation's foundation in 1179 (in exchange for 1,000 gold coins).

Aided by northern European crusaders, in 1147 Afonso Henriques attacked Lisbon. On St Crispin's Day, 25 October, a soldier called Martim Moniz led the invading force into the city, where they ran amok.

Later Afonso Henriques heard of a shrine in the Algarve where relics of St Vincent were guarded by ravens. An expedition of *moçarabes* was sent to retrieve the remains. According to myth, a boat bearing the corpse, circled by ravens, reached Lisbon in September 1173. The image of a boat and ravens subsequently became the city's symbol.

CAPITAL CITY

The last Moorish bastions in the Algarve fell in 1249 and Lisbon established itself as the capital, replacing Coimbra. The city huddled within the old walls, with the royal palace in the castle. The Sé cathedral (*see p70*) was built soon after the reconquest. Other houses of worship included the primitive chapels of Santos and St Gens (now Senhora do Monte). Moors and Jews could stay on outside the walls – in Mouraria, in the Baixa and in Judiarias in Alfama.

For centuries a provincial outpost, Lisbon was now a political and business centre. Portuguese ships plied routes as far as the Baltic, and south into the Mediterranean.

Medieval Portugal reached its height under poet-king Dom Dinis (1279-1325). He founded the University of Lisbon in 1290 (later moved to Coimbra), planted coastal pine forests to prevent erosion, and built castles to keep out Castilians and Moors. The national borders formalised in the 1297 Treaty of Alcanices with Castile are almost unchanged today.

By the late 1400s Lisbon's population was back above 14,000 and the walls expanded to enclose 60 hectares (148 acres). Commerce had moved downhill to the Baixa, with the diagonal Rua Nova (now disappeared) the main street and Rossio a busy open-air marketplace.

Lisbon suffered several earthquakes during this period. One, in 1321, destroyed part of the Sé. Another, in 1337, took place on Christmas Day. Yet another, in 1344, again damaged the Sé, while a tremor in 1356 set church bells ringing. And the Black Death struck in 1348 and 1349.

Despite quakes, plague and persistent grain shortages, Lisbon outgrew its walls once more, creeping up hills north and west of Rossio. When a Castilian raiding party laid waste to much of extramural Lisbon in 1373, Dom Fernando I had new walls built. The Cerca Fernandina was a little over five kilometres (three miles) long with 77 towers and 38 gates and circled Rossio, the Baixa and part of today's Chiado, enclosing 50,000 residents.

The Portas de Santa Catarina stood where two churches now face each other in Largo do Chiado. There are remnants of these walls downhill, partially hidden by new buildings.

When Fernando died in 1383, war broke out between his widow Leonor Teles and João, master of the Aviz Military Order. Leonor sought support in Castile. When the two sides

Wish you were here, wish I were there

Central to the Portuguese sensibility is a beautifully evocative word whose meaning can't really be captured in English. To feel *saudade* for a place, person or just about anything no longer in reach is to suffer an intense yearning or nostalgia that weighs heavily on the heart.

Fado, that melancholy national art, is replete with references to the *saudades* endured by this nation of hardy seafarers and emigrants. It shines a light into the soul of a nation where the sentimental fatalism of an Atlantic temperament seems to be in constant conflict with a sunnier Mediterranean side.

So what is it all about? *Saudade* is what villagers feel when their menfolk have been long at sea. Or perhaps it better describes the yearning of those men for their hearths, the comforting arms of their women and a stiff fish stew. *Saudade* is what the emigrant feels for his home town or city as decades of separation slip by.

Since the time voyagers first rounded the Cape of Good Hope, millions of Portuguese have resettled, seeking riches and a better life. Until recently economic hardship at home meant that a move to northern Europe or across the Atlantic was the clearest path to a better life, and the currency sent back by emigrants is still a tangible element of the balance of payments. Again, women did not always accompany their men abroad, and some spent most of their lives seeing little of loved ones.

But the men usually did come back, and that was because they were in the grip of *saudade*. Like the Spanish, many Portuguese believe their village, town or city is the most blessed patch of earth on the planet, and none of the finery of Paris or the nightlife of London would deter them from saving their cash for the day when they will settle in a fine house in the old town.

But all this is changing. You are unlikely these days to find many black-clad fishwives sending a heart-rending fado out across the waves. Portugal recently became a net recipient of immigrants for the first time, and young lisboetas are not so keen to leave their city. But there are still several million Portuguese living abroad, and *saudade* and the sea are still defining features of the national character.

Take a trip along the coast and, whatever the weather, you'll notice people of all ages parked up and simply gazing in silence at the waves. Some Portuguese gene seems to compel them to do this, and *saudade* is its name.

In medieval times Portuguese ships plied routes as far afield as the Baltic.

met in 1385 at Aljubarrota, a vastly outnumbered Portuguese force, assisted by English archers, trounced the invaders, cementing Portuguese independence.

João I thus founded Portugal's second ruling house, the Avis dynasty. In gratitude he ordered the construction of the magnificent monastery of Batalha. As a thank you to the archers, he signed the Treaty of Windsor, an alliance valid today (*see p93* **The Brit pack**).

THE DISCOVERIES

Portugal's first maritime foray was the 1415 conquest of Ceuta in North Africa. Key to organising and financing this assault was João I's wife, English princess Philippa of Lancaster. Among the participants was João's son, Henriques. Known as Infante Dom Henriques or Prince Henry the Navigator (**photo** *p16*), Henriques soon began training mariners. In 1415 and 1416 expeditions sailed to the Canary Islands; next Madeira was discovered around 1419; the Azores in the 1430s. Ships were dispatched to explore the African coast. The psychological barrier of Cape Bojador – people thought they'd fall off the edge of the world – was overcome and charted by Gil Eanes in 1434.

What prompted this sudden burst of activity? Portugal's identity was forged in battle, but it could not expand on land. So it went to sea, driven by greed, adventure and religious fervour – Prince Henry was a master of the Order of Christ, successor to the Knights Templar and a sworn enemy of Islam. After Ceuta, Portugal took Alcacer-Ceguer in 1458, and Arzila and Tangier in 1471.

Madeira and the Azores were by now settled and a brisk trade grew up with these additions to the 'Kingdom of Portugal, the Algarve and the Ocean Seas and Beyond in Africa'. Henry died in 1460, but by the mid 1470s Portuguese squadrons were active in the Gulf of Guinea and had crossed the equator.

'The slaves' corpses were cast into pits.'

Trade with Asia was controlled by Venice, Genoa and Cairo; the only way to reach Asia while avoiding these competitors was to sail around Africa. Later royals took up this challenge. Dom João II was nicknamed the Perfect Prince for his Machiavellian talents –

he had his rival the Duke of Braganza beheaded in Évora and personally stabbed to death his brother-in-law, the Duke of Viseu. Sailing under his orders, navigator Diogo Cão reached the Zaire river in 1482 and later explored the coast to Angola. Meanwhile, Bartholomew Dias rounded the Cape of Good Hope in 1488 and reported that Africa was circumnavigable.

In 1497 Vasco da Gama set out from Restelo (now Belém) with three caravels and a supply ship. Rounding the Cape in November, he sailed up the East African coast and across to India, putting in at Calicut on 20 May 1498. Portugal could now dominate Indian Ocean trade.

Its only rival was Spain. The 1479 Treaty of Alcaçovas was the two countries' first attempt to carve up the world. The 1494 Treaty of Tordesillas divided the world along a line 370 leagues west of Cape Verde. Portugal could take anything to the east (with the exception of the Canary Islands, already ruled by Spain). This division puts much of present-day Brazil within the Portuguese sphere. There is evidence the Portuguese knew of the South American landmass well before Pedro Álvares Cabral 'discovered' it in 1500.

FORTUNATE SON

Dom Manuel I was dubbed 'the Fortunate' because he came to the throne in 1495, just before Portugal won the India lottery jackpot, which he greedily controlled through royal monopolies. After Vasco da Gama returned with his cargo of spices, the city was overwhelmed by the 'vapours of India', an irresistible force that drew young and old overseas. Many did not return, victims of shipwreck, piracy or disease.

Lisbon's population was now 40,000; it grew west along the river as convents and palaces sprang up. Traders, moneychangers and booksellers jostled along the Rua Nova. The opulence in Europe's richest city was unrivalled – as was its depravity, as caricatured by Gil Vicente in his play *Auto da Índia*, depicting a wife at play while her husband travelled.

Dom Manuel spent part of his new-found fortune on two important monuments: the Torre de Belém (*see p88*) to guard the harbour entrance, and the Mosteiro dos Jerónimos (*see p86*) to thank God for the unexpected wealth. Both are masterpieces of the Portuguese late Gothic style known as Manueline, replete with oriental and maritime motifs.

In 1492 Ferdinand and Isabel of Spain had expelled all non-Christians after conquering Moorish Granada. Portugal at first welcomed fugitive Jews, but in 1496 expelled all Moors and Jews who refused baptism. Those who stayed were to form an underclass of 'New Christians'. In 1506 thousands were massacred in a riot that lasted for days. Not surprisingly, after this, most of the Jews fled to North Africa and northern Europe.

Prince Henry the Navigator. *See p15.*

Lisbon's population grew fitfully, to 72,000 in 1527 – another plague year. The city had its glories – Renaissance man Damião de Gois described seven of its buildings as wonders of the world, among them the Palácio de Estaus and Hospital de Todos-os-Santos on Rossio. None survived the 1755 earthquake. But other travellers complained of the stench of slaves' corpses cast into pits such as the Poço dos Negros, and crime was rampant.

RULING THE WAVES

The Indian Ocean, for centuries traversed by Roman, Arab, Indian and Chinese merchants, was surrounded by prosperous cities and states where standards of living and literacy were often higher than in Europe. The Portuguese sailed in, armed with bronze cannons that were previously unknown in the region.

In 1502 Vasco da Gama returned to Calicut in response to the massacre of Portuguese expatriates by local Hindus, a slaughter incited by Muslims. He took terrible revenge. Da Gama bombarded the city for three days, cutting off the ears, noses and hands of prisoners before burning them alive. Elsewhere he sank a ship of 700 Muslim pilgrims and sent longboats to spear survivors. Other prisoners were rigged up and used for crossbow practice.

In 1510 Viceroy Afonso de Albuquerque conquered Goa, which became the sumptuous seat of the 'pepper empire'. The taking of Malacca in 1511 opened the way to the Far East: caravels soon reached the Spice Islands (Moluccas) and Timor, and by 1513 were trading with China. In 1542 caravels reached Japan and in 1557 Portugal won the right to administer Macao on the southern coast of China. The poet Luís Vaz de Camões spent time here as well as in Africa, Goa and the East Indies during 17 years of travel. At one point he almost lost his epic poem, *The Lusiads*, in a shipwreck, but made it ashore with the poem and later completed it. Published in 1572, it chronicles Vasco da Gama's first voyage to India. Inspired by the origins of empire, Camões saw it come to an end. Young, heirless Dom Sebastião I led a disastrous expedition to Morocco in 1578 where he perished along with much of Portugal's nobility. In 1582 Philip II of Spain snatched the Portuguese crown.

THE SPANISH MOVE IN

The Habsburg Philip backed his claim to the throne by landing an army outside Lisbon and routing the Portuguese in the Alcântara district. As Philip I, he ruled from 1581 to 1598. After modernising the bureaucracy along Spanish lines, he cast his eyes further afield. In 1588 he assembled a fleet of 130 ships and 27,000 men in Lisbon and sent it to attack England. The invincible Armada lost to both the elements and the English, scuttling Spain's ambitions of global domination. In 1590 construction of the imposing Igreja de São Vicente de Fora (*see p75*) started, under Juan de Herrera of Escorial fame.

The Inquisition, which was an agent of the state rather than the church, had been in Lisbon since 1537, and in 1570 it took over the Estaus Palace on Rossio, where the Teatro Nacional Dona Maria II is now. The inquisitors requested more funds to expand overcrowded dungeons and organised the notorious autos-da-fé, which began with processions from the Igreja de São Domingos (*see p68*) and ended with the condemned being burned at the stake (*see p69* **Burning issues**).

The Portuguese chafed under Spanish rule – especially when Philip IV (III of Portugal) began appointing Spanish nobles to positions reserved for locals and ignoring the welfare of Portuguese overseas possessions. On 1 December 1640 conspirators overpowered the authorities in Lisbon and proclaimed the Duke of Braganza Dom João IV of Portugal. After a war of secession, Spain in 1668 recognised Portugal's independence and possessions, except Ceuta, Ceylon and Malacca. To bolster its position, Portugal in 1661 matched Catherine of Braganza with England's King Charles II (*see p93* **The Brit pack**); her dowry included the ports of Bombay and Tangier.

WEALTH AND RECONSTRUCTION

Portugal's new-found confidence was soon displayed in the reconstruction of the Igreja do Loreto in Chiado – the church of the Italian community, finished in 1663 – and a start to the building of the Panteão Nacional de Santa Engrácia (*see p75*). Then, in 1699, gold was discovered in Brazil. The flagship of the ensuing construction boom was the massive monastery-palace started by Dom João V in 1717 at Mafra (*see p217*).

Elsewhere, artisans created gilded baroque masterpieces behind the altars of the churches of Madre de Deus (at the Museu Nacional do Azulejo, *see p97*), Santa Catarina and São Roque (*see p77*), and ornate private carriages, some on display at the Museu dos Coches (*see p87*). The 1730s also saw construction of the indestructible Aqueduto das Águas Livres (*see p91*). But Lisbon was still mostly a medieval city of narrow lanes. The Bairro Alto became an entertainment centre, as popular theatres staged farces and comedies for plebeians. By 1755 the population was 190,000.

'The dust had barely settled when Pombal decreed: "Bury the dead, feed the living".'

On 1 November 1755 Lisbon was struck by a devastating earthquake that lasted six minutes and brought buildings crashing down. It was All Saints' Day, so the churches were packed, while at home candles had been lit in memory of the dead. Panic-stricken citizens racing down to the river were met by a tidal wave that engulfed the Baixa, and a dry north-east wind fanned fires for days. Dom José I's chief minister, Sebastião José de Carvalho e Melo, threw himself into recovery work.

Seen by some as an enlightened despot, by others as high-handed and dictatorial, he is known today as the Marquês de Pombal, a title awarded in 1769. The dust had barely settled when Pombal decreed: 'Bury the dead, feed the living'. Teams searched the rubble for bodies, while taxes on food were dropped and grain requisitioned: no one starved and no major epidemics followed a disaster that had killed some 15,000.

In the Baixa, hit by the triple scourge of earthquake, tidal wave and fire, Pombal opted to build a new city. The plan, drawn up by Eugénio dos Santos and Hungarian-born Carlos Mardel, was based on the grid scheme of a military encampment, the medieval maze overlain by straight roads earmarked for distinct trades, with right-angled corners.

Rubble was used as landfill to prevent flooding. Rossio was neatened into a rectangle, and the wide Rua Augusta cut down to the riverside Terreiro do Paço, renamed Praça do Comércio, where Lisbon's rebirth was celebrated 20 years on. The equestrian statue of Dom José I was unveiled in an incomplete square, wooden façades filling in the gaps.

Pombal's authoritarianism brought results but earned him enemies. He cowed the aristocracy after executing nobles accused of plotting to kill the king in 1758. The following year he expelled the Jesuits. He ended discrimination against New Christians and granted Brazil's Indians freedom from slavery.

José I was succeeded in 1777 by his daughter, Dona Maria I. She dismissed Pombal and cultivated links with France, a policy that had to be reversed after the 1789 revolution there. Her fragile health degenerated into insanity in 1791 and the prince regent, later Dom João VI, took over. She left one important legacy, the Basílica da Estrela (*see p91*), built between 1779 and 1789, while her consort, Pedro, oversaw building of the Palácio de Queluz (*see p216*), often called the Portuguese Versailles.

In Lisbon, the superintendent of police – or *intendente* – Diogo Inácio de Pina Manique, held sway from 1780. A social reformer, he was instrumental in founding the Casa Pia in 1780, which continues to this day doing good work for orphans and the poor. He also introduced Lisbon's first widespread street lamp-lighting scheme, oversaw the paving of streets, the laying of sewers, rubbish collection and subjected prostitutes to regular health inspections. At the other end of the social scale, he oversaw the construction of the Teatro Nacional de São Carlos (*see p169*) in 1793, and improved the city with 40,000 trees in 1799. Meanwhile the population continued to grow: in 1801 it was near 170,000.

PENINSULAR WARS

In 1801 France and Spain joined forces and invaded. After a brief campaign Portugal was forced into submission, ceding to Spain the town of Olivenza near Badajoz – still a bone of contention. During Napoleon's rise, Portugal tried quietly to maintain trade with England. But in 1806 he decreed a continental embargo. Portugal faced an unhappy choice: accede and see Britain take over its overseas possessions; or refuse and be invaded. Napoleon gave the Portuguese until September 1807 to declare war on England. Portugal stalled, France invaded,

British forces helped out the Portuguese during the **Peninsular Wars**.

Family trees

Most visitors to Portugal will soon notice, if they didn't know already, that it is an overwhelmingly Catholic country. Scratch under the surface, though, and you'll find a more complex story. Recent years have seen attempts to reclaim the country's Jewish and Islamic heritage. In some circles, it is not only acceptable but fashionable to have non-Catholic antecedents: Dom Duarte of Bragança, who claims Portugal's virtual throne, said in one interview that he is descended from both Muhammad and David. He may not be alone: Jews made up a large proportion of Portugal's population for centuries, and most of the country was ruled by Muslims.

Lisbon's first Jews probably came with the Phoenicians, and the community grew steadily in Roman times. It flourished under Islamic rule, as merchants and financiers settled in a city that re-emerged as a major entrepôt, trading everything from horses to spices, medicinal plants and fish. After the Christian reconquest in 1147, Jewish traders' links with their co-religionists in the Islamic world made them invaluable. Trade between Lisbon and towns from Andalusia to Constantinople was resumed, and new links forged with European ports that had been beyond the reach of Muslims. The Jewish community soon accounted for about one tenth of residents, and expanded hugely when the Spanish expelled all Jews in 1492. It also punched well above its weight thanks to its members' learning and business acumen.

Many Muslims had stuck around after the reconquest, too. In Lisbon, where the Sé Cathedral (*see p70*) was built on the site of the great, seven-domed mosque, they had to live beyond the walls in Mouraria, where a new mosque was founded in what is now Rua do Capelão. It was in a tavern here centuries later that the singer known as A Severa brought fado – in which many hear Moorish elements – to prominence (*see p171*).

For Oporto residents, southerners in general and lisboetas in particular are *mouros*. (It's not meant as a compliment.) Even the affectionate nickname for Lisbon natives, *alfacinhas* – little lettuces – comes from the Moorish practice of growing, on irrigated land, vegetables unknown up north. The term *saloio*, meaning bumpkin, derives from *salaio*, a tax paid by the Muslims who cultivated these plots.

Portugal's Jewish heritage is more geographically dispersed. The surnames taken by Jews forced to convert in 1496 – usually from animals or trees such as Pereira (pear tree) – are now among the most common. But it was in remote northeastern villages that crypto-Judaism – observance in secret to evade the Inquisition – held out. Crypto-Jews in the town of Belmonte only came fully out of the closet some 15 years after the 1974 Revolution, when they formed an Orthodox community; they now worship in a swanky foreign-funded synagogue. In 2005 a Jewish Museum was inaugurated in Belmonte by Portuguese and Israeli officials.

It is in the south – the Algarve and rural Alentejo, where communism vies with Christianity as the faith of choice – that Moorish traces are most evident, in everything from vernacular architecture to desserts. The town of Mértola, where archaeologists have made fascinating finds in what was once a major river port, now has an Islamic Museum and a biennial Islamic Festival. Among participants are visitors from Chefchaoun, the Moroccan town with which Mértola is twinned. It's an apt choice as it was founded by 'Moors' who fled Iberia after the Christian reconquest.

and the royal family fled to Brazil, staying for 14 years. Many followed their example: 11,000 passports were issued in short order.

The French invaded three times. In 1808 a British force led by General Arthur Wellesley (better known as the Duke of Wellington) sent them packing after the battles of Roliça and Vimeiro. The next year the French returned under Marshal Soult, but were ejected by Portuguese and British forces. In summer 1810 Marshal Masséna arrived, and after initial setbacks his forces marched on Lisbon. Wellington stopped them with fortifications (the Torres Vedras Lines) stretching north of Lisbon from the Tagus to the sea. The French fled. By 1814 they were back in Toulouse.

The Peninsular Wars left Portugal a wreck. Lisbon's population dipped to 150,000, regaining its turn-of-the-century peak only in 1860. Under the post-war British regency (read, occupation) of Marshal Beresford, unrest was never far from the surface (*see p93* **The Brit**

pack). New ideas took root and words such as 'liberal' and 'constitution' entered the dissident vocabulary. In 1820 Beresford went to Brazil to coax home Dom João VI, who was loath to trade the comforts of Rio for devastated Portugal.

In Beresford's absence, the regency was overthrown and liberal rule installed. Elections were held and the Cortes, or parliament, approved a constitution in March 1821.

Now João VI returned and swore allegiance to the new constitution. Crown Prince Pedro stayed in Brazil. In 1822, when the Cortes threatened to strip Brazil of its status as a kingdom, it declared itself independent, and Portugal lost her largest source of overseas income. An ensuing constitutional conflict split the royals. The Absolutists were led by Prince Miguel. The Liberals championed his brother Pedro, whom they proclaimed Dom Pedro IV when João VI died in 1826. Pedro, content as Emperor of Brazil, abdicated the Portuguese throne in favour of his seven-year-old daughter. When she was crowned Dona Maria II in 1828, Miguel declared himself king. So Pedro abdicated the Brazilian throne and returned to head a Liberal counter-revolt.

The war lasted from 1832 – with Lisbon captured by a Liberal army on 24 July 1833 – to 1834, when Miguel was forced into exile. Pedro died months after taking over as regent for the now 13-year-old Maria II, but oversaw the 1834 abolition of religious orders. Monks and nuns were turned out from their cloisters, which were annexed by public and private institutions. Parliament set up in the Mosteiro de São Bento, renamed the Palácio da Assembléia da República (*see p90*), while the Mosteiro da Graça and others became barracks. In 1836 Maria II married Ferdinand of Saxe-Coburg-Gotha, responsible for the fantasy Palácio da Pena on a hilltop at Sintra (*see p214*).

ROMANTICISM AND REFORM

In Lisbon, the era saw fado music and military uprisings. Maria Severa Onofriana, the prostitute known as 'A Severa', kept open house in Mouraria, her soprano voice attracting lovers who included the bullfighting Count of Vimioso. She died in 1846, at the age of 26.

Meanwhile there was a series of revolts, the bloodiest on 13 March 1838, when government troops fought rebellious national guardsmen in Rossio. Rossio itself underwent a major facelift in the following years. Black and white cobblestones were laid in 1840 and, in 1846, the new Teatro Nacional (*see p194*) was inaugurated by Dona Maria II. The driving force behind it was Romantic author Almeida Garrett, one of many intellectual former exiles.

The city they returned to was not a healthy one. In 1833 cholera killed 13,000; in 1856 it killed 3,000. The 1857 yellow fever epidemic killed 6,000. By mid century, political stability made possible a major building programme. The grand arch on Praça do Comércio was completed in 1873. Railways had arrived in the 1850s; by the 1860s trains steamed from Santa Apolónia station to Oporto and Madrid, and by the 1890s from neo-Manueline Rossio station towards Sintra. Prosperity fuelled public entertainment: the Coliseu dos Recreios opened in 1890, followed by the Campo Pequeno bullring in 1892.

During Pombaline reconstruction a green space had been opened north-west of Rossio. The Passeio Público, as it was called, was not a hit at first – the idea of both sexes strolling in a public garden grated with contemporary mores. In the 1830s it was remodelled as a Romantic garden and became popular with the emergent bourgeoisie. In the 1880s it was extended, becoming the tree-lined Avenida da Liberdade. At its southern end, at Praça dos Restauradores, a monument was raised to the 1640 restoration. The park laid out to the north was named after Britain's King Edward VII.

Other urban projects of the late monarchy period included the introduction of the first funiculars in 1884, using the water gravity system – a tram filled a tank of water at the top of the hill, and that weight on the downhill run would provide enough counterweight to pull up another car from the bottom. Electrification was begun in 1901, and the city was soon filled with electric trams.

THE NEW REPUBLIC

In the 1870s a group known as the Cenáculo dominated literary Lisbon. Among its number were storyteller Teófilo Braga, later President of the Republic; historian Oliveira Martins, whose pan-Iberian vision was to shape future generations; and Eça de Queiroz, whose novels *The Maias* and *Cousin Bazílio* paint an unrivalled vision of Lisbon life. Politically, intellectuals favoured republicanism, especially after the monarchy gave in to the 1890 British ultimatum that demanded Portugal withdraw from much of south-central Africa.

In 1905 Dom Carlos I appointed João Franco as chief minister. He stepped up censorship and persecution of republicans, but only inflamed the situation. On 1 February 1908 Dom Carlos, his wife Amélia and princes Luís Filipe and Manuel returned from a visit to the Alentejo. Their procession had reached the north-west corner of Praça do Comércio when a black-cloaked figure circled behind the carriage and opened fire. Another conspirator ran out from the arcade. Yet another fired from the central statue. The horse guards rampaged, killing two of the assassins and several bystanders. But the king and crown prince lay dead.

Carlos's second son lasted only two and a half years as Dom Manuel II until the Republican revolution of 4-5 October 1910. When warships shelled his Palácio das Necessidades residence, he fled to Ericeira and then into exile. At the Câmara Municipal (City Hall), the Republic was proclaimed.

NASCENT FASCISM

The optimism accompanying the provisional government set up on 5 October 1910 was soon betrayed by battles over the constitution. A persistent concern was to hang on to the African colonies, prompting Portugal to enter World War I on the side of the Allies. The Portuguese Expeditionary Force was virtually wiped out in the April 1918 battle of La Lys on the Western Front.

On 5 December 1917 an army major named Sidónio Pais led a revolt, taking the heights around Parque Eduardo VII and bombarding the ministries in Praça do Comércio. Loyalist troops counter-attacked and hundreds of soldiers died in a brief but bloody skirmish at Largo do Rato before Sidónio prevailed. What was arguably Europe's first fascist regime saw huge rallies, mass arrests of opposition leaders and heavy censorship. However, Sidónio's increasingly chaotic rule lost him allies, and he was assassinated in December 1918.

António Oliveira Salazar.

Competing local powers now threatened to rip Portugal apart. In January 1919 the monarchy was proclaimed in the north; Republican forces took a month to quell the rebellion. In Lisbon, the National Republican Guard (GNR) was heavily armed and often influenced government. On 19 October 1921 – the Noite Sangrenta or 'bloody night' – members of the GNR and navy revolted; several politicians were massacred, including Prime Minister António Granjo. The next government – the 31st since 1910 – lasted two weeks; 45 Republican administrations would fall before the military definitively took over in 1926.

Meanwhile, despite the political turmoil, intellectual life was thriving. In 1915 the only two issues of the magazine *Orfeu* appeared, introducing poets Fernando Pessoa and Mário de Sá Carneiro and painter José de Almeida Negreiros. In 1924 the Tivoli cinema opened on Avenida da Liberdade; in 1928 the Teatro Municipal de São Luíz in Chiado followed.

DICTATORSHIP

This cultural awakening was stifled by the Estado Novo, the 'New State' regime that prevailed after the May 1926 coup d'état led by Marshal Gomes da Costa. Two years later a conservative Coimbra professor, António Oliveira Salazar, was named finance minister.

'During World War II Portugal settled into uneasy neutrality.'

In 1932 Salazar became prime minister and ruled for almost four decades, backed by the infamous PIDE political police. In the early years the regime styled itself a dictatorship without a dictator, because it eschewed personality cults. But Salazar kept a tight grip by cracking down on the left while playing right-wing rivals off against each other. In 1940 the regime mounted the Exhibition of the Portuguese World in Belém, glorifying national achievements while ignoring World War II and the miserable conditions of rural and industrial workers.

WALKING THE TIGHTROPE

During the war Portugal was once more forced into a balancing act. When the threat of an Axis invasion evaporated in 1940, Portugal settled into uneasy neutrality, providing tungsten for the Nazi war effort while lending Azores air bases to the Allies. British and German

Some down-to-earth advice

It was the morning of All Saints' Day, 1755, and Lisbon's churches were full, when the ground began to shake. The earthquake, its epicentre off the Portuguese coast but felt as far away as Paris, is now believed to have reached 8.7 on the Richter scale in Lisbon. Even well-built structures – including dozens of palaces and convents – buckled. More people were killed in the ensuing tidal wave and fires that burned for days afterwards. Some 15,000 died in all.

The destruction of Lisbon – then Europe's grandest city thanks to the riches flowing in from Brazil and other colonies – gripped the contemporary imagination. As the news spread, it shook the faith of Christians perplexed that God sent this disaster on a holy day, crushing worshippers in packed churches. Voltaire seized on it to debunk rival philosophers' view that all was as it should be in the world. The Museu da Cidade (*see p94*) displays evidence of the event's international importance, in the form of engravings by foreign artists.

'Sometimes they put things that don't happen, but some are very true and show what happened to the big monuments in the city,' says curator Edite Alberto. She notes that not only school groups but many local adults are taken aback by the engravings: 'When people visit, it can come as a bit of a shock: they realise this can happen to Lisbon today or tomorrow and they start to be afraid'.

Fear generates taboos, and there are signs that public reluctance to discuss the subject has reduced the pressure to enforce building regulations that could prevent death and destruction. In 2005 President Jorge Sampaio felt moved at a conference marking the disaster's 250th anniversary to call on home-buyers to demand quality construction.

Seismologists and other experts want the authorities to do more. Earthquake engineers says that while the country has world-class specialists, funding is patchy. Building codes are tight, but inspection isn't. The key is awareness – and prevention.

Ministers routinely state that building safety and the protection of Lisbon's rich built heritage is a priority. But physicist João Duarte Fonseca, who's written a book that surveys both the scientific and cultural aspects of the 1755 earthquake, is sceptical. He finds it telling that the Ministry of Home Affairs, which oversees civil defence, is on Praça do Comércio – a riverside square – and says disaster prevention is not part of the culture. 'The Lisbon earthquake is very absent from our cultural references. If you look at the impact it had on European culture, it's surprising to see such a contrast. This situation is actually quite risky, because a psychological block leads to denial.'

Seismologists say that an earthquake the size of the one in 1755 comes round in this part of the world every few hundred millennia. But there are periodic minor tremors, and a moderate risk of a damaging one occurring in the next 50 years.

So whether ordinary citizens want to think about the subject or not, they must hope – if not necessarily pray – that policymakers do more soon to limit the potential damage and loss of life.

diplomats dodged one another at receptions, and Sintra airport was alone in Europe in offering scheduled flights to both London and Berlin.

Lisbon's cafés were crowded with refugees. Even the king of Romania passed through. *Casablanca* was to have been set here and Lisbon remained the hoped-for destination in the finished film. French airman-author Antoine de Saint Exupéry whiled away hours at the Estoril Casino in December 1940, awaiting passage to America; he eventually made it with refugee film director Jean Renoir. Ian Fleming also visited the casino, gleaning ideas for his main character by watching Yugoslav spy Darko Popov at the gaming tables.

The Allies' victory in 1945 put Portugal's right-wing dictatorship in a tricky position: celebrating the victory of democracy and communism over its natural allies. The Cold War came to the rescue, and after some cosmetic concessions, Portugal aligned with the West in 1949, as a founding member of NATO. Salazar had a scare in 1958 when General Humberto Delgado garnered support and enthused the opposition in show elections for the presidency. Delgado was forced into exile (and assassinated by PIDE agents in 1965) and internal repression was stepped up. Revolts in the African colonies in 1960 and 1961 became full-blown wars that were only resolved after the Revolution.

During the 1950s and 1960s Salazar kept Portugal closed to outside influences. Lisbon was one of the cleanest, quietest cities in

Europe: you could chat in the middle of Avenida da Liberdade during rush hour. In the older neighbourhoods, poverty was rampant. Keeping order were the police, who fined citizens for cursing or letting their laundry drip.

F THIS, F THAT AND F THE OTHER

Many emigrated. The rest hunkered down and swallowed the regime's three Fs: Fátima, Football and Fado. In 1917 the Virgin Mary supposedly appeared to three shepherd children at Fátima, north of Lisbon. The church had doubts, but the regime adopted the cult, building an enormous shrine that became a pilgrimage destination on the 13th of each month from May to October.

Football: always a national passion. Benfica (*see p199*) reached the heights of European football in the 1960s thanks to the peerless Eusébio. The national team, inspired by him, finished third in the 1966 World Cup.

Fado: the 1950s and 1960s were a golden age, dominated by the legendary Amália Rodrigues (for more, see the chapter on Fado). Down on Praça de Alegria, the Hot Clube turned Lisbon on to jazz (*see p181* **Hot and cool**).

Various major public works were undertaken by the Estado Novo, not least the bridge over the Tagus (Ponte Salazar, renamed Ponte 25 de Abril after the Revolution), linking Lisbon to Almada and its Cristo Rei statue, put up in 1958 in thanks for keeping Portugal out of World War II. The Metro was inaugurated in 1959. The city spread outwards. Art nouveau buildings on Avenida da República were demolished and replaced by the first concrete office blocks.

THE REVOLUTION

In 1968 Salazar was incapacitated by a stroke after a deck chair collapsed beneath him. No one had the heart to tell him that President Américo Tomás had appointed the reformist Marcello Caetano in his place; until his death in 1970 ministers held sham meetings at his bedside. Caetano proved unable to unravel the Estado Novo or answer the colonial question. Student demonstrations had been common in the 1960s; now the army joined in. On 25 April 1974 a military coup was masterminded by Otelo Saraiva de Carvalho. Caetano, holed up in the GNR barracks on Largo do Carmo, surrendered after a young captain, Salgueiro Maia, threatened the GNR with tanks, supported by a cheering populace. The only bloodshed came when crowds massed outside the PIDE headquarters on Rua António Cardoso. Shots fired from inside killed three. A plaque marks the spot (*see p66* **Walking Lisbon**).

General António Spínola headed a Junta de Salvação Nacional and on 1 May hundreds of thousands demonstrated on Avenida Almirante Reis to back the Revolução dos Cravos – Revolution of the Carnations – so-called after citizens stuffed soldiers' rifles with the flowers.

Spínola was out by September and for 14 months right and left, military and civilians, tussled for power. Fading murals from this time, peppered with hammers and sickles and party initials, are now fast disappearing. After the 'hot summer' of 1975, when the Communist Party, led by Álvaro Cunhal, seemed to gain the upper hand, Portugal settled down to being a parliamentary democracy.

'The once quiet streets of Lisbon became clogged with motor vehicles.'

In the Revolution's aftermath, the colonies won independence, prompting an exodus of hundreds of thousands of Portuguese citizens. These *retornados*, as the white and mixed-race returnees were called, flooded into a post-revolutionary shambles. Later waves of African immigrants came for economic or political reasons. Many found low-paid, insecure work in the construction industry, and homes in the shanty towns that have ringed the city for decades (*see p26* **Ethnic Lisbon**).

CATCHING UP

In the early 1980s Lisbon's image was one of genteel decay. Money was scarce, public works at a standstill, and emigration to northern Europe or North America continued. But, after Portugal joined the European Community in 1986, governments provided the stability for sustained development. The 1986 opening of the Amoreiras shopping centre saw the arrival of mass shopping culture; the logical conclusion was the Colombo mega-mall, opened in 1997.

The once quiet streets of Lisbon became clogged with motor vehicles, transforming the feel of a city now ringed by motorways and bypasses. The Ponte 25 de Abril is notorious for rush-hour jams, not eased by the newer rail service beneath the carriageway. Another bridge, the Ponte Vasco da Gama, opened in 1998, but merely drained off some weekend traffic; there are now plans to build a rail bridge.

Road-dependent dormitory communities have mushroomed on the outskirts. But in the old city, a few more streets are barred to traffic each year.

On 25 August 1988 fire broke out in the Chiado, ripping the heart out of the classy shopping district and ending its outdoor café

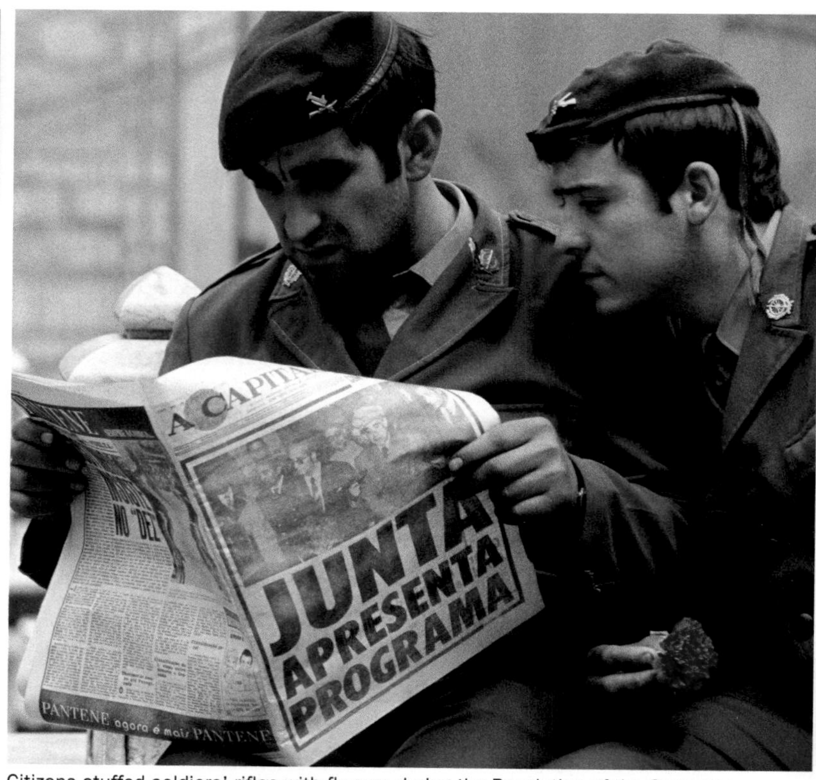

Citizens stuffed soldiers' rifles with flowers during the Revolution of the Carnations.

culture. Renowned Oporto architect Ávaro Siza Vieira was called in, and in the face of sloth-like city administration, his sensitive vision of reconstruction was realised.

Further redevelopment took place on the waterfront, where parks, promenades and marinas emerged from Belém to Santa Apolónia station. Upriver, the 1998 Expo was held on a swathe of former industrial wasteland.

Its stated purpose was to mark the 500th anniversary of Vasca da Gama's discovery of the sea route to India, its theme the oceans, and its hallmark the Oceanário (*see p98*) – a giant aquarium. After Expo ended on 30 September 1998, the site reopened as Parque das Nações (*see p98*), a residential and business district with extensive parkland stretching along the river beyond it. Another legacy is Portugal's confidence in its ability to organise big events, including football's Euro 2004, for which ten stadiums were built or overhauled.

Portugal's entry into the EU monetary union on 1 January 2000 underscored its European identity. At the end of 1999 it handed over its last colony, Macao, to China. Yet in autumn 1999, when Islamist militias in East Timor terrorised civilians who had voted for independence from Indonesia, the Portuguese mobilised on behalf of their former colony with a fervour that recalled revolutionary times.

The last few years have been difficult for many Portuguese. The country has struggled economically as development funds and foreign investment have switched to Eastern Europe. Its politicians lost credibility after the departure of three prime ministers in quick succession, each of whom had proved incapable of tackling deep-rooted problems. The election in 2005 of the first majority Socialist administration was seen as a mandate for reform. The focus has shifted from Portugal's history and on to how its people might build a sustainable future.

Lisbon Today

From marginality to modernity.

Perched at the western edge of Europe, from where ships set out to discover the rest of the world, Lisbon is today more of a destination than ever. After decades of being what its obscurantist dictator termed *orgulhosamente só* (proudly alone) – but most of his subjects saw as isolated and impoverished – Portugal has embraced the world.

The 1998 Lisbon Expo – which both surprised many locals by being a success and left an impressive physical legacy – gave the Portuguese the confidence to host other events, such as football's Euro 2004. There has even been talk of an Olympics bid. But perhaps more importantly for Lisbon, it aided more routine but profitable activities, such as the conference business and a series of smaller sporting events that help offset the seasonal nature of tourism.

All this comes in the wake of years of breakneck economic development as a result of joining the European Union. The EU – such a fraught issue in so many member states – is seen as a good thing by most Portuguese, because they associate it with democracy and prosperity. After Portugal joined the then European Economic Community in 1986, vast inflows of EU regional aid funded projects that transformed the structure of the economy and the expectations of the people.

There were losers as well as winners. Many – particularly pensioners but also unskilled workers – were left behind by the rising tide, never to catch up. But the investment boosted economic activity and potential, and income per head moved steadily nearer to the EU average. Portugal's success in qualifying for European monetary union slashed interest rates, triggering a building and credit boom that fuelled more growth.

Until a few years ago continued progress seemed assured. But even before EU enlargement started to switch regional aid away from Portugal and towards Eastern Europe, serious economic and financial problems emerged. And when in March 2001, a century-old bridge fell into the River Douro, taking with it a coach full of passengers, Portugal's dream went sour. The disaster soon symbolised the way funds had been funnelled into flagship projects to the detriment of

Ethnic Lisbon

It will probably come as no surprise that this former imperial capital has a rich ethnic mixture. Lisbon's ethnic communities tend to have their own enclaves and self-contained cultures, with many clubs, restaurants and bars to explore. For a taste of Africa, visit the Associação de Cabo Verde, on the eighth floor at Duque de Palmela 2 (21 353 1932/2098), in the heart of the city's business district. Here you can enjoy an inexpensive lunch of Cape Verdean dishes (noon-3pm Mon-Fri). On Tuesdays and Thursdays these are accompanied by live music: couples dance their lunch break away before filing back to their offices. There's a similar vibe during dinner on Fridays and Saturdays at the first-floor Espaço Cabo Verde (Travessa do Fala Só 9, 21 342 0333), just off the Elevador da Glória. See our music and nightlife chapters for other windows into Lisbon's African community.

The new 'Lisbon sound' has its roots in Africa too: 'progressive kuduro' takes a beat from the Angolan capital, Luanda, and electrofies it for the dance music crowd. Prime exponents are Buraka Som Sistema, from the Lisbon suburbs but now making inroads into dance floors abroad with their aptly named debut EP, 'From Buraka to the world'. Lisbon's ethnic mix has finally forged an urban sound of its own.

There are also myriad Brazilian bars where bands drive *brazucas* and locals alike into a state of delirium – for a selection, *see p179*. In fact, Brazil is all around you. It's not much more than a decade since the flow of emigration to Brazil went into reverse, but Brazilians have tended to integrate more easily than Africans. They plug key gaps in the job market – shaking up the advertising sector, for example, while less qualified immigrants provide construction muscle. More recently economic turbulence in Brazil sent over a wave of middle-class youngsters to provide service with more of a smile in shops, bars and restaurants, while unskilled workers have arrived in force from new areas such as the interior of São Paulo state.

Although some Portuguese harbour an image of Brazilians as tricksters, in general more unites than divides the two nations. This was shown by enthusiastic Portuguese support for Brazil's football team, although this seems to have waned as Portugal's own team's fortunes have improved. There is substantial anecdotal evidence of locals becoming less welcoming in recent years. Perhaps it is just that, where a Brazilian accent was once glamorous, it is now banal.

The Casa do Brasil community centre (Rua São Pedro de Alcântara 63, Bairro Alto, 1250, 21 347 1580, www.casadobrasildelisboa.pt) works hard to cope with the vast inflows of Brazilians, providing helpful job information, legal advice and Friday night dance parties.

India has had a special place in the Portuguese collective consciousness ever since Vasco da Gama discovered the sea route to India. Many Goans now live in the Lisbon area and the Navaratri festival (*see p153*), which happens every autumn, is the community's main event. It takes place at Lumiar's Hindu community centre (Alameda Mahatma Gandhi, 21 757 6524, www.comunidadehindu.org), and features traditional music and dancing.

Lisbon's small Timorese community, formed during the long Indonesian occupation of what has since become the world's newest country, has a focus at Espaço por Timor (Rua de São Bento 182-4, 21 396 1546). It has a community centre and library, and organises presentations and debates.

creaking basic infrastructure. The ensuing soul-searching reached self-flagellatory proportions, with one columnist describing Portugal's developed-nation status as a façade.

Socialist prime minister António Guterres, having sailed through his first term, resigned two years into his second. In a general election in 2002 the Social Democrats and the right-wing Popular Party garnered a majority, and formed a coalition headed by José Manuel Durão Barroso, a former foreign minister. Consumer confidence was then further undermined by gloom from a government whose priority seemed to be to blame its predecessor for the dire state of public finances. Consumption of anti-depressants in 2002 shot up and the number of divorces jumped by an improbable 46 per cent in a year.

Then came the lowest blow. An article in *Expresso* newspaper cited allegations by a former pupil of the Casa Pia, a 200-year-old state-funded network of orphanages and schools, of a paedophile ring at the institution. Among the prominent people arrested were a Socialist deputy, a former diplomat and a popular television presenter.

The plot thickened, with the phone of the leader of the opposition being tapped, anonymous letters accusing further public figures and countless leaks. There was fevered debate about reform of a justice system in which suspects can be held for a year without charge and defence lawyers use loopholes to delay interrogations of their clients. (In early 2007, there was still no indication of just when the trial would finally be concluded.)

Aided or abetted by these distractions, the government was wrestling with big economic and budget problems. Barroso himself, having said he would not go for the job of president of the European Commission, left to do just that. To the dismay and outrage of Portugal's tiny chattering class, his deputy at the top of the governing party, Pedro Santana Lopes, then mayor of Lisbon but best known as a socialite and former chairman of Sporting football club, stepped into the breach – despite not being a member of parliament.

'Portugal's president, Jorge Sampaio, dropped the so-called *bomba atómica*.'

A matter of months later, with consumer and business confidence on the rocks and after a series of ministerial mishaps, Portugal's president, Jorge Sampaio, dropped the so-called *bomba atómica*, exercising his constitutional power to dissolve parliament. In the subsequent general election, in February 2005, the Socialists won their first ever absolute majority, in what was seen as a mandate to bring some order to state affairs and tackle powerful vested interests from banks to public sector unions.

The new government surprised few by promptly reneging on a campaign pledge not to raise taxes, after 'discovering' (in the by now usual fashion) that the state accounts were worse than expected. Although the prime minister, José Sócrates, remains relatively popular despite a less than impressive economy, the jury is out as to whether his team will succeed in slaying the country's demons.

PLANS? WHAT PLANS?

In the capital, one legacy of Expo '98 has been a yearning for grandiose projects. You might ask how they fit into the city's overall planning framework, but don't expect an answer. There is no plan. Lisbon actually lacks key planning instruments required by law. The Câmara Municipal (city council) should have updated the Directive Plan by 2004. But so long as no revision of the old one is in force, it may release parcels of land for commercial development as it wishes. (Some lisboetas object to this, and have taken it to court.)

That is not to say that left-wing city administrations have been significantly better where planning is concerned. Gonçalo Ribeiro Telles, who probably knows more about Lisbon's urban structure and historical development than anyone, drew up a draft strategy when chief of urban planning back in 1997. Not only was it never implemented, neither were any of several alternatives.

City fathers of all parties are playing fast and loose with what is a very delicate urban environment. One of the first things to strike visitors to Lisbon, its challenging topography, is a clue as to why. As a city of hills and valleys, it is also a city of flowing – though mostly now subterranean – water.

This is particularly true in the Baixa, once a marsh where two tributaries of the Tagus met after flowing down what are now Avenida da Liberdade and Avenida Almirante Reis. The 18th-century buildings you see today stand on wooden piles driven vertically down through marsh and the rubble left by the 1755 earthquake; these are effectively pickled so long as they remain soaked. In recent years underground car parks and newly dug basements under chain stores have diverted the flow of water essential to preserve the piles.

Chat to the curator at the Núcleo Arqueólogico (*see p63*) – Roman remains under a high street bank – and he will tell of his concern at the soil getting drier yearly, with results visible in the form of crumbling wood at the top of the piles. Even that nearby symbol of uprightness, the Bank of Portugal, in Rua do Comércio, is subsiding.

The extension of the Metro from Baixa-Chiado to Santo Apolónia is complicating matters still further, since it is likely to block the entry into the ground under the Baixa of estuary water. Although work has been slow since the collapse of a tunnel several years ago

took with it part of the road on the river side of Praça do Comércio, it is advancing.

Elsewhere, the gradual disappearance of the traditional *quintais* – backyards – of the old city means fewer dispersed sources of groundwater from rainfall. There are ever more incidents of underground pipes snapping because the earth on which they rested has dried and shrunk. During rainstorms, flooding is common.

'Lisbon is a contradiction: a dry city by a river.'

A plan for the renovation of the Baixa was recently released, but to the shock of those who know the city's three hydrographic basins, none was mentioned in it. No wonder then that a project sketched out by star Italian architect Renzo Piano west of the centre recently had to be scrapped because, for lack of information, it did not take into account the *boqueirões* – inlets along the Tagus into which brooks once flowed (and whose tidal nature long made them ideal places to build and repair boats).

All the downtown car parks – of which half-a-dozen have been dug recently – need constant pumping, as do Baixa basements. Lisbon, the council's critics say, is being turned into a contradiction in terms: a dry city by a river.

All this is ironic given that Lisbon has been renewing its relationship with the Tagus after two centuries of trying hard to ignore it. This is very welcome news for residents and visitors alike. It all started in the 1990s with the Docas development at Alcântara – which brought many lisboetas into regular contact with their river for the first time – and has continued with ever more waterside bars and restaurants and patches of open space that are increasingly being joined up.

DEVELOPMENT HELL

Joined-up administration, however, is often lacking. Work on the *túnel do Marquês*, dug out to circumvent traffic snarl-ups around Lisbon's main downtown roundabout, was held up for months after it emerged that no statutory environmental study had been done. Above ground, an unbroken expanse of asphalt assaults the eyes, because no one thought to replace the trees uprooted earlier.

Meanwhile, silence has fallen over Parque Mayer – the sadly dark former theatreland off the Avenida da Liberdade. A few years ago, with the Portuguese media in eager attendance, then mayor Santana Lopes brought over Frank Gehry to talk up the plan he had drawn up for the area, which would include theatres, a hotel, shops, jazz club and performing arts school.

Although officially the project is still on (albeit amended after a preservation order was slapped on one of the derelict theatres), many believe it will now never go ahead. And it will probably be years before more modest plans are implemented.

No one is going to tear down the Baixa, of course, but there is perennial talk of repopulating it. One student residence has been inaugurated, and a few apartments have been prettified for foreign professionals. But at a time when there are tens of thousands of empty apartments in the fancy new Alcântara XXI development and at Alto de Lisboa in northern Lisbon, it is hard to see locals moving downtown.

While the Portuguese media is generally keen to expose corruption in public life, day-to-day oversight and the exposure of humdrum incompetence makes for less exciting sport. Nevertheless, while public engagement is traditionally limited – a legacy of lengthy dictatorship and historically low levels of literacy – there has of late been vigorous growth in citizens' movements, many relating to the protection of Lisbon's heritage.

Lisboetas love their luminous city and are convinced that everyone else should too. And after you've lost an afternoon wandering through Moorish alleyways, sat and nursed a beer on a *miradouro* as the sun sets over the city, been transported by the *saudade* in the voice of a fado singer, or joined late-night revellers in the Bairro Alto, you surely will.

Architecture

From Moors to modernism – and a marvellous Metro.

Although Lisbon's origins are lost in legend, its days as a Roman provincial city are recalled by the ruins that dot the centre in subterranean (but visitable) pockets. The **Teatro Romano** (*see p70*) is one of these. The centuries after the fall of Rome left little mark and the earliest physical evidence of urban civic life still found in the modern city is that planted during Moorish rule between the eighth and 12th centuries. Surrounded by the Cerca Moura, the Moorish siege walls that skirt the Castelo de São Jorge, Alfama was the city's core. Latticed window shutters to shield women from the glances of passers-by can still be seen on some houses, and the quarter retains the feel of a North African port. Popular style has changed little over the centuries, with the traditional *casa portuguesa* keeping simple lines and whitewashed walls with small windows.

Portuguese architecture advanced in the 15th century when Dom Manuel I, known as 'the Fortunate', put to use the riches gleaned from the sea route to the Indies. Palaces and churches were built and royal architects such as Francisco de Arruda devised a new, late-Gothic style known as Manueline. This featured plain walls but extravagant windows and portals decorated with flora and fauna, maritime motifs, the king's seal and the Vera Cruz, or True Cross.

Structures still visible today include, to the west, the **Torre de Belém** (*see p86*) and the **Mosteiro dos Jerónimos** (*see p86*), with its spectacular cloister and nave. At the eastern end of Lisbon is another example, the **Madre de Deus church**, now the **Museu Nacional do Azulejo** (*see p97*). Lioz, a local limestone, lent these massive buildings a light, airy look.

SPANISH STYLE

Philip II of Spain's ascension to the Portuguese throne in 1582 as Philip I brought a more monumental style. Sombre on the outside but gilded on the inside, many of Lisbon's grandiose churches date from this era. Still visitable are the **Igreja de São Vicente da Fora** (*see p75*), the **Igreja de São Roque** (*see p77*), the **Mercês** church on Largo do Chiado and the **Convento do Beato** on Alameda do Beato out east in Xabregas. **São Vicente**, white and imposing on the hill above Alfama, is a prime example. It typifies the mannerist style of the counter-Reformation, rich in ideology and imagery, and its twin bell towers served as models for local architects for two centuries. The interior houses some of Lisbon's most elaborate panels of *azulejos* (tiles).

Once imported from Seville but long since made in Portugal, these tiles have remained a consistent presence in Portuguese architecture (*see p32* **Lisbon's got the blues**).

This period also saw the first attempts at planning. In 1580 the Bairro Alto or 'Upper Town' (*see p77*) was laid out on a grid of streets then thought wide and regular, although now they seem cramped and maze-like.

SOBERING UP AND REBUILDING

Following the restoration in 1640, a sober style known as the Estilo Chão (Flat or Plain Style) developed, in which massive corner pillars framed horizontally organised façades, with simple balconies topped with stone balustrades or plain railings. Larger country houses and palaces began to mimic the French U-shaped style. Most surviving Lisbon palaces from this period are in Estilo Chão, including the **Palácio Galveias** (Campo Pequeno), now a library, and the **Palácio da Fronteira** (*see p95*).

Artistry and engineering flourished: the **Aqueduto das Águas Livres** (*see p91*) was completed; elaborate wood carving and sculpture became de rigueur in royal, church and public interiors; and façades with intricately painted blue and white *azulejos* multiplied.

Under Dom João V, the Magnificent, baroque triumphed in palaces such as the **Paço de Bemposta** (off Campo dos Mártires da Pátria), now a military academy, the **Igreja da Graça** (on Largo da Graça, *see p75*) and the **Palácio das Necessidades** (on Largo das Necessidades), today's Foreign Ministry. Many were inspired by the palace and convent at **Mafra**, north-west of Lisbon, designed by German architect João Frederico Ludovice.

The Great Earthquake of 1 November 1755 left a score of churches, the royal palace and dozens of other noble dwellings, and two thirds of the city's medieval housing in rubble. In the aftermath of the ensuing tidal wave and fires, the all-powerful minister of Dom José I, later known as the Marquês de Pombal, sought to impose modernity. He began by forbidding construction outside the city limits and reconstruction inside them until his plans were concluded. Pombal drafted three bright architects – Manuel da Maia, newly arrived Hungarian Carlos Mardel and Eugénio dos Santos. They plotted out a new Baixa of some 200,000 square metres (2.1 million square feet), on a grid of seven streets running north–south, christened after the trades that would operate on them, and eight streets running east–west.

Pombaline style is characterised by scant exterior decoration, although façades were given a glossy finish by pressing the fresh stucco with tin plates – a process called *estanhado*. The mainly four-storey houses were built around a *gaiola*, or cage, a flexible structure with wooden joists filled with brick, stone and plaster, aimed at resisting earthquakes. Another innovation was to raise the walls separating houses to a level higher than the roof joists, as a firewall. Fully equipped with modern sanitation, these blocks were the state of the art in urban planning.

'When Pombal fell from grace, Lisbon resumed its haphazard growth.'

As soon as Pombal fell from grace, however, Lisbon resumed its haphazard growth. Dom José's daughter, who became Dona Maria I, was a pious woman responsible for two beautiful churches – the **Igreja da Memória** in Ajuda (*see p87*) and the **Basílica da Estrela** (*see p91*). The latter is an imposing building in white stone, topped by an ornate dome that, when illuminated, dominates the western skyline. Inside is a finely crafted profusion of pink and black marble. The Igreja da Memória is reminiscent of the Basílica – both are mostly the work of Mateus Vicente – but smaller and more intimate. Also of note from this epoch are the 1792 **Teatro Nacional de São Carlos** (*see p169*), perhaps Lisbon's first neo-classical building, and the **Palácio da Ajuda** (*see p87*).

STAGNATION AND INDUSTRY

The first half of the 19th century was a turbulent time, and urban planning languished, although the **Teatro Nacional Dona Maria II** (*see p194*) was built between Rossio and the Passeio Público. The industrial revolution brought a new age of engineering (and Romantic nostalgia), epitomised in the neo-Manueline Rossio station and the more French neo-Gothic of the **Elevador de Santa Justa** (*see p63*), designed by Raul Mesnier du Ponsard. The **Campo Pequeno** bullring (*see p200*) and the Casa do Alentejo in Baixa reflect a neo-Moorish trend of the 1890s.

At the turn of the 19th century a new generation of architects emerged, designing art nouveau houses for wealthy industrialists, or *vilas*, residential complexes in working-class quarters such as Graça that often housed employer and employees.

Lisbon's distinctive paving, *calçada à portuguesa* (Portuguese paving), came into its own in 1849 with the completion of the dizzy-

Lisbon's got the blues

The Portuguese ornamental element that most catches visitors' fancy is the *azulejo*, or tile. These are everywhere: from palaces to the façades of the humblest houses, from butcher's shops to Metro stations. There is a **Museu Nacional do Azulejo** (*see p97*) in a former convent but sometimes the whole city seems like one big tile museum.

The word *azulejo* comes either from *zulej*, 'blue' in Persian, or from *al-zuleycha*, Arabic for polished stone. Tiles from Islamic Asia are on show at the **Museu Calouste Gulbenkian** (*see p96*), but the tradition has deep roots in Iberia. It was in the 14th century that tiles produced in Seville by Muslim craftsmen were first imported in large numbers; Sintra's **Palácio Nacional** (*see p215* **'Glorious Eden'**) has fine examples. But the craze only took off a century later, with the arrival of Italian *majolica* techniques. After Spain expelled all *mudéjars* (local Muslims) in 1610, new factories in Portugal produced flat painted tiles rather than the old relief designs. Made mainly for religious buildings, such as the **Igreja de São Roque** (*see p77*), they depicted biblical landscapes or popular saints.

Larger 'tile tapestries' appeared in the 17th century. Splendid examples survive in the **Igreja São Vicente** (*see p75*) and the **Palácio dos Marqueses de Fronteira** (*see p95*), whose Sala das Batalhas – full of panels representing battles of the Restoration – has been called 'the Sistine Chapel of tilework'. Mass production began in 1767 when the Marquês de Pombal founded the Real Fábrica do Rato to serve post-earthquake reconstruction. Tiles were used increasingly in façades, with a more restrained, neo-classical style.

The popularity of *azulejos* declined in the early 19th century with the Peninsular Wars, the court's departure to Brazil, and the dissolution of the monasteries (the Real Fábrica closed in 1835). The industrial age heralded a comeback: examples include the 1865 façade of Fábrica Viúva Lamego (which still sells tiles) on Largo do Intendente, and the façade on Rua da Trindade facing Largo Rafael Bordalo Pinheiro, depicting Progress and Science. The three firms from the period survive, hewing to old techniques and selling mostly to northern Europe.

The craft moved on. Particularly in Lapa, Campo de Ourique and Saldanha, colourful art nouveau tiles frame doors, windows and balconies. Artists such as Rafael Bordalo Pinheiro and Jorge Colaço created lavish façades and interiors. In later decades run-of-the-mill tiles were all too often slapped on to façades to provide colour or protect against rain. But the latter part of the 20th century saw a revival, with Portuguese and foreign artists designing *azulejos* for sale in specialist shops – and, of course, for Lisbon's Metro.

To name a few examples: **Campo Grande** is graced by Eduardo Néry's 'deconstructions' of traditional blue and white *azulejo* panels, while **Campo Pequeno**, two stops away, has bullfighting scenes that recall the nearby Praça de Touros. **Parque station** was clad in cobalt blue by Belgium's Françoise Schein and France's Federica Matta, with designs alluding to Portugal's maritime history and with suitably noble quotations from poets, philosophers and the Universal Declaration of Human Rights. Out at **Carnide**, José de Guimarães's inimitable style finds expression in neon and stone renditions of wobbly animal forms. At bustling commuter terminal **Cais do Sodré**, António da Costa's giant versions of the White Rabbit from *Alice in Wonderland* announce 'I'm late'.

The Oriente (red) line, opened just in time for Expo 98, is the biggest publicly funded showcase of recent times. While the euphoria of that time has evaporated, the exuberant art and architecture remain. At brash **Olaias** (photo *p30*), love-him-or-hate-him architect Tomás Taveira produced a dizzying mosaic of primary colours and restless patterns. For the next station, **Bela Vista**, Querubim Lapa mixed geometric patterns and naïve designs. **Chelas** integrates architecture by Ana Nascimento and decoration by Jorge Martins: tunnels plunge into blue limestone walls with no visible support, slashed by bold rents and asymmetric windows. **Olivais** (*below*) is one of the network's deepest stations, with fittingly profound artwork by Nuno de Siqueira: panels with images of adversity, war and revolution hint at Portugal's contribution to modernity, while phrases such as 'a thing is not only what we see but also what it signifies' comment obliquely on the artist's own work. At **Cabo Ruivo**, David de Almeida set white Stone Age hunting images on black walls. As your train passes, these flash between pale blue arches, creating a moving-image effect.

The line terminates at **Oriente**, designed by Sanchez Jorge. It's a gallery of huge panels on maritime themes by renowned Portuguese and international artists including Hundertwasser and Erró. Upstairs, the **Gare do Oriente** train and bus station by Spain's Santiago Calatrava, with its glass and steel palm-tree structures, leads you into a feast of bravura architecture in what is now the Parque das Nações.

looking **Rossio Square** (only recently restored after decades of being eaten into by asphalt). Even today *calcário* (limestone) is hewn into tiny blocks to decorate walkways with traditional and modern designs. Each stone is cut and laid by hand, but no longer by skilled workers.

Portugal's early 20th-century experiment in democracy produced the first district of social housing in Arco do Cego, today dwarfed by state bank Caixa Geral de Depósitos, and the Parque Mayer – a cluster of variety theatres off the Avenida da Liberdade that included the ultra-modern **Teatro Capitólio**, built between 1925 and 1931. It comprised technical innovations such as reinforced concrete, a naturally lit auditorium and Portugal's first escalator. Long derelict and recently threatened with demolition as part of a development sketched out for the council by star Canadian architect Frank Gehry, it is now the subject of a vigorous campaign to restore it.

With the rise of Salazar, architecture took on a pseudo-fascist look. Monumental buildings such as the **Palácio da Justiça** at the top of Parque Eduardo VII and the **Biblioteca Nacional** (*see p94*) symbolised the regime's power. Modernism struggled on, for example in Cassiano Branco's Eden theatre, whose skeleton is preserved as the **Aparthotel VIP Eden** (*see p42*), and the **Instituto Superior Técnico**, Portugal's first campus, an 'acropolis' of learning by Porfírio Pardal Monteiro. But the regime favoured the Portuguese Modern Traditional style, which featured touches such as galleries with round arches and bas-reliefs. The **Igreja da Nossa Senhora da Fátima** on Avenida da Berna and the twin-towered **Igreja São João de Deus** on Praça de Londres are outstanding examples.

By 1940 nationalism was in full flood and the Exposição do Mundo Português, the Exhibition of the Portuguese World, was held in Belém. It centred on the chauvinistic **Padrão dos Descobrimentos** (*see p86*), in which giant statues of Henry the Navigator and his brave courtiers, mapmakers and sailors advance along a plinth towards unknown seas. The building now housing the **Museu Nacional de Arte Popular** (*see p86*) was part of the exhibition. Elsewhere in Lisbon, the fountain on Alameda Dom Afonso Henriques, decked with Tagus nymphs and mythical creatures from Camões's *Lusiads*, stems from the same period.

However, it would be simplistic to write off the Salazar era. It saw the construction of Pardal Monteiro's impressive modernist **Gare Marítima de Alcântara** (1943), with murals by José de Almada Negreiros. The hyperactive minister of public works Duarte Pacheco was a visionary, laying out three large residential neighbourhoods – Alvalade, Restelo and Olivais – and starting the first dual-carriage highway. By the 1960s Portugal could no longer avoid international trends: the first Metro line opened in 1960, the **Ponte Salazar** (now Ponte 25 de Abril) was built in 1966, and the **Fundação Calouste Gulbenkian** (*see p96*) in 1969.

MODERN TIMES

After the 1974 Revolution much harm was done to the city's fabric. In the 1970s and '80s corrugated-iron shanty towns sprang up and dormitory suburbs were built, largely illegally. Portugal's 1986 entry into the European Community generated wealth at a time of minimal public awareness of urban planning and Mayor Nuno Kruz Abecassis permitted the rape of several historic zones. On Largo de Martim Moniz a shopping centre was built on the back of a tiny, ancient chapel; architect Tomás Taveira tested local humour with his pink and smoked-glass **Amoreiras shopping centre** (*see p132*), which juts out from an old hilltop district; while at the corner of Avenida 5 de Outubro and Avenida de Berna an office block echoes the form of a Portuguese guitar.

In 1992 Portugal inaugurated the **Centro Cultural de Belém** (*see p161*) to host the EU presidency. Plonked opposite the Mosteiro dos Jerónimos, the lioz block designed by Vittorio Gregotti and Manuel Salgado caused a controversy that has never fully died away.

After the 1988 Chiado fire reconstruction was handed to Portugal's leading architect, Álvaro Siza Vieira. He rescued 18 of the 20 damaged façades and rebuilt the gutted insides. The centrepiece is the former Armazéns do Chiado department store, now a shopping centre and luxury hotel.

The most important urban project of recent years, though, was **Expo 98**, which required the rehabilitation of a stretch of the eastern waterfront polluted with disused oil refineries, munitions factories and a slaughterhouse. Now called **Parque das Nações** (*see p98*), the architectural highlights of the area are Peter Chermayev's **Oceanário**; Regino Cruz's UFO-like **Pavilhão Atlântico**; Siza's **Pavilhão de Portugal** (for all, *see p98*) with its concave concrete canopy; and Santiago Calatrava's imaginative Gare do Oriente.

Built in conjunction with Expo were the 17-kilometre (10.5-mile) **Ponte Vasco da Gama** and a remarkable Metro line (*see p32* **Lisbon's got the blues**).

A few years on Gehry is one of the big names that Lisbon's right-of-centre administration is looking to for architectural pzzazz. Renzo Piano, Jean Nouvel and Norman Foster all have plans to develop portions of a mostly neglected riverside.

Where to Stay

Features

Hotel Miragem Cascais. *See p54.*

Where to Stay

More choice than ever, from palaces to pensões.

Lisbon's hotel boom began in the run up to Expo 98 and has continued in the wake of the Euro 2004 football championship. Dozens of large new establishments have opened in recent years, as Lisbon overtook the Algarve in terms of visitor numbers. City officials have encouraged businesses to convert crumbling mansions into luxury hotels, and there are more schemes on the drawing board. Los Angeles-based architect Frank Gehry, the man behind Bilbao's Guggenheim Museum, has drawn up plans for the dilapidated theatre district Parque Mayer that include yet more hotels. Add to that the towers built in Parque das Nações, the former Expo site, and Lisbon caters abundantly for the well-heeled, while continuing to welcome the backpackers and mid-market tourists that were long its speciality. Luxury gaffs are springing up along the Estoril coast, too, including the **Miragem Cascais** (*see p54*) and the **Grande Real Villa Itália Hotel & Spa** (*see p54*).

We've divided places to stay into areas corresponding to those used elsewhere in this guide, although bear in mind that in a small city such divisions are rather artificial. Most hotels cluster between the Baixa and Parque Eduardo VII. Up around the Castelo de São Jorge, there are now scenic options catering for all categories – including the **Palácio Belmonte** (*see p46*) for the lottery winners among you. One of the four hotels owned by the family-run Heritage chain, **Solar do Castelo** (*see p46*), is also in the castle. It now has a local challenger, the plush **Olissippo Castelo** (*see p46*).

Although you can still find cheap hotels in Lisbon (usually designated *pensões*), even downmarket ones have been forced to upgrade their facilities in recent years – and so raise prices. That shouldn't alarm those on a shoestring; rates are still cheap compared with much of Europe. In many mid-range to lower-priced hotels it is worth asking about deals, as prices may be negotiable. Even in fancier establishments, there are bargains to be had if you book ahead or online.

PRICES AND FACILITIES

Area sections are sub-divided by price: Deluxe, Expensive, Moderate and Budget. A single room in a Deluxe hotel, taking the average winter 2006 price, will cost from around €250 upwards; Expensive is €150-€250; Moderate €50-€150; and Budget under €50. Camping sites and hostels – defined as anywhere with dorms – are listed separately, after the hotels. They're not necessarily cheaper than *pensões* but they have kitchen and other facilities and tend to be more social; some are very central.

Art nouveau: **Hotel Metrópole**. *See p37*.

In general, even budget accommodation is clean, partly because the authorities are strict. Some places also have surprising features for their price category: the **Pensão Portuense** (*see p42*) and **Residencial Marisela** (*see p52*) both offer breakfast in your room, and the Marisela also has a basketball court, of all things. Another cost-saving option is the aparthotel. We list two – the **Clube do Lago** (*see p55*) in Monte Estoril and the **Aparthotel**

VIP Eden (*see p42*) downtown – and give contact details for the Real Residência and Chiado Residence (*see p45* Dom Carlos Park). All have self-catering apartments rented out by the day, week or month. For longer lets, the choicest apartments are found by word of mouth. If you are not well connected, check ads in *Diário de Notícias*, *Correio de Manhã* or the weekly classifieds rag *Ocasião* (on its website www.ocasiao.pt click on 'ImOcasião' then 'Arrendamentos'). For more on gay and GLBT-friendly accommodation, *see p164*.

Prices can as much as double in summer, particularly on the Estoril coast. Book at least two weeks in advance in July and August, especially if you want to be near a beach. In Lisbon hotels, rates can depend on the size of the room, the view and whether there's a bathroom. Unless we've stated otherwise, the price includes breakfast and the cost of parking quoted is per day. Also, all places listed have telephones in rooms unless otherwise stated (or, in the case of budget hotels, if we say there's a payphone). Most allow an internet connection from your room if you use a laptop, but from the UK you'll need an adaptor plug if it's not wireless. It's increasingly common for hotels to offer broadband access (and/or Wi-Fi in common areas), but some cheaper places may have analogue connections. You can configure your laptop for a free ISP connection like Sapo, Clix or Oninet which will hook you up at local rates, or visit a cybercafé. For more places to go online see the Directory chapter.

Booking

Associação Portuguesa de Pousadas de Juventude (Youth Hostels Association)

Avenida Duque de Ávila 137, Saldanha, 1069-017 (21 356 8120/www.pousadasjuventude.pt). Metro Saldanha. **Open** *Winter* 9am-6pm Mon-Fri. *Summer* 9am-7pm Mon-Fri. **Map** p248 L5

Portugal's hostels association is an arm of state run outfit Movijovem (21 723 2100, http://juventude.gov.pt/Portal/Movijovem), whose own website is also very informative, albeit in Portuguese. Staff at this downtown shop will provide advice on hostels and a booking service. They also supply general information for young travellers, such as how and where to find discounts. You can use their internet, reference library and photocopiers. To book hostels yourself, call 707 203 030, email reservas@movijovem.pt or check individual hostel listings (*see p58*).

Empresa Nacional de Turismo (Enatur)/Pousadas de Portugal

Rua Soares de Passos 3, Alto de Santo Amaro, 1300 (21 844 2000/reservations 21 844 2001/www.pousadas.pt). Train to Alcântara Mar from Cais do Sodré then bus 738, 742. **Open** 10am-1pm, 2-5pm Mon-Fri. **Credit** AmEx, DC, MC, V.

A privately managed state agency that handles bookings for *pousadas* (the luxury hostels that are situated in converted monuments) around Portugal. It also has an online booking service for some upmarket hotels in the Lisbon region.

Lisboa Welcome Centre

Rua do Arsenal 15, Baixa, 1100-038 (21 031 2700/www.visitlisboa.com). Metro Baixa-Chiado/tram 15, 18. **Open** 9am-8pm Mon-Fri. **Map** p250 L10

Lisboa Welcome Centre provides limited help with finding accommodation and on-the-spot bookings but it has no advance reservation service. Also a long list of hotels, but these are not categorised.

Where to Stay

Baixa & Rossio

Expensive

Hotel Metrópole

Praça Dom Pedro IV (Rossio) 30, 1100-200 (21 321 9030/www.almeidahotels.com). Metro Rossio or Restauradores. **Rates** €123-€160 single; €134-€170 double; €43-€50 extra bed. **Credit** AmEx, DC, MC, V. **Map** p250 L9 ❶

The best Hotels

For a slap-up breakfast on a budget
Pensão Portuense (*see p42*).

For ocean views
Estalagem do Muchaxo (*see p57*), Farol Design Hotel (*see p54*), Hotel Miragem Cascais (*see p54*), Hotel Albatroz (*see p55*).

For the bars of Bairro Alto
Pensão Globo (*see p47*), Pensão Londres (*see p47*), Residencial Camões (*see p48*).

To drink Caipirinhas while admiring panoramic views
Albergaria Senhora do Monte (*see p46*), Bairro Alto Hotel (*see p47*), Lisboa Regency Chiado (*see p47*).

To pamper your body
Lapa Palace Hotel (*see p48*), Pestana Palace (*see p48*), Four Seasons Hotel Ritz Lisbon (*see p41*).

To play a round of golf
Hotel Palacio Estoril (*see p54*), Penha Longa (*see p54*).

Located above the famous Café Nicola, the Hotel Metrópole combines art nouveau with modern comfort. The interior is a throwback to the 1920s, with individually decorated rooms containing period furniture. Bathrooms are spacious and decorated in white marble. The bar faces Rossio; it was from these windows that political leaders such as Mário Soares addressed the people during the 1974 Revolution. It's peaceful now, though: rooms are double-glazed and quiet at night. **Photo** *p36.*
Bar. Disabled-adapted room. Room service. TV.

Avenida da Liberdade

Moderate

Hotel Lisboa Tejo

Rua dos Condes de Monsanto 2, Rossio, 1100-090 (21 886 6182/www.evidenciahoteis.com). Metro Rossio. **Rates** €80-€105 single; €85-€120 double; €135-€150 suite. **Credit** AmEx, DC, MC, V. **Map** p251 M9 ❷
One of the most surprising hotels in Lisbon, the Lisboa Tejo (not to be confused with the Tivoli Tejo) offers cool style at reasonable prices. A Gaudí- and Braque-inspired lobby bar is open to all and is a good place to hang out even if you are not lucky enough to be staying at the hotel. Recommended.
Bar. Disabled access. Internet. Payphone. Room service. TV.

Hotel Mundial

Rua Dom Duarte 4, Rossio, 1100-198 (21 884 2000/www.hotel-mundial.pt). Metro Rossio/tram 12, 28. **Rates** €107-€150 single; €117-€160 double; €35 extra bed. **Credit** AmEx, DC, MC, V. **Map** p251 F9 ❸
Opened in 1958, the Mundial isn't pretty to look at and its size makes it somewhat impersonal but staff work hard to ensure you have a pleasant stay. A rooftop grill with a garden that looks on to the castle serves cheap local grilled fish and meat dishes. Rooms have decent views and are quiet thanks to double glazing, although many are rather poky or have strange dimensions. A large extension has been added recently, but it's still good value.
Bar. Disabled-adapted rooms. Internet (wireless & pay terminal). Parking (free). Restaurant. Room service. TV (pay movies).

Hotel Portugal

Rua João das Regras 4, Rossio, 1100-294 (21 887 7581/www.hotelportugal.com). Metro Rossio/tram 12, 28. **Rates** €55-€60 single; €65-€70 double; €75-€90 triple. **Credit** AmEx, DC, MC, V. **Map** p251 F9 ❹
One block east of Praça da Figueira, this two-star hotel has 60 modest, clean rooms at reasonable prices. Built in 1872, it retains its pretty tiled hallways, antique furniture and original moulded ceilings. Rooms look either to the street or towards the castle. The spacious bathrooms are clean and come with power showers.
Bar. Parking (€10/day). TV.

Budget

Pensão Coimbra e Madrid

Praça da Figueira 3, Rossio, 1100-240 (21 342 1760/fax 21 342 3264). Metro Rossio/tram 12, 15. **Rates** €25-€30 single; €35-€50 double. **No credit cards. Map** p250 M9 ❺
Once you get past the tacky hallway covered in blue and green tiles, things start to look up. It's a lively place to stay, attracting backpackers and InterRailers, who mingle or watch videos in the TV lounge. Some rooms have bathrooms and a view of the castle. The *pensão* is centrally located but not centrally heated, so it could be chilly out of season. All rooms have phones; most share bathrooms.
Payphone.

Pensão Ibérica

Praça da Figueira 10-2, Rossio, 1100-085 (21 886 5781/fax 21 886 7412). Metro Rossio/tram 12, 15. **Rates** €15-€20 single (shared toilet); €30-€40 double (own toilet). **No credit cards. Map** p251 M9 ❻
Cheap and cheerful hotel on Praça da Figueira. Inside, the decoration has an African motif, perhaps thanks to the Mozambican family who run the place. A generous buffet breakfast is served in an airy breakfast room and some bedrooms have en suites; all are bright and very clean. Good value for money.
TV.

Pensão Praça da Figueira

Travessa Nova de São Domingos 9-3E, Baixa, 1100-372 (tel/fax 21 342 4323/www.pensaopracada figueira.com). Metro Rossio/tram 12, 15. **Rates** €18-€40 single; €30-€60 double. **Credit** AmEx, DC, MC, V. **Map** p250 M9 ❼
Still the best value for money of the pensões overlooking Praça da Figueira, especially after a recent refurbishment. The rooms are large with decent views; all have showers. Friendly and upbeat atmosphere with good service.
Internet. TV.

Pensão Prata

Rua da Prata 71-3, Baixa, 1100-414 (21 346 8908/pensao_prata@netcabo.pt). Metro Baixa-Chiado/bus 9, 28, 39, 46. **Rates** (excl breakfast) €15-€25 single; €22-€30 double; €30-€35 triple. **No credit cards. Map** p250 M10 ❽
This central *pensão* has decent-sized rooms with shower, sink and bidet; toilets are just outside the rooms. The owners, Carlos and his son, both speak English and are helpful. Breakfast is not included, but there are lots of cafés nearby. Recommended.

Residencial Duas Nações

Rua da Vitória 41, Baixa, 1100-150 (21 346 0710/www.duasnacoes.com). Metro Baixa-Chiado/tram 28. **Rates** €25-€35 single/double; €50-€75 with bathroom. **Credit** AmEx, DC, MC, V. **Map** p251 M9 ❾
One of the best bargains in the Baixa. Rooms are simple and comfortable; the more expensive ones have private bathrooms with showers. Try and avoid rooms along Rua Augusta, which can be

Praça da Figueira.

noisy; the rest are fairly quiet. You can order a basic continental breakfast in bed. The modest bar at the back can get quite animated in summer.
Bar. TV.

Residencial Rossio

Rua dos Sapateiros 173-2F, Baixa, 1100-577 (tel/fax 21 342 7204/pensao-rossio@hotmail.com). Metro Rossio/tram 12, 15. **Rates** €15-€25 single; €30-€35 double. **No credit cards**. **Map** p250 M9 ⑩
If you really are on a shoestring budget, this very basic hostel-like residence is safe, clean and friendly. A few rooms have their own bathrooms; others have basins and share other facilities. Be aware that if you stay here you are on the edge of Lisbon's red-light area, so hanging around alone late at night may not be a great idea.

Restauradores & Avenida da Liberdade

Deluxe

Four Seasons Hotel Ritz Lisbon

Rua Rodrigo da Fonseca 88, Marquês de Pombal, 1099-039 (21 381 1400/www.fourseasons.com/lisbon). Metro Marquês de Pombal. **Rates** (excl breakfast) €370 single; €395 double; €895-€920 suite. **Credit** AmEx, DC, MC, V. **Map** p246 D6 ⑪
Run by the Four Seasons chain, the Ritz now boasts the most impressive health spa in central Lisbon, with Zen-like decoration throughout and an indoor lap pool, solarium, steam room and sauna. Treatments such as the 'tranquillity massage' and 'heavenly nectar papaya wrap' are as good as they sound and a spa menu adds relish to relaxation. The penthouse fitness centre – with rooftop running track – has breathtaking views over the Parque Eduardo VII. The outstanding Varanda restaurant (*see p105*) attracts lots of outside custom. An art collection worthy of a museum adorns the lounge and lobby areas. Rooms are as luxurious as you'd expect, with decoration on the conservative side. All have private terraces and, although the less expensive rooms are on the lower floors, they still offer fine views over the park because of the hotel's elevated position. Even the smallest have a dressing area with two walk-in closets.
Bar. Business centre. Concierge. Disabled access. Gym. ISDN line. No-smoking rooms. Parking (free). Pool (indoor). Restaurant. Spa. Room service. TV (/in-house movies/radio/pay movies).

Hotel Tivoli Lisboa

Avenida da Liberdade 185, 1269-050 (21 319 8900/www.tivolihotels.com). Metro Avenida. **Rates** €113-€300 single; €118-€420 double; €197-€630 suite. **Credit** AmEx, DC, MC, V. **Map** p246 L8 ⑫
Halfway up the Avenida de Liberdade, this landmark is a good choice for convenience as well as creature comforts. It opened in 1933 but the interior is swish 1950s. Business people, honeymooners, families and tour groups keep returning for the plush rooms. Upon entry, you face a cavernous lobby scattered with clusters of comfy sofas and a piano bar at the back serviced by attentive waiters. The rooftop Terrace Grill has great views and traditional cuisine, while the Beatriz Costa buffet restaurant honours the Portuguese actress who lived in the hotel for years. At the rear, far from the city bustle, a secluded tropical garden (closed in winter) with oval pool is ideal for discreet sunbathing, and a tennis court and cocktail bar are also at hand. For the newer Tivoli Tejo, *see p53*.
Bars (3). Concierge. Gym. Internet. Parking (€14). Pool (outdoor). Restaurants (2). Room service. TV (pay movies).
Other locations: Tivoli Jardim, Rua Júlio Cesar Machado 9, Avenida da Liberdade, 1250 (21 359 1100).

Expensive

Hotel Altis

Rua Castilho 11, Avenida da Liberdade, 1269-072 (21 310 6000/www.altishotels.com). Metro Avenida. **Rates** €185-€205 single; €205-€225 double; €325-€350 suite. **Credit** AmEx, DC, MC, V. **Map** p246 K7 ⑬
Halfway between the gay hangouts of Príncipe Real and the offices and shops of Avenida da Liberdade, the Altis offers modern comforts at a competitive price. It attracts a mix of tourists and business travellers (there's an enormous conference centre). The Grill Dom Fernando has traditional cuisine and panoramic views, while the Girassol Restaurant serves a varied buffet. There is a small health club with heated indoor pool on the top floor.
Bars (2). Business centre. Concierge. Disabled-adapted rooms. Gym. Parking (€9). Pool (indoor). Restaurants (2). Room service. TV.
Other locations: Altis Park Hotel, Avenida Engenheiro Arantes e Oliveira 9, Olaias, 1900-221 (21 843 4200).

Hotel Heritage Avenida Liberdade

Avenida da Liberdade 28, 1250-145 (21 340 4040/www.heritage.pt). Metro Avenida. **Rates** €192-€230 single; €206-€255 double; €236-€325 triple. **Credit** AmEx, DC MC, V. **Map** p246 E7 ⑭
For review, *see p55* **Palatial by design**.
Bar. Business centre. Concierge. Gym. Internet (wireless). No-smoking rooms. Restaurant. Room service. TV (CD/DVD).

Hotel Lisboa Plaza

Travessa do Salitre 7, Avenida da Liberdade, 1269-066 (21 321 8218/www.heritage.pt). Metro Avenida. **Rates** (excl breakfast) €146-€183 single; €156-€195 double; €183-€229 triple; €260-€320 suite. *Breakfast* €14. **Credit** AmEx, DC, MC, V. **Map** p246 L8 ⑮
Opened in the early 1950s, this grand hotel was designed in bold neo-classical style by architect Lucínio Cruz. Graça Viterbo, one of Portugal's best-known interior designers, was let loose on the foyer, and a cream-coloured marble floor now blends with

the soft pastels of the carpets and furniture. The spacious rooms are also in Viterbo's style, with comfortable furnishings and light, airy bathrooms. A fantastic buffet breakfast is served in the restaurant, which also has a very good à la carte menu.
Bar. Concierge. Disabled-adapted rooms. Internet (wireless). No-smoking rooms. Parking (€16). Restaurant. Room service. TV (LCD/CD/DVD).

Hotel Marquês de Pombal

Avenida da Liberdade 243, 1250-143 (21 319 7900/ www.hotel-marquesdepombal.pt). Metro Marquês de Pombal. **Rates** €132-€170 single; €144-€182 double; €234-€260 suite. **Credit** AmEx, DC, MC, V. **Map** p246 L7 ⑯

A new four-star hotel that has 123 soundproofed rooms, including three top-floor suites. The decoration is understated contemporary, the hotel aimed at the business market: all rooms have a large desk and free broadband internet (RJ45 ethernet plug), and there's PC and printer rental. But families aren't forgotten: cots are free on request and there are discounts on extra beds for little ones. The health club, with sauna and steam bath, is for all. Don't be deceived by the piano in the restaurant; the hotel has no live music licence.
Bar. Business centre. Concierge. Gym. Internet (datapoint, high speed). Parking (€12.50). Room service. TV (pay movies/music/DVD on request).

Hotel NH Liberdade

Avenida da Liberdade 180B, 1250-146 (21 351 4060/www.nh-hotels.com). Metro Avenida. **Rates** €170-€220 single; €185-€240 double; €323-€366 suite. **Credit** AmEx, DC, MC, V. **Map** p246 E7 ⑰

This central, Spanish-owned hotel in a shopping complex caters mainly for corporate clients but also serves weekending families and couples. Its rooftop terrace bar and swimming pool have bird's-eye views of the castle. The Do Teatro restaurant serves traditional Portuguese cuisine. Spacious rooms are more like mini-suites, with separate lounge and kitchenette minimally decorated in matt black, and little luxuries such as PlayStation on call.
Bar. Business centre. Disabled-adapted rooms. Internet (wireless). Parking (€14). Pool (outdoor). Restaurant. Room service. TV (pay movies/video games/music).
Other locations: NH Campo Grande, Campo Grande 7, 1700-087 (21 791 7600); NH Parque Lisboa, Avenida António Augusto Águiar 14, 1050-016 (21 351 5000).

Moderate

Aparthotel VIP Eden

Praça dos Restauradores 24, 1250-187 (21 321 6600/www.viphotels.com). Metro Restauradores. **Rates** (excl breakfast) €89-€125 single/double/ studio; €129-€180 apartments. *Breakfast* €5. **Credit** AmEx, DC, MC, V. **Map** p250 L9 ⑱

This aparthotel is popular with young tourists and business travellers for its central location and reasonable prices, although it is perhaps showing its age. Named after the Eden cinema it once was, it retains most of the art deco façade, with a sweeping entrance and corridors lined with old film posters. All 75 studios and 59 air-conditioned apartments are comfortable and quiet, and have fully equipped kitchenettes. Most top floor rooms have balconies but the crown jewel is the swimming pool on the roof terrace, complete with bar and patio, where you can have breakfast with a view.
Bar. Disabled-adapted rooms. Pool (outdoor). TV.

VIP Inn Veneza

Avenida da Liberdade 189, 1250-141 (21 352 2618/www.viphotels.com). Metro Avenida. **Rates** (excl breakfast) €85 single/double; €114 triple. *Breakfast* €6. **Credit** AmEx, DC, MC, V. **Map** p246 E7 ⑲

Formerly plain Hotel Veneza, the edifice was built in 1886 by Portuguese lawyer Adriano Antão Barata Salgueiro and its interior is fabulously over the top. Beyond the stained-glass window above the entrance, a colourful mural of Lisbon ascends the elegant spiral staircase. Thankfully, the large rooms are not quite so kitsch, but all have a colour motif. The hotel, run by the expanding VIP chain, has few services but is cheaper than rivals.
Bar. Parking (€10.50). Room service. TV.

Budget

Hotel Suíço Atlântico

Rua da Glória 3-19, 1250-114 (21 346 1713/www. grupofbarata.com). Metro Restauradores. **Rates** €40-€46 single; €49-€59 double; €61-€70 triple. **Credit** AmEx, DC, MC, V. **Map** p250 L8 ⑳

Located next to where the Elevador da Glória leads to Bairro Alto, the Hotel Suíço Atlântico is five minutes' walk from the Praça dos Restauradores and the main tourist office. There is a pleasant TV lounge off the main foyer next to the pub-like Taverna bar. The surrounding area can get pretty noisy and seedy at night but the hotel itself is quiet. Rooms could be a little brighter and cleaner but the staff are friendly.
Bar. TV.

Pensão Portuense

Rua das Portas de Santo Antão 151-53, 1150-167 (21 346 4197/www.pensaoportuense.com). Metro Restauradores. **Rates** €32-€44 single; €47-€50 double. **Credit** MC, V. **Map** p250 F9 ㉑

A first-floor *pensão* run very efficiently by an upbeat, helpful family. The location is fine if you want to be on a street full of restaurants, but it can get noisy at night. Rooms are well furnished and comfortable and have clean, modern bathrooms with decent high-pressure showers. There are enterprising touches not often seen in this price category such as room service – a generous and fresh continental breakfast can be served in your room, as well as other snacks – and internet. Prices are low for what you get and it has a good vibe.
Internet (pay terminal). Room service. TV.

Pensão Residencial 13 da Sorte

Rua do Salitre 13, 1250-198 (21 353 9746/www.trezedasorte.no.sapo.pt). Metro Avenida. **Rates** €35-€40 single; €45-€50 double; €55-€60 triple. **Credit** AmEx, MC, V. **Map** p246 L8 ㉒

With 21 clean, simple rooms – each with a bathroom and views of the Avenida – over five floors, this *pensão* never feels crowded. The friendly owners go to great lengths to make the 'Lucky 13' attractive with pretty curtains and fresh flowers. Good value.

TV.

Residencial Alegria

Praça da Alegria 12, 1250-004 (21 347 5522/www.alegrianet.com). Metro Avenida. **Rates** €43-€58 single/39-€60 double; €53-€68 triple. **Credit** AmEx, MC, V. **Map** p246 L8 ㉓

This warm and welcoming guesthouse in a somewhat seedy area has 35 rooms but still feels like a family home. The best rooms are the spacious doubles at the back overlooking the palm tree-lined square. All have large, sparkling clean bathrooms. Decent value.

Payphone. TV.

Residencial Dom Sancho I

Avenida da Liberdade 202, 1250-147 (21 354 8648/www.domsancho.com). Metro Avenida. **Rates** €55-€75 single; €65-€85 double; €85-€100 triple. **Credit** AmEx, MC, V. **Map** p246 E7 ㉔

This good, cheap, central guesthouse is impeccably run. The room decor may be a bit old-fashioned, but it offers services which are usually only found at more expensive hotels.

Bar. Internet (high speed, shared terminal). TV.

Residencial Florescente

Rua Portas de Santo Antão 99, Restauradores, 1150-266 (21 342 6609/5062/www.residencialflorescente.com). Metro Restauradores. **Rates** €35-€45 single; €40-€55 double; €65-€80 triple. **Credit** AmEx, MC, V. **Map** p250 L8 ㉕

Across from one of Lisbon's most important live music venues, the Coliseu, this friendly place has decent sized rooms (including twins), that are chintzy but immaculate, with bright bathrooms. Rooms have free Wi-Fi; for guests without a laptop there's an internet PC. The lounge has no TV, making it a place to read or just relax. The walls of both it and the breakfast room are hung with naïve style paintings of Portuguese scenes.

Internet (Wireless). Parking (€15). TV.

Marquês de Pombal & Parque Eduardo VII

Expensive

Hotel Britania

Rua Rodrigues Sampaio 17, 1150-278 (21 315 5016/www.heritage.pt). Metro Marquês de Pombal or Avenida. **Rates** €157-€225 single; €167-€245 double; €196-€300 triple; €350-€450 suite. **Credit** AmEx, DC, MC, V. **Map** p246 L7 ㉖

The Britania is housed in a carefully restored 1940s building that was designed by leading Portuguese architect Cassiano Branco, and attracts a mix of media business types and sightseeing couples. Rooms are generously sized with marble bathrooms

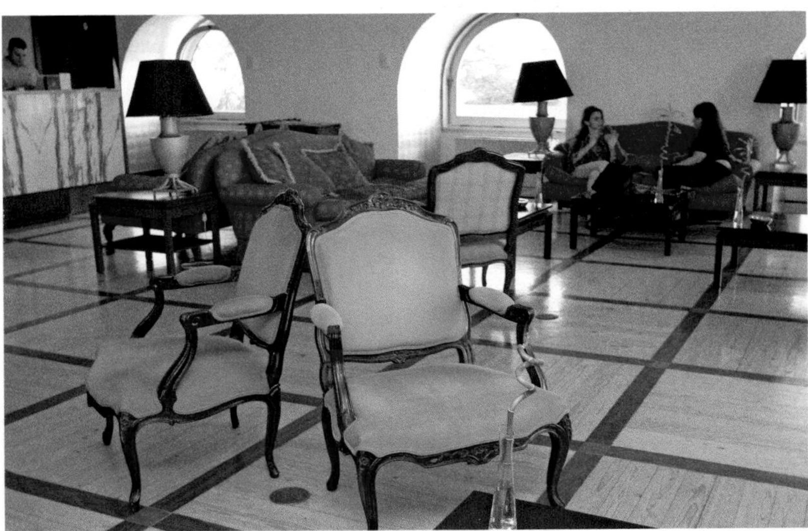

Slick service and wonderful views at the **Lisboa Regency Chiado**. *See p47.*

and classical furniture that suits the building, as well as offering five-star comforts at three-star prices. There's also a huge buffet breakfast. The receptionists all speak good English. Recommended.
Bar. Concierge. Internet (wireless). No-smoking rooms. Parking (€9). Room service. TV.

Moderate

Hotel Astoria

Rua Braancamp 10, 1250-050 (21 386 1317/www.evidenciahoteis.com). Metro Marquês de Pombal. **Rates** €45-€55 single; €50-€65 double; €65-€85 triple. **Credit** AmEx, MC, V. **Map** p246 K7 ㉗
This art deco guesthouse – which has a reputation for friendliness and comfort – has been totally modernised. All rooms have bathrooms and are surprisingly quiet for somewhere so close to Marquês de Pombal. Good value if you want somewhere central.
Bar. Internet (pay terminal). Room service. TV.

Hotel Dom Carlos Park

Avenida Duque de Loulé 121, 1050-089 (21 351 2590/www.domcarloshoteis.com). Metro Marquês de Pombal. **Rates** €90-€102 single; €106-€123 double; €126 triple; €31 extra bed. **Credit** AmEx, DC, MC, V. **Map** p246 L7 ㉘
Owned by the same chain as the nearby Dom Carlos Liberty, this place is more spacious and comfortable. Despite the location, right by Praça Marquês de Pombal, it is surprisingly secluded, overlooking a leafy square. Bedrooms are comfortable and quiet with roomy en suite marble bathrooms. The cosy, 1970s bar can rustle up light snacks at any time. A sister hotel down the road has a rooftop terrace and small gym, while the rental flats in the Chiado cater to long-stay visitors. Good value.
Bar. Internet (dataport, high speed). Parking (€10 per night). Room service. TV (pay movies).
Other locations: Chiado Residence, Rua da Misericórdia 22, Chiado, 1200-273 (21 781 5770); Dom Carlos Liberty, Rua Alexandre Herculano 13, Marquês de Pombal, 1150-005 (21 317 3570).

Casa de São Mamede. *See p47.*

Hotel Jorge V

Rua Mouzinho da Silveira 3, 1250-165 (21 356 2525/www.hoteljorgev.com). Metro Marquês de Pombal. **Rates** €70.50-€87.50 single; €82.50-€102.50 double; €105-€135 suite; €20 extra bed. **Credit** AmEx, DC, MC, V. **Map** p246 K7 ㉙
Run by friendly staff, the Jorge V offers simple, modern services and 49 compact but well-organised rooms, all with clean en suite bathrooms and 24 of them with private terraces boasting great views. There is a garish TV lounge with a rather dull adjoining bar that serves light snacks.
Bar. Internet (dataport, high speed). No-smoking floors. Parking (€10.50). TV (radio/pay movies).

Hotel Miraparque

Avenida Sidónio Pais 12, 1050-214 (21 352 4286/www.miraparque.com). Metro Parque. **Rates** €58-€90 single; €67-€100 double; €82-€125 triple. **Credit** AmEx, DC, MC, V. **Map** p246 E6 ㉚
This three-star 1950s hotel is set in a tranquil location overlooking the Parque Eduardo VII, near the El Corte Inglés shopping complex. Rooms are on the cramped side and plainly furnished, but a friendly atmosphere and helpful English-speaking staff go some way to making up for that. A rather featureless restaurant serves local cuisine.
Bar. Restaurant. Room service. TV.

Budget

Residencial Horizonte

Avenida António Augusto de Aguiar 42, 1050-017 (21 353 9526/www.hotelhorizonte.com). Metro Parque. **Rates** €35-€42 single; €50-€60 double; €60-€70 triple. **Credit** AmEx, DC, MC, V. **Map** p246 E6 ㉛
A refurbished *pensão* that is a popular choice for young business folk on a budget. Each room has a modern private bathroom with powerful hot showers. There's a bar in the lobby. The nearby sister hotel is more expensive and comfier.
Bar. TV.
Other locations: Hotel Nacional, Rua Castilho 34, Marquês de Pombal, 1250-070 (21 355 4433).

Residência Mar dos Açores

Rua Bernadim Ribeiro 14, Estefânia, 1150-071(21 357 7085/noristeves@gmail.com). Metro Marquês de Pombal/Picoas. **Rates** €25-€35 single; €35-€45 double; €50-€75 triple. **Credit** MC, V. **Map** p246 M6 ㉜

Away from Lisbon's busiest avenues but only five minutes from two metro stations, this *pensão* comes recommended. The rooms are neat and clean, and the generous continental breakfast includes a choice of fresh breads and juices. Unusually for this price bracket, there's one room with en suite bathroom, accessible by a wheelchair. The Azorean owners are friendly and transmit a can-do attitude to staff. They also rent out nearby apartments that at €65 (including breakfast) for three beds are even cheaper.
Disabled-adapted room. Room service. TV.

East of Baixa

Deluxe

Palácio Belmonte

Pátio Dom Fradique 14, Castelo, 1100-624 (21 881 6600/www.palaciobelmonte.com). Tram 12, 28/bus 37. **Rates** €300-€800 suites; €700-€800 apartments. **Credit** AmEx, DC, MC, V. **Map** p251 M9 ㉝
Just a small plaque gives away the presence of this boutique hotel in a patio near the castle. The result of the drive and imagination of French ecological entrepreneur Frédéric Coustols, the Belmonte is a 15th-century palace (itself built into Roman and Moorish walls), painstakingly renovated using modern materials and methods. Fifty-nine tile panels commissioned by the palace's owners in the 18th century, comprising some 30,000 *azulejos*, were restored and remounted. The garden, too, contains local plants and vegetables (as well as a stylish black granite pool). The hotel's library has 4,000 books, publications and papers in a variety of languages. Service is discreet and efficient. The eight suites and three apartments were individually designed and furnished with antiques and contemporary art. The largest, the Bartolomeu de Gusmão suite, has four floors and its own terrace.
Concierge. Internet. No-smoking rooms. Parking (free). Pool (outdoor). Restaurant. Room service.

Expensive

Solar do Castelo

Rua das Cozinhas 2, Castelo, 1100-181 (21 887 0909/7/www.heritage.pt). Tram 28/bus 37. **Rates** €183-€220 single; €196-€305 double; €225-€310 triple. **Credit** AmEx, DC, MC, V. **Map** p251 M9 ㉞
Opened in 2003, Solar do Castelo is the fourth in the family-run Heritage chain and its best to date. This 18th-century Pombaline building within the castle walls once housed the Alcáçova Palace kitchens. There's a medieval fountain in a courtyard that serves as a sunny eating patio; all is serenity as cars are kept out of the castle. The designers have preserved the feeling of living inside castle walls, while functional furnishings let you relax in comfy surroundings. Staff are chatty and reliable.
Bar. Concierge. Disabled-adapted rooms. Internet (wireless). No-smoking rooms. Restaurant. Room service. TV.

Moderate

Albergaria Senhora do Monte

Calçada do Monte 39, Graça, 1170-250 (21 886 6002/www.senhoramonte.blogspot.com). Tram 28. **Rates** €75-€90 single; €95-€110 double. **Credit** AmEx, DC, MC, V. **Map** p251 N8 ㉟
Set atop one of Lisbon's seven hills, with the old town at its feet and the castle and the river beyond, this place is totally removed from the bustle of the city. It's great for romantic night-time views – so long as you don't mind skimping on modern facilities. The rooms are simple, done in pink pastels and white. The top-floor café-bar and terrace serves a modest breakfast and, throughout the day, drinks and light snacks. The pricier air-conditioned rooms have balconies with beautiful views.
Bar. Room service. TV.

Olissippo Castelo

Rua Costa do Castelo 112-126, Castelo, 1100-179 (21 882 0190/www.olissippohotels.com). Metro Martim Moniz then 10min walk/tram 12/tram 28 then 4min walk. **Rates** €100-€160 single; €125-€170 double; €160-€200 suite. **Credit** AmEx, MC, V. **Map** p251 N9 ㊱
Tucked away on a cobbled street, this new four-star hotel below the castle walls has won prizes from local conservationists and plaudits from foreign visitors. The 24 rooms and two suites are plush and elegant, and some have balconies with fabulous views. Space elsewhere is at a premium and although breakfast is included there's no restaurant, just a lobby bar. The hotel is a steep walk up from the Baixa, but its larger sister hotels can't match its charm. Extraordinarily good value.
Bar. Internet (wireless). Parking (€10). Room service. TV.
Other locations: Olissippo Marquês de Sá, Avenida Miguel Bombarda 130, Saldanha, 1050-167 (21 791 1014); Olissippo Oriente, Avenida Dom João II Lote 1.03.22, Parque das Nações, 1900-083 (21 892 9100).

Budget

Pensão Residencial Ninho das Águias

Costa do Castelo 74, Castelo, 1100-150 (21 885 4070). Tram 12, 28/bus 37. **Rates** (excl breakfast) €25-€40 single; €40-€60 double. **No credit cards.** **Map** p251 M9 ㊲
Nestling below the castle, far from both nightlife and traffic, this turreted guesthouse offers simple lodgings with five-star panoramas. It's a fair walk from Baixa through steep cobbled streets, then a further climb up a spiral staircase to a precipitous patio. At the top of another spiral stairway is an octagonal tower with rickety seats where you can admire the view on three sides. Try and get room 12 on the northern corner to feel really on top of the world. The rooms are clean but spartan; most share bathrooms.
Payphone.

Pensão São João da Praça

Rua São João da Praça 97 2º, Alfama, 1100-519 (tel 21 886 2591/fax 21 888 0415). Tram 12, 28/ bus 37. **Rates** €30-€35 single/double (shared bathrooms); €40-€50 (shower); €45-€55 (full bathroom); €55-€60 suite; €15 extra bed. **Credit** MC, V. **Map** p251 N10 38

Conveniently located for the Sé cathedral, this family-run guesthouse is a little worn but clean, with decent-sized rooms that are nicely decorated and light. All have heating and a phone; many have great views and en suite bathroom. Breakfast is taken in a nearby café. One of the *pensão*'s best aspects is that you get your own key and so face no curfew. The owner has a larger, similarly priced *pensão* next to the French embassy.

TV.

Other locations: Pensão Maná, Calçada Marquês de Abrantes 97 R/C, Santos, 1200-718 (21 393 1060/fax 21 397 3196).

Sé Guesthouse

Rua de São João da Praça 97 1º, Alfama, 1100-301 (21 886 4400). Tram 12, 28/bus 37. **Rates** €50-€90 double. **Credit** AmEx, V. **Map** p251 M10 39

Named after the neighbouring medieval cathedral, this simple guesthouse is run by a family from Mozambique who have created a very welcoming atmosphere. The rooms are clean and bright, and all have bathrooms. A generous continental breakfast is included in the price. It's in the same building, but a floor below, the Pensão São João da Praça. Highly recommended.

West of Baixa

Deluxe

Bairro Alto Hotel

Praça Luís de Camões 2, Bairro Alto, 1200-243 (21 340 8222/www.bairroaltohotel.com). Metro Baixa-Chiado. **Rates** €220-€290 single; €280-€350 double; €450-€560 suite. **Credit** AmEx, DC, MC, V. **Map** p250 L9 40

For review, *see p55* **Palatial by design**.

Bar (2). Concierge. Gym. Internet (wireless). No-smoking rooms. Parking (€15). Restaurant. Room service. TV (LCD/DVD).

Expensive

Lisboa Regency Chiado

Rua Nova do Almada 114, Chiado, 1200-290 (21 325 6100/www.regency-hotels-resorts.com). Metro Baixa-Chiado. **Rates** €153-€252 single; €173-€270 double; €304-€388 suite; €60 extra bed. **Credit** AmEx, DC, MC, V. **Map** p250 L10 41

At the bottom of Rua Garrett, the Regency is one of Lisbon's best-located hotels, with postcard views. Designed, like much of the area, by Álvaro Siza Vieira (*see p34*), its success is most apparent in the morning, when a big bay window frames the best breakfast backdrop in Lisbon. The interior is in a refreshing style, with hip furniture, and complemented by efficient service. Rooms have oriental and western furnishings; they're roomy and light with touches of luxury such as fresh flowers. **Photo** *p43.*

Bar. Internet (dataport, web TV). No-smoking rooms. Restaurant. Room service. TV (pay movies).

Moderate

Casa de São Mamede

Rua da Escola Politécnica 159, Príncipe Real, 1250-100 (21 396 3166/fax 21 395 1896). Metro Rato. **Rates** €60-€65 single; €60-€75 double; €85-€90 triple. **Credit** MC, V. **Map** p246 K8 42

Midway between Príncipe Real and Rato, convenience is the main selling point here, but this religiously austere 18th-century *pensão* is as good as it gets for the price. Friendly, no-nonsense middle-aged ladies rotate shifts on reception, acting as sentries to filter out the riff-raff and make sure guests behave. Rooms are big and reasonably comfortable, with decent bathrooms. A basic breakfast is served. If you're looking for somewhere calm and child-friendly, it's ideal; if you plan to stagger in at 4am after a bar crawl, best look elsewhere. **Photo** *p45.*

TV.

Residencial Borges

Rua Garrett 108, Chiado, 1200-205 (21 346 1951/ www.hotelborges.com). Metro Baixa-Chiado/tram 28. **Rates** €65 single; €75 double. **Credit** AmEx, DC, MC, V. **Map** p250 L9 43

This Chiado hotel is one of Lisbon's oldest, and despite cursory renovations remains endearingly rough around the edges. Service is far from outstanding; it is the sheer history of the location that makes a stay worthwhile. The best rooms look out on to Rua Garrett, so you can window shop from your bed. Added luxury: a decent breakfast can be taken in your room.

TV.

Budget

Pensão Globo

Rua da Teixeira 37, Bairro Alto, 1200-459 (tel/fax 21 346 2279/www.pensaoglobo.com). Metro Baixa-Chiado/tram 28/bus 44, 45. **Rates** €20-€25 single; €25-€30 double; €45-€50 triple. **No credit cards. Map** p250 L9 44

One of the best choices for value and proximity to trendy restaurants and clubs, this friendly, well-run guesthouse is tucked away on a quiet street, thus avoiding night-time noise. More expensive rooms have en suites with showers; cheaper interior rooms are windowless and share facilities. Rooms are clean. No breakfast, but cafés abound here.

Bar. Payphone.

Pensão Londres

Rua Dom Pedro V 53, Bairro Alto, 1250-092 (21 346 2203/www.pensaolondres.com.pt). Metro Baixa-Chiado/tram 28. **Rates** €40-€52 single; €47-€67 double. **Credit** DC, MC V. **Map** p250 L8 45

A decent option, though a bit faded. Some more expensive rooms have en suites, satellite TV and phone. Its location at the Príncipe Real end of Bairro Alto means it's not too noisy, but close to the city's nightlife. Get a room with a view across Lisbon; the alternative is views of the street behind. Staff are friendly, though not all have fluent English.
Payphone.

Pensão Luar

Rua das Gáveas 101, Bairro Alto, 1200-207 (21 346 0949/www.pensaoluar.com). Metro Baixa-Chiado/ tram 28. **Rates** €15-€20 single; €22.50-€40 double; €45-€50 triple. **No credit cards. Map** p250 L9 46
This lesbian-friendly *pensão* opened in mid 2005. It has just ten rooms, all clean and with bathroom. There's no breakfast but you're spoiled for choice in the area.
TV.

Residencial Camões

Travessa do Poço da Cidade 38, Bairro Alto, 1200-334 (21 346 7510/www.pensaoresidencial camoes.com). Metro Baixa-Chiado/tram 28. **Rates** €15-€30 single; €30-€35 double; €40-€45 triple. **No credit cards. Map** p250 L9 47
Popular with backpackers, the Residencial Camões is well located with large, comfy, clean rooms, each with a shower. The chirpy family that run it speak good English. The main drawback is noise from the streets below at weekends, although the double-glazing helps. Breakfast is included in the price only from April to September.
Bar. Payphone. TV.

Residencial Santa Catarina

Rua Dr Luís de Almeida e Albuquerque 6, Santa Catarina, 1200-154 (21 346 6106/www.pensao santacatarina.com). Metro Baixa-Chiado/tram 28. **Rates** €30-€35 single; €43-€55 double; €50-€60 triple. **Credit** AmEx, MC, V. **Map** p250 K9 48
A quiet, family-run guesthouse, a short walk from the nightlife of the Bairro Alto. Rooms are clean, with private bathrooms and central heating, and some have great views of the river. Recommended.
TV.

Western waterfront/Ajuda

Deluxe

Pestana Palace

Rua Jau 54, Ajuda, 1300-314 (21 361 5600/ reservations 808 252 252/www.pestana.com). Tram 18/bus 738, 742. **Rates** €390-€410 single; €410-€430 double; €500-€700 suite. **Credit** AmEx, DC, MC, V. **Map** p244 E9 49
You would never guess that this 18th-century palace had been left abandoned for more than 50 years until lovingly restored by Portugal's Pestana Group a few years ago. Once home to the Marquês Valle Flor, this national monument now houses a vast collection of rare Portuguese 19th-century paintings, sculpture, frescoes, tapestries and furniture – although most guests stay in the modern wing. From its hilltop in Alto de Ajuda, the hotel commands fine views of the Tagus. There are sumptuous gardens, a health spa that does amazing things with hot stones and hot chocolate, and an exquisite chapel. The hotel's award-winning restaurant (*see p121*) is run by Aimé Barroyer, a charismatic Frenchman who insisted on planting his own herbs within the grounds. This is a good place to spot visiting celebs. **Photo** *p49.*
Bar. Business centre. Concierge. Internet (pay terminal). ISDN line on request. Parking (€15). Pools (1 indoor, 1 outdoor). Restaurant. Room service. Spa. TV (pay movies/DVD).

Moderate

Vila Galé Ópera

Travessa do Conde da Ponte, Ajuda 1300-141, (21 360 5400/www.vilagale.pt). Train to Alcântara Mar from Cais do Sodré/tram 15/bus 28, 49, 27, 51, 42. **Rates** €90-€150 single; €120-€220 double. **Credit** AmEx, DC, MC, V.
This opera-themed hotel (each room is named after a singer) is an excellent option in terms of location, price and facilities. Right under the Ponte 25 Abril, it is between the sights of Belém and the bars of Docas. There's live jazz on Tuesday and Thursday evenings in the river-facing Falstaff restaurant, which has an excellent à la carte menu. A well-equipped gym and indoor pool, with jacuzzi and sauna, are further attractions.
Bars (2). Disabled-adapted rooms. Gym. Internet (wireless). No-smoking rooms. Parking (€4.50). Pool (indoor). Restaurant. Room service. TV (pay movies).

Budget

Pensão Beira-Tejo

Calçada Marquês de Abrantes 43, 2E, Santos, 1200-718 (tel/fax 21 397 5106/residencial-beira-tejo @clix.pt). Tram 15, 18/tram 28 then 5min walk. **Rates** (excl breakfast) €20-€30 single; €25-€30 double; €30-€35 triple; €35-€40 quadruple. **No credit cards. Map** p245 J9 50
A friendly *residencial* high above the bars of Santos, Beira-Tejo is not exactly luxurious (its rooms have basins and showers, but loos are shared) but since it works with embassies it keeps up a decent standard. All ten rooms have small balconies, some with river views. Breakfast is not on offer as there are three cafés just outside.
Internet (pay terminal). Payphone. TV.

Lapa

Deluxe

Lapa Palace Hotel

Rua do Pau da Bandeira 4, 1249-021 (21 394 9494/www.lapa-palace.com). Tram 25, 28/bus 27. **Rates** €340-€450 single/double; €975-€1,150 suite. **Credit** AmEx, DC, MC, V. **Map** p245 H9 51

Pestana Palace. *See p48.*

OUR CLIMATE NEEDS
A HELPING HAND TODAY

RECIBO VENDA

N. Sequencial do Recibo 2 71 3 1-240495

Metropolitano de Lisboa, E.P.
Nº de Contribuinte: 500 192 855

Data: 22-11-2009 09:53

Título de Transporte	Qt.	Preço
1 Dia Ca/ml Rede (24h)	1	3,70
Cartao Sete Colinas	1	0,50
Nº. Cartão 7C: 153081486		
1 Dia Ca/ml Rede (24h)	1	3,70
Cartao Sete Colinas	1	0,50
Nº. Cartão 7C: 153081485		
Total:		Eur 8,40

Inclui IVA à taxa legal

Cliente: ____________________
Nº Contribuinte: ____________________

Processado por Computador

Set in tranquil gardens with wonderful views, this former aristocratic residence is one of Lisbon's classiest hotels, and has been frequented by the likes of Robbie Williams, Cher and George Bush. The interior is positively opulent and there are excellent facilities for fans of health and beauty treatments and exercise, including sizzling hot stone therapy. Each room has a terrace or balcony looking over the lush garden or the dome of the Basílica de Estrela. The Cipriani restaurant (*see p119*) has outstanding Mediterranean food and there's an amazing breakfast buffet, including chilled champagne.
Bars (2). Business centre. Concierge. Gym. Internet (datapoint, high speed). Parking (free). Pools (1 indoor, 1 outdoor). Restaurants (2). Room service. Spa. TV (DVD/in-house movies).

Expensive

As Janelas Verdes

Rua das Janelas Verdes 47, 1200-690 (21 396 8143/www.heritage.pt). Tram 25/bus 27, 40, 49, 60. **Rates** €174-€265 single; €187-€295 double; €215-€305 triple. **Credit** AmEx, DC, MC, V. **Map** p245 C10 52

It's said that this late 18th-century mansion was once the home of the Portuguese novelist Eça de Queiroz and inspired his magical novels *O Ramalhete* and *Os Maias*. It is now a charming hotel. As well as examples of his books and paintings, the hotel is cluttered with antiques and there's a lovely garden with an ivy-clad patio and a reading room with river views. The Museu Nacional de Arte Antiga (*see p84*) is next door.
Bar. Concierge. Internet (wireless). No-smoking rooms. Parking (€9). Room service. TV.

York House

Rua das Janelas Verdes 32, 1200-691 (21 396 2435/ www.yorkhouselisboa.com). Tram 25/bus 27. **Rates** (excl breakfast) €135-€200 single; €155-€230 double; €20-€30 extra bed. *Breakfast* €15. **Credit** AmEx, DC, EC, V. **Map** p245 J10 53

With Graham Greene and John le Carré among past guests, there can't be many better places to find literary inspiration. Behind a wall at the top of a flight of stairs is a courtyard filled with flowers, trees and plants. Arranged around it are 36 rooms, a dining room, a café and bar. Solid furnishings provide the air of a country retreat, but the cool corridors and ecclesiastical artefacts betray a pious past – until 1834 this was a Carmelite convent. The name came in 1880, when a pair of Yorkshirewomen turned it into a guesthouse. Rooms vary from deluxe modern boutique style, refurbished by celebrated interior designer Filipa Lacerda, to the original opulence of gilt mirrors and 19th-century artworks. The gourmet restaurant serves Mediterranean fusion dishes based on traditional Portuguese cuisine. During the summer you can eat out under the stars in the courtyard.
Bar. Business centre. No-smoking rooms. Restaurant. Room service. TV.

Northern Lisbon

Deluxe

Sheraton Lisboa Hotel & Towers

Rua Latino Coelho 1, Estefania, 1069-025 (21 312 0000/www.sheraton.com/lisboa). Metro Picoas. **Rates** €380 single; €400 double; €600 suite; €50 extra bed. **Credit** AmEx, DC, MC, V. **Map** p246 L6 54

A popular choice with foreign business travellers and families, with all the essentials for mobile office work. The outside is rather ugly but inside is luxury itself: spacious bedrooms with super-snug beds, and gleaming marble bathrooms. The 26th floor Panorama bar and the Lounge command fine views of the city and river. Service is excellent. On the upscale Towers floor, rooms and suites come with butler service. At the time of writing an overhaul was underway, including the installation of a spa.
Bars. Business centre. Concierge. Gym. Internet (dataport). No-smoking floors. Parking (from €20). Pool (indoor). Restaurants (2). Room service. Spa. TV (pay movies).

Expensive

Hotel Real Palácio

Rua Tomas Ribeiro 115, Picoas, 1050-228 (21 319 9500/9150/1/2/www.hoteisreal.com). Metro Picoas or Parque. **Rates** €125 single; €135 double; €160 triple; €240 suite. **Credit** AmEx, DC, MC, V. **Map** p246 L6 55

A charming five-star hotel built into a 17th-century palace and the neighbouring building. The palace's features are still very visible and it is decorated in period style, but the transition between it and the other space is sensitively managed. Although there are 135 rooms, four of them suites, the place feels cosy, while small artworks dotted about add an air of sophistication. The main restaurant opens on to an inner courtyard, the bar has jazz three times a week, and the health club – to which guests have access – has a lovely jacuzzi, sauna and Turkish bath. Children are well provided for with special furniture, toys and menus. The same chain also has a four-star sister hotel round the corner and an aparthotel nearby.
Bar. Business centre. Concierge. Disabled-adapted rooms. Gym. Internet (datapoint, high-speed & wireless). Parking (€6). ISDN lines. No-smoking floor. Restaurants (2). Room service. TV (pay movies).
Other locations: Hotel Real Parque, Avenida Luís Bivar 67, Saldanha, 1069-146 (21 319 9000); Real Residência Suite Hotel, Rua Ramalho Ortigão 41, Praça de Espanha, 1070-228 (21 382 2900).

Moderate

Hotel Lutécia

Avenida Frei Miguel Contreiras 52, Avenida de Roma, 1749-086 (21 841 1300/fax 21 841 1311/ www.luteciahotel.com). Metro Roma. **Rates** €100-

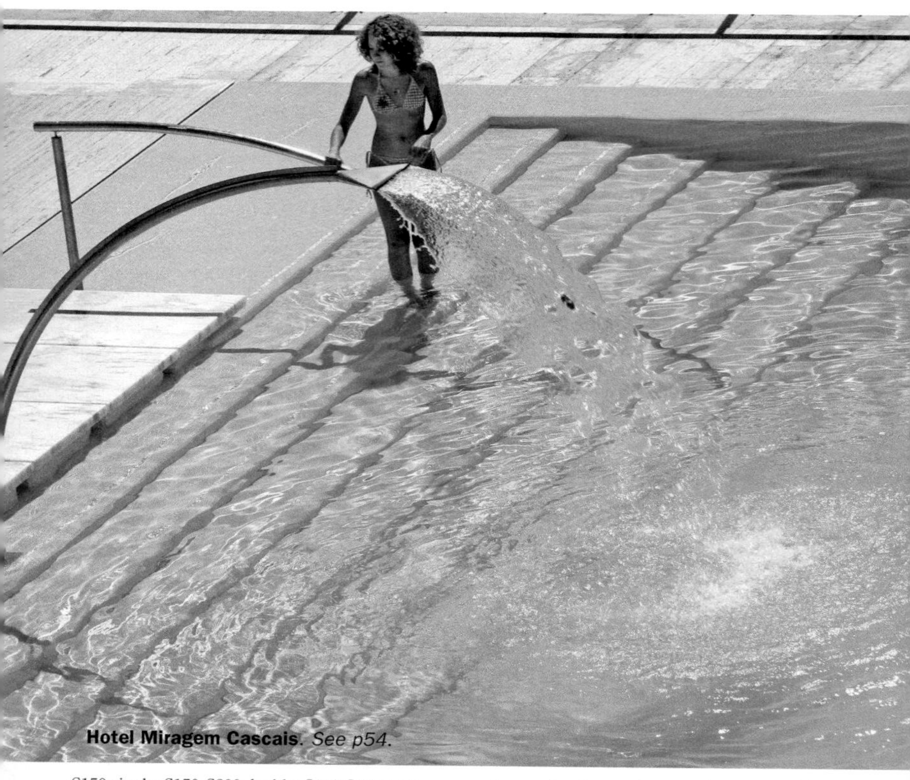

Hotel Miragem Cascais. *See p54.*

€150 single; €150-€200 double; €150-€300 triple; €30 extra bed. **Credit** AmEx, DC, MC, V. **Map** p249 N3 56

A recently renovated four-star hotel, Lutécia is now one of Lisbon's most modern and best run. The decoration is along clean modern lines, and the restaurant will soon be turning out fusion dishes to match. Many rooms have breathtaking views. Though not right in the centre the hotel is next to the metro.

Bar. Business centre. Disabled-adapted room. Internet (datapoint, high speed & wireless). No-smoking rooms. Restaurant. Room service. TV.

Budget

Pensão do Sul II

Avenida Almirante Reis 34, Anjos, 1100-018 (21 814 7253/fax 21 813 6297). Metro Anjos/tram 28. **Rates** (excl breakfast) €20-€35 single; €35-€45 double; €55-€75 triple. **Credit** MC, V. **Map** p250 L9 57

A decent, first-floor *pensão* that compares favourably with other budget options in the area. The decor is austere but the comfortable and large rooms, most with en suites, make up for this. The house-proud family who run the place really try to please guests. Breakfast is not included but there are good cafés nearby. The sister hotel is smaller and slightly dearer.

Payphone. Phone. TV.

Other locations: Pensão do Sul, Praça Dom Pedro IV (Rossio) 59 2, 1250-093 (21 342 2511).

Pensão Residencial Estrela dos Santos

Avenida Almirante Reis 53, Anjos, 1150-011 (21 317 1030/fax 21 315 1397). Metro Anjos. **Rates** €25-€50 single; €30-€60 double. **Credit** AmEx, MC, V. **Map** p247 G7 58

Modern, homely, family-run guesthouse with ten spacious rooms, all with private baths. Being next to Anjos Metro station you can be in central Lisbon in ten minutes, but traffic can be noisy.

Phone. TV.

Residencial Marisela

Rua Filipe Folque 19, Saldanha, 1050-111 (21 353 3205/www.residencialmarisela.pt). Metro Picoas or Saldanha. **Rates** €30-€40 single/double; €45-€55 triple. **Credit** AmEx, MC, V. **Map** p248 L5 59

A little out of the centre but with good transport links, this somewhat dingy guesthouse, run by Dona Marisela and her family, has a good atmosphere and one enterprising feature: there's an outdoor basketball court. The prices are pretty reasonable considering the decent breakfast, a private lavatory with most rooms, and central heating. Some of the rooms have water beds.
Internet. Payphone. Room service. TV.

Residencial Saldanha

Avenida da República 17, Saldanha, 1050-185 (21 354 6429/fax 21 354 6552/www.residencial saldanha.pt). Metro Saldanha. **Rates** (excl breakfast) €35-€37 single; €38-€40 double; €50-€60 triple; €5 extra bed. *Breakfast* €3. **Credit** AmEx, DC, MC, V. **Map** p248 M5 60

Residencial Saldanha is a plush guesthouse with reasonable rates. All the bedrooms are attractively decorated, with spacious bathrooms, and have central heating. The guesthouse is also handily located for the cinemas and shops dotted around Praça Duque de Saldanha.
TV.

Parque das Nações

For budget accommodation in this area, *see p58* **Youth hostels**.

Expensive

Tivoli Tejo

Avenida Dom João II, 1990-083 (21 891 5100/www. tivolihotels.com). Metro Oriente. **Rates** €170 single; €190 double. **Credit** AmEx, DC, MC, V.

The Tivoli Tejo is right by the former Expo 98 site, which is handy for Lisbon airport and just a ten-minute train ride from the futuristic Oriente station to the centre of town. The rooms have breathtaking views of the Tagus, of the Expo site and of the Vasco da Gama bridge. The hotel itself is popular with business clients and media types, but the swish facilities, great value and traditional food attract a more family-oriented clientele during the summer. Another attraction is the health club with sauna and Turkish bath but the highlight is the large swimming pool, which you often have to yourself.

Bar. Business centre. Internet (dataport, high speed & wireless). No-smoking floor. Parking (€12). Pool (indoor). Restaurants (2). Room service. TV (pay movies).

Cascais & Estoril coast

Deluxe

Grande Real Villa Itália Hotel & Spa

Av Rei Umberto II, 2750 Cascais (reservations 21 319 9150/1/2/www.hoteisreal.com). Train to Cascais from Cais do Sodré, then bus 405, BusCas. **Rates** €350 single/double; €450 junior suite; €550 suite; €650 executive suite; €2,500 penthouse; €50 extra bed. **Credit** AmEx, DC, MC, V.

The Grande Real Villa, scheduled to open in March 2007, is housed in the former residence of exiled King Umberto II of Italy and a neighbouring mansion, near the Boca do Inferno. It is the latest link in the chain that runs Lisbon's Real Palácio (*see p51*), and its name signals what much of the €25 million budget was spent on: a spa that claims to be the first of its kind in Cascais: with a treatment pool, Turkish bath, sauna, hydro-massage, massage, ice fountain and jet, and Vichy showers. Interior decoration is by Graça Viterbo in a 'classical revisited' style with lots of marble and Venetian mosaic, and traditional and modern Portuguese tiling. Rooms are in blue and grey, giving a nautical feel; suites are in warmer colours. All have views of the sea or the garden. Two penthouses have a jacuzzi, the third an outdoor pool.

Bar. Business centre. Gym. Internet (datapoint, high speed). Pools (2 outdoor seawater). Parking. Restaurants (2). Spa.

Hotel Miragem Cascais

Avenida Marginal 8554, Monte Estoril, 275-536 Cascais (21 006 0600/www.cascaismirage.com). Train to Monte Estoril from Cais do Sodré. **Rates** €260 single; €290 double; €475 suite. **Credit** AmEx, DC, MC, V.

The gleaming new Miragem has replaced the Estoril Sol as the favourite of visiting showbiz stars. Its outstanding feature is its giant terrace with pool, edged with cafés and restaurants. Inside, rooms are large and plush; most have balconies with ocean view. Each suite is decorated in a different style, with 'oversize' marble bathrooms, and all have balconies. Children are spoiled: as well as a play area, there's PlayStation 2, cartoon DVDs, toys on request and a free extra bed for under-nines. **Photo** *p52.*

Bars (3). Concierge. Internet (wireless). No-smoking rooms. Parking (€12). Pool (outdoor). Restaurants (3). Room service. TV (music).

Hotel Palacio Estoril

Rua do Parque, 2769-504 Estoril (21 464 8000/ www.palacioestorilhotel.com). Train to Monte Estoril from Cais do Sodré then 5min walk. **Rates** €290-€325 single; €320-€350 double; €400-€500 suite. **Credit** AmEx, DC, MC, V.

The Palacio Estoril, which faces the Casino Estoril, has a grand 1930s exterior and a lavish interior – marble halls, high stucco ceilings decorated with crystal chandeliers – that has been tastefully restored and filled with classic 19th-century French and English furniture. This is pure luxury with none of the stuffiness that is often found in establishments of similar quality. If you don't fancy the beach or the casino, note that the hotel owns the Golfe do Estoril course (*see p201*) and guests can play a round at special rates (from €22).

Bar. Concierge. Parking (free). Pool. Restaurants (2). Room service. TV.

Penha Longa Hotel & Golf Resort

Estrada da Lagoa Azul, Linhó PT, 2714-511 Sintra (21 924 9011/www.penhalonga.com). Train to Estoril from Cais de Sodré then bus 403 to Malveira. **Rates** €350 single; €370 double; €700-€1,200 suite. **Credit** AmEx, DC, MC, V.

Half an hour from the airport, a ten-minute drive from Estoril (there's a shuttle bus) or a short taxi ride from Malveira, this country club retreat is a golfer's paradise with two challenging courses (*see p201*), as well as tennis courts and swimming pools, all set in a rolling pine forest below the Sintra hills. There are reduced green fees for guests, from €20 per hour. The resort is modern, but there's a beautifully restored 13th-century monastery in its grounds that makes an original party or wedding venue.

Bars (3). Business centre. Concierge. Gym. Internet (wireless). Parking (free). Pools (1 indoor, 1 outdoor). Restaurants (2). Room service. Spa. TV.

Expensive

Farol Design Hotel

Avenida Rei Humberto II de Italia 7, 2750-461 Cascais (21 482 3490/www.cascais.org). Train to Cascais from Cais do Sodré, then bus 405, 415, BusCas. **Rates** €110-€230 single; €150-€270 with seaview; €130-€250 double; €170-€300 with seaview; €200-€370 designer room; €250-€450 suite. **Credit** AmEx, DC, MC, V.

Architect Carlos Miguel Dias and the celebrity designers – among them Ana Salazar, Augustus, Fátima Lopes and João Rôlo – who decorated the 34 rooms and suites have made this a uniquely stylish place to stay. Rates remain fair (varying according to room and view) and everyone gets a jacuzzi. The Farol is well placed if you want to explore Cascais (it's next to the marina, walking distance from the town centre) and the coast to the north. Kitsch decoration makes the common areas look a little like a set from *Buck Rogers* but you won't find a robot chef in the Rosa Maria restaurant, just immaculate service and inspired food – although perhaps it overdoes the trance music a bit. A deck terrace overlooks the pool, and prompt waiter service makes this ideal for lounging. In the morning punters come straight from the nearby Nuts Club to nurse their hangovers.

Bar. Internet (dataport, ISDN lines). Parking (free). Pool (outdoor). Restaurant. TV.

Palatial by design

Portugal's capital is full of *palácios* and *palacetes*, while its pumping nightlife has made it one of Europe's coolest cities. Hardly surprising, then, that hoteliers and designers are joining forces to turn ever more old mansions into luxury pads. As a result, a new type of visitor is being drawn to Lisbon, following the waves of backpackers in the 1980s and clubbers in the '90s: fad conscious and moneyed, they are discovering a city that is finally ready to pamper them as they demand.

At the heady end of the market, the Palácio Belmonte (*see p46*) led the way with its offbeat luxury. The Hotel Regency Chiado (*see p47*) brought design to the clued-up middle classes and the Farol Design Hotel (*see p54*) took it a step further. **Bairro Alto Hotel** (*see p47*) sums up the current state of things, with its tasteful mix of Portuguese old and global new. The decor of this boutique hotel, opened in October 2005 in a building that once housed the Grande Hotel Europa, recalls that establishment's 19th-century heyday – when opera divas and thespians such as Sarah Bernhardt stayed between performances at the São Carlos theatre – but with modern touches. The 51 rooms and four suites, in tones of blue, red, yellow or ivory, with hand-painted designs of native birds, all have plasma screen TVs. Bathrooms are in bourgeois style; the suites have freestanding tubs. The rooftop bar and terrace have fine river views, while the ground floor Igloo lounge is a cosy refuge.

Managed by a company with hotels in Paris and Mustique, this place dances to an international beat – sometimes literally, thanks to a house DJ in the lobby bar. The concept, 'a design-hotel basic' in some cities, in the words of one blasé American visitor, 'is still considered a novelty here'. Lisbon has been getting more US coverage of late, as some Americans at least defy a sagging dollar and finally discover just how cool the city is.

Meanwhile, even implausible fashion victims are picking up on the design trend. Portugal's VIP Hotels (www.viphotels.com), which in Lisbon has one basic Inn and one Aparthotel (the VIP Eden, *see p42*) targeting business travellers, is gestating a 'Zen concept' VIP Grand, to open in mid 2007 in the former headquarters of state TV broadcaster RTP. The Zen influence is already in evidence at the Ritz (*see p41*), whose giant spa has proved a hit with locals, and prompted copycat efforts at rival hotels.

Another combination of the old and the new is the **Heritage Avenida Liberdade**, opened in July 2005 by the Lisbon company that owns As Janelas Verdes (*see p51*), Solar do Castelo (*see p46*) and the Hotel Lisboa Plaza (*see p41*). The old is supplied by the late 18-century mansion the hotel occupies, the new by the interior design of Miguel Câncio Martins, architect of Paris's Buddha Bar and London's Strictly Hush. The hotel has 42 rooms and suites, all with plasma screen TVs.

Hotel Albatroz

Rua Frederico Arouca 100, 2750-353 Cascais (21 484 7380/www.albatrozhotels.com). Train from Cais do Sodré to Cascais. **Rates** €165-€215 single; €195-€255 with beach view; €210-€270 double; €245-€320 with beach view; €290-€405 suite. **Credit** AmEx, DC, MC, V.

Overlooking the Conceição beach, this luxurious gem is small enough for truly personalised service. The interior has a relaxed, oriental flavour that just makes you want to sit on the floor and meditate. A stylish mosaic oval pool looks on to the harbour. A beachside restaurant serves delicacies such as stuffed crab, lobster salad or stone bass ceviche (main courses from €15). The Albatroz Palace opposite has spacious suites, a library, business services and a cooking school, while the nearby Villa Cascais has lower rates and an acclaimed fish restaurant, and shares the Albatroz's pool.

Bar. Business centre. Internet. Parking (free). Restaurant. Room service. TV.

Other locations: Albatroz Palace, Rua Frederico Arouca 100, 2750-353 Cascais (21 484 7380); Villa Cascais, Rua Fernandez Tomás 1, 2750-342 Cascais (21 486 3410).

Moderate

Clube do Lago

Avenida do Lago 4, 2765-420 Monte Estoril (21 464 7597/www.hotelclubedolago.com). Train to Monte Estoril from Cais do Sodré. **Rates** €60-€99 single studio; €77-€128 double studio; €112-€170 penthouse suite. **Credit** AmEx, DC, MC, V.

This swish health club-cum-aparthotel is the best bargain on the Estoril coast. Prices may seem high, but split it between a group of friends and it becomes reasonable to a point with which nowhere else in Lisbon can compare. With indoor and outdoor pools,

Perfect pitch: escape the rat race at newly revamped **Lisboa Camping**. *See p57*.

gym, jacuzzi, Turkish bath, sauna, solarium, squash and tennis courts, indoor and poolside bar, games room and restaurant, it is paradise for sporty types. The mini-apartments are spacious, all with kitchenette, terrace and sofabeds; some have their own washing machines. A generous cooked buffet breakfast is served in the restaurant, which doubles as a charcoal grill. Rooms can be rented for up to a year at reduced rates. Recommended.
Bars (2). Gym. Internet (pay terminal). Parking (€5). Pools (2 outdoor). Restaurant. Spa. TV.

Estalagem do Muchaxo

Praia do Guincho, 2750-642 Cascais (21 487 0221/342/www.muchaxo.com). Train to Cascais from Cais do Sodré then bus 405, 415, BusCas. **Rates** €51-€77 single; €55-€98 with seaview; €60-€90 double; €65-€115 with seaview. **Credit** AmEx, DC, MC, V.
An atmospheric converted fort, with a modern annexe whose rooms are a bit pricier, Estalagem do Muchaxo overlooks the huge Guincho beach. Rooms are basic and comfortable; some have sea views but the view from the airy lounge is just as good. There's a saltwater pool out back (open June-Sept) with its own bar and internet corner. The hourly bus into town takes some 15 minutes. The restaurant has its own lobster bed, and prices compare well with the posh gaffs along the coast road. But beware: the electric organ is in action at weekends.
Bar. Concierge. Parking (free). Pool (outdoor, seawater). Restaurant. TV.

Hotel Baia

Avenida Marginal, 2754-509 Cascais (21 483 1033/www.hotelbaia.com). Train to Cascais from Cais do Sodré. **Rates** €55-€110 single; €75-€135 double; extra bed half cost of room. **Credit** AmEx, DC, MC, V.
Popular with Brits due to its location near a string of pubs, the Hotel Baia is a stone's throw from the beach (although swimming here is not recommended), and also has an indoor rooftop pool for cooling down in summer. Modestly priced for what it offers, the hotel has 113 spacious, double-glazed and comfy rooms and suites, some with a balcony overlooking the sea. There's a spacious ground floor and a restaurant, the Grill, that's worth a visit.
Bar. Business centre. Restaurant. Parking (€10). TV.

Hotel Inglaterra

Rua do Porto 1, 2765-271 Estoril (21 468 4461/ www.hotelinglaterra.com.pt). Train to Estoril from Cais do Sodré then 5min walk. **Rates** (excluding breakfast) €55-€64 single; €72-€80 double; €110-€130 suite. **Credit** AmEx, MC, V.
This beautifully converted cream-coloured mansion is now part of the Best Western chain. Rooms are spacious and the breakfast generous; you can have it served on your terrace or in the café-bar by the elegant pool. Recommended.
Bars (2). Business centre. Internet (dataport). Parking (€10). Pool (outdoor). Restaurant. Room service. TV.

Budget

Pensão Pica Pau

Rua Dom Afonso Henriques 48, 2765-185 Estoril (21 466 7140/www.picapauestoril.com). Train to Estoril from Cais do Sodré. **Rates** €35-€50 single; €50-€75 double; €65-€97 triple. **Credit** AmEx, DC, MC, V.
The Pica Pau (literally, 'woodpecker') is a friendly, English-run guesthouse with lots of character and a place to meet other travellers. It's right by the beach and has a great outdoor pool area. Rooms are well decorated and some look out on to the garden area, with its pool and jacuzzi. Breakfast is excellent; there's also a pleasant shellfish restaurant with reasonable prices. The large bar area comes to life at night. Recommended.
Bar. Pool (outdoor). Restaurant. TV.

Residencial Solar Dom Carlos

Rua Latino Coelho 8, 2750-408 Cascais (21 482 8115/fax 21 486 5155/www.solardomcarlos.net). Train to Cascais from Cais do Sodré. **Rates** €30-€50 single; €40-€65 double; €60-€100 triple. **Credit** DC, MC, V.
Housed in a former royal residence, the Residencial Solar Dom Carlos is a clean, family-run *pensão* that has recently been made more cosy and modern. In the centre of Cascais, it is ideal for backpackers keen to sample the local nightlife. A basic continental breakfast is served in a grandish dining room. The large, air-conditioned rooms have solid furniture and decent-sized bathrooms. The manager is chatty and speaks good English – ask to see the 17th-century chapel behind the building. The secluded garden next door is open to guests.
Room service. TV.

Camping & caravanning

Camping Orbitur-Guincho

Estrada da Areia, 2750-053 Cascais (21 487 0450/ bungalow reservations 21 811 7070/www.orbitur.com). Train to Cascais from Cais do Sodré/bus 405, 415. **Rates** €2.70-€5.10 per tent; €50-€87 bungalow (sleeps 2-6). **Credit** DC, MC, V.
A great location among low pine trees, just ten minutes from Guincho, one of Europe's best windsurfing beaches, makes this a popular hangout for water bunnies. It's five kilometres (three miles) from Cascais. There are plenty of facilities and it can get busy in the high season but the crowd usually provides a good party atmosphere. An open area is available for motor homes.
Disabled facilities. Restaurant.

Lisboa Camping

Estrada da Circunvalação, Parque de Monsanto, 1400-041 (21 762 8200/fax 21 762 8299/www.lisboacamping.com). Bus 714, 750. **Rates** €4.10-€5.80 per tent; €18-€25 camping pitch (2 people); €63-€103 bungalow (sleeps 2-6). **Credit** AmEx, MC, V.

Located in Monsanto park, Lisboa Camping is set amid woods and can accommodate up to 400 tents. It has 170 fully equipped camping pitches and 70 furnished four- to six-person bungalows. After a revamp, the campsite now boasts new facilities such as two multi-sports areas, a mini-golf course, two tennis courts, a pool area with solarium and terrace, a common room and an amphitheatre. **Photo** *p56*.
Bar. Pool (outdoor). Restaurant.

Youth hostels

Easy Hostel

Rua São Nicolau 13, 4D, Baixa, 1100-547 (21 886 4280/lisboneasyhostel@sapo.pt). Metro Baixa-Chiado. **Rates** €18-€20 bed. **No credit cards. Map** p251 M10 61

At the top of a shabby 18th-century building (don't worry – there's a lift), this bare but cheerful new hostel joins an emerging trend of backpackers' joints with DIY facilities (kitchen, washer and dryer) absent from your traditional *pensão*. It has 30 bunk beds in rooms sleeping four or six, four shared showers (towels are provided), a lounge with free internet PC (there's also Wi-Fi), guitar and dartboard, and a smaller one with plasma TV for games or DVDs (also provided). A basic breakfast is included.
Internet (shared terminal).

Lisbon Lounge Hostel

Rua de São Paulo 111, 2, Cais do Sodré, 1200-427 (21 346 2061/www.lisbonloungehostel.com). Metro Cais do Sodré. **Rates** (excl breakfast) €18-€20 per person (dorm); €20-€22 double. *Breakfast* €3. **No credit cards. Map** p250 K8 62

Modernity, style and comfort are the goals here, and it's done well on all counts. There are four dormitories sleeping four or six, and one double room; all beds boast crisp linen and fluffy pillows. Rooms are bright if bare; each has a basin but guests share two bathrooms, three showers and three loos. The hostel has a funky lounge, internet access and helpful staff. The neighbourhood is scruffy (it is one of Lisbon's red light districts) but has some of the city's most offbeat bars, such as the reggae club Jamaica. The hostel is open 24 hours – handy given its location halfway between the nightlife areas of Bairro Alto and Docas. But of course, by the same token it can get a bit noisy. The hostel may move in the next couple of years, so check.
Internet (pay terminal).

Lisbon Poets Hostel

Rua do Duque 41, Chiado, 1200 (21 346 1058 (www.lisbonpoetshostel.com). Metro Baixa-Chiado. **Rates** (excl breakfast) €18-€20 dormitory; €40 double; €65 studio. *Breakfast* €3. **No credit cards. Map** p250 L9 63

A funky downtown hostel in an immaculately restored building, part of which dates from the 17th century. Over four floors it has 30 single beds in dorms and two double rooms – all sharing access to a kitchen, four bathrooms and an *azulejo*-lined lounge with free internet that's a great place to chat with fellow travellers – plus a ground floor studio with its own facilities. The poetry theme is a bit of a gimmick but overall the place is recommended.
Internet (shared terminal).

Pousada de Juventude de Catalazete

Estrada Marginal (junto ao INATEL), 2780 Oeiras (21 443 06 38/reservations 707 203 030/www.pousadasjuventude.pt). Train to Oeiras from Cais do Sodré, then 15min walk. **Rates** dorm €9-€13; double €24-€28; with bathroom €30-€36; apartment €55-€70. **Credit** MC, V.

A 20-minute train ride from Lisbon on the Estoril coast, this youth hostel, in a building put up by the Marquês de Pombal after the 1755 earthquake, is well located for water sports enthusiasts. It overlooks Oeiras beach (rather cleaner than it used to be), and Carcavelos is just around the headland. Lunch and dinner can be eaten on the terrace. The place is well run, with friendly staff. Close by are the Oeiras marina and a fun seawater pool (open June-Sept), and the Jamor sports complex (*see p198*) is a short bus ride away. Book ahead in summer: phone, email catalazete@movijovem.pt or go online.
Bar. Internet (pay terminal). Parking (free). Payphone.

Pousada de Juventude de Lisboa

Rua Andrade Corvo 46, Saldanha, 1050-009 (21 353 2696/reservations 707 203 030/www.pousadasjuventude.pt). Metro Picoas. **Rates** €16 per person (dorms sleep 4 or 6); €43 double. **Credit** MC, V. **Map** p246 L6 64

The more central of Lisbon's two youth hostels is cheap, well run and pleasantly clean. There is a conference room and good facilities for the disabled, but no internet access. Rooms are basic but comfortable and some have their own bathrooms. Lunch and dinner are served in the campus-like canteen. The decent bar serves drinks on a large sunbathing patio in high season. This is not the best place for night owls as reception closes at midnight. Email for booking is lisboa@movijovem.pt.
Bar. Disabled-adapted room. Self-service canteen.

Pousada de Juventude do Parque das Nações

Rua de Moscavide 47-101, 1998 (21 892 0890/reservations 707 203 030/www.pousadasjuventude.pt). Metro Oriente. **Rates** €11-€13 per person (dorms sleep 4 or 6); €30-€36 double. **Credit** MC, V.

A modern hostel at the former Expo site, and probably the best option for backpackers in Lisbon. Everything is available, from internet access to shared cooking facilities, in a friendly atmosphere. Rail links are good and it's also very handy for the airport. There's a self-service breakfast available from 8.30am. The doors are closed at midnight, although they are not actually locked. Email lisboaparque@movijovem.pt.
Disabled-adapted rooms. Parking (free). Payphone. Self-service canteen.

Sightseeing

Features

Palácio dos Marquêses da Fronteira. *See p96*.

Introduction

Between the river and the sea.

Most people arrive in Lisbon by air these days, and flight paths usually sweep over the city centre. The view from the right side of the plane takes in the great curve of the River Tagus and the breadth of its estuary, with the tangle of city-centre streets below. But, traditionally, visitors would arrive by water – on a cruise ship or one of the ferries that cross the Tagus from the south to dock at the Cais do Sodré or Praça do Comércio terminals.

Miradouros

For coffee and a view
Chapitô (*see p187*) or the café of Teatro Taborda (*see p195*).

For a drink before hitting the Bairro Alto
Esplanada do Adamastor (*see p82*).

For flower-edged romance
Santa Luzia in Alfama (*see p72*); Nossa Senhora do Monte in Graça (*see p75*); Jardim de São Pedro de Alcântara (*see p80*).

For sunset
Esplanada da Igreja da Graça (*see p75*).

To see the city
Castelo de São Jorge (*see p72*); Elevador de Santa Justa (*see p63*).

Trains coming into the city of Lisbon from the Algarve mostly now cross the river under the Ponte 25 de Abril, comparable in size and design to San Francisco's Golden Gate Bridge. At its southern foot, the statue of Cristo Rei ('Christ the King') presides. If you come from the south or east by car, you'll traverse either this bridge or the newer Ponte Vasco da Gama, far to the east.

Whichever way, there are few more spectacular entrances to a major European city: across the vast Tagus estuary, the 'peaceful harbour' – 'Alis-Ubbo' in Phoenician – from which Lisbon probably took its name. The mouth of the Iberian peninsula's longest river is one of the world's largest natural harbours.

The 18th-century heart of the city – Baixa, literally 'low' – is fronted by a grand square, the Praça do Comércio, that opens out on to the water. From here, the city scrambles up on to its alleged seven hills. Above the clutter of terracotta rooftops, the skyline is topped by the brooding castle, the Castelo de São Jorge, with white-domed churches to the east and west – the Panteão Nacional de Santa Engrácia just below it, and the Basílica da Estrela way over to the west.

If the Praça do Comércio was the city's welcome mat – and remains so for tens of thousands of commuters who cross from the south bank every day – the front door is the bold Arco Triunfal on the square's northern side, through which leads Rua Augusta, the Baixa's main thoroughfare. And don't forget the *miradouros*, the lookout points dotted through Lisbon that bring new vistas into view.

Central Lisbon

Baixa from the rubble.

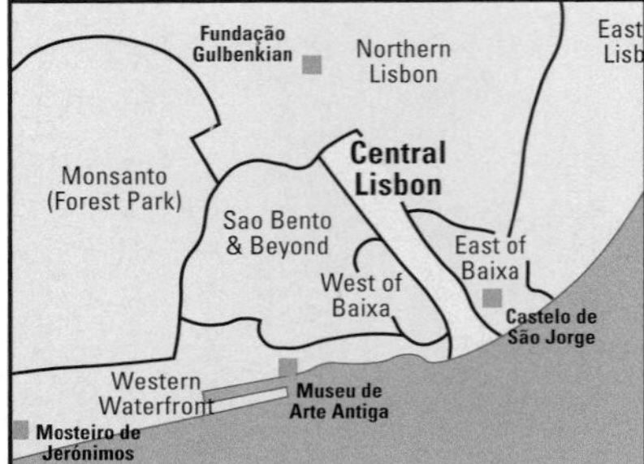

The Baixa

A walk around the Baixa, Lisbon's traditional downtown, gives a flavour of how things were done in the days before shopping malls. Old fashioned emporia, long driven out of business in other cities, here survive thanks to rent controls. Thus you can wander down streets where trades have clustered for centuries: jewellers linger on Rua do Ouro (also marked on some maps by its old name, Rua Aurea), Rua dos Sapateiros is still a 'street of shoemakers' and Rua dos Fanqueiros is home to a number of textile merchants and fabric shops, as it has always been.

Or at least since the mid 18th century. Before then, the heart of medieval Lisbon was a labyrinthine tangle of narrow streets. Then, as now, the poles were two squares: the Terreiro do Paço on the waterfront, later remade as the Praça do Comércio but still often known by its old name; and the Rossio (now officially Praça Dom Pedro IV) at its upper end where the low ground splits into two valleys. The centre of commerce was the Rua Nova, which cut east-west across the lower end of the modern grid. The largest of Lisbon's Jewish quarters, the Judiaria Grande, occupied a big chunk of the Baixa, centred around the synagogue that stood between Rua da Conceição and Rua de São Nicolau, at their eastern end.

The 1755 earthquake put paid to all that. Charged with the job of reconstruction, the Marquês de Pombal (*see p17*) based his plan on a military encampment, with each street having a specific function. The orderly rows still stand as he planned them, though some took until the next century to finish – the **Arco Triunfal** (Triumphal Arch) capping Rua Augusta was completed in 1873. That's Glory on top of the arch, holding wreaths above the heads of Genius and Bravery. Below are Viriatus, Nun'Álvares Pereira, Vasco da Gama and the Marquês de Pombal. The Tagus is the River God on the left, the Douro is on the right.

This grid retains nothing of medieval Lisbon, yet has accumulated a patina of history in the past 250 years. In the waterfront **Praça do Comércio**, Pombal wanted a majestic square to rival anything found in Europe, and architects Carlos Mardel and Eugênio dos Santos more or less gave him what he wanted. It was designed with one side open to the river and the other three for government ministries, with the centrepiece Joaquim Machado de Castro's 14-metre-high (46-foot) equestrian statue of Dom José I, monarch at the time of the earthquake. Long condemned to be a car park, the centre of the square is once again used as a public space – even an outdoor sculpture gallery. Traffic still surges around the edges, though, severing it from the river, and rush-hour crowds pour on and off buses, trams and

Riding high on **Praça do Comércio**.

ferries, the square being the entry point into the city for many inhabitants of the southern suburbs. On the square's north-east corner, the Café Martinho da Arcada (*see p126*) has been open since 1782. Lisbon's iconic poet Fernando Pessoa was a regular in the 1920s and '30s (*see p78* **Walking Lisbon**). On the north-west corner is a tourist office and a fine restaurant, Terreiro do Paço (*see p104*). Next door is the Sala Ogival (21 342 0690, open 11am-7pm Tue-Sat), a space run by national winemakers' association ViniPortugal where you can taste wines for free. Next to it is the Lisbon Welcome Center, with a walk-in tourist bureau.

The **Paços do Concelho**, housing Lisbon's Câmara Municipal (city council) sits on the west side of the Baixa on the Praça do Município. Built in 1867, it was renovated after a 1996 fire that mysteriously broke out in the department of financial records. If you want a peep inside, check at the desk about guided visits (usually two Sunday mornings a month). The Câmara's grand balcony was where the Portuguese Republic was proclaimed on 5 October 1910, and the square is the setting for annual Republic Day celebrations. The Rua do Arsenal running west from here to the Cais do Sodré waterfront district is principally famous for the smell of *bacalhau* emanating from its storefronts.

Many of the Baixa's streets are now pedestrianised, notably the main drag, **Rua Augusta**. The end by the arch has a few raggedy stalls that locals call the 'Mercado dos Hippies'. On and around Rua Augusta are café esplanadas, buskers, shops and fast-food joints. The workaday lunch crowd head for the cluster of cheap restaurants on Rua dos Correeiros or more obscure eateries, doorways devoid of signage that offer sustenance for local workers. At night the Baixa has no real bar life.

Many businesses hereabouts still have appealing old fronts, such as the dilapidated art nouveau button shops and haberdashers on Rua da Conceição. Between the tram tracks near the junction with Rua da Prata, a rectangular manhole cover marks the way down to some Roman tanks, often referred to as 'baths' or fish-salting tanks, but probably the foundations of a temple or other large building. They are normally flooded and open to the public only once a year, in the autumn. Those interested in Roman Lisbon should step into the **Núcleo Arqueológico** on Rua dos Correeiros, or head east to the **Museu do Teatro Romano** (*see p70*).

The area's tallest landmark is the **Elevador de Santa Justa**, the 19th-century solution to the problem of getting up to the Chiado without breaking into a sweat. Today the series of escalators in Baixa-Chiado Metro station do part of the job, but are underground.

Going up: **Elevador de Santa Justa**.

Walking Lisbon Revolution

A visit to **Rossio** helps explain how the 1974 military coup that ended 48 years of dictatorship in Portugal came to be known as the Revolução dos Cravos, or Carnation Revolution. Amid jubilant celebrations, flower sellers in the square pressed red carnations on the young soldiers who had toppled the old regime. The motif of the flower in a rifle barrel, evoking the relatively bloodless nature of the coup, remains a powerful symbol of Portugal's transition to democracy.

The florists are still here, although fewer in number and, since a refurbishment a few years ago, in discreet modern kiosks at the southern end of the square rather than in the centre. There is a carnation-strewn march down Avenida da Liberdade every 25 April, the date of the coup, but fewer people seem to take part every year as the Revolution recedes into history.

Looking up and south-west from Rossio you'll see, high above the rooftops, the ruined arches of the **Convento do Carmo** (*see p77*), left as a permanent reminder of the calamity. It was in the cobbled square beside this church that the main confrontation of the 1974 Revolution took place.

Following the map, take Calçada do Carmo, which leads from the west side of Rossio to a steep flight of steps opposite the side entrance to Rossio railway station. From the top of the steps turn left and follow the same street into a tree-lined square, **Largo do Carmo**. On the left you pass the arched entrances, designed for cavalry, of the headquarters of the Guarda Nacional Republicana, Portugal's paramilitary national guard. A soldier in the GNR's grey and green uniform usually stands on sentry duty.

It was to this barracks that the leaders of the old regime fled after the uprising. These

Elevador de Santa Justa

Rua do Ouro (21 342 7944). Metro Baixa-Chiado. **Open** 7am-9pm daily. **Admission** €2.40 (return). **No credit cards**. **Map** p250 L9.

The industrial-age iron tracery of the Santa Justa lift – sometimes called the Elevador do Carmo – is one of Lisbon's most beloved landmarks but became a national monument only in 2002. The 45m (147ft) elevator was built by Portuguese-born Eiffel disciple Raul Mesnier de Ponsard, and officially opened in August 1901, linking downtown Rua do Ouro with the square next to the Carmo church up above. The 15m (50ft) viaduct at its head, bridging the Rua do Carmo, was reopened in 2006 after several years of engineers shoring up buildings in the wake of works on the Metro. On the top floor, up a spiral staircase, a café offers 360° views. The elevador is part of the Carris public transport system; a one-way trip is the equivalent of one bus journey, but on board the lift only return tickets are on sale, so if you want a single it's better value with a pass.

Núcleo Arqueológico da Rua dos Correeiros

Rua dos Correeiros 9 (21 321 1700). Metro Baixa-Chiado/tram 12, 28. **Guided tours** *Portuguese* 3pm, 4pm Thur; 10am, 11am, 3pm, 4pm Sat. *English* noon, 5pm Sat. **Admission** free. **Map** p250 M10.

Underneath the Millennium BCP bank headquarters in Rua Augusta (enter round the back), the Archaeological Centre offers a glimpse of what's lurking below the Baixa. In Roman times this was a river beach. The locals made sauces with fish and shellfish bits mixed with salt, spices and herbs. The ingredients were then put in tanks and left to rot over time into a suitably tasty decomposed mush. When the bank wanted to redo its head office in 1991, the construction teams unearthed the ancient included Marcello Caetano, who had taken over from Salazar as prime minister in 1968, President Américo Tomás, and several government ministers. In support of the rebel troops, crowds packed into the square, cheering from the tops of tanks for their surrender. Caetano told Captain Salgueiro Maia, the young rebel officer demanding his capitulation, that he feared 'power would fall to the mob' and as a matter of dignity he should surrender only to a general.

General António de Spínola, a charismatic, monocle-wearing figure, was telephoned and agreed to intervene, although he had played no part in the coup. He spoke with the rebel officers and entered the barracks. As word came that he had accepted the unconditional surrender of Caetano and his colleagues, the crowd rejoiced. The next day the deposed leaders flew to exile in Brazil.

A few streets away another confrontation was unfolding. Leaving Largo do Carmo by Travessa do Carmo and turning left into Rua Serpa Pinto takes you past the now dilapidated **Avis** restaurant on the left. Avis was once a glittering gathering place for the rich and famous. After most of its patrons fled following the Revolution, left-wing visitors like Jean Paul Sartre, Simone de Beauvoir and some of the young 'Captains of April' who had led the coup helped keep it in business.

Turn right into Rua Garrett and then second left into Rua Antónia Maria Cardoso. On the right, opposite the **Teatro São Luiz**, a few faded graffiti panels remain as a reminder of the revolutionary art that proliferated for years after the 1974 coup but has now all but disappeared. No.26, at the end of the street on the left, was the headquarters of the **PIDE**, the despised and feared secret police of the Salazar-Caetano regime. A plaque on the wall commemorates the four people who were killed when PIDE agents fired into the crowd that surrounded the building on 25 April 1974. Their deaths represented the last violent throes of the regime.

That plaque is currently somewhat obscured by a construction site; the building is controversially being turned into a residential complex. It had stood abandoned for decades, not least because of its powerful associations. The PIDE's crimes were not on the scale of its Nazi or Soviet counterparts, but it was a violent tool of repression: the building was used to detain, interrogate and torture opponents of the regime.

The decision to turn former prisoners' cells into luxury apartments outraged some Portuguese, who wanted the building made into a museum commemorating the resistance to the dictatorship. The campaign failed, and while an alternative has been suggested in the form of the Aljube prison, for now the only keeper of the flame is the Associação 25 de Abril.

Double back to Largo do Chiado, turn left and then right up Rua da Misericórdia to No.95. The association's members include some of the – now greying – young officers who revolted back in 1974.

Sightseeing

complex. Experts were called in and the centre opened to the public in 1995. On display are artefacts found during the digging, ancient walls, a holding tank and an intact section of mosaic floor.

Rossio

Most people moving around the city will pass through Rossio at least once a day. It's also a central meeting point, and was once a market. Flowers are still sold at its southern end; it was here that a flowerseller on 25 April 1974 is supposed to have given a carnation to a soldier, thus earning the Revolution the nickname Revolução dos Cravos. But most of the cafés that the nervous dictator Salazar had 15 years earlier ordered to ban *tertúlias* – informal discussion groups – have disappeared. Of those that remain, Café Nicola (*see p126*), here in one form or another since the late 18th century, has the most historical resonance. Around the square, crowds of commuters queue for buses and tourists browse at kiosks selling foreign-language newspapers.

Meanwhile, Africans cluster around the steps of the **Teatro Nacional Dona Maria II** (*see p194*), catching up with news from Guinea-Bissau or Angola: the area first became a magnet for them because the nearby **Igreja de São Domingos** traditionally had a black priest. In the square in front of the church, businessmen peruse the paper during a lunchtime shoeshine, shopworkers fortify themselves with a nip of *ginjinha*, the cough syrup-like brandy made from morello cherries that is served from stand-up bars in the area (*see p191* **Cherry aid**), and taxis frequent one of Lisbon's busiest ranks.

Supposedly built on the site of the Roman hippodrome, medieval Rossio was the open marketplace at the top of town. Pombal intended his more rectangular version to be secondary to the Praça do Comércio. Instead, Rossio increased in importance as the city expanded north. Its official name, Praça Dom Pedro IV, is something you'll only see on maps or the odd business card. Dom Pedro IV is the chap on top of the square's 23-metre (75-foot) central column. Or at least, that's who the bronze figure nominally represents. Rumour has it that it is actually a likeness of Emperor Maximilian of Mexico. In 1870 a ship bearing his statue was docked at Lisbon, en route from Marseille to Mexico, when word came of his assassination. By chance Portugal had ordered a statue of Pedro IV from the same French sculptor, Elias David, and a deal was struck. The figures you see around the base represent Justice, Wisdom, Courage and Restraint.

Restraint was not always Rossio's hallmark. The Teatro Nacional stands on the site of a royal palace that was taken over by the Inquisition and many an auto-da-fé (public judging of heretics) ended with the condemned being burned at the stake in the square. 40,000 people were judged guilty during the history of the Portuguese Inquisition, of which 1,800 were consigned to the flames.

Next to Rossio lies the less gracious **Praça da Figueira**. Every Portuguese city has a square where people sell seeds to feed the pigeons and this is Lisbon's. Here the statue is of Dom João I, erected in 1971. If you've visited before and could have sworn the plinth has moved a jot, you're right: when replaced after the construction of an underground car park, it was aligned with the vista down Rua da Prata, instead of returning to the square's centre. Praça da Figueira is ringed with nonedescript shops, the exception being the Hospital das Bonecas (*see p148*), a sweet doll's hospital. At night the square's population runs from skateboarders to ageing whores; in winter the homeless warm themselves over the Metro vents. Round the corner, in the lobby of the Hotel Lisboa Tejo (*see p39*), the **Poço de Borratem** is an ancient well whose water was long used to cure itching and liver ailments.

The Rua das Portas de Santo Antão is a pedestrian-only street behind the Teatro Nacional. It's full of tourist-trap restaurants where signs advertise tripe or pig's ear salad.

If you have to stop and eat here, try the grilled fowl at Bonjardim (*see p104*). One discreet doorway nearer Rossio marks the **Casa do Alentejo** (No.58, 21 346 9231), a home from home for *alentejanos* with an amazing neo-Moorish decor that's worth stepping in for. Its restaurant, which serves regional dishes, is open to all, but the food is nothing special.

Portas de Santo Antão is also the address of the cavernous **Coliseu dos Recreios** (*see p169*), the Lisbon Coliseum, opened in 1890 and nowadays a concert venue, hosting both classical and rock. A smaller entrance in the same building, at No.100, leads into the Sociedade de Geografia and its **Museu Etnográfico**. Further along is the **Elevador**

Rossio.

Avenida da Liberdade.

da Lavra, a funicular that allows weary lisboetas and wearier tourists to ascend up to Campo de Santana. For a non-touristy lunch option, keep walking until you're on Rua de São José, which is lined with eateries serving local office workers.

Igreja de São Domingos

Largo de São Domingos (21 342 8275). Metro Rossio/tram 12, 15. **Open** 7.30am-6.40pm daily. **Map** p250 M9.

A succession of natural catastrophes has laid waste to this Dominican church since it was founded by Dom Sancho II in 1242 – most notably the earthquakes in 1531 and 1755 and then, most recently, a fire in 1959. It took 38 years to renovate, reopening in 1997, but the still flame-ravaged interior gives the church a striking cave-like look. The high altar was completed in 1748 to the designs of Ludovice, architect of the monastery of Mafra. The Dominicans were central to the Inquisition, which was based across the square, and autos-da-fé often included a procession that began from here.

Museu Etnográfico

Sociedade de Geografia, Rua das Portas de Santo Antão 100 (21 342 5068). Metro Restauradores. **Open** by appointment. **Admission** free. **Map** p250 L8.

The antiquated Ethnographical Museum, founded in 1892, is a monument to colonial plunder. Glass cases are crowded with textiles, masks, wooden sculptures and ceramics from Portugal's former dominions. There's little context on offer, but the collection does serve as an interesting example of the attitudes of the colonial era. The building – constructed at the very end of the 19th century – is also of interest, particularly the magnificent main hall, with its painted wooden galleries.

Restauradores & Avenida da Liberdade

The Avenida da Liberdade began as an extension of the Passeio Público, a late 18th-century garden promenade. This busy boulevard, built on the Champs-Elysées model, was completed in 1886, forming an axis that connects the 18th-century downtown with the new areas built in the 19th century. Where Lisbon had previously clustered along the river, now it expanded inland to the north. Carrying several lanes of traffic between the Praça dos Restauradores and the Praça Marquês de Pombal roundabout, the Avenida da Liberdade has been spruced up in recent years and is now an elegant home to office blocks, big hotels and upmarket fashion shops.

At the southern end, just north-west of Rossio, the neo-Manueline façade is that of Rossio station, completed in 1892. It is built against the hillside, its main hall and platforms on the top floor. This is normally the terminus of the Sintra line, but delays in repairs to the tunnel though which trains exit Lisbon mean it is closed for now.

The obelisk in Praça dos Restauradores commemorates the 1 December 1640 restoration of independence from Spain, inscribed with dates of decisive battles in the 28 years of war. The Eden cinema here was once an outstanding art deco landmark, but is now an Aparthotel (*see p42*), retaining only the façade and a monumental staircase. Next door, the Palácio Foz housed a notorious nightclub in the 1920s, and later the Ministry of Propaganda. Its ground floor is now home to Lisbon's main

Burning issues

Several Lisbon squares, including Rossio and Praça Martim Moniz, serve as outdoor social centres for immigrants. On sunny days Largo de São Domingos fills with Guinea-Bissauans, some of whom regularly bring cardboard to place on the dirty stone benches before settling in to catch up on the gossip. The area conveys an image of tolerance, with people of various ethnic backgrounds milling about as shoppers bustle past. Yet it was here, in 1506, that a terrible event helped trigger centuries of persecution.

It all started on the Sunday after Easter, when a mob went on a three-day rampage, raping, torturing and killing 2,000 to 4,000 Jews or suspected Jews – dubbed New Christians after being obliged to convert.

A contemporary chronicler, Garcia de Resende, wrote: 'They incited low people and villeins against the new Christians... Some of them they burned alive, children they tore to pieces, they performed great cruelties, great robberies, and vileness on all those they found.'

The frenzy was unleashed when a supposed miracle – a cross in the church of São Domingos brightly illuminated by candlelight or a ray of sunlight – was doubted by an onlooker. A group of women seized the sceptic, who may not even have been Jewish, dragged him outside and beat, killed and quartered him.

A prolonged drought had brought hunger and plague to the city, prompting the Court to move out and those left behind to seek succour in religiosity. There had also been social upheaval with the arrival some years earlier of thousands of Jews expelled from Castile whose knowledge and capital Dom Manuel welcomed as Portugal engaged in its seaborne Discoveries. He prevented them from leaving, forcing them to convert but barring anyone from probing the genuineness of their faith. That stoked resentment as well-educated individuals long subject to special laws suddenly won access to positions open only to Christians.

The killing was whipped up by Dominican friars angered at the king's indulgence of unbelievers. From the square a rumour spread that killing a Jew brought 100 days' absolution. Hundreds fanned out, murdering many on the spot and taking others barely alive to burn before São Domingos.

The next day the hunt continued for those in hiding. Officials who intervened fell victim to the enraged mob. Pregnant women were thrown on to stakes. Only on the third day, after a royal shield-bearer was killed, did troops restore order. The king ordered murderers punished and condemned the turbulent friars to death.

But the balance of power was shifting and soon the Inquisition was ensconced in the Hospital de Todos-os-Santos in Rossio (where the Teatro Nacional de Dona Maria II now stands). 'Heretics' were burned at the stake after processing around Rossio in an auto-da-fé. Those Jews who could, fled.

Five hundred years after the 1506 massacre, the victims were remembered in a candlelight vigil and small-scale official events. Already in 2000 the Cardinal of Lisbon had apologised for the massacre and the Inquisition (in the wake of the Pope's apology for the sins of the Church). But the anniversary was a catalyst. Researchers in Sephardic (Iberian Jewish) Studies at Lisbon University promised a book on the massacre, which had been largely ignored by academics and wiped from the collective memory.

Not far from São Domingos, a different Christian attitude had its roots, in Jesuit institutions frequented by the man who became **St Francis Xavier**. Born in Navarre, now in Spain, Xavier came to Lisbon in 1540 in answer to an appeal by Dom João III for missionaries to the Orient, and in 12 years of travel made countless conversions in India, Malaysia and Indonesia. But two years in Japan, with its emphasis on courtesy, high levels of literacy, and blend of rationality and spirituality convinced him of the need for a missionary to be 'a good philosopher, trained in dialogue'.

Sites associated with St Francis Xavier include the world's first Jesuit foundation (1542), the **Convento de Santo Antão-o-Velho** (*see p76*), and the nearby Colégio dos Meninos Orfãos. Xavier lived in Rossio, in the now vanished Palácio dos Estaus. The sacristy of the nearby Sao José hospital (the former Convento de Santo Antão-o-Novo, which replaced its namesake as the Jesuits' activities expanded) is dedicated to the saint, as is a chapel in the Igreja de São Roque.

He, at least, would feel at home among the Indians, Chinese and other immigrants.

tourist office, a shop selling replicas from Portugal's museums that make good souvenirs, and the tourist police. There are also late afternoon concerts some Wednesdays in a wonderful gilded room upstairs. The central post office is across the square, as is the **ABEP** kiosk (*see p169*) selling tickets for films, plays, bullfights and other sports and cultural events.

On the tree-lined lower end of the Avenida, there is often music and dancing on the shady walkways. This stretch is a tolerated prostitution zone, spilling out from the red-light district around the green Praça da Alegria, also home to Lisbon's venerable jazz venue Hot Clube (*see p181* **Hot and cool**). A few blocks north on the west side, two art deco pillars mark the entrance to **Parque Mayer**, a decaying 1920s complex that was home to Portuguese *revista* – revue theatre – but where all stages but one have now gone dark. The city council in 2002 commissioned architect Frank Gehry to produce a plan to redevelop the area, and earmarked revenues from the planned new Lisbon Casino to fund it, but there's no sign of work starting. In the meantime one of the disused theatres, the Capitólio, has been listed, so Gehry's plan will have to be modified.

By Avenida Metro station, the São Jorge cinema, completed in 1950 to a design by Fernando Silva, is the last of Lisbon's big old movie theatres, now council owned and used only for festivals. By contrast, the Cinemateca Portuguesa (*see p159*) round the corner in Rua Barata Salgueiro has a packed programme of Portuguese and international classics and art movies. On the next road north, the **Fundação Medeiros e Almeida** boasts one of Portugal's finest collections of decorative arts.

There's little life on the Avenida at night; it's a daytime boulevard where tourists mix with office workers. The exception is the neo-classical Teatro Tivoli on the east side, a former cinema. Built in 1924 by Raul Lino, it was renovated at the end of the 1990s and now pulls in the punters with slick Brazilian comedies. The striking kiosk in front was installed in 1925 by the owners of the *Diário de Notícias*, whose modernist editorial offices (1936) stand further north.

Fundação Medeiros e Almeida

Rua Rosa Araújo 41 (21 354 7892/www.fundacaomedeirosealmeida.pt). Metro Marquês de Pombal. **Open** 1-5.30pm Mon-Fri; 10am-5.30pm Sat (last tickets 5pm). **Admission** €5 (guided visit €6); €3 concessions; free under 10s. Free for all 10am-1pm Sat. **Credit** AmEx, MC, V. **Map** p246 K7.

The legacy of years of hoarding by late businessman António Medeiros e Almeida, the foundation he created in 1973 has 2,000 pieces (of a total of 9,000) on show in 26 rooms on two floors. They include Chinese porcelain, clocks, paintings, furniture, gold and jewellery, sacred art, sculpture and textiles. It's a varied but fairly coherent collection, as its founder devoted several years to complementing the treasures he had begun picking up to decorate the mansion where he lived for 30 years, before finally donating it and its contents to the nation. The 19th century mansion was previously the Vatican's embassy.

Marquês de Pombal & Parque Eduardo VII

At the top of the Avenida stands the enormous column from which the statue of the Marquês de Pombal lords it over Lisbon's worst traffic headache – the Praça Marquês de Pombal roundabout, a seething, honking mass of cars. Some of the arteries have been even more chaotic of late as work continues on a tunnel to relieve the congestion. High above, the Marquês, in the bronze company of a lion, serenely overlooks the distant Baixa that he imposed upon the city.

Behind him is the **Parque Eduardo VII**, laid out in the late 19th century as the natural extension of the Avenida da Liberdade axis, and later named after the British king Edward VII during his 1903 visit to Portugal. The layout of much of the park is rather formal, but the **Estufa Fria** gardens and greenhouse on its west side provide welcome shade.

Two fascist pillars at the park's upper end now enclose a pile of stones – purportedly, a sculpture by João Cutileiro – that is supposed to commemorate the 1974 Revolution. A pond garden in the upper eastern corner has a café with pleasant outdoor *esplanada*. At night this part of the park is a gay cruising area and rent boys, many feeding heroin habits, solicit passing traffic. At the top of the park, beyond Alameda Cardeal Cerejeira, is a garden named after fado singer Amália Rodrigues (*see p172*) and Lisbon's most serene esplanades, the Linha d'Água. At the opposite, lower end of the park, near the Marquês de Pombal, gypsy fortune-tellers lurk in ambush in the daytime, leaping out to offer palm readings.

Estufa Fria

Parque Eduardo VII (21 388 2278). Metro Marquês de Pombal. **Open** *Summer* 9am-5.30pm daily. *Winter* 9am-4.30pm daily. **Admission** €1.53; free under-11s. **No credit cards**. **Map** p246 K6.

This greenhouse garden on the north-west side of Parque Eduardo VII was completed in 1930. The promenade around the pond leads into three areas: the Estufa Quente, or hothouse, for plants that require hot air and humidity; the Estufa Fria itself, a cool greenhouse; and the Estufa Doce, the 'sweet' greenhouse, with drier conditions. The foliage, statues and cascades are ideal for a romantic stroll.

East of Baixa

The castle on the hill.

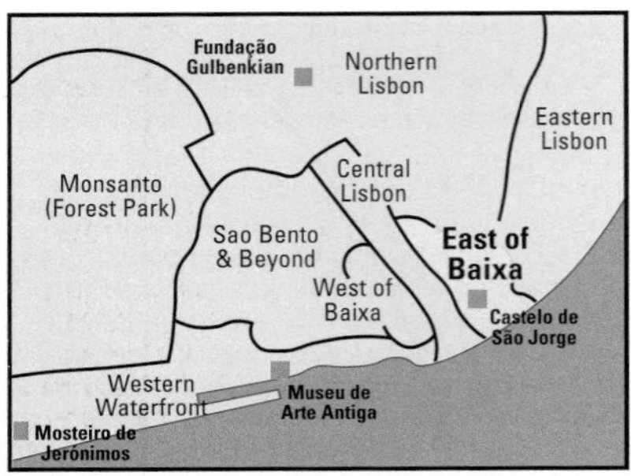

Santo António.

Sé

Lisbon's most picturesque tram ride – the No.28 east from the Baixa and up to Graça – leads past the **Igreja de Santo António**, built on the birthplace of the city's favourite saint, and the neighbouring **Museu Antoniano**, and then on past the 12th-century **Sé Catedral**. As it skirts the hill below the Castelo, the street changes names so many times locals often refer to it as 'Rua do Eléctrico da Sé' – the Street of the Tram of the Cathedral.

Unlike nearby Alfama, this area was greatly modified after the 1755 earthquake, giving way to wider streets and elegant houses. On the tram route there are many fascinating if expensive antique shops. Also of interest is the apparently innocuous Instituto de Reinserção Social (Institute of Social Placement), once the Salazarist secret police prison.

The Teatro Romano, Portugal's only known Roman amphitheatre, was begun during the reign of Augustus and rebuilt under Nero in AD 57. A section can be seen fenced off under a shed on Rua de São Mamede. It is difficult to discern the lie of the place; a video at the neighbouring **Museu do Teatro Romano**, which has entrances on Rua de São Mamede and from the tram route, shows a virtual reconstruction. The theatre was first surveyed in 1798 by the architect royal, Italian Francisco Xavier Fabri, but he failed to convince his bosses that it should be preserved. The ruins were rediscovered in 1964, and when stone benches were unearthed, the council demolished a building on the site.

If you follow any one of the narrow alleys that run downhill from the right of the Sé, you'll eventually pop out on to the Campo das Cebolas (Field of the Onions). A big, open square lined with souvenir shops and cheap restaurants, its main attraction is the spiky façade of the Casa dos Bicos, a 16th-century house built by a rich merchant who wanted to be located near the new royal riverfront palace. It now houses a department of the city council and is not open for visits. Turning west on Rua da Alfândega brings into view the medieval stone façade of the **Igreja da Conceição-a-Velha**.

Igreja da Conceição-a-Velha

Rua da Alfândega (21 887 0202). Tram 18, 25. **Open** 8am-6pm Mon-Fri; 8am-4pm Sat; 10am-2pm Sun (for mass). **Map** p251 M10.

This site originally housed a church adapted in 1534 from what was Lisbon's former Great Synagogue and dedicated to Nossa Senhora Nossa Senhora da Misericórdia (Our Lady of Mercy), who can be seen above the portal sheltering various notables under her mantle (among them Dom Manuel and João III's wife Queen Leonor, founder of Portugal's main house of charity, the Casa da Misericórdia). The 1755 earthquake demolished the building, leaving only the stone Manueline-style façade. In 1770 the church reopened to house the congregation of Nossa Senhora da Conceição-a-Velha, whose original house of worship, a converted synagogue in the Baixa, had been flattened. The simple post-earthquake interior has only one nave and contains an image of Our Lady of Restelo, donated to the earlier Conceição church by Prince Henry the Navigator. As of writing the church was closed for extensive restoration work.

Igreja de Santo António

Largo de Santo António da Sé (21 886 9145). Tram 12, 28/bus 37. **Open** 8am-7pm daily, with 30-45min breaks at 11am & 5pm for mass. **Map** p251 M10.

This small baroque church opened in 1787, 20 years after construction began. It replaced a structure destroyed in the 1755 earthquake, on the spot where Fernando Bulhões, later known as St Anthony of Padua, was born around 1190. St Anthony became famous in his own day as a constantly travelling preacher and a miracle worker, the latter charism still being frequently invoked, particularly in his capacity as the patron saint of things lost. St Vincent may be Lisbon's official patron, but lisboetas prefer their native son perhaps because he gets them an extra day off in June. Mass marriages for those too poor to afford individual ceremonies, known as 'St Anthony's weddings', are held here then (*see p152*).

Museu Antoniano

Largo de Santo António da Sé 24 (21 886 0447). Tram 12, 28/bus 37. **Open** 10am-1pm, 2-6pm Tue-Sun. **Admission** €1.23; free concessions. **No credit cards. Map** p251 M10.

The Museum of Anthony, next to the church dedicated to the saint, contains iconographic sculptures, paintings and biographical documents, but also some rather more offbeat representations of the saint in the form of soft furnishings and collages.

Museu do Teatro Romano

Pátio do Aljube 5, Rua Augusto Rosa (information 21 751 3200). Tram 12, 28/bus 37. **Open** 10am-1pm, 2-6pm Tue-Sun. **Admission** free. **Map** p251 M10.

The Roman Theatre Museum was created in 2002 in belated recognition of the importance of what was probably Portugal's only Roman amphitheatre. Thought to have seated 5,000, it is proof that Olisipo, as Lisbon was known, was a major outpost. The museum occupies a renovated 19th-century factory around which excavations continue – to work out, among other things, how a first-century wall was designed to prevent the whole pile sliding down the slope. (The wall is visible in the upper part of the museum, next to a pretty covered patio.) There is also a smattering of columns and other decorative bits, including the inscription dedicating the theatre to Nero and a sculpture (a copy) of Silenus. To find the museum, look out for the banner on the left as you climb past the Sé. To go straight to the theatre, turn left up Rua da Saudade (where the museum also has a back entrance), a little further on.

Sé Catedral

Largo da Sé (21 887 6628/3258). Tram 12, 28/bus 37. **Open** *Church* 9am-7pm daily. *Cloisters* 10am-6pm Mon-Sat; 2-6pm Sun. *Treasury* 10am-5pm Mon-Sat. **Admission** *Treasury* €2.50. *Cloister* €2.50. Both free under-12s. **No credit cards. Map** p251 M10.

Lisbon's Cathedral or Sé is a symbol of the Christian Reconquest, having been built in the 12th century on the site of the main mosque, under the supervision of Gilbert of Hastings, the Englishman who became bishop after Lisbon was conquered in 1147. It was enlarged in subsequent centuries and facelifts were made necessary by earthquake damage, particularly after the 1755 quake: the south tower collapsed and the interior chancel, chapels and high altar were damaged. The Sé's current appearance is the result of restoration work completed in 1930 that removed many baroque trappings. The rose window was reconstructed at this time from fragments of the original. In the original Romanesque scheme the Sé was laid out in the form of a Latin cross, with three naves. Gothic cloisters were added under Dom Dinis (early 14th century). The Sé once housed the relics of St Vincent, Lisbon's patron saint, but his urn was

The view from **Castelo de São Jorge**. *See p72.*

destroyed in the 1755 quake. The treasury has artefacts and vestments, but visitors may be more interested in the dig going on in the cloisters, where parts of the mosque wall have been uncovered. A section of Roman road and remains from the Visigothic occupation have also been found.

Castelo

Lisbon began on the hill of the Castelo, with an Iron Age settlement that was later occupied successively by Romans, Visigoths and Moors, all of whom added their own fortifications. Some of the oldest segments, thought to be of Roman origin, are near the 37 bus stop. These are the outer walls, enclosing both the **Castelo de São Jorge** itself and the small *intramuros* ('within the walls') neighbourhood.

From here the way in is through the Arco de São Jorge, where on the left a niche houses an image of St George, the castle's – and also Portugal's – dragon-killing patron. The ticket office for the castle proper is beyond it; at the top of the rise is the Casa do Governador, an official shop selling classy souvenirs, including well chosen fado CDs. Off to the right, narrow streets lead into a neighbourhood where the number of older residents living in rent-controlled flats is dwindling, while newcomers pay fortunes for renovated places. The public bathhouse at Rua da Santa Cruz do Castelo 29 is still in business, though. At the end of that street, the **Igreja da Santa Cruz do Castelo** stands on the shady Largo of the same name and contains a statue of St George. The original church was built on top of a mosque right after the 1147 reconquest; the present post-earthquake version dates from 1776.

The open square just past the entrance to the Castelo proper has fine views over the city. The cannons projecting over the parapet recall the castle's original purpose, but today overlook orange and lemon trees in the gardens of the houses below. Further in, a series of bumpy paths lead to the inner walls that contain the open courtyards and ramparted walkways that make up the heart of the medieval castle. In an inner tower is a Cámara Oscura in which you can scan the streets below.

At the far end of the Chão da Feira from the Arco de São Jorge is an unusual urinal, much photographed by tourists despite its characteristic odour. The Palácio Belmonte, through the archway around the corner, was renovated with the help of city council funds and is now a top-class hotel. In the small courtyard is its more accessible, arty café, which stays open late in summer.

The tunnel through to the Pátio de Dom Fradique is still a public passageway; take it to pass through a square now surrounded by tumbledown houses with a view west towards the dome of the Panteão Nacional de Santa Engrácia. Through the arch at the bottom is the **Rua dos Cegos** – the Street of the Blind – where the 16th-century house at No.20 is one of Lisbon's oldest. The large church to your left, the baroque **Igreja do Menino de Deus** (open for mass 8.30am Sat & Sun), has an octagonal shape that is unique in Portugal. From here, the streets lead on to the Alfama and Mouraria.

The street circling just below and around the castle in the other direction from the Arco de São Jorge is called Costa do Castelo for much of its length. It rewards walkers with views over the city, including from the esplanades of the Chapitô (*see p194*) theatre and restaurant, and the café of the restored 19th-century Teatro Taborda (*see p195*). Back at the southern end, a staircase, Escadinhas de São Crispim, follows the course of the old Moorish walls down to the Sé.

Castelo de São Jorge

Castelo (21 880 0620/0626). Tram 12, 28/bus 37. **Open** *Mar-Oct* 9am-9pm daily. *Nov-Feb* 9am-6pm daily. *Cámara Oscura* 10am-1pm, 2-5.30pm Mon, Wed-Sun (last entry 12.30pm & 5pm). *Olisipónia* 10am-1pm, 2-5.30pm daily (last entry 12.30pm & 5pm). **Admission** €5; €2.50 concessions; free under-10s, over-64s. **Credit** DC, MC, V. **Map** p251 M9.

The hilltop was fortified even before the arrival of the Roman legions; in later centuries the castle walls were strengthened by Visigoths and Moors before falling to Portugal's first king, Afonso Henriques, in 1147. His statue stands in the square just past the main gate. From the 14th to the 16th centuries Portuguese kings resided in the Palácio de Alcaçovas, the remains of which now house a restaurant, a café and multimedia exhibit called Olisipónia. It offers an overview of the city's history – from prehistoric origins to today's development plans – that is fairly accessible to non-Portuguese speakers, and a video-wall sequence that includes a curious simulation of the 1755 earthquake. The Castelo itself has gone through numerous transformations. In the 1930s several government offices and a firehouse were removed from the grounds, thus baring the walls, which were then topped off with some new authentic-looking battlements. There have been cosmetic clean-ups since then (the latest to justify the recent introduction of paying admission). The battlements have ten towers, which can be climbed, plus a steep staircase leading down to the Torre de São Lourenço. **Photo** *p71.*

Alfama

A *miradouro* (lookout point) with a beautiful view on the 12 and 28 tram lines introduces visitors to Alfama. The **Miradouro de Santa Luzia**, just below Largo das Portas do Sol, has a rose garden, wading pool and grapevine trellises

Bargain or browse at **Feira de Ladra** flea market. *See p75.*

that combine to provide one of Lisbon's most serene views. On the outside wall of the nearby church, the **Igreja de Santa Luzia** (which is headquarters of the Order of Malta in Portugal), are two tile panels: one maps downtown before the 1755 quake, the other depicts Christians storming the castle in 1147. Another twist of the road up the hill leads to the **Largo das Portas do Sol** (Sun Gate Square) graced by a statue of Lisbon's patron, St Vincent, bearing the city's symbol, a boat with two ravens.

On the southern side of the square, the former city palace of the Visconde de Azurara is now occupied by the **Museu-Escola de Artes Decorativas**, while the adjacent Cerca Moura bar and café (*see p126*) is in an old stone tower that was once part of the Moorish siege walls. Its terrace overlooks an expanse of red Alfama roofs where TV antennas sprout like weeds. Over the next hill, the white marble churches of **São Vicente** and **Santa Engrácia** mark the western boundary of Alfama. The ugly slab in the foreground to the left is the roof of the quarter's controversial new car park.

Running down the south-eastern slope of the hill topped by the Castelo, Alfama is Lisbon's oldest *bairro* (quarter). It's an appealing warren of narrow streets and blind alleys, stooping archways and twisting staircases. Some buildings stand on foundations dating back to the Visigoths, but the street pattern is Moorish. Canaries twitter from cages hung outside small windows. Washing flutters everywhere. Children chase through alleys as grown-ups chatter outside shops and cafés, many of them mere holes in the wall.

The most densely populated of Lisbon *bairros*, Alfama is still a community. The poor linger in tiny rent-controlled apartments, though rooftop flats are much sought after by wealthier newcomers. It looks cheerful and postcard-perfect in summer, and the city, aware of the area's attractiveness to visitors, subsidises the maintenance of façades. But many houses are in dire need of renovation, being draughty and cold in winter.

The name Alfama probably comes originally from the Arabic word *al-hama*, which means springs or fountains. Most of this well-watered neighbourhood stood outside the Moorish siege walls, which from the Portas do Sol descended along Rua Norberto Araújo and Rua da Adiça down to the river. The fountain in Largo do Chafariz de Dentro, after which the square is named, has been in use since medieval times, while the Chafariz d'el Rei on Rua Cais de Santarém has also been producing water for more than seven centuries. In the 17th and 18th centuries the taps were segregated: blacks used the tap on one side, whites the other.

The narrow Rua de São Pedro is a fishmarket on weekday mornings. Here you can tune in to the singsong patter of the fishwives (much of it unprintable) while dodging trays of slippery squid. At the end of the street the Largo de São Rafael opens on to a remaining portion of the Moorish siege walls, complete with a private lemon-tree garden on top. Below this, a small side street is called the Rua da Judiaria, in medieval times home to Alfama's Jewish community.

The **Largo de São Miguel** is a sloping square centred around a palm tree and fronted by the white façade of the **Igreja de São Miguel** – like so many churches a post-earthquake reconstruction of an earlier one. The narrow Rua de São Miguel leads off from it; this is a main street of sorts, with grocery stands, butchers and tiny *tascas* where the buzzing of flies is drowned out by televisions tuned to the football. The tiny alleys off the Rua de São Miguel lead up into wondrous networks of staircases, terraces and gardens.

What's missing in Alfama is the sound of motor vehicles. They can't get in here – a factor that acts as a brake on gentrification. Morning rush hour in Alfama is accompanied by the sound of birds singing and footsteps scurrying to work. The traffic gathers down on the Largo do Chafariz de Dentro, where tourist buses decant their camera-toting contents. On summer evenings crowds head into Alfama looking for an outside table, a dinner of grilled sardines and plenty of red wine. A number of fado houses crowd the bottom end of the neighbourhood. The Parreirinha de Alfama (*see p172*) on Beco do Espírito Santo is one of the city's most renowned. Just across the main road at the bottom of Alfama is the Casa do Fado e da Guitarra Portuguesa, a museum devoted to this traditional form of music. Its restaurant also hosts shows.

A good way to get a more intimate look at Alfama is to step up (via Rua dos Remédios) to the **Igreja de Santo Estevão**, whose veranda-cum-*miradouro* provides yet another fine view. From here you can see grapevines growing in the back lots of some houses. Leading off here are streets up to the Igreja de São Vicente de Fora and the neighbourhood named after it, and to the more bustly Graça.

But the best way to get to know Alfama is simply to wander around and get a little lost – something visitors will find almost impossible to avoid. Be watchful, though, as pickpockets do operate, so don't flash fancy cameras around.

Museu-Escola de Artes Decorativas

Largo das Portas do Sol 2 (21 888 1991/www.fress.pt). Tram 12, 28/bus 37. **Open** 10am-5pm Tue-Sun. *Library* 1-6pm Mon-Fri. **Admission** €5; €2-€2.50 concessions; free under-13s. **Credit** MC, V. **Map** p251 N9.

Banker Ricardo do Espírito Santo Silva – admirer of Salazar, lover of *fadista* Amália, and builder of the Ritz Hotel – was also a leading collector of Portuguese applied arts. In 1947 he bought a 17th-century former palace and created the Museum of Applied Arts and attached school. The collection of 16th- to 19th-century Portuguese, French and English furniture is the most important in Portugal, and is displayed in reconstructions of the original rooms. Tapestries, silverware, porcelain, antique books and tiles make up the rest of the exhibits. The shop sells items produced in the school and workshops, whose 100-strong staff are skilled in 21 different crafts.

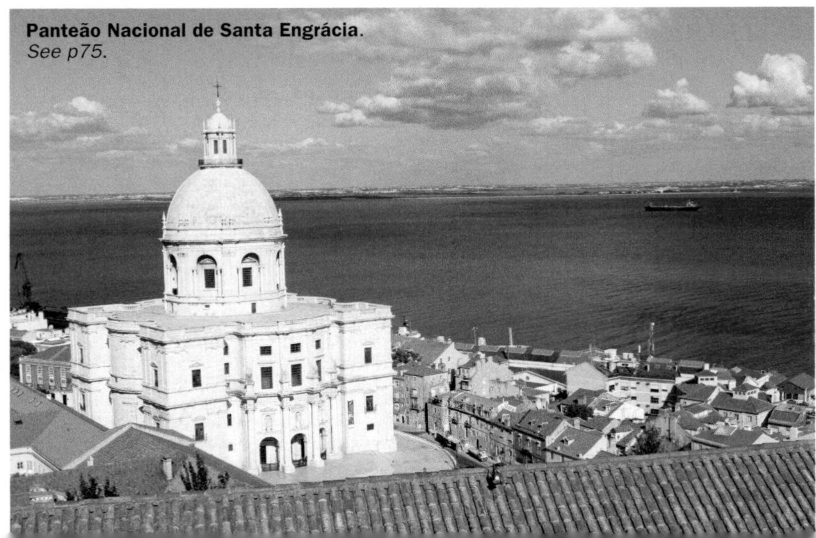

Panteão Nacional de Santa Engrácia. *See p75.*

São Vicente & Graça

Between the **Igreja de São Vicente de Fora** and the white dome of the **Panteão Nacional de Santa Engrácia** – both of whose roofs offer fabulous views of Lisbon – lies the hillside space known as the **Campo de Santa Clara**. Here, from dawn until early afternoon on Tuesdays and Saturdays, the **Feira da Ladra** flea market (photo *p73*) is held. The name sounds like 'thieves' market' in Portuguese (although its origins are disputed) and this is more car boot sale than open-air auction house, but bargains can be had if you come early.

Whereas Alfama feels like a busy village, Graça, on the hill above São Vicente, is more like a small town – and indeed boasts several *vilas operários*, built by the more enlightened late 19th-century industrialists to house their workers in decent conditions, with patios and verandas. The No.28 tram stops at Largo da Graça, site of one of the largest, Vila Sousa. (If it whets your appetite, you can find others off the nearby Rua da Senhora da Glória and Rua do Sol à Graça, and a whole *bairro operário*, the Bairro Estrela de Ouro at the northern end of Graça, off Rua Virgínia.) To the west is the Esplanada da Igreja da Graça (*see p127*), an open-air café with great sunset views. The **Igreja da Graça** is one of Lisbon's oldest churches, originally built in 1271 though enlarged in the mid 16th century. The attached monastery became a military barracks after religious orders were dissolved in 1834.

The small promontory above Graça (turn left on Rua Damasceno Monteiro, and then bear right up the Calçada do Monte) is the highest of Lisbon's hills, topped by the chapel of **Nossa Senhora do Monte** (open 3-6pm daily). The *miradouro* here is a favourite of lovers and another fine place to catch the sunset. In front of the chapel is a glass-encased image of the Virgin, inside the stone chair of St Gens, a bishop martyred during Roman times, after whom the chapel was originally named. A sit down here is supposed to ease the pangs of childbirth; the chair was popular with Portuguese queens over the centuries.

Igreja da Graça

Largo da Graça (21 887 3943). Tram 28/bus 34. **Open** 9.30am-noon, 3-6pm Mon-Sat; 9.30am-noon, 5.30-7pm Sun. **Admission** free. **Map** p251 N9.

The original monastery of Graça was built in 1271, and completed with an image of Nossa Senhora da Graça (Our Lady of Grace), salvaged from the sea off Cascais that same year. Renovated in the mid 16th century, most of the church came tumbling down in the 1755 earthquake. The later renovation reduced three naves to one, and removed much austere marble in favour of more flamboyant rococo decoration. During Lent the church organises the Senhor dos Passos procession (*see p160*), Lisbon's longest-standing religious parade.

Igreja de São Vicente de Fora

Largo de São Vicente (21 882 4400/cloisters 21 888 5652). Tram 28/bus 34. **Open** *Church* 9am-6pm Tue-Sun. *Cloisters* 10am-6pm Tue-Sun. **Admission** *Church* free. *Cloisters* €4; €2 concessions; free under-12s. **No credit cards. Map** p251 N9.

Portugal's first king, Afonso Henriques, laid the foundation stone for the first church of St Vincent de Fora (Outside) beyond the city walls in 1147, hardly a month after taking Lisbon from the Moors. He was fulfilling a vow to construct Christian houses of worship on the sites where Portuguese soldiers and northern European crusaders lay buried. In 1580 Portugal's then ruler King Philip II of Spain decided to start from scratch and brought in his own architect, Juan Herrera (builder of the Escorial outside Madrid), who, accompanied by Italian architect Filippo Terzi, designed a new Igreja de São Vicente in the Italian mannerist style. The church was inaugurated in 1629, but severely damaged in the 1755 earthquake, when the main dome and roof collapsed on a crowded house of worshippers. The beautiful cloisters are richly decorated with many early 18th-century tile panels, some of which illustrate the fables of La Fontaine. Inside you'll also find the royal pantheon of the Braganza family, the last dynasty to rule Portugal. The figure of a weeping woman kneels before the twin tombs of Dom Carlos I and Crown Prince Luís Filipe, who were cut down by assassins' bullets in 1908.

Panteão Nacional de Santa Engrácia

Campo de Santa Clara (21 885 4820). Tram 28/bus 34. **Open** 10am-5pm Tue-Sun. **Admission** €2; €1 concessions; free under-14s. Free for all Sun to 2pm & holidays. **No credit cards. Map** p247 N9.

The dome of this church was completed in 1966, a mere 285 years after the building was begun; hence the Lisbon expression 'a job like Santa Engrácia' – one that takes forever. The church is on the site of an earlier one, which was torn down after being desecrated by a robbery in 1630. A Jew was blamed and executed, but later exonerated. Before dying he is said to have prophesied that the new church would never be completed because an innocent man had been convicted. The first attempt at a new Santa Engrácia duly collapsed in 1681 (construction error, compounded by a storm, may have been to blame) and work restarted from a new plan the following year. This plan by master stonemason João Antunes bears many similarities to Peruzzi's plans for St Peter's in Rome, and marble in various colours dominates the interior. In 1916 the Republican government decided that the then still roofless Santa Engrácia would become the national Pantheon, a temple to honour dead Portuguese heroes. Among those since laid to rest here is General Humberto Delgado, an opposition leader assassinated by

Salazar's secret police in 1962, and one woman – fado diva Amália. Her remains were transferred here in 2001, within two years of her death, after a special session of parliament changed the law requiring a five-year hiatus. Her tomb is constantly besieged by flowers. You can, guides say, tell which are from friends: the meadow blooms she loved rather than hothouse products. **Photo** *p74*.

Mouraria & Intendente

Mouraria is the district wedged on the hillside between the north side of the Castelo and Graça. The defeated Moors were allowed to settle here. In the 12th and 13th centuries two mosques were still functioning; a 1471 Muslim petition to the king mentions that Mouraria was enclosed by walls and that residents locked the gates at night. Twenty-five years later non-Christians were either converted or expelled from the country. In the 19th century Mouraria was known for its prostitutes, seedy *tascas* and fado houses. The most famous tavern was in Rua do Capelão and run by the singer known as A Severa; a plaque at the bottom of the street recalls it. The area is still scruffy, but no less lisboeta than Alfama on the other side of the hill.

Mouraria's main street is the Rua dos Cavaleiros/Calçada do Santo André, which the No.12 tram climbs. The lower part of it has been taken over by Indian-run discount stores, and the Centro Comercial Mouraria, down in Praça Martim Moniz, bustles with Asian and African shops. The wholesalers here attract large numbers of market traders, many of them black-clad Portuguese gypsies, in search of bargains.

This multi-ethnic area is, appropriately enough, the part of Lisbon where the Society of Jesus began its work of training missionaries (such as St Francis Xavier) to send out to the far corners of the world explored by Portuguese mariners. On Rua Marquês de Ponte de Lima is the former Convento de Santo Antão-o-Velho, which in 1542 became the world's first Jesuit foundation. It is now the parish church of **Socorro** (21 886 0973; open 8.30-11am, 4-6pm daily). Its oil paintings, tile panels and vestry date back to the 18th century; the cloister (entrance next door; open 9am-12.30pm, 2-5.30pm Mon-Sat) to the early 16th century. Downhill in Rua da Mouraria, through a Manueline doorway next to a police station, is the former **Colégio dos Meninos Orfãos**. Founded as a hostel for orphans in the 13th century, it was restored in the 16th and taken over by the Jesuits, who turned it into a unique educational experiment. Today it houses various social organisations and even a gym. The narrative tile panels in the entrance hall and up the staircase are worth a detour.

At the southern end of Rua Marquês de Ponte de Lima, turn right to reach the Rua de São Lourenço, which changes its name four times as it runs along the west slope of the castle, leading past several budget African restaurants to the white **Igreja de São Cristovão**. Behind this church is a small square, the Largo da Achada, with a handful of pre-earthquake houses.

Mouraria meets the Baixa in **Praça do Martim Moniz**. The area this now covers was once the heart of Mouraria, but in the 1950s and 1960s old byways, patios and churches were bulldozed in the name of urban renewal. For some three decades what is now a large square was a maze of rubble and temporary sheds put up to house displaced shopkeepers. Successive city administrations inflicted architectural atrocities on the area – for example tacking the Centro Comercial Mouraria on to the back of the tiny chapel of Nossa Senhora da Saúde and dotting the square with strange metal kiosks. Most that remain now house African and Chinese cafés, serving the immigrants who have adopted the square as a meeting place.

Running north of Martim Moniz towards the airport, the Rua da Palma/Avenida Almirante Reis axis is a workaday contrast to the glitzier Avenida da Liberdade. At this end it's a down-at-heel shopping district and devoid of landmarks, save for the municipal **Arquivo Fotográfico** at Rua da Palma 246, which has regular exhibitions and a pleasant bar-café, and the red-light district around Largo do Intendente. This is a round-the-clock precinct of sleaze featuring dodgy bars and occasional stabbings.

Campo de Santana

Rising in the fork between the two Avenidas, Almirante Reis and da Liberdade, is a mixed bag of a neighbourhood with an uncommon number of hospitals. This makes it the perfect location for the statue of Sousa Martins, which stands on the well-greened square of Campo dos Mártires de Pátria (invariably still known by its original name of Campo de Santana) outside the Faculdade de Medicina.

José Thomaz de Sousa Martins died in 1897 having gained great favour among the poor for his even-handed approach to curing the sick. Though the man himself was entirely secular in outlook, grateful locals have since made him a religious cult hero and many keep candles burning in his memory. The stone plaques around the base have been left in thanks for miracle cures attributed to the divine medic.

The **Jardim de Torel**, a small park on Rua de Júlio de Andrade, has fine views. The nearby Lavra funicular descends to Largo da Anunciada off the Avenida da Liberdade.

West of Baixa

Chiado your mind at a Bairro Alto bar.

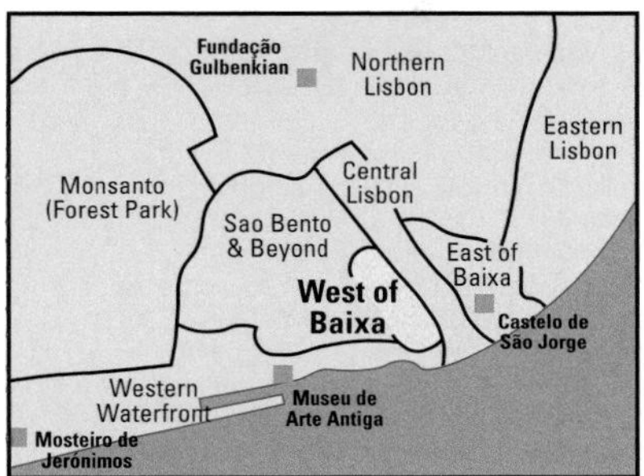

Chiado

During the 19th and early 20th centuries the **Chiado**, with Rua Garrett as its main axis, was the centre of Lisbon's intellectual life. The dictatorship, not keen on the life of the mind, first pressurised this inheritance and then in August 1988 much of what remained went up in smoke when fire reduced Lisbon's only two department stores to ruins. Reconstruction was overseen by the renowned Oporto architect Alvaro Siza Vieira but took longer than it should have. Still, he ensured that some of the former grandeur endured in this neighbourhood of cafés and booksellers, theatres and boutiques.

The ascent from Rossio up the Rua do Carmo and then along Rua Garrett is reasonably gentle and leads into the heart of the quarter. On the way, as the road passes under the viaduct of the Elevador da Santa Justa, modern boutiques rub shoulders with ancient establishments selling first editions or fine gloves. As you climb Rua Garrett you pass Portugal's oldest bookshop, Livraria Bertrand (*see p133*), founded in 1773. On the Largo do Chiado, Café a Brasileira (*see p127*) is a traditional meeting point, though too expensive for most locals actually to eat anything. Once a haunt of writer Fernando Pessoa, whose bronze likeness has a seat on the terrace (*see p78* **Walking Lisbon**), today it serves both tourists and locals.

Downhill towards the river, the **Museu do Chiado** (*see p162*) houses a collection of Portuguese art from the 19th and 20th centuries. The nearby **Teatro Nacional de São Carlos** (*see p169*) was built in 1793 and modelled after La Scala in Milan. The **Teatro Municipal de São Luíz** (*see p194*) is more notable for the ironwork fire escapes that lace its plain back façade on Rua Duque de Bragança, by the excellent Café no Chiado (*see p128*).

On the other side of Rua Garrett, the Largo do Carmo is one of Lisbon's prettiest squares, fronted by the ruined **Convento do Carmo**, next to the former headquarters of the paramilitary National Republican Guard. This was the scene of one of the most memorable moments of the 1974 Revolution, being the final refuge of prime minister, Marcello Caetano. (*See also p66* **Walking Lisbon**).

Convento do Carmo/Museu Arqueológico

Largo do Carmo (21 346 0473). Metro Baixa-Chiado/ tram 28. **Open** 10am-5pm Mon-Sat. **Admission** €2.50; €1.50 concessions; free under-14s. **No credit cards**. **Map** p250 L9.

The Gothic lines of the Church of Our Lady of Mount Carmel went up on the orders of Nun'Álvares Pereira, who helped Dom João I consolidate the rule of Portugal's second dynasty, the House of Avis. Pereira, known as the Condestável, or Constable, founded the church and convent to fulfil a pledge made before a battle, and was adamant in his choice of location – despite the nearby precipice and various false starts after foundations caved in. During the 1755 earthquake the roof fell in on a crowd of All Saints' Day worshippers, leaving the structure near collapse with only the walls and some vault ribbing still standing. Said by many to be the most beautiful church in Lisbon, it has been left roofless ever since, and now a grassy lawn carpets what was once the central nave. The Archaeological Museum, a ragbag of finds from around Europe, is in the back end of the church.

Bairro Alto

When Dom Manuel I moved his residence down from the castle to the waterfront in the early 1500s, the axis of Lisbon's development shifted westward: harbour activity expanded along Cais do Sodré, while up the hill the level ground outside the Fernandine walls was divided into lots and sold off to aristocrats and the emerging merchant class. The Jesuits set themselves up in the **Igreja de São Roque** and the quarter became known as the **Bairro Alto de São Roque** (upper neighbourhood of St Roch).

Wealthy merchants later gave way to small shopkeepers and for a while there were many print shops and newspaper offices. Both Rua de

Walking Lisbon Coffee with Pessoa

A marble-top table, black coffee, absinthe and endless cigarettes. These were the materials that **Fernando Pessoa**, Portugal's greatest modern poet, needed to write. At **Café Martinho da Arcada** (*see p126*), tucked in the bottom left-hand corner of Praça do Comércio as you face the river, you'll find the table he wrote at night after night, preserved as if he were expected back at any moment.

Pessoa (1888-1935) earned his living as a commercial translator and would arrive at the café after work to write, drink, dream and talk until late. Only one of his works, the epic poem *Mensagem*, was published in his lifetime. Many of his great poems, written under 72 different 'heteronyms' or alter egos, each with their own distinctive character, were discovered in a trunk after his death.

'Melancholy, mysterious, mildly paranoid, incontestably Portuguese… Pessoa hived off separate personalities like swarms of bees,' wrote the English critic Cyril Connolly.

Painter José Almada Negreiros told how he once found Pessoa cowering behind his table when a storm broke. Negreiros, with characteristic braggadocio, had gone to the door to shout, 'Long live the lightning! Long live the rain!' Being photographed was another horror for Pessoa. Some of the few existing photos of him are on the café walls.

The Martinho da Arcada, founded in 1782 under another name, has always been a favourite of artists. Another table is dedicated to the novelist José Saramago, a regular customer and winner of the Nobel Prize for literature in 1998. Saramago's *The Year of the Death of Ricardo Reis* takes its title from one of Pessoa's alter egos.

The main body of the café is now a restaurant, frequented by officials from the ministries around the square. But there's still a café attached, famous for its *pastéis de nata*. Or, for a true touch of nostalgic decadence, there's always absinthe.

The image of the bespectacled Pessoa writing at a café table in his bow tie and fedora is one of the iconic images of 20th-century Portugal, endlessly reworked by artists. The most famous version is Almada Negreiros's portrait, painted in 1954. One of two original versions of this painting can be seen at the Casa Fernando Pessoa in Campo de Ourique, where the room in which Pessoa lived during the last 15 years of his life has been preserved in its original form.

But the writer's image can be found within walking distance too. To see a life-size Pessoa, head for another café – A Brasileira (*see p127*). Turn right as you leave Martinho da Arcadia up Rua da Prata and then take the sixth left into Rua da Assunção. It was here in an office on the second floor of No.42 that Pessoa met Ofélia Queiroz, the only known love of his life. He fell in love with the 19-year-old typist when he was 31, writing her many captivating letters and poems. She responded warmly but the affair is thought to have remained platonic.

O Século and Rua do Diário de Notícias are named after papers once based here. Here too is the **Museu Maçónico Português**, which transmits some sense of the major influence of republican, anti-clerical freemasonry in Portuguese history.

Though maps differ, the Bairro Alto is essentially bounded by Rua do Século (as it's usually written) to the west, Rua Dom Pedro V to the north, Rua de São Pedro de Alcântara and Rua da Misericórdia to the east and Rua do Loreto to the south. This layout predates the Baixa; this was the first district in Lisbon to have straight, regular streets. Straight and regular by the standards of the time, that is. In many ways it's as maze-like as other old quarters, with enough kinks and dead ends that even locals get confused as to what's where – especially after a crawl through the neighbourhood's many bars.

During the day the Bairro Alto is relatively quiet, especially since almost all cars were banished from the area a few years ago. Children play ball in the streets while old ladies chat and hang out the laundry. Interesting shops are dotted about, many of which are at the cutting edge of Lisbon's fashion scene. There are also plenty of second-hand bookstores, specialist record shops and a couple of art supplies places on Rua da Rosa. But still, it's mainly a residential area and by day streets rarely bustle.

At night it's another story. Every weekend thousands of revellers cram into these narrow streets, hopping from bar to bar or jamming nexus points, such as on Rua do Diário de Notícias outside Cafédiário and Café Suave (*see p183*), or at the junction of Rua da Atalaia and Travessa da Queimada outside Portas Largas (*see p185*) and the original Bairro Alto club Frágil (*see p185*). The area is also full of

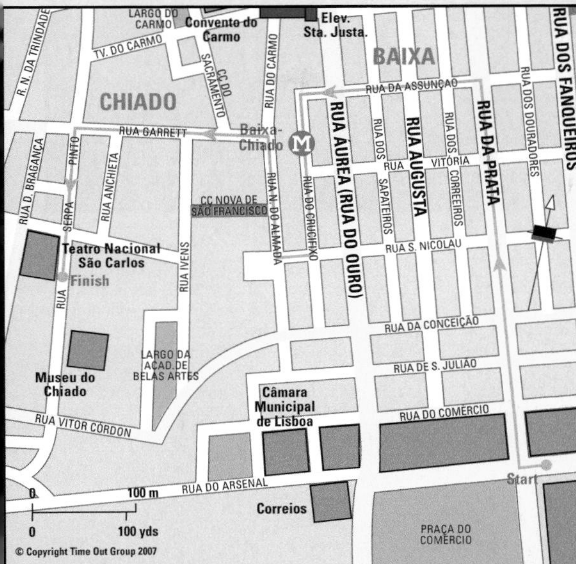

Cross Rua Áurea into Rua do Crucifixo, follow it round to the left and turn right after the Metro entrance up the steps, right on Rua Nova de Alamada and left into Rua Garrett. The café is at the top of the street on the right, No.120. The bronze statue of Pessoa seated at an outside table is by Lagoa Henriques. In the 1920s A Brasileira was a meeting place for artists, one of a number of favoured local venues for the Portuguese institution of *tertúlia*, a mixture of philosophical discussion and gossipy chat. This tradition was discouraged under Salazar and has all but disappeared today.

Cross the small square, past the statue of Chiado, a 16th-century poet, into Rua Serpa Pinto to Largo de São Carlos, dominated by the neo-classical 18th-century opera house, the Teatro Nacional de São Carlos. A little further down, in a fourth-floor apartment that overlooked the Tagus, Pessoa was born. Forty-seven years later, he died of cirrhosis in a Lisbon hospital. Although he had partly grown up in South Africa, and wrote his first juvenile poems in English, he spent his adult life and produced his greatest works amid the streets and cafés of central Lisbon.

'My homeland,' he once said, 'is the Portuguese language.'

Sightseeing

restaurants, varying from traditional *tascas* to purveyors of smart cosmopolitan cuisine.

The Bairro Alto also has Lisbon's largest collection of fado houses – 20 or so – which have been in this quarter since long before the more fashionable bars and clubs began opening up in the early 1980s. Café Luso at Travessa da Queimada 10 is Lisbon's oldest; Adega Machado (*see p173*) on Rua do Norte is almost as venerable; while Tasca do Chico (*see p174*) is cheaper and more informal. All these places are after tourists but Portuguese visit them too. And sometimes, as the Bairro Alto begins to close down around 2am, rising above the clatter and chatter, you'll hear someone singing fado on the street – a lament for the end of the night.

There are three open spaces on the southern and western edges of the Bairro Alto. The first is the **Praça Luís de Camões** at the south end of the neighbourhood, a square ringed with umbrella pines and adjoining the Largo do Chiado to the east. A monumental statue designed by Vítor Bastos was unveiled in 1867 in its centre; it represents the 16th-century epic poet Luís de Camões, standing on a pedestal ringed by smaller statues of Portuguese authors – all now atop a new underground car park. A short way down Rua da Misericórdia is another literary statue, of 19th-century novelist and scourge of hypocrisy Eça de Queirós unveiling Truth.

Going in the opposite direction, at No.95 the **Associação 25 de Abril** (21 324 1420, 9.30am-11pm Mon-Sat) strives to keep memories of the 1974 Revolution alive, with changing exhibitions on the ground floor and a sociable first-floor restaurant (21 342 0030, 11am-3pm, 7-11pm Mon-Sat). Further uphill, in front of the Igreja de São Roque, is the **Largo de Trindade Coelho**, although lisboetas prefer to call it the Largo da Misericórdia, after

Gilt gone mad at **Igreja de São Roque**.

the Santa Casa da Misericórdia charity institution whose head offices are on the square. (This also explains the bronze statue of a lottery ticket seller – Misericórdia has the monopoly on the lottery.) This end of the Bairro Alto is where antiquarian and second-hand bookshops cluster. There are plenty on the Rua Nova da Trindade, which also boasts the **Teatro da Trindade** (*see p193*) and the Cervejaria Trindade (No.20C, 21 342 3506), a beer hall built into the walls of a former monastery that has fabulous *azulejos* but not particularly fabulous food.

A scenic staircase, the Calçada do Duque, leads down to Rossio, passing a few cheap restaurants, including a reasonable veggie canteen, and more bookshops. The third open space bounding the Bairro Alto is the **Jardim de São Pedro de Alcântara**, a garden *miradouro* laid out in the early 19th century and offering splendid views over the Avenida da Liberdade business district, the Baixa, Castelo and river. The Casa do Brasil, on the first floor above gay fado dive Harry's Bar (Rua São Pedro de Alcântara 57-61, 21 346 0760), overlooks the park and everyone runs out here to celebrate whenever Brazil win a football game.

The **Elevador da Glória** funicular has been whisking passengers down and up the steep Calçada da Glória between Jardim de São Pedro de Alcântara and Restauradores since 1885. The fit climb on leg power alone; those who tire can hitch a handhold on the back of the car and get pulled up. The Solar do Vinho do Porto, the Port Wine Institute, complete with bar (*see p138* **Port-able**), is opposite its upper terminal point. Its building was once known as the Palácio Ludovice, after the architect of Mafra, who built it as his city residence in 1747 at a time when Bairro Alto was the 'in' neighbourhood. The building is organised around an inner courtyard and takes up an entire block.

The street running north up the side of the park is named after the active nunnery of São Pedro de Alcântara at its upper end. The doors are barred to visitors but it's worth having a look at the blue-tile depiction of St Peter of Alcantara's stigmata, on the wall by the entrance.

The northern end of the Bairro Alto was barely affected by the 1755 earthquake. Today it is relatively quiet. An alley halfway down Rua da Rosa leads to the Colégio dos Inglesinhos, founded in 1628, at a time when English Catholics were forced to flee their country or be thrown in prison. It closed in 1973, and is now somewhat controversially being developed into luxury apartments. On the Bairro Alto's western edge, the Rua do Século is a quiet street, home to Portugal's constitutional court, galleries and a dance conservatoire in a palace that was the boyhood home of the Marquês de Pombal. Another former religious institution at No.123, the Convento de Cardaes (21 342 75 25, 2.30-5.30pm Mon-Sat), does guided tours.

Igreja de São Roque/Museu de São Roque

Largo de Trindade Coelho (church 21 323 5000/ museum 21 323 5380/1). Metro Baixo-Chiado then 10min walk/Restauradores then Elevador da Glória. **Open** *Church* 8.30am-5pm Mon-Fri; 9.30am-5pm Sat, Sun. *Museum* 10am-5pm Tue-Sun. **Admission** *Church* free. *Museum* €1.50; €1.20 concessions. Free to all Sun. **No credit cards**. **Map** p250 L9.

The Igreja de São Roque was built for the Jesuits with the assistance of Filippo Terzi on the site of an earlier chapel dedicated to São Roque (St Roch). Most of the single-nave structure was built between 1565 and 1573, though it remained roofless for almost another decade. The ceiling is a wonder of sorts. The original architect had planned a vaulted roof, but in 1582 a decision was made to flatroof the space in wood, and sturdy timber was then richly painted after being brought in from Prussia. The paintings in the inner sacristy are worth seeing but the main attraction is the side chapel dedicated to St John the Baptist; its lavish use of ivory, gold and lapis lazuli attests to Portugal's colonial wealth and extravagance. Built in Rome and shipped to Lisbon in 1749 after being blessed by the pope, it took four years to reassemble, not least because of the detailed mosaic above the altar. The museum contains items from the chapel, including Italian goldsmiths' work, paintings and vestments; it is closed for renovation at least until the end of 2007.

Museu Maçónico Português

Rua do Grémio Lusitano 25 (21 342 4506). Metro Baixa-Chiado then 10min walk/Restauradores then Elevador da Glória. **Open** 2.30-5.30pm Mon-Fri. **Admission** €2. **No credit cards**. **Map** p250 L9.

Freemasonry has long played a prominent role in Portuguese history, providing an anti-clerical counterweight to the power of the Church and, later, a non-Marxist pole of thought on the left. Masons took a leading role in events such as the 1820 revolution against absolutist monarchy and are well represented in the upper echelons of the army. As a result, the influence of freemasonry is not a target of left-wing criticism as in Britain. This museum provides an introduction to this private world.

Príncipe Real

Rua Dom Pedro V leads north to the **Praça do Príncipe Real**. There are antique and book shops along here, and the Pavilhão Chinês (*see p186*), the bar with the best interior decor in Lisbon. In some ways Príncipe Real is little more than a continuation of the Bairro Alto, especially for the gay and lesbian community for whom there are plenty of bars and clubs within easy distance of one another.

The Praça do Príncipe Real is one of Lisbon's most romantic garden settings, with a café and esplanade on which to linger. The park was laid out in 1860, with lots of exotic imported greenery. On sunny afternoons knots of old men play cards at one end, while lovers curl up on benches under the century-old cedar tree, bent out horizontally to provide more shade. Directly under the garden, accessible via some steps just to the side of the central pond, is an octagonal cistern, the **Reservatório da Patriarcal** (open 10am-6pm Mon-Sat), built at the same time as the park to store water carried into the city by the aqueduct. The complex includes 31 ten-yard-high pillars and three galleries leading off it. Taken out of service in the 1940s, it was renovated in 1994, and like other antique water infrastructure, is looked after by the Museu da Água (*see p97*).

The *praça* is ringed by pastel-painted buildings, the most notable of which is the Arabesque palace at No.26, built in the late 19th century as the Palácio Ribeiro da Cunha and now housing a university department. The streets between Príncipe Real and São Bento are a gridiron of townhouses that are home to, among others, the British Council on Rua de São Marçal. Eça de Queiroz's famous novel *Cousin Bazílio* portrays the life of a bored, upper-class 19th-century housewife living in this neighbourhood.

Rua da Escola Politécnica is home to the **Museu de Ciência**; the path lined with spindly palm trees leads to the faculty's **Jardim Botânico**.

Jardim Botânico da Faculdade de Ciências

Rua da Escola Politécnica (21 392 1893). Metro Rato. **Open** *Winter* 9am-6pm daily. *Summer* 9am-8pm daily. **Admission** €1.50; €0.60 concessions; free under-6s. **No credit cards**. **Map** p246 K8.

The shaded walkways of the Botanical Garden were laid out between 1858 and 1878 and contain about 10,000 plants. Highlights include palm-ferns that have been around since the time of the dinosaurs. There's a second entrance on Rua da Alegria, so you can use the garden as a verdant shortcut down towards the Avenida da Liberdade. **Photo** *p82*.

Museu de Ciência

Museu de Historia Natural, Rua da Escola Politécnica 56 (21 392 1808/www.museu-de-ciencia.ul.pt). Metro Rato. **Open** 10am-1pm, 3-5pm Mon-Fri; 3-6pm Sat. **Admission** €2.50; €1.50 concessions; free under-6s. **No credit cards**. **Map** p246 K8.

Jardim Botânico: *See p81.*

The Science Museum, part of the Museu de Historia Natural collective of small museums, was founded in 1985. It is interactive, child-friendly and accessible to all. Phenomena such as momentum, centripetal force, the properties of a vacuum and the speed of sound are demonstrated in entertaining and practical ways. The museum also has a collection of antique instruments and organises temporary exhibitions, lectures and courses for non-specialists. It has a planetarium, with sessions on Wednesday and Thursday, usually at 10am, 11am, noon, 3pm and 4pm. (They're for school groups, but you can book yourself in if there's space.) In the same building is the Museu Bocage (21 392 1817), comprising an odd assortment of stuffed animals, models of marine mammals and seashells. Round the back is the Museu do Laboratório Mineralógico e Geológico, a collection of minerals from Portugal and Brazil, but whose space is frequently used to exhibit contemporary art. These latter two museums close at the weekend.

Bica

The **Bica** funicular snails its way up a steep street between Cais do Sodré and the lower end of the Bairro Alto, beginning its journey in a yellow building marked 'Ascensor da Bica' on Rua de São Paulo. It climbs through one of Lisbon's quirkiest old *bairros*, an area where fashionable restaurants and bars coexist with tatty grocers and taverns.

The lie of the land here was formed when a landslide swept away much of an earlier Bica during an earthquake in 1598. Topping out the neighbourhood is the Esplanada do Adamastor (also known as Santa Catarina *miradouro*), where the kiosk often serves drinks deep into a summer night. Crowds gather to admire the wonderful view over the Tagus, or lie out on the lawn under the statue of the Adamastor – the mythical monster who guarded the Cape of Good Hope in Camões's *The Lusiads*. The big pink building that backs on the square above the *miradouro* is the headquarters of the pharmacists' association, with its excellent **Museu da Farmácia**.

The 18th-century **Palácio Verride** on the eastern side of the square is to house another museum, MUDE, showcasing the vast design and fashion collections bought by the city council from publishing executive Francisco Capelo. Many of the items drew crowds to the Museu do Design in the Centro Cultural de Belém from 1999, but moved out in 2006 to make room for the Berardo collection (*see p163* **Money talks...**)

If you like to wash away your sins in gilt, head over to the **Igreja de Santa Catarina** on Calçada do Combro. The original building dates to 1647, though it was remodelled after the 1755 earthquake. The adjoining monastery is now a National Guard barracks with an interesting military library upstairs, but the main church is still in use and contains giltwork dating back to the late 17th century, as well as a ceiling that is a masterpiece of 18th-century rococo painting.

Museu da Farmácia

Rua Marechal Saldanha 1, Santa Catarina (21 340 0600). Metro Baixa-Chiado/tram 28. **Open** 10am-6pm Mon-Fri; 2-6pm last Sun of mth. **Admission** €5; €2.50 concessions. **No credit cards**. **Map** p246 K9.

The idea of a Pharmaceutical Museum may not grab you, but this is a treasure house of fascinating items. They include European medical implements and model infirmaries from medieval times onwards, as well as ancient Roman and Greek artefacts, Tibetan medical charts and Arab medicine chests.

Western Waterfront

Lisbon realises it won't melt.

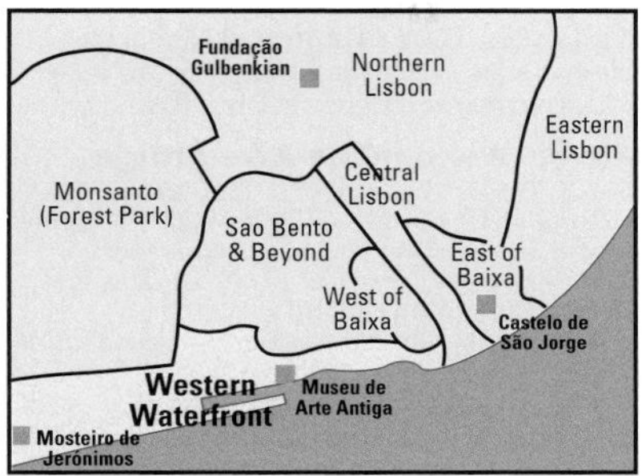

Lisbon has woken up to its waterfront. In the past the riverbank was the site of shipyards that outfitted the caravels of the Discoveries. Today's waterfront is hopping with bars, restaurants and joggers, especially at the city's western and eastern limits.

Cais do Sodré

Immediately west of the Praça do Comércio is a walkway along the river to the **Cais do Sodré** train, Metro and boat stations. Much of this area, however, has been torn up for the construction of a traffic tunnel under the Praça and the dump trucks will be staying for a while. The giant red sculpture here was erected to mark Lisbon's 1994 term as Europe's cultural capital.

At rush hour this area is swollen by commuters heading every which way (and in summer, by beachgoers too). It's the end of the line for many buses, trains on the Cascais line, and the Metro's green line. It's also the boat terminal for ferries to Cacilhas.

Cais do Sodré has a port-like red-light neighbourhood just in from the river. Many clubs bear the names of old ports-of-call, while the prostitutes who loll around the Praça de São Paulo are a reminder of a whorier heyday.

The flipside is a slew of trendier bars, among them two Irish pubs, that have joined the old British Bar (*see p187*) – a fixture since before World War II. A number of long established restaurants in this area are famed for their seafood, including Porto de Abrigo (*see p114*), while shoppers looking for that extra oilskin may find it in one of the local ships' chandlers. The **Mercado da Ribeira** (photo *p87*), built in 1882 on what was only recently discovered to be the remains of the old port, is a market hall on Avenida 24 de Julho; its bar opens early and is a spot for late-night revellers to sip hot chocolate in winter while waiting for the first train home. A little later, stallholders are unpacking fruit and veg, and in the afternoons the place is transformed into a blaze of colour when the flower sellers take over. Strenuous efforts have been made to use more of the market's first floor, with a large crafts shop, restaurant Espaço da Ribeiro (*see p114*) and live music bar RibeirArte (*see p179*), and regular book and music fairs. Behind it is the **Museu das Comunicações**.

Museu das Comunicações

Rua do Instituto Industrial 16 (21 393 5106/ www.fpc.pt). Metro Cais do Sodré/tram 18. **Open** 10am-6pm Mon-Fri; 2-6pm Sat. **Admission** €2.50; €1.25 concessions; free under-13s. **No credit cards. Map** p246 K10.

This post and telecommunications museum has a collection of models including old mail coaches and

Museums

For applied arts
Museu-Escola de Artes Decorativas (*see p73*); Museu Nacional de Azulejo (*see p97*).

For educational fun
Museu da Marioneta (*see p154*); Museu da Ciência (*see p81*); Pavilhão do Conhecimento (*see p154*).

For engineers
Museu da Água (*see p97*); Museu da Electricidade (*see p87*).

For global artistic excellence
Museu Calouste Gulbenkian (*see p96*).

For Portuguese art
Mosteiro dos Jerónimos (*see p87*); Museu Nacional de Arte Antiga (*see p84*).

For transport buffs
Museu da Marinha (*see p88*); Museu Nacional dos Coches (*see p89*).

modern delivery vans, and telephone equipment going back to 1810, plus a fair amount on new technologies. The museum also has stamps on show upstairs, including some issued by Madeira and the Azores, and a pleasant café.

Santos

The nightlife builds westward, particularly with nightclubs such as the rather kooky Kremlin and the upper-krust Kapital (for both, *see p189*). (K is not traditionally used in Portuguese, being rendered as qu.) During the day Avenida 24 de Julho is pretty empty, but at night clubbers are often out until dawn. Fast-food stops in **Santos** stay open late, serving *caldo verde* (cabbage soup with a slice of sausage) and *pão com chouriço* (sausage bread), warm from the brick oven.

The neighbourhood was named after three saintly Christian siblings – Verissimus, Julia and Maxima – who according to tradition were martyred by the Romans on the beach in the early fourth century. The only hint of sand now is the Escadinhas da Praia – Staircase of the Beach – which has the entrances to two nightclubs on its short length.

Santos is also home to crumbling monasteries and nunneries, and there are tales of secret tunnels used by enterprising monks in search of lonely nuns. One old royal palace on Rua de Santos-o-Velho is now the French Embassy; legend has it that Christopher Columbus was introduced to his future wife here.

The road running west is Rua das Janelas Verdes – Street of the Green Windows – named after the nickname of the old Alvor Palace that now houses the **Museu Nacional de Arte Antiga**. Its rear garden serves as the esplanade of the museum's café, but is accessible without a ticket. It's a favourite of visiting artists and writers, thanks to the area's literary associations: Graham Greene and John le Carré are among past guests of nearby Pensão York House (*see p51*), while As Janelas Verdes (*see p51*), a charming hotel, was once the home of Portuguese novelist Eça de Queiroz and is said to have inspired two of his novels. There's also a small park at the museum's far western end where you can watch ships lining up at the quay below.

Museu Nacional de Arte Antiga

Rua das Janelas Verdes (21 391 2800/www.mnarteantiga-ipmuseus.pt). Tram 15, 18, 25. **Open** 2-6pm Tue; 10am-6pm Wed-Sun. **Admission** €3; €1.50 concessions; free under-15s. Free to all Sun to 2pm. **Credit** V. **Map** p245 H/J10.

Lisbon's largest state-run museum, housed in a 17th-century former palace, the National Museum of Ancient Art is the only place that offers a truly comprehensive view of Portuguese art from the 12th to the early 19th centuries. Its most prized possession is Nuno Gonçalves's enigmatic late 15th-century masterpiece that is usually known as the *Panels of St Vincent*, although in fact its subject is hotly disputed; some say the central figure is Dom Fernando, the Infante Santo (holy prince) who died in captivity in Fez in 1443 after years as a hostage. The collection also includes Flemish Renaissance paintings (including a triptych by Hieronymous Bosch), Chinese porcelain, Indian furniture and African carvings. There are some fascinating products of the stylistic mix fostered by the 15th- and 16th-century Discoveries and empire, such as Indo-Portuguese cabinets with legs in the form of buxom women or snarling tigers. Other treasures include two Japanese lacquer screens depicting the landing of the Portuguese 'longnoses' on the islands in the 1540s. The shop is one of the best of any museum in Lisbon and the garden esplanade is an oasis.

Ponte Vasco da Gama. *See p85.*

Alcântara & Docas

The westernmost end of Avenida 24 de Julho meets the **Alcântara** district in the shadow of the Ponte 25 de Abril, its two towers rising 190 metres (635 feet) above the level of the water. With a main span of 1,013 metres (3,323 feet), it was the longest suspension bridge in Europe when it was built in 1966 as the Ponte Salazar. Its four lanes were then more than enough to handle all foreseeable traffic, but by the mid 1990s it was Lisbon's biggest traffic bugbear, with rush-hour jams that lasted hours. By the time work started on a new suspension bridge, the **Ponte Vasco da Gama** (photo *p84*), to relieve the pressure, more than 50 million vehicles each year were squeezing over the old bridge. The new link, opened in 1998, has done nothing to solve beach-related jams, and with car ownership and use still on the rise, overall traffic has not eased significantly despite the addition of a sixth lane. In 1999 a rail track that was part of the bridge's original design but never installed was finally suspended underneath. The railway links Entrecampos in northern Lisbon with commuter settlements around Almada and beyond.

Alcântara itself was transformed in the 1990s, with nightclubs and restaurants such as the classy Alcântara Café (*see p117*) carved out of old warehouses. Across the tracks and under the bridge is the **Docas de Santo Amaro**, a yachting marina with outdoor *esplanadas* and indoor bars. Most of the restaurants offer conveyor-belt cuisine, and if you hate noise and crowds, don't venture here on weekend nights. The Doca de Alcântara, to the east, is a better place to moor if you live on a boat and are thinking of stopping. There are smart new restaurants and cafés and the Fundação Oriente, which has a vast collection of Asian art, is installing what is expected to be a splendid Museu do Oriente in a former cold store, the Armazéns Frigoríficos do Bacalhau. The bas-relief façade, by Barata Feyo, is a fine example of the 1940s Estado Novo aesthetic, but inside there were problems eliminating that characteristic *bacalhau* smell. At the time of writing the museum was set to open in early to mid 2007.

Also worth a look from the same period is the **Gare Marítima de Alcântara**, designed by Porfírio Pardal Monteiro as a state-of-the-art receiving passenger ship terminal. Its western end has been taken over by a nightclub but the central hall – used for special events – has the original murals by the painter Almada Negreiros. One focuses on Lisbon daily life, particularly on the waterfront; another on the legend of Dom Fuas Roupinho, a medieval knight and naval hero who would have followed an evil hart over a foggy cliff if the Virgin Mary hadn't appeared and warned him back.

Inland, on the eastern side of the Alcântara valley, are the pink walls of the **Palácio das Necessidades**, now the Foreign Ministry. Its leafy park contains a notable collection of exotic plants, including one of Europe's oldest cactus gardens. Down below, lining the highway north, are the colourful blocks that house former residents of Casal Ventoso, a hillside slum that won a degree of international fame as a drugs hypermarket and no-go area for police in the 1990s. It was cleared in 2001, but the site still draws addicts.

On the western side of the valley is the **Tapada de Ajuda**, a former royal hunting ground where guided walks are organised at the weekends (21 363 8161). A little further west is the hilltop 16th-century **Capela de Santo Amaro**. At the bottom of the road is the tram terminal housing the Museu da Carris.

Capela de Santo Amaro

Calçada de Santo Amaro, Santo Amaro (21 361 7190). Tram 15, 18/bus 742. **Open** *Mass* 10am first Sun or by appointment (phone 4-7pm Mon-Fri). **Map** p244 E9.

This pretty, round hermitage was built in 1549. Its early 17th-century polychrome tile panels recount the life of St Amaro. Other 18th-century panels tell the building's story. Legend has it that the original chapel was founded by grateful Galician sailors saved from shipwreck offshore, and this was indeed long a centre of worship for Lisbon's large Galician community. The appropriately ship-shaped courtyard has sweeping views over river and bridge. St Amaro is also patron saint of the handicapped, and inside are replicas of arms and legs turned over to his care in the hope of obtaining a miracle cure.

Belém

Belém itself could be called a museum: its varied 'collection' ranges from the Manueline, late Gothic Torre de Belém to the fascistic Padrão dos Descobrimentos, from the Mosteiro dos Jerónimos, a temple to God, to the Centro Cultural de Belém, a temple to culture. Tourists troop through daily and on Sundays lisboetas crowd the lawns and promenades along the river, lunch at *esplanadas*, gorge themselves on tarts or flock to art exhibitions.

The area was once separate from the city of Lisbon, and bore the name Restelo (now limited to the residential region uphill). The lower part was dubbed Belém (Bethlehem) in the early 16th century by Dom Manuel I. Once a prime anchorage spot, its history is intertwined with the Discoveries. In 1415 the first overseas expedition left Restelo beach on the way to conquer Ceuta in Morocco. In March 1493

Christopher Colombus stopped in on his way back from discovering the Americas and in 1497 Vasco da Gama departed with his fleet to discover a maritime route to India – a scene recorded in the 16th-century epic poem *The Lusiads* by Luís de Camões. In 1588, during Spanish rule, Belém was the assembly point for the Spanish Armada sent against England.

So, take a trip through history, starting at the **Torre de Belém**, a curious little fortress put up between 1514 and 1520, and one of Lisbon's most recognisable symbols. Nearby, almost under the adjacent road overpass, is a V-shaped monument that pays homage to Portugal's dead in the African colonial wars that raged through the 1960s, ending only with the 1974 Revolution.

In 1940, to divert attention as World War II raged around neutral Portugal, the Salazar regime put on a show called the Exhibition of the Portuguese World, celebrating various historical anniversaries, including 300 years since the restoration of Portugal's independence from Spain. The waterfront at Belém was dolled up and the grandiose Praça do Império levelled out in front of the Mosteiro dos Jerónimos. Remnants of the show are the reflecting pools, the Museu Nacional de Arte Popular (now closed, its fate uncertain) and a building that houses a beer hall. Another leftover is the monolithic **Padrão dos Descobrimentos**, which stands by the marina.

Inland, the **Mosteiro dos Jerónimos** is one of Portugal's most famous and beautiful landmarks, containing the tombs of Vasco da Gama and Luís de Camões, both laid to rest here in the 19th century. The longer wing, facing the Praça do Império, was built in the 19th century and now houses, in the middle, the **Museu Nacional de Arqueológia**, and at the far end, the **Museu da Marinha** and the **Planetário Calouste Gulbenkian** (*see p156*). On the hill above Jerónimos are Belenenses, the football club with the best view in Lisbon, and the **Museu Nacional de Etnologia**.

The modern complex facing the Praça do Império is the **Centro Cultural de Belém** (*see p161*), or CCB, erected as a showpiece for Portugal's 1992 presidency of the European Union. Originally controversial for its cost, this striking building soon settled into its role as host of cultural events and, from 1999, an excellent design museum, now being shifted to central Lisbon to make way for the Berardo collection of modern art (*see p163* **Money talks...**) The CCB is a favourite with visitors, who can see travelling exhibits, listen to jazz, buy books and records, or idle away afternoons in the upstairs garden overlooking the river.

One block of the old residential district of Belém survives amid the monumentality. The houses along the Rua de Belém were once on the river, which has since retreated to the other side of the train tracks. Here, the Antiga Confeitaria de Belém (*see p130*) has been serving its lovely speciality, *pastéis de Belém*, a creamy custard tart topped with cinnamon and sugar, since 1837; the place is often mobbed.

On the western end of the block, a small alley on the right leads into a square with a column. The five bands on the *pelourinho* (pillory) stand for the five members of the aristocratic Távora family who were executed here in 1759, condemned by the Marquês de Pombal for complicity in an assassination attempt against Dom José I. The Marchioness of Távora was decapitated; her husband and sons tortured and their bones crushed. Salt was spread on their property so nothing would grow there; today the *pelourinho* stands all but forgotten, and weeds peek up among the cobbles.

Just round the corner is one of two botanical gardens in the area. Created in 1906 as the Jardim do Ultramar, the **Jardim Museu-Agrícola Tropical** (Calçada do Gavão, 21 396 2262) consists of tropical gardens with ponds and exotic lush outgrowth. One building houses the Xiloteca, a scholarly collection of woods from some 15,000 species of tree, with each specimen varnished and waxed to preserve it (visits by appointment only).

Further up the Calçada do Galvão is a lovely church, the **Igreja da Memória**.

Between the eastern end of the Rua de Belém and the river is the shady Praça Afonso de Albuquerque, named after the fiery Indian Ocean governor who established Portugal's pepper empire in the early 16th century. The salmon-coloured building opposite is the official residence of the president of Portugal. Its museum (21 361 4660, www.museu.presidencia.pt, closed Mon) has curiosity value, with glass cases displaying official decorations and gifts from foreign heads of state, but the palace itself is more interesting (by appointment, 11am-5pm Sat), not least because it contains specially commissioned paintings by Paula Rego depicting the life of the Virgin Mary: an unusual subject for an artist known for more secular concerns but recalling the area's Biblical name. In summer there are guided tours of the lovely gardens (June-mid Aug, 2-6pm Sun).

Next door is tourist favourite the **Museu Nacional dos Coches**. On the other side of the railway tracks, a short walk towards Lisbon, is the **Museu da Electricidade**, housed in what was Portugal's first power station.

The Calçada de Ajuda runs up the side of the Coach Museum and past the 18th-century **Jardim Botânico da Ajuda** (21 362 2503, www.jardimbotanicodajuda.com, closed Wed).

Portugal's first botanical garden, it was created by order of Don José I to grow plants from around the world. Further uphill is the **Palácio da Ajuda**, begun in 1802 but left unfinished.

Beyond Ajuda is **Monsanto Forest Park**, created in the 1930s at the behest of Salazar's energetic minister of public works, Duarte Pacheco. Comprising almost one eighth of Lisbon's area, it is the city's 'lung', freshening the west wind as it breezes in. On the map, so much green space looks inviting, but it was long a notorious haunt of prostitutes and drug dealers. There are pockets of civilisation, and recently the City Council has been trying to make better use of Monsanto, with open-air concerts in summer and a variety of activities for children in particular (*see p157*).

Igreja da Memória

Largo da Memória, Calçada do Galvão, Ajuda (21 363 5295). Tram 18/bus 729, 732. **Open** 2-7pm Mon-Sat (mass 6pm); 8am-1pm Sun (mass 10am). **Map** p244 C9.

The neo-classical Church of the Memory was built on the spot where Dom José I survived assassination on 3 September 1758. The suspected conspirators – the Távora family – were brutally put to death in Belém four months later. Designed by Italian Giovanni Carlo Bibienna, who died a few months after construction began, the church took more than two decades to complete. It was restored after a lightning strike in 1985.

Mosteiro dos Jerónimos

Praça do Império, Belém (21 362 0034/www.mosteirojeronimos.pt). Train to Belém from Cais do Sodré/tram 15/bus 28, 714, 727, 751. **Open** *Oct-Apr* 10am-5pm Tue-Sun (last entry 4.30pm). *May-Sept* 10am-6pm Tue-Sun (last entry 5.30pm). **Admission** *Church* free. *Cloisters* €4.50; €2.25 concessions; free under-15s. Free for all Sun to 2pm. **No credit cards. Map** p244 B9/10.

Jerónimos is the masterpiece of the Manueline style that is the Portuguese twist to late Gothic. Construction of the church and cloisters for the Hieronymite religious order began in 1502 on the orders of Dom Manuel I, in thanks for the divine favour bestowed through the Discoveries. The site had previously housed a chapel dedicated 50 years earlier by Prince Henry the Navigator. The monastery was to commemorate Portugal's maritime prowess, and master architect Diogo de Boytac set to work. The west-facing entrance to the church is now obscured by the 19th-century extension housing the Museu Arqueológia (*see p77*), but the sculptural relief of the south lateral entrance still captivates visitors. The hierarchic pile of stonework saints is topped by the image of St Mary of Bethlehem (Belém), patron saint of church and monastery. Immediately inside the church are the stone tombs of Vasco da Gama and Luís de Camões. Jerónimos is famed for the almost mystic quality of light that sweeps into the nave during the day: a visit during a choir performance is enough to make the wicked long for redemption. The exquisite cloisters, designed by Boytac and completed by João de Castilho, are often the setting for concerts , and other events. Boytac is also thought to have overseen the construction in 1514 of a pretty hermitage uphill, the Capela de São Jerónimo, guided visits to which (Wed only) can be booked at the monastery. **Photo** *p88*.

Museu da Electricidade

Avenida de Brasília, Belém (21 363 1646). Train to Belém from Cais do Sodré/tram 15/bus 27, 28, 56, 714, 727, 732, 751. **Open** 10am-7.15pm Tue-Thur;

Mercado da Ribeira.
See p83.

See heaven in stone at **Mosteiro dos Jerónimos**. *See p87.*

10am-9.15pm Fri, Sat; 10am-7.15pm Sun.
Admission €10; free under-8s. **No credit cards**.
Map p244 D10.

Although highly visible, this cathedral-like former power station by the river is not that easy to get to. The best way is probably on foot, via the footbridge at Belém rail station. The Central Tejo, as it originally was, powered Lisbon for three decades from 1918, before being relegated to the status of a back-up powerplant. Its boilers and generators, many dating from the 1930s, were last used in 1972. The museum opened in 1990 and was given a revamp in 2005 to turn it into a real technology museum (a leaflet in English is available), with a new children's area. But fans of industrial architecture will just enjoy wandering among giant machines in this tall red-brick building with arched windows, pilasters, pediments and cornices. It makes a dramatic backdrop for the art and fashion shows that are often held here and there's a riverside café.

Museu da Marinha

Praça do Império, Belém (21 362 0019/http://museu.marinha.pt). Train to Belém from Cais do Sodré/tram 15/bus 28, 714, 727, 729, 751. **Open** *Oct-Mar* 10am-5pm Tue-Sun. *Apr-Sept* 10am-6pm Tue-Sun.
Admission €3; €1.50 concessions; free under-7s.
No credit cards. **Map** p244 B10.

The Naval Museum boasts an enormous collection, all owned by the Defence Ministry. The display starts with scale models of every type of Portuguese boat, and ends with a hangar full of gilded royal barges. Along the way are maps, navigational instruments, and crypto-fascist statues and murals from the Salazar years of sanctifying Portugal's maritime history. The library (entrance next to Jerónimos church) holds 10,000 books on maritime affairs. Its photographic archive, which includes negatives from the mid 19th century, is open by appointment. There's a café by the museum's exit and a shop selling cufflinks with nautical motifs, ships in bottles and reproductions of old maps. An English leaflet is available.

Museu Nacional de Arqueológia

Praça do Império, Belém (21 362 0000/www.mnarqueologia-ipmuseus.pt). Train to Belém from Cais do Sodré/tram 15/bus 28, 714, 727, 729, 751.
Open 10am-6pm Tue-Sun. **Admission** €3; €1.50 concessions; free under-15s. Free to all Sun to 2pm.
No credit cards. **Map** p244 B10.

Although the Archaeological Museum has been housed in a wing of the Mosteiro dos Jerónimos for more than a century, it has only existed in its current form since 1990. There isn't enough space to display more than a small proportion of the permanent collection at any one time, but on show are usually an impressive collection of Egyptian artefacts and temporary exhibitions (which can often be excellent) from around Portugal. Access to the specialised library is by request (10am-noon, 2-5pm Tue-Fri).

Museu Nacional de Etnologia

Avenida da Ilha da Madeira, Alto do Restelo (21 304 1160/9). Bus 28, 714, 732. **Open** *Museum* 2-6pm Tue; 10am-6pm Wed-Sun. *Library* 9.30am-5.15pm Mon-Fri. **Admission** €3; €1.50 concessions; free under-15s. Free for all Sun to 2pm. **No credit cards**.
Map p244 B8.

The National Museum of Ethnology has a vast collection of items from rural Portugal and the former colonies that are regularly rotated and displayed in well-researched temporary exhibitions. A permanent show on rural life is also available for visits (guided if pre-booked) at 3pm on Tuesday and at 11am and 3pm from Wednesday to Friday. The staff are very helpful and the shop has books in English for sale. The café is on the minimalist side, so best trek down to Belém for your custard tarts.

Museu Nacional dos Coches

Praça Afonso de Albuquerque (21 361 0850/www.museudoscoches-ipmuseus.pt). Train to Belém from Cais do Sodré/tram 15/bus 28, 714, 727, 729, 751. **Open** 10am-6pm Tue-Sun. **Admission** €3; €1.50 concessions; free under-15s. **No credit cards**. **Map** p244 C10.

Housed in an 18th-century royal riding hall (commissioned by Dom João V in 1726), the Coach Museum claims to have the world's largest and most valuable collection of horse-drawn coaches – 45 of them. The oldest is an early 17th-century one used by Spanish incomer Philip II (Philip III of Spain), which was outwardly austere so as not to stoke resentment among his new subjects, but plush inside. The art of coach-making reached its height in three Italian baroque confections sent to Pope Clement XI by Dom João V; even their wheels are elaborately carved. There are ambitious plans for a large new museum, so the riding hall can house displays of horsemanship currently put on only in summer at Queluz palace (*see p216*).

Padrão dos Descobrimentos

Avenida de Brasília (opposite Praça do Império) (21 303 1950). Train to Belém from Cais do Sodré/tram 15/28, 714, 727, 729, 751. **Open** *Oct-May* 10am-6pm Tue-Sun. *June-Sept* 10am-7pm Tue-Sun. **Admission** €2.50; €1.50 concessions; free under-13s. **No credit cards**. **Map** p244 B10.

The original temporary Monument to the Discoveries was put up for the 1940 Exhibition, and the permanent stone Salazarist glorification of the Discoveries opened to the public only in 1960. From the side, it takes the form of a tall oblong marker; at the base sculpted figures of discoverers line a stylised prow jutting over the Tagus. They're led by Prince Henry the Navigator. Viewed head on, the monument appears as a giant sword-cum-cross, its point embedded in the riverbank, marking the entrance to the little exhibition space. Inside is a multimedia overview of Portugal's history (shows 11am, noon, 1pm, 3pm, 4pm & 7pm; reservations 21 301 0619); a lift carries visitors to the top for fine views. As the sun follows its course, the shadow of the monument's cross-section traces Portuguese explorers' progress around a marble map of the world on the square below. Key dates, such as Vasco da Gama's rounding of the Cape of Good Hope in 1498 and Pedro Álvares Cabral's landing in Brazil in 1500, are marked.

Palácio da Ajuda

Largo da Ajuda, Ajuda (21 363 7095). Tram 18/bus 729, 732. **Open** 10am-5pm Mon, Tue, Thur-Sun. **Admission** €4; €2 concessions; free under-15s. Free to all Sun to 2pm. **No credit cards**. **Map** p244 D8.

Where's the rest of that palace? Construction began in 1802 but was interrupted in 1807 when the royal family high-tailed it to Brazil to escape Napoleon's armies. The palace was never finished and still looks sawn in half. Nevertheless, it served as a royal residence in the late 19th century (when Dona Maria Pia imposed her rococo taste) and is classified as a national monument. Some wings are open as a museum, while others house the Ministry of Culture.

Torre de Belém

Praça da Torre de São Vicente, Belém (Mosteiro 21 362 0034). Train to Belém from Cais do Sodré/tram 15/bus 723, 729. **Open** *Oct-Apr* 10am-5pm Tue-Sun. *May-Sept* 10am-6.30pm Tue-Sun. **Admission** €3; €1.50 concessions; free under-15s. **No credit cards**. **Map** p244 A10.

The Tower of Belém was put up to guard the river entrance into Lisbon harbour. Built on the orders of Dom Manuel the Fortunate, it has stonework motifs recalling the Discoveries, among them twisted rope and the Catholic Crosses of Christ. Other sculptures depict St Vincent, patron saint of Lisbon, and – under the north-west watch-tower – an exotic rhinoceros that is said to have inspired Dürer's drawing of the beast. The tower was originally some distance from the riverbank; it is now easily accessible by wooden walkway from a lovely green park.

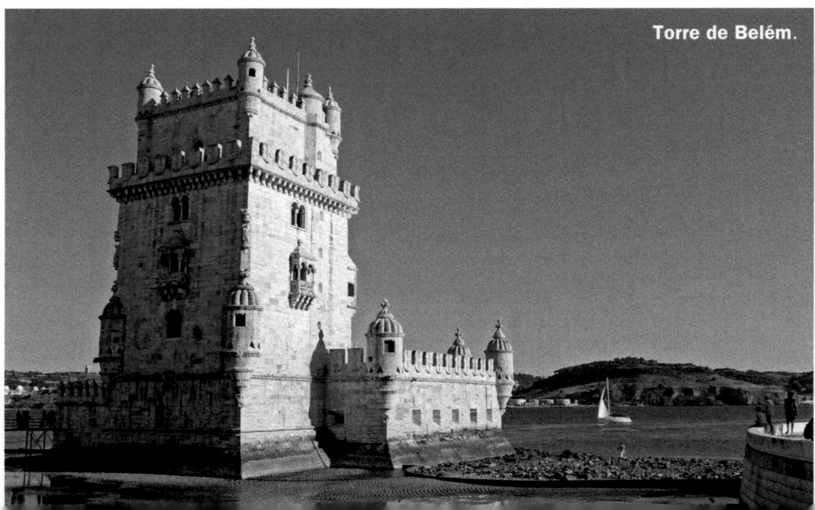

Torre de Belém.

São Bento & Beyond

Home to diplomats, divas and dearly departed Brits.

The neighbourhood in front of the Palácio de São Bento, the massive old Benedictine monastery that now houses the Portuguese parliament, takes its name from the building. Perhaps the best approach to the *palácio* is from the narrow Travessa da Arrochela, a typical old street with laundry hanging out. Capping the view at the bottom of the street are the enormous pediment and columns of the palace, now known as the **Palácio da Assembléia da República** (*see below*).

Up Rua de São Bento is the former home of the greatest 20th-century fadista, Amália. It is now the **Casa-Museu Amália Rodrigues** (*see below*). In the other direction, the broad Avenida Carlos I leads down to Santos.

In the 16th century the area around the busy Rua do Poço dos Negros (Well of Negroes) to the east of Avenida Dom Carlos I reeked of rotting bodies – African slaves dumped in a depository at the bottom of the hill after serving their use. It's now a lively residential area served by cheap *tascas*. There's an African feel as well, with live music from Cape Verde at the splendid **B.leza** (*see p179*) down on the Rua da Boavista, and hungry nighthawks trooping into the semi-legal Cape Verdean kitchen Cachupa (upstairs at Rua do Poço dos Negros 73) in the early hours.

Tucked between the parliament and the river is one of Lisbon's most enduring traditional neighbourhoods – Madragoa. A feast of fado and fishwives, it once housed a colony of African fishermen; their waterfront irreverence contrasting with the holy orders dwelling in the many nearby houses of religion. Since those days the rail line and Avenida 24 de Julho have cut the neighbourhood off from the river, while religious orders were abolished in Portugal in 1834. The former Convento das Berardas on Rua da Esperança now hosts the **Museu da Marioneta** (*see below*) and a fine restaurant, the Luso-Belgian **A Travessa** (*see p114*).

Casa-Museu Amália Rodrigues

Rua de São Bento 193, São Bento (21 397 1896). Metro Rato/bus 6, 727. **Open** 10am-1pm, 2-6pm Tue-Sun. **Admission** *Guided tours* €5. **No credit cards**. **Map** p246 K8.

Inaugurated weeks after her body was transferred to the National Pantheon in 2002, fado diva Amália Rodrigues's house is a shrine to the memory of this greatest exponent of Lisbon's soulful music (see the chapter on Fado for more about her). Lined with 18th-century *azulejos*, it has been restored and adapted, displaying portraits of the star by leading Portuguese artists, her favourite outfits, jewellery, and decorations awarded by adoring politicians. Rodrigues, who died in October 1999 after a career that spanned decades, won the hearts of her compatriots, and fame in Italy, France and Brazil. The guided tour is conducted in Portuguese or English.

Museu da Marioneta

Convento das Bernardas, Rua da Esperança, Madragoa (21 394 2810). Tram 15, 18, 25 then 5min walk. **Open** 10am-1pm, 2-6pm Tue-Sun (last entry 12.30pm, 5.30pm). **Admission** €2.50; €1.50 concessions; €0.75 under-6s. **No credit cards**. **Map** p245 J9.

The Puppet Museum was installed a few years ago in a grand 18th-century former convent. It contains more than 800 marionettes from Portugal and around the world, some created for operas staged by the museum's founders, puppet-maker Helena Vaz and late composer João Alberto Gil. The latest acquisition, in 2006, was some 500 puppets, shadow figures and masks from south-east Asia. The convent's former chapel serves as a theatre; shows are mainly for schools, but you can look in.

Palácio da Assembléia da República

Largo das Cortes, à Rua de São Bento, São Bento (21 391 9000/www.parlamento.pt). Tram 25, 28/bus 6, 713, 727, 773. **Open** Session viewings normally from 3pm Wed, Thur; from 10am Fri. **Admission** free. **Map** p246 J9.

The imposing façade of the São Bento palace seems as if it ought to face more than just a huddle of red-roofed neighbourhoods kept at bay by the stone lions of parliament. Portugal's national assembly is housed in the former convent of São Bento (St Benedict), which was turned over to parliament in 1834 when religious orders were abolished. Major renovation work since then has left little evidence of the original late 16th-century structure; the building is now noteworthy for some of the artwork contained inside, especially the upstairs murals painted between 1920 and 1926 by Rafael Bordalo Pinheiro. The house and gardens behind it are the official residence of the prime minister.

Lapa, Estrela, Campo de Ourique, Rato & Amoreiras

West of São Bento the neighbourhoods are more well-to-do. Lapa, on a hillside facing south over the river, is home to Lisbon's diplomatic community. A walk along Rua do Sacramento, Rua do Caetano or Rua de São Domingos shows what Lisbon has to offer in the way of luxury. Estrela is the area based around the late 18th-century **Basílica da Estrela** (*see p92*). Tram 28 passes by here, on the west end of its run up and down old Lisbon. The **Jardim da Estrela** (*see p92*) opposite the church is a popular stop for parents with children in tow.

Beyond the roundabout at its eastern end is an art nouveau building housing the free **Museu João de Deus** (Avenida Álvares Cabral 69, 21 396 0854, closed Sat, Sun), dedicated to the poet-pedagogue but most interesting for its 19th-century paintings. There's one by José Malhoa in the office to the right of the lobby, another by Rodrigo Soares in one on the left. Inside, in the conference room, there are cartoons and a vase by the multi-talented late 19th-century artist Bordalo Pinheiro.

On the other side of Rua de São Jorge, the **Cemitério Inglês** (*see p92*) contains the remains of Henry Fielding, among others. The area has other features of relevance to British expats, *see p93* **The Brit pack**.

Campo de Ourique is a middle-class district above Estrela that was laid out last century on a grid pattern. The house on Rua Coelho da Rocha where poet Fernando Pessoa spent the last 15 years of his life is now the **Casa Fernando Pessoa** (*see p92*), one of Lisbon's more active small cultural institutions. At the far west end of the neighbourhood is the enormous municipal cemetery Prazeres ('pleasures') with a city of the dead spread beneath lonely cypresses. Campo de Ourique is staunchly bourgeois and has an indoor market with quality fruit and veg.

A pile of pastel postmodernism marks the north end of Campo de Ourique and the beginning of the Amoreiras business district. Architect Tomás Taveira (*see p32* **Lisbon's got the blues**) boasted in the mid 1980s that his goal with the **Amoreiras towers** (*see p34*) – which look like giant Liquorice Allsorts made of smoked glass – was to provide a skyline counterbalance to the Castelo de São Jorge. Most feel he missed the mark, but the towers are still there and Amoreiras is one of the capital's most popular malls. Just down the Rua das Amoreiras, above the busy Largo do Rato, one can escape the reflecting glass and take a shady seat in the delightful Jardim das Amoreiras, located under the arches at the end of the **Aqueduto das Águas Livres** (*see p92*) before it terminates in the **Mãe de Água** (*see p93*). A café in the garden serves light lunches.

Aqueduto das Águas Livres. *See p92.*

Across the street is the **Fundação Arpad Szenes-Vieira da Silva** (21 388 0044/53, www.fasvs.pt), which exhibits a permanent collection of the work of Portuguese modernist painter Maria Helena Vieira da Silva and her Hungarian husband Arpad Szenes. Entry is free on Mondays. The museum is housed in the former royal silk and textile workshop; the whole neighbourhood was set up as an industrial park in the late 18th century, which is why so many of the streets are named after factories, such as Travessa da Fábrica dos Pentes (Comb Factory Way).

Lisbon's central synagogue – set well back, as non-Catholic places of worship were not permitted to front on to the street when it was built a century ago – is off Largo do Rato, at Alexandre Herculano 59. You can book a visit on 21 393 1130.

Aqueduto das Águas Livres

Access from Calçada da Quintinha (EPAL gate), Campolide. Bus 2. **Guided tours** *Apr-Oct* organised by Museu de Água (21 810 0215, 10am-6pm Mon-Fri). **Map** p245 H6.

Lisbon's aqueduct spans the valley of Alcântara. The best views of it are from Campolide train station or roads leading south to Ponte 25 de Abril.

A very British burial: **Cemitério Inglês.**

Construction began in 1731 and by 1748 the first water was flowing down the line from the main source 58km (36 miles) to the north-west. The aqueduct's main span is nearly 940m (3,133ft) long and bridges the valley of Alcântara on a series of 35 arches, the largest of which rises 64m (213ft) from the ground; giddy heights if you book a guided visit and walk along the parapet. When built these were the tallest stone arches in the world. Sturdy too: they survived the 1755 quake unscathed. The aqueduct was only taken out of service in 1967. **Photo** *p91.*

Basílica da Estrela

Praça da Estrela, Estrela (21 396 0915). Tram 25, 28. **Open** 7.30am-8pm daily. **Map** p245 J8.

The ornate white dome of the Basílica da Estrela is one of Lisbon's best loved landmarks. It was built on the orders of Dona Maria I to fulfil a promise over the birth of a male heir. Construction took ten years, from 1779 to 1789, with statues sculpted by artists from the Mafra School. The church is richly decorated inside with Portuguese marble, although many of the paintings are by Italian masters.

Casa Fernando Pessoa

Rua Coelho da Rocha 16, Campo de Ourique (21 391 3270/7). Tram 25, 28/bus 9. **Open** 10am-6pm Mon-Wed, Fri; 1-8pm Thur. **Admission** free. **Map** p245 H8.

Dedicated to poetry in general and Pessoa in particular, the Casa Fernando Pessoa contains a library specialising in his work, organises poetry readings, and produces several publications annually. It also frequently stages exhibitions by young artists.

Cemitério Inglês

Rua de São Jorge à Estrela, Estrela (21 390 6248/ 21 469 2303). Tram 25, 28/bus 9, 720, 738. **Open** 9am-1pm daily. **Map** p245 H8.

Across the street from the top end of the Jardim da Estrela a tall wall encloses the English cemetery, which dates back to a 1654 agreement between Dom João IV and Oliver Cromwell over the need for a Protestant burial ground in Lisbon. Intentions were made good seven decades later, and the first customer officially laid to rest in 1729. Among them is 18th-century novelist Henry Fielding, who came to Lisbon to improve his health and promptly died. A small Jewish area is hidden behind a wall on the west side. To enter the cemetery, ring loudly (and repeatedly) at the gate and somebody should come and let you in.

Jardim da Estrela

Praça da Estrela, Estrela (21 396 3275). Tram 25, 28/bus 9, 720, 738, 773. **Open** 7am-midnight daily. **Map** p245 H8.

Also known as the Jardim Guerra Junqueiro, the Estrela Garden was laid out in 1842 across the street from the Basílica. The bandstand near the top end of the park once graced the public promenade that became the Avenida da Liberdade, and was moved here in the 1930s. There is a swan pond with neighbouring café and a large playground.

The Brit pack

There's some corner of a Lisbon field that is forever England, and it's opposite the Jardim da Estrela. The **Cemitério Inglês** (*see p92*) is, naturally enough, attached to the city's Anglican church, **St George's** (*see p234*). In the same large block can be found several other Anglo institutions: the **British Hospital** (*see p229*), known to taxi drivers as 'O Hospital Inglês', **Estrela Hall** (*see p194*), home of amateur theatre troupe the Lisbon Players (founded 1947), and the British-Portuguese Chamber of Commerce.

This little ghetto has its origin in a 1654 agreement in which the Portuguese conceded the right to bury Protestant dead on Catholic soil, albeit in a walled cemetery. There was demand because the British community in Portugal – and particularly the 'Factory', as its merchants were known – was flourishing. How and why the British came to wield such influence is something that, not all that long ago, every English schoolboy could tell you: Portugal is 'our oldest ally'.

English crusaders were prominent among the invaders who seized Lisbon from the Moors, and Gilbert of Hastings was the city's first bishop subsequently. But it was the 1386 Treaty of Windsor – signed a year after English archers helped Portugal clinch its independence – that foresaw a 'perpetual alliance', cemented by the marriage of João I and Philippa of Lancaster.

Three centuries on the knot was retied by Charles II and Catherine of Braganza, a scion of the family that had led a rebellion against the ruling Spanish. Portuguese schoolchildren in turn learn how Catherine's yearning for *marmelada* (quince jelly) prompted the invention of marmalade, and how she introduced tea to England. Such cartoon history masks hard-nosed calculations. Portugal needed a counterweight to its larger neighbour, and Britain a foothold in its continental power struggles.

Trade also benefited both sides but overall the weaker party got a raw deal. The 1703 Methuen Treaty secured a market for Portuguese wine, but by throwing Portugal open to English textiles entrenched its underdevelopment. It became a virtual economic colony.

In the Peninsular Wars, Wellington's forces expelled Napoleon's armies, but the heavy-handedness of postwar administrator Marshal Beresford caused such outrage that members of the local Masonic order (ironically, set up on the British model) plotted against him. The site of their 1817 execution in Lisbon, later renamed Campo dos Mártires da Pátria after these 'martyrs of the fatherland', recalls another British-inflicted scar.

The nadir was the 1890 Ultimatum, in which Britain demanded that Portugal give up territory between Angola and Mozambique. The decision to yield sparked riots, a Republican rebellion in Oporto, and despair at the fecklessness of Portugal's rulers.

Over the centuries numerous other institutions with a British connection sprang up around Lisbon. The Colégio dos Inglesinhos, on the eponymous Travessa in the Bairro Alto, housed Catholics forced to flee England during the Reformation. They developed a complex relationship with the mother country, at times even helping with diplomatic deals. Though closed in 1973, the building still towers over the area; it is currently being turned, somewhat controversially, into luxury apartments.

Today many British expats live along the rail *linha* to Cascais, send their children to St Julian's in Carcavelos, and prompt accusations of not engaging with the host culture. A number of old Anglo-Portuguese families remain, making money from traditional businesses such as cork; it was their forefathers' relationship with local employees and associates that threw up phrases such as '*para inglês ver*' ('for Englishman to see', meaning done for show) and made *pontualidade britânica* synonymous with rigorous time-keeping.

Mãe de Água

Jardim das Amoreiras, Rua das Amoreiras, Rato (21 325 1646). Metro Rato/bus 74. **Open** 10am-6pm Mon-Sat. **Admission** €2.50; €1.50 concessions; free under-13s. **Map** p246 K7.

The Aqueduto das Águas Livres ends at the Mãe de Água (Mother of Water), a large stone building that looms behind the Socialist Party headquarters on Largo do Rato. Construction began in 1745 and work carried on until 1834. Inside, the central tank has a capacity of 5,500 cubic metres, and the cool stone interior the feel of an eerie grotto. Arriving water tumbles into the central pool over a fantastic sculpture. The walkways around the tank and a floating platform are used for art exhibitions. Visitors can climb the stairs to peer down the aqueduct passage.

Northern Lisbon

One of Portugal's finest museums, and its most famous football team.

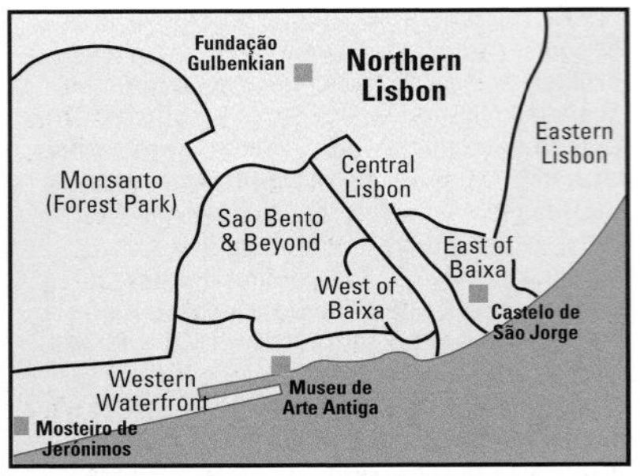

Saldanha & Avenidas novas

The office blocks along the new avenues off the Avenida da República is where Lisbon does its business. Yet bits of an older, gentler city remain: **Pastelaria Versailles** (*see p131*) at the beginning of the Avenida da República near Praça Duque de Saldanha retains its bourgeois appeal; Galeto opposite is a prime example of 1960s cafeteria style; at No.38 is a building in the art nouveau style, the Clube dos Empresários (Businessmen's Club), with its rather formal restaurant. And the **Casa-Museu José Anastácio Gonçalves** (*see below*) is a monument to tasteful bourgeois acquisitiveness.

Halfway up Avenida da República, ringed by brick-red cupolas, is the neo-Moorish Praça de Touros or bullring (*see p200* **No death in the afternoon**), built in 1892. The Avenida continues north to leafy Campo Grande, home of the Biblioteca Nacional (No.83, 21 798 2000), Portugal's main copyright library. To consult any publication, bring ID and fill in a form stating what you're looking for. The library regularly holds exhibitions.

Further up Campo Grande are the **Museu da Cidade** and **Museu Rafael Bordalo Pinheiro** (for both, *see below*); beyond the northern end is Sporting's flashy **Estádio de Alvalade** (*see p198*), built in time for the 2004 European football championship finals. A few blocks east, Avenida da Roma cuts through Alvalade proper, a smart residential area. North of Alvalade, beyond Lisbon's main ring road, the Segunda Circular, is Portela airport and remnants of the shanty towns that dotted the city's periphery for decades.

Casa-Museu José Anastácio Gonçalves

Avenida 5 de Outobro 8, Saldanha (21 354 0823). Metro Picoas. **Open** 2-6pm Tue; 10am-6pm Wed-Sun. **Admission** €2; €1 concessions; free under-14s. Free to all Sun to 2pm. **No credit cards. Map** p248 L5.

Originally commissioned by painter José Malhoa, who had his atelier upstairs, and decorated in art nouveau style, the house was bought by art enthusiast Dr Gonçalves. He favoured landscapes and portraits by his chum Silva Porto, and Mário Augusto and Bordalo Pinheiro. He also amassed a collection of Chinese porcelain from the Ming and Transition periods that rivals that of the Gulbenkian, along with lots of 18th- and 19th-century English, French and Portuguese furniture.

Museu da Cidade

Campo Grande 245 (21 751 3200). Metro Campo Grande. **Open** 10am-1pm, 2-6pm Tue-Sun. **Admission** €2.55; free under-13s. Free to all Sun. **No credit cards. Map** p248 L5.

In 1962 the city council took over the 18th-century Pimenta Palace with a view to founding a museum to chart Lisbon's history. While some displays are skimpy, they cover the ground as best they can, starting with the Stone Age and working through Roman times to the Visigoths and Moors. There is a reminder of the links between Portugal and Britain (*see p93* **The Brit pack**) in the form of a bust of Dona Beatriz, the illegitimate daughter of Dom João I who married the fifth Earl of Arundel. Also worth seeing is a large model of Lisbon before the 1755 earthquake, the fabulously tiled palace kitchens, and the formal garden with its peacocks. The displays have Portuguese labels only, but there is a (poorly translated) English leaflet.

Museu Rafael Bordalo Pinheiro

Campo Grande 382 (21 755 0468/www.museubordalopinheiro.pt). Metro Campo Grande. **Open** 10am-6pm Tue-Sun. **Admission** *Museum* €2; free concessions. Free to all Sun. *Temporary exhibitions* Free. **No credit cards. Map** p248 L1.

Portuguese architect and artist Rafael Bordalo Pinheiro (1846-1905) had his own ceramics factory in Caldas da Rainha, where he produced fantastic and colourful designs. Examples here include a pig's head on a platter, lobsters in baskets, and frogs sitting on plates or climbing up vases and poles. He was also a prolific caricaturist, using his Portuguese everyman character Zé Povinho to puncture the pomposity of public figures. This recently renovated museum has a series of rooms dedicated to his output, and rotates its large permanent collection through them.

Lumiar

North of Campo Grande, the Avenida Padre Cruz winds past Telheiras, where the results of a decade-long building boom fuelled by cheap mortgages are much in evidence, towards Lumiar. Once a sleepy village, it is now a dreary suburb choked with traffic that has not been much eased by the recent arrival of the Metro. The **Museu do Traje** and **Museu do Teatro** (for both, *see below*) are housed in wings of an 18th-century former palace that overlooks the Parque Monteiro-Mor, one of Lisbon's prettiest parks and a reminder of more bucolic times.

Further north, just outside the city limits, is the Convento de São Dinis de Odivelas (Largo Dom Dinis, Odivelas). Founded at the end of the 13th century, it was rebuilt after the devastation of the 1755 earthquake. Gothic elements remain while wonderful *azulejos* were added. Visits may be booked through Odivelas council (21 934 4870).

Museu do Teatro

Estrada do Lumiar 10, Lumiar (21 756 7410/9/ www.museudoteatro-ipmuseus.pt). Metro Lumiar. **Open** 2-6pm Tue; 10am-6pm Wed-Sun. **Admission** €3; €1.50 concessions; free under-14s. **Credit** V.
Opened in 1985, this theatre museum has more than 300,000 items, including costumes, stage designs, manuscripts and 100,000 photographs. It has its own café, with a shaded terrace from which to study the overgrown formal garden. Entry also gives admission to the Museu do Traje (*see below*).

Museu do Traje

Largo Júlio Castilho 2, Estrada do Lumiar, Lumiar (21 759 0318/www.museudotraje-ipmuseus.pt). Metro Lumiar. **Open** 10am-6pm Tue-Sun. **Admission** €3; €1.50 concessions; free under-14s. **No credit cards**.
The Costume Museum has a limited display, but it is worth a visit just to poke your head into the prettier parts of the former Palácio de Angela-Palmela. Walls are decorated with garlands and musical instruments in pastel colours, and most original wall tiles remain in place. You may also catch one of the temporary exhibitions on Portuguese costume. Behind the palace is a restaurant. Entry includes admission to the Museu do Teatro (*see above*).

Praça de Espanha, Sete Rios & Benfica

The Praça de Espanha, to the west, is infamous at rush hour; the grassy space in the middle now sports an aqueduct arch that used to constrict traffic further downtown until it was uprooted to here. On one side is the Palácio de Palhavã, the official residence of the Spanish ambassador. Opposite the palace is the Fundação Calouste Gulbenkian, one of Lisbon's most important cultural institutions. Its **Museu Calouste Gulbenkian** (*see p96*) has a rich collection of artefacts, while at the other end of the foundation's lovely wooded garden, the **Centro de Arte Moderna** (*see p161*) showcases modern art and, in summer, stages open air jazz concerts.

There are more shows on offer on the south-western corner of Praça de Espanha, at the **Teatro Aberto** (*see p194*) and the **Teatro da Comuna** (*see p195*). On the northern side of Praça de Espanha is a ramshackle market with a whiff of the souk, where stalls sell everything from buckets to imitation designer T-shirts. Some locals calls it the *Centro comercial do céu-aberto* – the Mall of the Open Skies. Continue past it along Avenida Columbano Bordalo Pinheiro to reach the **Jardim Zoológico de Lisboa** (*see p156*).

Sete Rios is now a sprawl of bank headquarters and airport-style hotels, but old jewels are still scattered about, such as the **Palácio dos Marquêses da Fronteira** (*see p96*), famed for its gardens and *azulejos* depicting exotic hunting scenes. A little further north is the **Biblioteca-Museu República e Resistência** (*see p96*). Nearby is the **Museu da Música** (*see p96*), which melds with Alto dos Moinhos Metro station. From here it's a short walk to the giant **Estádio da Luz** (*see p199*), home of Benfica. A powerhouse of European football in the 1960s, the club is a perennial candidate, with FC Porto and Sporting, for the Portuguese league title.

Across the ring road is the massive **Centro Colombo** (*see p132*), a shopping mall that is billed as Iberia's largest. Beyond is the once quiet town of Benfica, today a concrete suburb.

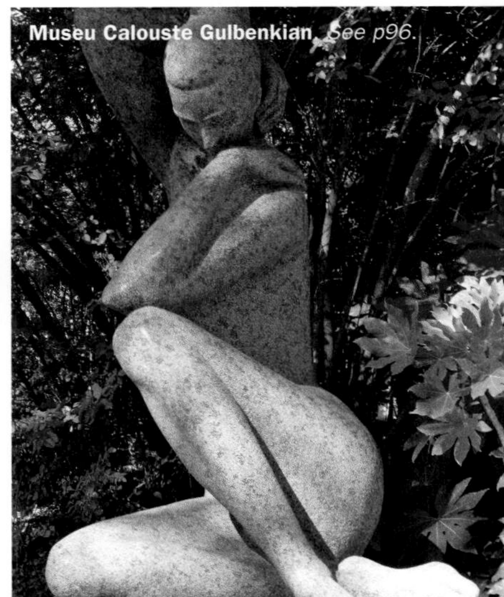
Museu Calouste Gulbenkian. *See p96.*

Baroque rules at the 17th-century **Palácio dos Marquêses da Fronteira**.

Biblioteca-Museu República e Resistência

Estrada de Benfica 419, Benfica (21 771 2310/29). Metro Alto dos Moinhos. **Open** 10am-6pm Mon-Fri. **Admission** free.

This historical archive of Portuguese republicanism and resistance to fascism is crammed into a late 19th-century building put up to house the workers of entrepreneur Francisco Grandela (owner of the eponymous department store on Rua do Carmo in Chiado, now invaded by chains). Containing 5,000 books dating from the 1870s to the present day, including the archives of trade unions and social organisations, it organises seminars, exhibitions, screenings and tours. There is another, modern site in Entrecampos (Rua Alberto de Sousa 10A, 21 780 2760; open 10am-6pm, Mon-Fri), with a library.

Museu Calouste Gulbenkian

Avenida de Berna 45, Praça de Espanha (21 782 3461/50/guided visits & children's activities 21 782 3455/6/7/www.museu.gulbenkian.pt). Metro Praça de Espanha. **Open** *Museum/Centro de Arte Moderna (CAM)* 10am-6pm Tue-Sun. *Library* 9.30am-7pm Mon-Fri. **Admission** *Museum/CAM* €3; free concessions. Free for all Sun. *Museum & CAM* €5. **No credit cards**. **Map** p248 K4.

It is difficult to know where to start in this, one of the world's great museums, whose exhibits date from 2000 BC to the early 20th century. From the ancient world come Egyptian scarabs, Greco-Roman jewellery and a larger-than-life Assyrian bas-relief in alabaster of a warrior from the ninth century BC. The most outstanding rooms are the two containing Islamic and oriental art: carpets, robes, tapestries, tiles and glassware, mainly from 16th- and 17th-century Persia, Turkey, Syria and India, plus porcelain, jade, paintings and lacquered boxes from China and Japan. Squeezed in among the Islamic art are artefacts from Christian Armenia – a nod to the founder's origins. The section on European art boasts medieval manuscripts and ivory and wood diptychs. Further on are Italian Renaissance majolica ware and tapestries, and a selection of mainly 18th-century French furniture and silverware. Among painters represented are Domenico Ghirlandaio, Roger van der Weyden and Jan Gossaert, Rubens, Hals and Rembrandt, Gainsborough, Manet and Corot. Save time for the final room and its breathtaking glass and metal art nouveau jewellery by René Lalique. Note that if you intend to stay in the museum after 5pm, you should check your things into the downstairs cloakroom; the upstairs one closes early. Also downstairs are the Gulbenkian art library, an excellent cafeteria and a small gift shop. There's a larger bookshop upstairs. The Centro de Arte Moderna (*see p161*) is to be found at the other, northern end of the Foundation's lovely gardens. **Photo** *p95*.

Museu da Música

Alto dos Moinhos Metro station, Benfica (21 771 0990/www.museudamusica-ipmuseus.pt). Metro Alto dos Moinhos. **Open** 10am-6pm Tue-Sat. **Admission** €2; €1 concessions; free under-15s. **No credit cards**.

A newish state museum, containing 700 musical instruments and related documents. The collection boasts instruments dating from the 16th to 20th centuries, including Portuguese guitars and an outstanding selection of baroque harpsichords. The museum shop has a good range of books and scores of classical CDs, as well as miniature instruments.

Palácio dos Marquêses da Fronteira

Largo de São Domingos de Benfica 1, Sete Rios (21 778 2023). Metro Parque Zoológico then 15min walk or bus 70. **Tours** *June-Sept* 10.30am, 11am, 11.30am, 12.30pm Mon-Sat. *Oct-May* 11am, noon Mon-Sat. **Admission** *Palace & gardens* €7.50. *Gardens* €3; free under-14s. **No credit cards**.

The idyllic setting of this palace, at the foot of Monsanto Forest Park, is in sharp contrast to the concrete jungle of Sete Rios. The palace was built for the Mascarenhas family, who still own it today. The Jesuit super-missionary St Francis Xavier supposedly said mass in the chapel here before leaving for India in 1541. The palace itself was mostly put up in the 1670s, then rebuilt after the 1755 earthquake. The Sala das Batalhas is decorated with 17th-century *azulejos* depicting battles against Spain during the war of restoration (1640-68), while the rest of the complex of halls, courtyards and gardens is a veritable museum of baroque statuary. Guided tours last about an hour; arrive a few minutes early.

Eastern Lisbon

Relax by the river.

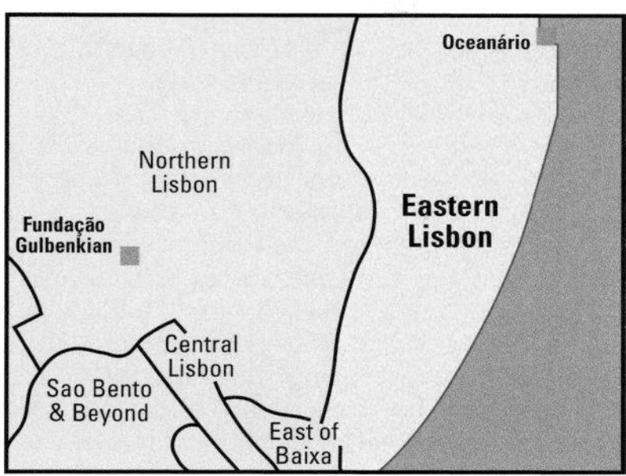

In the mid 19th century the romantic writer Almeida Garrett described the low hills above the eastern Lisbon waterfront as being full of gardens and orchards. The districts of Chelas, Xabregas and Marvila were garden getaways within easy reach of the city. Indeed, the valley of Chelas has a history that rivals that of Lisbon itself. Legend has it that Chelas is a corruption of Achilles, and that it was here that the Greek warrior disguised himself as a woman to avoid combat at Troy. To no avail. Odysseus found his hideaway, near where today's Oriente Metro line emerges into the open between Olaias and Bela Vista stations, and enticed Achilles to war, glory and death outside the walls of Ilion.

The railway that links Lisbon with Madrid and Oporto radically altered this area. By the 1860s trains were chugging along a line parallel to the river, leaving in their wake industries and warehouses. The contrasts can be disconcerting. There are still small farm plots, though many *azinhagas* (narrow stone-walled country lanes) end in concrete blocks of social housing. High-rise apartment blocks look out to the river on one side and to tin-roof slums on the other.

This 'forgotten' Lisbon faces the Mar de Palha – the inland 'Sea of Straw' – wide enough that the morning mist often obscures the other side, and so named either because bales of straw used to be shipped over from Alcochete and Montijo, or because its waters glow with a golden hue at sunset. This is the home of the Tágides, the river nymphs of Camões' *Lusiads*. Since 1998 the broad highway along the river has linked Praça do Comércio with the Expo 98 site – now renamed Parque das Nações – and the Gare do Oriente rail station.

Santa Apolónia & Madre de Deus

The Santa Apolónia rail station at the foot of Alfama is the end of the line for lines going to Oporto, Madrid, Paris and beyond. Long the city's main station, it has lost some of that status to the monumental new Gare do Oriente rail station up the line near Parque das Nações.

Santa Apolónia was built in the 1860s on the Cais dos Soldados – 'Quay of the Soldiers' – where troops departed on their way to Africa and India, Timor and Macao. Fittingly, the **Museu Militar** is opposite the station. In the 19th century there was no road to the right of the station; ships would tie up directly alongside the tracks. Nowadays the port warehouses that sprang up on landfill across the way have been cleared. A new cruise ship terminal has been installed, along with a string of restaurants and nightclubs such as Lux (*see p192*) and the diverse bunch in the Jardim do Tabaco complex a little nearer to Praça do Comércio.

Other old industrial and monument spaces in eastern Lisbon have been turned over to new uses, such as the award-winning **Museu da Água**, in an old pumping station back on Rua do Alviela, and the **Museu Nacional do Azulejo**, which in 1980 took up residence in one of the city's most important Manueline landmarks, the 16th-century Convento da Madre de Deus. This once stood on the waterfront but is now separated from the river by a bewildering assortment of streets, overpasses, railways and cranes. The **Convento do Beato** upriver was built in the 16th century. In the mid 19th century it was annexed to the Nacional biscuit factory but has been restored and is occasionally used for special events. Old warehouses and even former churches in the area are also used for theatre and music performances.

Museu da Água

Rua do Alviela 12, Santa Apolónia (21 810 0215/ http://museudaagua.epal.pt). Bus 794. **Open** 10am-6pm Mon-Sat. **Admission** €2.50; €1.50 concessions; free under-13s. **No credit cards**. **Map** p247 O9.

Like Belém's Museu da Electricidade (*see p87*), the Water Museum and its contents are important parts of Portugal's industrial archaeology and still run by a utility, in this case, state water company EPAL.

Housed in the first main pumping station to serve Lisbon, the museum is dominated by four huge steam engines from the 1880s, which were used as pumps. One is set in motion every month or so. The rest of the displays trace the history of Lisbon's water supply from Roman times to the present. The museum also organises visits to the 18th-century aqueduct spanning the Alcântara valley.

Museu Militar

Largo do Museu do Artilharia, Santa Apolónia (21 884 2569). Bus 6, 9, 12, 28, 34, 38, 39, 81, 82, 90, 746, 759, 794. **Open** 10am-5pm Tue-Sun. **Admission** €2.50; €1.30 concessions; free under-11s. Free Wed under-19s, over-64s. **No credit cards**. **Map** p247 N9.

A former 17th-century weapons factory provides an appropriate setting for the Military Museum. Tiles and paintings on walls and ceilings depict real or imagined battles. The tour begins upstairs, with two rooms devoted to the Napoleonic invasions, and a display on World War I. Note the traditional ridged helmet used by the Portuguese until they realised it wouldn't stop bullets and switched to the smooth British model. A series of rooms with elaborately carved and gilded decoration leads to a comprehensive display of Portuguese arms up to the 20th century. Downstairs are a plethora of cannons and a mind-boggling variety of weaponry captured from adversaries during the colonial wars of the 1960s and 1970s. Labels are in Portuguese, but there is an leaflet in English.

Museu Nacional do Azulejo

Rua da Madre de Deus 4, Madre de Deus (21 810 0340/www.mnazulejo-ipmuseus.pt). Bus 39, 718, 742, 794. **Open** *Summer* 2-6pm Tue; 10am-6pm Wed-Sun (last entry 5.30pm). *Winter* 2-6pm Tue; 10am-noon, 2-6pm Wed-Sun (last entry 5.30pm). **Admission** €3; €1.20-€1.50 concessions; free under-15s. Free to all Sun to 2pm. **No credit cards**. **Map** p247 P8.

A favourite with tour groups, the Tile Museum, housed in a former convent, charts the development of the art of Portuguese *azulejos* from the 15th century onwards. The building itself is a treat, including a tiled mural depicting Lisbon before the 1755 earthquake, a tiny Manueline cloister, and a barrel-vaulted church where the gilt baroque ornamentation of the altar contrasts with the cool blue of the tiled walls. The museum shop, not surprisingly, has many superior tiles for sale.

Parque das Nações

Few would have thought it possible. In 1990 the area around Cabo Ruivo was a wasteland of near-derelict warehouses, the municipal abattoir, a munitions factory, an oil refinery and dozens of oil tanks. It had not always been so. In the area's heyday the Companhia dos Diamantes on Avenida Marechal Gomes da Costa (now the headquarters of state broadcaster RTP) had overseen Africa's diamond trade, and Pan-American Clipper seaplanes docked on the Olivais quay – where the über-modern **Oceanário** now stands.

Those days were a distant memory by the mid 1990s, when a site measuring 330 hectares (815 acres) was levelled as armies of bulldozers and workers wrought the transformation that readied the area for the opening of Expo 98 on 22 May 1998. The four-month World's Fair was timed to coincide with the 500th anniversary of the discovery of the sea route to India, and had the theme of the oceans. It introduced lisboetas to a different city that looked east over the Mar de Palha. To shuttle visitors to and from the site, a new Metro line was built, with an expensive and impressive artistic input (*see p32* **Lisbon's got the blues**). The Galp petroleum company tower, at the southern end of the precinct, remained – and remains – as a reminder of the area's industrial past.

Expo closed its doors on 30 September 1998, reopening as an urban district dubbed Parque das Nações in which development of hotels, offices and residential complexes has continued ever since. The centrepiece is the Oceanário, one of the world's largest aquariums. Nearby, cable cars dangle above the riverside walkway as they move towards the Torre Vasco da Gama, Lisbon's tallest 'building'. On the other side of the dock, the Pavilhão de Portugal, designed by Álvaro Siza Vieira, hosts irregular exhibitions but lacks a permanent vocation. The futuristic beetle-shaped building next door is the Pavilhão Atlântico, designed by Regino Cruz and built around a wood framework like a giant caravel.

Pavilhão Atlântico.

Parque das Nações.

It has hosted everything from rock concerts to ice spectaculars. Nearby is a tourist booth (21 891 9333) where you can pick up a local map and information on facilities in the area. South of the Oceanário, the Pavilhão do Conhecimento (*see p154*) continues to delight children and their parents with hands-on science exhibits. By the river, the Teatro Luís de Camões (*see p169*) is home to the Companhia Nacional de Bailado and hosts classical music concerts.

But the most pleasant legacy of Expo is simply the open space along the Tagus. The promenades extend north through the green **Parque do Tejo** to the new Ponte Vasco da Gama and beyond. The Tagus is up to ten kilometres (six miles) wide here, and this is the only place in town where you can relax by the river without the noise of passing trains or cars. Lisboetas appreciate this; at weekends they flock here, and not just to shop or see films in the Centro Vasco da Gama (*see p132*). They stroll around (or cycle – you can hire bikes) revelling in the well-swept pavements and neatly tended vegetation – such a contrast from central Lisbon – fill the cafés and restaurants, or even visit trade shows at the Feira Internacional de Lisboa (21 892 1500).

By night, bars and clubs cater for young out-of-towners who don't want the hassle of driving across the city. The latest addition to local nightlife is the Casino Lisboa (21 466 7700), which as well as some 1,000 slot machines and 22 gaming tables has a restaurant and auditorium that is an excellent place to catch big-name jazz performers and the like.

Beyond the Parque das Nações is the Ponte Vasco da Gama, briefly Europe's longest bridge (before the link between Sweden and Denmark was built). Its construction – aimed at relieving jams on the Ponte 25 de Abril and linking up with new motorways to Spain – was a long process, dogged by controversy. There was an outcry at the choice of location – between Sacavém and Montijo – not only because of the likely effects on the nature reserve east of the latter, to which birds flock, but because studies had favoured a link downriver to serve the teeming south bank suburbs of Almada and Barreiro. Then in 1994, when the government announced plans to hike charges on the old bridge to help pay for the new one, commuters flipped and there were violent incidents at the toll gates as they mounted *buzinhão* ('big honk') blockades that were democratic Portugal's first big single-issue protests.

But construction of the new bridge went ahead. Financed by a mix of EU, national and private grants and loans, 17.2 kilometres (10.5 miles) of bridge and viaduct – 11 kilometres (seven miles) of it over water – opened in March 1998. That year the project accounted for one per cent of Portugal's gross domestic product.

Oceanário

Esplanada Dom Carlos I, Doca dos Olivais, Parque das Nações (21 891 7002/6/www.oceanario.pt). Metro Oriente. **Open** *Summer* 10am-8pm daily (ticket office closes 7pm). *Winter* 10am-7pm daily (ticket office closes 6pm). **Admission** €10.50; €5.25-€9.50 concessions; free under-4s. **Credit** AmEx, MC, V.

The world's second-largest aquarium (the biggest is in Osaka), Lisbon's Oceanarium was designed by the American specialist Peter Chermayeff. Around an enormous central tank are four smaller ones representing the Antarctic, Indian, Pacific and Atlantic Oceans, each topped by a room representing the respective coastal habitat. There are observation decks on two levels so you may catch an underwater glimpse of the penguins or otters you saw lolling about upstairs, while around every corner myriad mini aquariums showcase exotic species. Many of the fish in the main tank, from hammerhead sharks to rays, would not be found together in the wild, but their presence here is dazzling, if disconcerting.

South of the River

Take a trip across the Tagus for some capital views.

Ferries criss-cross the Tagus between Lisbon and the south bank suburbs of Trafaria, Porto Brandão, Cacilhas, Seixal, Barreiro, Montijo and Alcochete. These boats are the equivalent of commuter trains in other cities and are packed at rush hours, but a trip across the Tagus at off-peak hours is an indispensable part of any visit to Lisbon, if only for the view of the capital on the return journey. The bulk of commuter traffic docks in Cacilhas, about ten minutes by boat from Cais do Sodré (the other route, from Terreiro do Paço ferry station near Praça do Comércio, is currently closed). This terminal serves Almada, a burgeoning metropolis whose cultural life includes Portugal's most important theatre festival (*see p151*). In summer, the crowds piling off at Cacilhas are headed for the buses to the beaches of the Costa da Caparica.

The statue of **Cristo Rei**.

Near the quay are some moderately priced seafood restaurants. Further west along the river on the Cais do Ginjal are a dirty river beach and the esplanadas of restaurants Atira-te ao Rio (*see p124*) and Ponto Final. On the cliff at the end is Almada's cute old town: the Boca do Vento elevator whisks you up to the *miradouro* behind the Câmara Municipal (City Hall) for great views. Further west, the statue of **Cristo Rei** (*see below*), arms outspread, guards the southern anchorage of the Ponte 25 de Abril.

Visitors crossing into eastern Lisbon on the Ponte Vasco da Gama pass over a large area of old salt pans near Alcochete. This is the start of the Reserva Natural do Estuário do Tejo, covering much of the marshland at the north end of the Mar de Palha. It's a birdwatcher's paradise. Besides kingfishers, herons and other waders, there is one of Europe's largest colonies of pink flamingoes, which spend their summers in mud flats within easy sight of eastern Lisbon. Though the Ponte Vasco da Gama was completed in 1998, its full impact will stretch far into the future. The edges of the mud flats are being stealthily reclaimed by developers and ecologists say that car-related noise and pollution from developments such as Europe's largest outlet centre (selling discounted brands), near Alcochete, are disturbing the birds.

To the west, a building boom around the once sleepy town of Montijo has left dozens of empty apartment blocks. If and when the economy recovers more fully from the recession of recent years, the south bank between the bridges will once again be a prime target for development, especially if a third crossing is built. For now, budget constraints have put plans for this on ice, although there is still talk of a rail link.

Santuário do Cristo Rei

21 275 1000. Ferry to Cacilhas from Cais do Sodré, then bus 101. **Open** 9.30am-6pm daily (last entry 5.45pm). **Admission** €4; €2 8-14s; free under-8s. **No credit cards**.

This stiff echo of Rio's statue of Christ the Redeemer gazes across at the city, an observation deck at its feet. Worth the trip, not least for the weird sensation of looking down on the towering Ponte 25 de Abril.

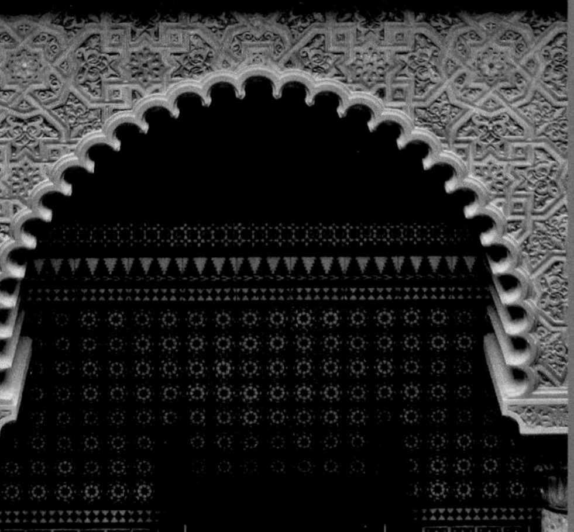

Eat, Drink, Shop

Features

Casa do Alentejo. *See p67.*

Restaurants

Cuisine rooted in tradition, offset by a history of exploration.

The Portuguese take time with food. 'Olive oil, wine and friendship – the older the better' runs a proverb. And if you also take from this maxim that the local cuisine is simple, honest fare, you'll be right. Globalised fast food is largely confined to shopping malls, while even in the ubiquitous *tascas* – cheap eateries with paper tablecloths and chipped white crockery – the proper rituals are observed. After all, as one of the best-known fado songs observes, '*Cheira bem, cheira a Lisboa*' – 'it smells good, it smells of Lisbon' and no one is going to change that.

The capital is one of the best places in Europe for seafood. Cod is always salted and dried – *bacalhau* – but fresh fish and seafood abounds. (To work out what's on offer, with this and other Portuguese food, *see p108* **What's on the menu?**) Generally speaking, the oilier fish give a juicier result; the traditional Portuguese sardine is one of the oiliest. Grilling them outside – once a badge of poverty – is now seen as rather cool. In posher places, fish and shellfish are often sold by weight, so keep an eye on the process.

Caldeirada is Portugal's bouillabaisse and was created by the *fragateiros* who worked on the *fragatas*, the graceful barges that once sailed up and down the Tagus. The crew would make *caldeirada* with whatever fish they could catch, plus potatoes, onions, tomatoes and bell peppers bartered with peasants along the way. The dish was cooked on board and served on a bed of sliced bread. Today you can find it at **Doca do Espanhol** (*see p117*). It is supposed to contain 24 kinds of seafood, but the impracticality makes this a rarity.

For diehard carnivores – or on Mondays when lisboetas steer clear of fish because the fleet stays home on Sundays – hearty dishes such as steak in Madeira sauce topped with a fried egg, or *feijoada* (a rich stew of beans, pork and sausage) are popular, made according to the chef's mother's recipe, of course. Portuguese steak (*bife*) is a slice of fried beef or pork served with fried potatoes and black olives. Pork is usually tasty, particularly ribs (*entrecosto*) and the strips of pork known as *febras*. Roast suckling pig (*leitão assado*) is a speciality of the Bairrada region, but widely available. The free-range, acorn-fed *porco preto* or Iberian black pig yields delicious meat: look for *costoletas* (chops) or *lombo* (loin). Lamb (*borrego*) is usually excellent – commonly in the form of grilled *costoletas*, but rich stews (*ensopado*) may also feature. Kid (*cabrito*) is a speciality and can be delicious roasted, but the animal is terribly young. Rabbit (*coelho*) is also fairly common; as with pork, the meat is often marinated. Portugal is of course famed for its grilled chicken – a real budget standby. Duck is less common, except in *arroz de pato*, which when baked to a T so the top is crunchy, can be divine.

Options for those who shun animal products are limited in traditional restaurants, but vegetarian dishes are gaining in popularity (*see p118* **Green shoots**). One standby is thick vegetable soup, usually containing olive oil, beans, cabbage, carrots or potato – but remain on the alert for pieces of meat.

Lisbon has a huge number of bakeries and bread – usually wonderful – is served with every meal. Cornbread, *broa*, is common. Bread has acquired an almost mythical status in Portuguese culture; it and cakes are strongly associated with Catholic holidays.

To wash all this down, lisboetas still prefer wine. Portugal produces a lot, most of it cheap and drinkable. For more, *see p123* **Grape**

The best Restaurants

For a hearty meal on a budget
Casa Liège (*see p107*); Pastelaria Nascer do Sol (*see p118*); Espaço Ribeira (*see p114*).

For city views
Cipriani (*see p119*); Via Graça (*see p111*); La Pararrucha (*see p110*).

For traditional food with a twist
Alcântara Café (*see p117*); Varanda (*see p105*); Na Ordem (*see p121*).

For traditional food with no twist
Charcutaria (*see p107*); Stop do Bairro (*see p119*); D'Avis (*see p122*).

For a meal al fresco
Doca do Espanhol (*see p117*); Clube dos Jornalistas (*see p119*).

Eleven. *See p105.*

Jardim dos Sentidos. *See p107.*

stuff. If you are a stickler for etiquette, note that *bacalhau* is accompanied with red. House wine comes in the bottle, unless it's bought in bulk, in which case it's served in jugs (*jarros*). Beer (*cerveja*), usually draught (imperial), is popular with seafood – and on this note, Lisbon's ***cervejarias*** are bustling beer halls that specialise in surf and turf. Usually open late, they're good for a snack while drinking in the atmosphere and, of course, the beer.

If you order water in a restaurant, you will invariably be asked whether you want it *com ou sem gás* (sparkling or still) and *fresca ou natural*. This last query is confusing to the uninitiated, suggesting that the water might not be natural. Don't panic – *fresca* means served cold, natural at room temperature.

If you intend to eat well over several days, consider buying the **Lisboa Restaurant Card**, available at tourist offices, which offers discounts of 10 per cent to 20 per cent at 35 restaurants over a 72-hour period. It limits your options but several of the eateries we list participate in the scheme and you could claw back the outlay (€6.15 single, €8.10 double, €10.75 family of four) in just one meal. For restaurant food delivered to your door, *see p143*.

In restaurants and cafés a tip of anything between two and ten per cent is normal.

Baixa, Rossio & Restauradores

Portuguese

Bonjardim

Travessa de Santo Antão 12, Restauradores (21 342 7424). Metro Restauradores. **Open** noon-11.30pm daily. **Main courses** €7-€15. **Credit** AmEx, DC, MC, V. **Map** p250 L8 ❶

A favourite for a quick, cheap meal. Chicken grilled over charcoal comes with chips, mixed salad and the ubiquitous (and thankfully optional) hot piri-piri sauce. There are other dishes but the place aims for quick turnover, so service can be brusque. Of the two buildings on either side of the street, upstairs in the southern one is the 'local' option.

Terreiro do Paço

Lisboa Welcome Centre, Praça do Comércio, Baixa (21 031 2850/www.terreiropaco.com). Metro Baixa-Chiado. **Open** 12.30-3pm, 8-11pm Mon-Fri; 8-11pm Sat. **Main courses** €16-€48. **Credit** AmEx, MC, V. **Map** p250 M10 ❷

Portuguese celebrity chef Vítor Sobral pays homage to his nation's food without being trapped by it. In atmospheric surroundings under 18th-century stone arches, he uses fine regional ingredients – such as olive oils from remote Trás-os-Montes – in dishes from the straight-up baked Atlantic cherne to the more exotic duck with ginger cream, baked banana and manioc. Not cheap, but the tasting menus make it a good place to sample Portuguese food.

Indian

Everest Montanha

Calçada do Garcia 15, Rossio (21 887 6428). Metro Rossio. **Open** 11.30am-3.30pm, 7pm-midnight daily. **Main courses** €4.50-€6. **No credit cards**. **Map** p250 M10 ❸

Up an alley off Largo de São Domingos, this was the first in a string of friendly Nepali-owned restaurants offering tasty food at low prices. The menu has lots of Indian standards, among them several vegetarian and vegan dishes. Recommended.

Other locations: Avenida do Brasil 130C, Alvalade (21 847 3195); Rua Ernesto da Silva 20B, Algés (21 411 3532).

Avenida da Liberdade & Parque Eduardo VII

Portuguese

O Manel

Parque Mayer, Avenida da Liberdade (21 346 3167). Metro Avenida. **Open** noon-4pm, 7-10pm Mon-Fri; noon-4pm Sat. **Main courses** €8-€11. **Credit** AmEx, MC, V. **Map** p246 L8 ❹

Lisbon's former theatreland, Parque Mayer, is hidden just off Avenida da Liberdade (on the left, near the northernmost Metro exit). Even better hidden is O Manel, a family-run restaurant, drawing a faithful clientele for homely Portuguese cooking.

Cervejarias

Ribadouro

Avenida da Liberdade 155, Avenida da Liberdade (21 354 9411/www.cervejariaribadouro.pt). Metro Avenida. **Open** noon-1am daily. **Main courses** €9-€15. **Credit** AmEx, MC, V. **Map** p246 L8 ❺
One of the two archetypal beer halls that gave the Portugália chain success by purveying decent seafood at decent prices. Specialities include *marisco à marinheira* (shellfish with parsley, garlic and wine) and *bacalhau a brás*. There are now Portugálias in shopping centres and on the Tagus, but only this and the original (Avenida Almirante Reis 117, 21 314 0002) are anything special.
Other locations: throughout the city.

Solmar

Rua das Portas de Santo Antão 108, Baixa (21 346 0010). Metro Restauradores. **Open** noon-2am daily. **Main courses** €8-€20. **Credit** AmEx, DC, V. **Map** p250 M9 ❻
A grand old beer hall anchored in the 1950s – as the neon lighting, pebble-dashed walls and station clock testify. The kitchen closes after 10pm, but there's still a bewildering choice of seafood and game to munch on until the wee hours. Something of a tourist trap but a real eye-filler nevertheless.

Indian

Maharaja

Rua do Cardal de São José 21-3, Avenida da Liberdade (21 346 9300). Metro Avenida. **Open** 12.30-3pm, 7-11pm Tue-Sun. **Main courses** €6-€10. **Credit** AmEx, MC, V. **Map** p246 L8 ❼
A favourite with expats, this red-plush den built up its clientele by word of mouth; it had to, since you could hardly stumble across it. From Avenida Metro station, it's up Rua das Pretas, first left, first right and first left. The cook, from New Delhi, turns out lovely tandoori kebabs (*espetadas*), coconut shrimp curry (*gambas com côcô*) and the like.

International

Eleven

Rua Marquês de Fronteira, Parque Eduardo VII (21 386 2211/www.restauranteleven.com). Metro Parque. **Open** 12.30-3pm, 7.30-11pm Mon-Sat. **Main courses** €20-€40. **Credit** AmEx, DC, MC, V. **Map** p248 K5 ❽
The city's only Michelin-starred restaurant was founded in 2006 by the eponymous 11 shareholders. Inside a large concrete box (bar one floor-to-ceiling window affording panoramic views) Lisbon's elite coo over the elegant Mediterranean cuisine of head chef Joachim Koerper: wild black truffles with scallop and pumpkin ravioli, monkfish on lemon-flavoured risotto, or veal with tagliatelle al pesto and wild mushrooms. Desserts, such as apricot amandine with vanilla ice cream, are divine. Yet while the results caress the palate, they rarely take one by surprise; there are chefs in Lisbon, such as at the Varanda (*see below*), that are preparing more exciting work. But the venture overseen by Koerper in Coimbra has one Michelin star, his restaurant in Spain two, so it was no surprise to anyone that Eleven made the culinary grade so soon after its opening. The minimalist decor – wood, iron and stone – makes it feel like a place geared towards the businessman, and the €39 lunchtime 'express menu' fits with that. **Photo** *p103*.

Varanda

Ritz Four Seasons Hotel, Rua Rodrigo da Fonseca 88, Marquês de Pombal (21 381 1400). Metro Marquês de Pombal. **Open** 12.30pm-3pm; 7.30pm-10.30pm daily. **Main courses** €27-€35. **Credit** AmEx, DC, MC, V. **Map** p246 D6 ❾
Housed in one of Lisbon's top hotels (*see p41*), the Varanda attracts a steady stream of locals looking for interesting twists on traditional food. Executive chef Stéphane Hestin has vast experience from his time in Michelin three-star restaurants La Côte d'Or (where his colleague Sebastien Grospellier also worked) and George Blanc, complementing it with a passion for Portuguese food. The à la carte menu has fabulous dishes such as saddle of lamb with polenta croquette and olives, and tuna medallions wrapped in cured ham with choucroute of fennel and *chouriço de porco preto*. There are daily specials and lots of seafood, but the pickings for vegetarians are meagre. At €55 the set menu sounds dear, but gives a sense of the talent in action. Formal atmosphere.

Italian

Luca

Rua de Santa Marta 35, Marquês de Pombal (21 315 0212/www.luca.pt). Metro Marquês de Pombal. **Open** 12.30-3pm, 8-11pm Mon-Thur; 12.30-3pm, 8pm-midnight Fri; 8pm-midnight Sat. **Main courses** €8-€25. **Credit** AmEx, DC, MC, V. **Map** p246 L7 ❿
Luca is currently Lisbon's most fashionable eaterie – and deservedly so as the price/quality ratio is unbeatable. Owner Luca is from Turin and feels no need to prove his Italian credentials: the *fritto misto* starter is a variant on Portuguese *peixinhos da horta* (green beans in batter) with added seafood; game is from the Pyrenees; the wines are mostly local; and while the grizzled faces in the photos on the walls could be Sicilian peasants, they're actually Portuguese. There are some fairly standard Italian dishes but also pumpkin ravioli, gnocchi with langoustine and Moroccan tiramisu. Luca draws a business crowd for lunch but loosens its collective tie at night, when it also functions as a tapas bar (6-11pm). On Saturdays there's a DJ.

Mezzaluna

Rua da Artilheria Um 16A, Marquês de Pombal (21 387 9944/www. mezzalunalisboa.com). Metro Marquês de Pombal. **Open** 12.30-3pm, 7.30-11pm Mon-Fri; 7.30-11pm Sat, Sun. **Main courses** €8-€22. **Credit** AmEx, DC, MC, V. **Map** p246 K7 ⓫

More formal than other local Italians, this is a business haunt at lunchtime and is patronised by well-heeled couples in the evening. They come for the fresh, delicious Mediterranean dishes produced with panache by chef Michael Guerrieri (who comes from a Neapolitan family but grew up on Long Island). The starters are a treat for vegetarians fed up of scrawny salads: grilled aubergine or spinach salad with goat's cheese sauce, as well as carpaccio of salmon or beef. For mains, there's magret of duck in prune sauce and fillet of redfish with lemon and pine nuts; liberal use is made of Portuguese ingredients, in chicken stuffed with *farinheira*, and penne with radicchio and *porco preto*.

Vegetarian

Jardim dos Sentidos

Rua Mãe d'Água 3, Avenida de Liberdade (21 342 3670/www.jardimdosentidos.com). Metro Avenida then 10min walk. **Open** noon-3pm, 7-11pm Mon-Fri; 7-11pm Sat. **Main courses** €8-€11.50. **No credit cards. Map** p248 L8 ⓬

The delightful garden with its palm trees is the main attraction here, as the menu is limited: vegetarian lasagna, stuffed aubergine and so on. The €7.50 lunch buffet is best value; there's also a €7 children's menu. The interior is stylishly simple, with original stone window frames dividing up the space and an attached alternative therapy centre. **Photo** *p104*.

Os Tibetanos

Rua do Salitre 117, Avenida (21 314 2038/www. tibetanos.com). Metro Avenida. **Open** *Buddhist centre* 10am-3pm, 4.30-7pm Mon-Fri. *Restaurant & shop* noon-3pm, 7.30-11pm Mon-Fri. **Main courses** €7-€12. **No credit cards. Map** p246 L8 ⓭

For a long time Os Tibetanos was the only place in Lisbon you could have a vegetarian dinner. It's attached to a Buddhist centre and offers Tibetan *momo*, *seitan* steak, tofu sausages and the like. The lunchtime set menu is a snip at €8.20, and there's French cider to sample if you don't fancy one of the many herbal teas. Seating in the dining room (which you can book) is rather cramped and the kitchen closes at 9.30pm, so this is not a place to relax over a long meal. There is a lovely patio and no smoking.

Chiado

Portuguese

Carvoaria

Rua das Flores 6 (21 342 6704). Metro Baixa-Chiado/tram 28. **Open** noon-3pm Mon-Sat. **Set menu** €4.50-€5. **No credit cards. Map** p250 L9 ⓮

Who says you have to get the plastic out for top-notch grub? This dive churns out generous portions of charcoal-grilled fish and meat for lucky construction workers working on nearby sites. Arrive early to get a table in what is a stone-floored aromatic oven of a restaurant.

Charcutaria

Rua do Alecrim 47A (21 342 3845). Metro Baixa-Chiado/tram 28. **Open** 12.30-3pm, 8pm-midnight Mon-Fri; 7-11pm Sat. **Main courses** €6.50-€16.50. **Credit** AmEx, DC, MC, V. **Map** p250 L10 ⓯

Alentejo farmhouse cuisine – *polvo grelhado com batatas a murro* (small baked potatoes), *alheira de caça com grelos* and various *bacalhau* dishes – that is excellent, and excellent value. The bread and cheese are fantastic too, but leave room for puddings such as *bolo de noz e ovos* (egg and walnut cake). A decent wine list includes lots of Alentejo reds, although they're not cheap.

Other locations: Rua Coelho da Rocha 97, Campo de Ourique (21 396 9724).

Argentinian

Café Buenos Aires

Calcada do Duque 31 (21 342 0739). Metro Rossio/ Baixa-Chiado/Restauradores. **Open** 6pm-1am Mon-Sat. **Main courses** €7-€15. **No credit cards. Map** p250 L9 ⓰

A cosy, dimly lit place with chunky wooden furniture and walls lined with old posters, Buenos Aires draws a boho crowd. The alternatives to steak don't go much beyond tartines and salad, but there's chocolate cake or tiramisu to finish off with, the wine list is decent and the esplanade buzzes in summer.

Vegetarian

Oriente Chiado

Rua Ivens 28 (21 343 1530). Metro Baixa-Chiado. **Open** noon-3pm, 7.30-10.30pm Mon-Thur; noon-3pm, 7.30-11pm Fri; 7.30-11pm Sat; noon-3.30pm Sun. **Buffet** *lunch* €9.20; *dinner* €11.90. **No credit cards. Map** p250 L9/10 ⓱

The buffet at this French-run place is vegetarian and represents macrobiotic food at its best: pure with unexpected flavours and combinations (asparagus with mango, vegetarian *feijoada*, spicy chocolate cake). The atmosphere is informal but fairly sophisticated, drawing local creative types.

Bica

Portuguese/International

Casa Liège

Rua da Bica de Duarte Belo 72 (21 342 2794). Metro Baixa-Chiado/Resauradores/tram 28. **Open** noon-3pm, 6.30-10.30pm Mon, Wed-Sat; 6.30-10.30pm Tue. **Main courses** €4.35-€5.60. **No credit cards. Map** p250 L9 ⓲

What's on the menu?

Portuguese tourist menus have their share of mistranslations and spelling mistakes – is 'sulking pig' suckling pig or something more moody? – which can prompt nervous visitors to stick to a linguistically and gastronomically unchallenging diet of grilled chicken and omelettes. Most restaurants, of course, don't translate their menus into any kind of English.

However, all is not lost. A typical Portuguese restaurant will store fresh produce in display cases, so diners can see what's available. Those specialising in seafood – *marisqueiras* – often have a fridge built into the window, and you can check the wares before stepping in.

The only restaurants that don't have such displays are either the very cheap, in which case it might be best to avoid the fish, or the untypically modern or posh. Even in the latter, however, you can ask to see a particular fish or cut of meat before ordering.

Basics

alho garlic; **almoço** lunch; **azeite** olive oil; **azeitona** olive; **coentro** coriander; **conta** bill; **dose** portion; **ementa** menu; **entrada** starter; **jantar** dinner; **lanche** snack; **lista da vinhos** wine list; **manteiga** butter; **meia**- half-; **ovo** egg; **pão** bread; **petisco** nibble; **piri-piri** chilli; **sal** salt; **salsa** parsley; **sandes** sandwich.

Cooking styles & techniques

açorda bread that has been soaked with olive oil, garlic, herbs and egg; **assado** roasted; **bem passado** well done; **caril** curry; **cebolada** cooked with onions; **caseiro** home-made; **churrasco** barbecue; **cozido** boiled; **espetada** skewer; **estufado** braised; **forno** oven; **frito** fried; **gratinado** baked with cheese on top; **grelhado** grilled; **guarnecido** garnished; **guisado** braised; **mal passado** rare; **massa** pastry/pasta; **médio** medium rare; **molho** sauce; **na brasa** charcoal-grilled; **no forno** oven-baked; **picante** spicy; **quente** hot/warm; **recheado** stuffed; **salteado** sautéd.

Sopas/ensopados (soups/stews)

Caldo verde shredded kale in potato broth; **canja** chicken broth; **cozido à portuguesa** stew of meats, sausages and cabbage; **feijoada** bean stew made with meat, seafood or snails.

Marisco (shellfish)

amêijoa clam; **camarão** shrimp; **gamba** prawn; **lagosta/lavagante** spiny/Norway lobster; **mexilhão** mussel; **ostra** oyster; **perceve** goose-necked barnacle; **sapateira** crab; **vieira** scallop.

Peixe (fish)

atum tuna; **bacalhau** salted cod (**...a brás** shredded, fried with potato and scrambled egg; **...a Gomes Sá** shredded, fried with onion and served with boiled potato, egg and black olives; **...com natas** shredded, baked with cream and potato; **...cozido com grão** boiled, served with chickpeas, potato and greens); **besugo** sea bream; **cação** dogfish; **caldeirada** fish stew; **cantaril** redfish; **carapau** mackerel; **cataplana** a copper pan for steaming fish; **cavala** horse mackerel; **cherne** large grouper; **choco** cuttlefish; **corvina** croaker; **dourada** gilthead bream; **enguia** eel; **espadarte** swordfish; **garoupa**

A friendly *tasca* at the top of the Elevador da Bica Casa Liège is great for carnivores on a budget. For three decades the cook has turned out local favourites such as *pernil de porco* (leg of pork) and, in summer, grilled meats. It also serves lots of fish and omelettes.

Toma Lá Dá Cá

Travessa do Sequeiro 38 (21 347 9243). Metro Baixa-Chiado/tram 28. **Open** noon-2.45pm, 7.30-11pm Mon-Sat. **Main courses** €6-€12. **Credit** AmEx, DC, MC, V. **Map** p250 L8/9 ⑲

On an alley between the Elevador da Bica and the Adamastor esplanade, this restaurant lacks a fancy façade but serves food that is pretty fancy for the price. Dishes range from pork steak gratiné to fondue, and a dozen types of fish, including grilled tuna and salmon. The *nacos de vitela* (veal chunks) are extremely succulent.

Bairro Alto, Príncipe Real & Rato

Portuguese

1° de Maio

Rua da Atalaia 8, Bairro Alto (21 342 6840). Metro Baixa-Chiado/tram 28. **Open** noon-3pm, 7pm-midnight Mon-Fri; 7pm-midnight Sat. **Main courses** €8-€15. **Credit** AmEx, MC, V. **Map** p250 L9 ⑳

The queue outside the saloon-style swing doors at about 8.30pm every weeknight testifies to the popularity of this budget classic. At lunchtime, too, canny regulars cram round snugly fitted tables, tucking into grilled fish or meat dishes, served fast and with a smile, at reasonable prices.

grouper; **imperador** cardinal fish; **joaquinzinho** whitebait; **linguado** sole; **lula** squid; **pargo** rosy sea bream; **pastel de bacalhau** deep-fried cod croquettes; **peixe espada** scabbard fish; **peixe-galo** John Dory; **pescada** hake; **polvo** octopus; **pregado** turbot; **raia** skate/ray; **robalo** sea bass; **salmão** salmon; **salmonete** red mullet; **sardinha** sardine; **sargo** white bream; **solha** plaice; **truta** trout.

Carne (meat)

bifana slice of braised pork; **bife** steak (though not necessarily beef); **bitoque** slice of fried beef, served with chips and a fried egg; **borrego** lamb; **cabrito** kid; **caracois** snails; **chouriço** smoked sausage; **costoleta** chop; **dobrada** tripe; **entrecosto** pork rib; **entremeada** pork-belly; **febras** boned slices of pork; **fiambre** uncured ham; **figado** liver; **ganso de vitela** topside of veal; **iscas** sliced liver; **leitão** suckling pig; **língua** tongue; **linguiça** spiced sausage; **lombinhos** tender pieces of meat; **lombo** loin; **medalhões** medallions; **mãozinha** trotter/hock; **morcela** blood sausage; **paio** cured sausage; **peito** breast; **perna** leg; **porco** pork; **porco preto** black pig; **prego** slice of beef, grilled; **presunto** cured ham; **posta** thick slice of meat (or fish); **rins** kidneys; **rojões** cubes of pork that are marinated and fried; **salpicão** spiced sausage; **salsicha** sausage; **toucinho** lard; **tripas** tripe; **vaca** cow/beef; **vazia** prime cut of beef; **veado** venison; **vitela** veal.

Aves e caça (poultry & game)

cabidela chicken with giblets; **codorniz** quail; **coelho** rabbit; **faisão** pheasant; **frango** chicken; **galinha** broiler chicken; **ganso** goose; **javalí** wild boar; **pato** duck; **perdiz** partridge; **perú** turkey.

Arroz, massa e feijão (rice, pasta & beans)

arroz rice; **esparguetes** spaghetti; **favas** broad beans; **feijão(ões)** bean(s); **grão** chickpeas; **lentilhas** lentils.

Legumes (vegetables)

alface lettuce; **batata (doce)** (sweet) potato; **cebola** onion; **cenoura** carrot; **cogumelo** mushroom; **couve** cabbage; **ervilhas** peas; **espargos** asparagus; **espinafres** spinach; **grelos** tender greens; **hortaliça** mixed vegetables; **pepino** cucumber; **pimenta** pepper.

Fruta (fruit)

ananás pineapple; **cereja** cherry; **laranja** orange; **limão** lemon; **maçã** apple; **maracujá** passion fruit; **melancia** watermelon; **melão** cantaloupe; **meloa** melon; **morango** strawberry; **pêssego** peach; **uva** grape.

Sobremesa (dessert)

arroz doce rice pudding; **baba de camelo** dessert of yolks and sugar; **barriga de freira** dessert of breadcrumbs, sugar, egg and nuts; **bolo** cake; **gelado** ice-cream; **leite** creme custard; **pudim** caramel pudding; **toucinho do céu** dessert of almonds, eggs and sugar.

Queijo (cheese)

queijo de ovelha sheep's cheese; **queijo fresco** cottage cheese; **requeijão** ricotta-type cheese.

Fidalgo

Rua da Barroca 27-31, Bairro Alto (21 342 2900). Metro Baixa-Chiado/tram 28. **Open** noon-3pm, 7-11pm Mon-Sat. **Main courses** €8-€13. **Credit** AmEx, MC, V. **Map** p250 L9 ㉑

Fidalgo is a *tasca* at heart that grew up into a more sophisticated restaurant. You'll find well-prepared dishes such as *arroz de garoupa, medalhões de javalí, queijo da serra* (gooey sheep's cheese), and the occasional faddish effort at modernity. Desserts are delicious: try the profiteroles or wild berry tart.

Frei Contente

Rua de São Marçal 94, Príncipe Real (21 347 5922). Metro Rato/tram 28. **Open** 7pm-2am daily. **Main courses** €8-€13. **Credit** V. **Map** p248 K8 ㉒

The Happy Friar serves traditional dishes in a cosy, romantic setting: *bacalhau com broa* (with cornbread), *arroz de pato*, and, of course, steaks. The food is reasonably low on cholesterol, with plenty of tasty salads on offer, and a decent wine list. Funky background music complements the friendly vibe.

Pap' Açorda

Rua da Atalaia 57, Bairro Alto (21 346 4811). Metro Baixa-Chiado/tram 28. **Open** 8-11.30pm Mon; 12.30-2.30pm, 8-11.30pm Tue-Sat. **Main courses** €14-€31. **Credit** AmEx, DC, MC, V. **Map** p250 L9 ㉓

To see and be seen, take a deep breath, push open the heavy door, sidestep the velvet curtain and fabulous flower arrangements, and run the gauntlet along the bar past three huge Murano chandeliers. Owners Fernando and Zé make sure everything runs like clockwork – and there are certainly few culinary surprises. As the name suggests, the signature dish is *açorda* – with prawns.

Primavera do Jerónimo

Travessa da Espera 34, Bairro Alto (21 342 0477). Metro Baixa-Chiado/tram 28. **Open** noon-3pm, 7.30-11.30pm Mon-Sat. **Main courses** €9-€14. **No credit cards**. **Map** p250 L9 ㉔

If you want simple Portuguese grub, look no further than this long-established haven, known simply as Primavera, where you can get a full meal with wine for no more than €20. The menu features hearty soups, clams in white wine, braised liver and other meaty concoctions from the north, grilled fish and *bacalhau*. The kitchen is on full view from the tiny dining room, where shiny pans and pots, tiles bearing Portuguese proverbs, framed articles, and a photograph of Josephine Baker above the table where she ate all make for good talking points.

Portuguese/International

Charcutaria Francesa Pettermann

Rua Dom Pedro V 54, Bairro Alto (21 343 2389/ 91 758 8281). Metro Baixa-Chiado or Rato/tram 28 then 10min walk/bus 58, 790. **Open** 9am-6pm Mon; 9am-6pm, 8pm-midnight Tue-Thur; 9am-6pm, 8pm-1am Fri, Sat. **Main courses** €5-€12. **Credit** MC, V. **Map** p250 L8 ㉕

A French-style charcuterie that offers traditional roasts with gravy as well as healthier grilled fish and vegetables, and a delicious Brazilian *feijoada*. It's both elegant and excellent value – a three-course meal with wine might cost €15. If it's full or closed, there's Portuguese home cooking with menus at €6.50 at No.96 (Antiga Casa Faz Frio, 21 346 1860).

Olivier

Rua do Teixeira 35, Bairro Alto (21 343 1405/ www.restaurante-olivier.com). Metro Baixa-Chiado/ tram 28. **Open** 8pm-midnight Mon-Sat. **Set menu** €33. **Credit** AmEx, DC, V. **Map** p250 L9 ㉖

Olivier da Costa's inventive Mediterranean delicacies have made his food some of the most drooled over in the capital. The set menu at this smaller of his two restaurants gets you a choice of six cold starters, six warm starters, main course and dessert. You might get mushrooms with pesto and Alentejo cheese, octopus carpaccio, *alheira* wrapped in grelos with poached quail's egg, cuts of *porco preto* with mango chutney in raspberry vinegar, and a divine soft-centred chocolate cake. There are 40 places so book ahead – or head for Olivier's larger place (with the same hours) down the hill, with its darkly luxurious decor and a DJ on duty from Thursday to Saturday (when there's also valet parking). The food is superb, but if you decide to order à la carte there it becomes difficult to match the excellent value of da Costa's original restaurant.

Other locations: Olivier Café, Rua do Alecrim 23 (21 342 2916/91 866 0609).

Argentinian

La Pararrucha

Rua Dom Pedro V 18, Bairro Alto (21 342 5333). Metro Baixa-Chiado then 15min walk/bus 58, 790. **Open** noon-3pm, 7.30pm-2am Mon-Fri; 1-4pm, 7.30pm-2am Sat, Sun. **Main courses** €10-€18. **Credit** AmEx, DC, MC, V. **Map** p250 L8 ㉗

Score some Brazilian food at **Comida de Santo**. *See p111.*

Eat, Drink, Shop

La Pararrucha remains the place in Lisbon for fine imported beef. There are tasty starters – *empanados tucuman* (a kind of meat pasty) and *secretos* with *abacaxi* (grilled fatty pork with pineapple) – and a lunch buffet (€9) that on Wednesdays includes *cozido à portuguesa*, but plump for steak and you can't go wrong. The esplanade affords dizzy views across the Baixa to the castle. The restaurant can be reached via the Elevador da Glória, if it is in operation.

Brazilian

Comida de Santo

Calçada Engenheiro Miguel Pais 39, Príncipe Real (21 396 3339). Metro Rato. **Open** 12.30-3.30pm, 7.30pm-1am daily. **Main courses** €12-€16. **Credit** AmEx, DC, MC, V. **Map** p246 K8 ㉘

One of the first and most deservedly enduring restaurants of its kind, serving good, hearty Brazilian food in good, hearty Brazilian surroundings: greenery, papier mâché toucans and other tropical tat. Its *feijoada* and other classic dishes are as good as any in town – not to mention the Caiprinhas – but the real secret is the cosy atmosphere. **Photo** *p110.*

Italian

Casa Nostra

Travessa Poço da Cidade 60, Bairro Alto (21 342 5931). Metro Baixa-Chiado/tram 28. **Open** 8-11pm Mon; 12.30-3pm, 8-11pm Tue-Fri; 8-11pm Sat. **Main courses** €8.50-€16. **Credit** AmEx, DC, MC, V. **Map** p250 L9 ㉙

This staple of the Bairro Alto dining scene offers authentic designer pasta from its owner, Maria Paola. Occasionally, the urge to experiment takes the cooking down something of a blind alley (watch out for chillies in the bolognese) but by and large the pasta is fresh, the risotto just so, the aubergines grilled to a T and the dishes not overloaded with cream. Ask for a table in the bright front room, designed by architect Manuel Graça Dias.

Moroccan

Flor da Laranja

Rua da Rosa 206, Bairro Alto (21 342 2996). Metro Baixa-Chiado then 15min walk/bus 58, 790. **Open** 7.30-11.30pm Mon-Sat. **Main courses** €12-€16. **Credit** DC, MC, V. **Map** p250 L9 ㉚

The most authentic of Lisbon's few Moroccan eateries, with decent helpings of couscous royale or lamb tagine with prunes, and passion fruit pudding to finish. The set menus (€16-€22) are good value. There's belly dancing from 9pm on Friday and Saturday. Lunch only for group bookings.

Vegetarian

Terra

Rua da Palmeira 15, Príncipe Real (21 342 1407/ reservations 707 108 108/www.terra.vg). Metro Rato. **Open** *Restaurant* 12.30-3.30pm, 7.30pm-midnight Mon-Sat. *Tea Room* 4-6.30pm Mon-Sat. **Buffet** *lunch* €8.90; *dinner* €11.90. **Credit** AmEx, MC, V. **Map** p246 K8 ㉛

Buffet lunching and dining only, with a plethora of vegetarian delights made from organic ingredients: sushi through kebabs to *cozido* (stew), plus homemade vegan ice-cream and crumble. Drinks – the juices are organic (try the ginger), soft drink, beer and wines – all cost extra though. The restaurant is to be found in an 18th-century building, its two separate dining areas filled with Portuguese furniture and decorative items from around the world. Out back there are more tables in a garden with a tinkling fountain; ensuring both you and the world get warmer, this area is heated in winter. There's no smoking indoors or out.

East of Baixa

Portuguese

Antiga Casa de Pasto Estrela da Sé

Largo de Santo António da Sé 4, Sé (21 887 0455). Tram 12, 28. **Open** noon-3pm, 7-11pm Mon-Fri (kitchen closes 9.30pm). **Main courses** €7-€12. **No credit cards. Map** 251 M10 ㉜

Lisbon's old *casas de pasto* – which means grazing houses – have all but died out. This one opposite the Sé cathedral is a classic. The food is tasty if plain – fish or meat, rice and salad – but the best feature is the curtained wooden booths that divide up the space. In the prudish 19th century they allowed a modicum of amorous activity during meals.

Santo António de Alfama

Beco de São Miguel 7, Alfama (21 888 1328). Tram 12, 25, 28 then 10min walk. **Open** 8pm-2am Mon, Wed-Sun. **Main courses** €10.50-€14. **Credit** AmEx, DC MC, V. **Map** p251 N10 ㉝

This restaurant became an Alfama fixture by being a tad more sophisticated than its local rivals. It has a wide variety of starters and desserts, and some decent main courses, though steak dominates. Perhaps a little overpriced (though at lunchtime they let you order half a steak) and the pictures of film stars are a bit beside the point. Nice esplanade, though.

Via Graça

Rua Damasceno Monteiro 9B, Graça (21 887 0830). Tram 28. **Open** 12.30-3pm, 7.30-11pm Mon-Fri; 7.30-11pm Sat, Sun. **Main courses** €16-€25. **Credit** AmEx, DC, MC, V. **Map** p251 N8 ㉞

Via Graça has one of Lisbon's best views, attentive but not pushy service, and excellent food, rooted in Portugal but influenced by European flavours. Tuck into duck marinated in Moscatel or game stew with chestnuts, accompanied by a chunky Alentejo red, while gazing at the illuminated ramparts of the castle or the busy streets down below. The portions are hearty, so if you want to do the meal justice, don't overdo the delicious titbits staff ply you with before your meal. You might want to take a taxi up to the place, although the tram stop is nearby.

CarbonNeutral® flights

Time Out
Lisbon

African

Cantinho do Aziz

Rua São Lourenço 3-5, Mouraria (21 887 6472). Metro Martim Moniz/tram 12, 28. **Open** noon-4.30pm, 7pm-midnight Mon-Sat. **Main courses** €5-€11. **Credit** MC, V. **Map** p251 N8 ㉟

For a real taste of Africa in Europe, you could do far worse than Cantinho do Aziz. Tasty meals are served at tables with paper tablecloths, mismatched cutlery and Duralex beakers, to the sound of Brazilian *telenovelas* blaring on TV. The cuisine is Mozambican (with some Goan recipes thrown in for good measure): we recommend the *frango à Zambeziana* (spicy grilled chicken).

Restaurante São Cristovão

Rua de São Cristovão 28-30, Castelo (21 888 5578). Metro Rossio/tram 28. **Open** 11am-midnight daily. **Main courses** €5. **No credit cards.** **Map** p251 M9 ㊱

The non-stop chatter of this *tasca*'s owner, Maria do Livramento – Mento for short – will either charm or unnerve first-time visitors to her restaurant. As she cooks and serves Cape Verdean dishes, members of Mento's extended family usually enter and depart. The food is passable – the *cachupa* has more bones than meat – but there's a great vibe, especially if you've picked the night of an impromptu jam session. If all else fails, Mento's *ponche* (honey spirit) will wipe out any doubts.

Chinese

Hua Ta Li

Rua dos Bacalhoeiros 109-15, Alfama (21 887 9170). Tram 15, 18, 28. **Open** 11am-3.30pm, 7-11.30pm daily. **Main courses** €8-€13. **Credit** MC. **Map** 251 N10 ㊲

A busy restaurant hard by Praça do Comércio, Hua Ta Li has the feel of the real McCoy – or is that the real Chen? A lot of care goes into preparing and serving food, right down to the fresh garnishes. The decor is a bit plasticky, but the waiters are abundant and fast, and portions generous.

Indian

Arco do Castelo

Rua Chão da Feira 25, Castelo (21 887 6598). Tram 12, 28 then 5min walk/bus 37. **Open** 12.30pm-midnight Mon-Sat. **Main courses** €7-€10. **Credit** AmEx, MC, V. **Map** p251 M9 ㊳

From the check tablecloths and bottle-lined walls you might think this tiny place was a typical cheap Italian eaterie, but in fact it's one of Lisbon's few genuinely Goan restaurants. The menu only runs to two pages, but includes *xacuti* (chicken with coconut and aromatic spices), *balchão de porco* and *sarapatel* – both pork dishes, the former in a rich sauce containing dried shrimp, the latter in a rich ginger gravy. Booking is essential for dinner.

Delhi Palace

Rua da Padaria 18-20, Sé (21 888 4203/http://delhipalace.restaunet.pt). Tram 12, 28/bus 37. **Open** noon-3.30pm, 6.30pm-midnight Tue-Sun. **Main courses** €7-€15. **Credit** AmEx, MC, V. **Map** p251 M10 ㊴

Trying to offer something for everyone is a risky business but Delhi Palace makes a decent fist of Indian and Italian specialities. The friendly crew that run it are from the Punjab, but the cook spent eight years working in an Italian restaurant. The pizzas are nothing special, but there's a decent choice of pasta. As for the north Indian fare, the spices are fresh and the sauces thick. Vegetarians are well served, with crispy pakoras, a good range of dals, a rich vegetable korma and half-a-dozen salads. For carnivores we recommend the tandoori chicken and Goan prawn curry. Puddings include creamy *badam* (almond) *kulfi*. Takeaways are available.

Hawli Tandoori

Travessa do Monte 14, Graça (21 886 7713). Tram 28. **Open** noon-3pm, 6-10.30pm Mon, Wed-Sun. **Main courses** €6-€20. **No credit cards.** **Map** p251 N8 ㊵

Despite its gaudy decoration, this neon-lit, brown-and-orange tiled restaurant serves some of the best Indian food in Lisbon. Hamini and his brothers hail from Portuguese India and their menu is influenced by the culinary mixing that went on there. Vegetarians are well catered for. Arrive early for dinner, to avoid the queues.

Other locations: Calcuta, Rua do Norte 17, Bairro Alto (21 342 8295); Restaurante Caxemira, Rua Condes de Monsanto 4 1°D (first floor, right), Baixa (21 886 5486).

Paladares de Goa

Rua do Zaire 2A, Anjos (21 814 5089/93 330 0038/www.paladaresdegoa.com). Metro Anjos. **Open** noon-3pm, 7.30-11pm Mon, Tue, Thur-Sat; noon-3pm Wed. **Main courses** €4.50-€7. **Credit** AmEx, MC, V. **Map** p247 N7 ㊶

One of Lisbon's oldest Goan restaurants. On the menu are *bojé* (bhajis), *xeque xeque de caranguejo* (crab curry) and *sarapatel*, with *bebinka* (a Goan tiramisu) to finish. It may seem out of the way but it is round the corner from Anjos Metro station. At No.17B is the newer, larger Sabores de Goa (21 812 9144, 96 258 5253, http://saboresdegoa.restaunet.pt; closed Mon, Tue, Sun lunch).

International

Viagem de Sabores

Rua de São João da Praça 103, Alfama (21 887 0189). Tram 12, 28. **Open** *Summer* 12.30-2.30pm, 8-10.30pm Mon-Thur; 8-11.30pm Fri, Sat. *Winter* 8-10.30pm Mon-Thur; 8-11.30pm Fri, Sat. **Main courses** €9-€13. **Credit** DC, MC, V. **Map** p251 M10 ㊷

The name means 'Journey of Flavours', and this cosy restaurant serves a bewildering selection, from Basque *bacalhau* soup to 'Iraqi lamb' (with dried

Stop do Bairro. *See p119.*

fruit and cinnamon). There are a couple of vegetarian options that are nothing special – couscous and the like. All in all, not gourmet dining and the mixture of flavours can be overpowering, but there's lots to choose from, it is good value and the wine list is respectable. If you come by tram, get off at the Sé cathedral, then walk down its right side. Cars are best parked below Alfama in Campo das Cebolas.

Cais do Sodré & Santos

Portuguese

A Travessa

Travessa do Convento das Bernardas, 12, Madragoa (21 390 2034/21 394 0800/www.atravessa.com). Tram 25, 28. **Open** 12.30-3.30pm, 8pm-midnight Mon-Fri; 8pm-midnight Sat. **Main courses** €17-€30. **Credit** AmEx, MC, V. **Map** p245 J9 ㊸

This Luso-Belgian restaurant is in the Convento das Bernardas – a former monastery that also houses the Museu da Marioneta (*see p90*). Owners Viviane Durieu and António Moita are usually on hand to guide you through the seasonal menu which includes five fish and five meat dishes, plus several steaks. Look out for *tamboril flamejado* (seared monkfish), *raia a vapor* (steamed ray), *pernil da pata negra assado* (roast shank of black pig) and *bifes de lombo* with pepper, sheep's cheese and Dijon mustard. The wine list is exhaustive, and of course there's also Belgian beer on offer. Saturday night is moules night but if you don't like mussels, there's always a fish or meat option. The setting and antique furniture are superb and in summer tables are set out in the courtyard. The entrance, round the back, is accessible by wheelchair. If you come by car, park in the lot in Largo Vitorino Damásio in Santos and call 96 893 9125 for a lift to the door.

Espaço Ribeira

Mercado da Ribeira, 1st floor, Avenida 24 de Julho, Cais do Sodré (21 031 2602/http://espacoribeira.pt). Metro Cais do Sodré. **Open** noon-3pm Mon, Tue; noon-3pm, 8-11.30pm Wed-Sat. **Main courses** €10.50-€13. *Buffet lunch* €7.75. **No credit cards.** **Map** p250 K8 ㊹

Portuguese standards – *bacalhau, polvo à lagareiro* (roasted) and *naco de lombo com gambas* – are served in a 'space' above the market where the ingredients are sold. There's live music Thursday to Saturday evenings. *See also p179.*

Porto de Abrigo

Rua dos Remolares 16-18, off Rua das Flores, Cais do Sodré (21 346 0873). Metro Cais do Sodré/tram 25. **Open** noon-3pm, 8-10.30pm Mon-Sat. **Main courses** €5-€12. **No credit cards.** **Map** p250 L10 ㊺

Tucked away behind the Mercado da Ribeira, Porto de Abrigo is a piece of ungentrified docklands: a neighbourhood restaurant whose prices and quality have remained stable. The name means safe harbour and it is, unless you happen to be an octopus, in which case you'll be thrown into a pot with rice and a secret cocktail of condiments and served up as *arroz de polvo*. The duck in olive sauce is also good.

Restaurante do Montado

Calçada Marquês de Abrantes 40A, Santos (21 390 9185/wwwdomontado.com). Tram 25/tram 28 then 10min walk. **Open** 12.30-3pm, 8pm-3am Tue-Fri; 8pm-3am Sat. **Main courses** €12.50-€16. **Credit** MC, V. **Map** p245 J9 46

Here's an idea: farmers opening a restaurant in Lisbon to serve meat from their own grass-fed cattle (native breeds only) and *porco preto*. You can be pretty sure your steak was munching grass the shortest possible time ago. The place is laid out on two levels in a 300-year-old building with cool stone arches. Better known Brasserie de l'Entrecôte (Rua do Alecrim 117, Chiado, 21 347 3616) might tempt you but we suggest making the short trip to Santos.

Tromba Rija

Rua Cintura do Porto de Lisboa, Edifício 254, Armazém 1, Santos (21 397 1507/www.tromba rija.com). Train to Santos from Cais do Sodré/ tram 15, 18. **Open** 12.30-3.30pm, 8-10.30pm. **Set menu** €25 Mon-Fri; €27.50 Sat, Sun; free under-5s, half-price 5-10s. **Credit** AmEx, MC, V. **Map** p245 J10 47

The Lisbon branch of one of Portugal's most famous restaurants, in Leiria, operates on the same basis: pay your money and stuff your face. Everything is included, from an aperitif through swillable house red or white wine to port, *aguardente* or liqueurs – these last accompanied with nuts and figs for those with gargantuan appetites. As for the meal itself, it kicks off with dozens of starters and a fine selection of Portuguese cheeses. There's less choice for the main courses, which are hearty but a little on the greasy side. All told, good value and a place for people watching, especially at weekends or on holidays.

Brazilian

Uai

Rocha do Conde de Óbidos, Cais das Oficinas, Armazém 114, Santos (21 390 0111/http://uai. restaunet.pt). Tram 15, 18 then 10min walk. **Open** 8-11pm Tue, Wed; 1-3pm, 8-11pm Thur-Sat; 1-3pm Sun. **Buffet** €20-€22. **Credit** AmEx, MC, V. **Map** p245 H10 48

A dockside restaurant, Uai is the only one in Lisbon dedicated to the cuisine of Brazil's Minas Gerais region. That means not only *feijoada*, a black bean stew that is virtually the national dish, but pumpkin stuffed with chicken, traditional sausages, okra, *couve à mineira* (dark Galician cabbage) and ground manioc galore. Start with a *pão de queijo* cheese-bread and finish with a delicious pumpkin jam with coconut or milky *doce de leite*. There's music from Minas Gerais to get you into the mood, an esplanade, disabled access, and parking. If you are driving, get on to the river side of the railway at Cais do Sodré; by public transport, alight at Santos to use the footbridge, then head west.

International

Café Malacca

Clube Naval de Lisboa, Cais do Gás, Armazém H, first floor, Cais do Sodré (21 347 7082/96 710 4142/93 866 5099). Metro Cais do Sodré. **Open** noon-3pm, 7-11pm Tue-Thur; noon-3am 7am-2pm Fri, Sat; 7-11pm Sun. **Main courses** €9.50-€12.50. **No credit cards. Map** p246 K10 49

A homely space above a boat club in an area full of slick eateries. Its menu is inspired by the voyages of 15th- and 16th-century Portuguese navigators: tempura and yakitori, satay, Thai salad, red and green curries, Korean beef (stir fried with peppers and mushrooms) and spicy steamed fish, plus a vegetarian option. Desserts include *arroz preto* (black sticky-rice pudding) and green-tea ice-cream.

Yasmin

Rua da Moeda 1, Cais do Sodré (21 393 00 74). Metro Cais do Sodré/tram 25. **Open** 7pm-2am Mon-Sat. **Main courses** €11-€18. **Credit** MC, V. **Map** p246 K10 50

A studiedly hip restaurant – black and white with floral motifs, and an in-house DJ to boot – Yasmin is the latest addition to Lisbon's burgeoning fusion cuisine scene. It has a large range of starters, from cured ham julienne with mint, through chilled cantaloupe and melon soup, to escabeche of quail with salad garnish and pine-nut olive oil. Continuing the theme the main dishes available include tuna steak on a bed of vegetables, tornedo of beef with chop suey, and confit of *bacalhau*. Next door, the longer established La Moneda (No.1C, 21 390 8012, closed Sun) tries hard but is rather noisy.

Alcântara & Docas

Portuguese

Alcântara Café

Rua Maria Luísa Holstein 15, Alcântara (21 363 7176/www.alcantaracafe.com). Tram 15, 18. **Open** 8pm-1am daily. **Main courses** €16-€40. **Credit** AmEx, DC, MC, V.

An eating-out landmark since the mid 1980s, this former industrial building, embellished with faux-classical steel pillars and yards of velvet, remains a centre of 'new Portuguese' cuisine (but with proper old-fashioned generous portions). On the menu are prawns in creamy lemon sauce, partridge with breadcrumbs and foie gras, and classics such as glazed duck. For a kitscher flight of fancy by the same designer, António Pinto, nip round the corner to Espaço Lisboa (Rua da Cozinha Económica 16, 21 361 0212, closed lunch), where tables are laid out in a mock-up of a Lisbon square with *típico* shops, but the food is less stylish.

Doca do Espanhol

Doca Alcântara C, Armazém 12, Docas (21 393 2600). Train to Alcântara Mar from Cais do Sodré/ tram 15, 18 then 5min walk. **Open** noon-1am Mon-Sat; noon-6pm Sun. **Main courses** €16-€25. **Credit** AmEx, MC, V. **Map** p245 G10 (51)

There are few eateries that stand out in the Docas area but this is great for Sunday lunch if you like seafood. In summer sit outside on the dock, in the shadow of the Ponte 25 de Abril. As well as *caldeirada* there's a great *arroz de tamboril.*

Kais

Cais da Viscondessa, Avenida 24 de Julho, Alcântara (21 393 2930/www.kais-k.com). Tram 15, 18. **Open** 8pm-1am daily. **Main courses** €16-€28. **Credit** AmEx, MC, V. **Map** p245 J10 (52)

Owned by the Rocha brothers, founders of nearby clubs Kremlin and Kapital (*see p189*), this cavernous place takes its name from the word *cais* (quay), housed as it is in a century-old riverside warehouse. The old pulleys and chains remain but the effect is more glam than industrial. The food is standard Portuguese fare and service often blasé, but the young, upwardly mobile crowd doesn't seem to mind.

Thai

Ban Thai

Rua Fradesso da Silveira 2, Loja 9, Alcântara Rio, Alcântara (21 362 1184/96 101 0560/www.restaurantebanthai.com). Train to Alcântara Mar from Cais do Sodré then 10min walk/tram 15, 18. **Open** 12.30-3pm, 7.30-11.30pm Tue-Sat. **Main courses** €11-€17. **Credit** DC, MC, V. **Map** p245 G9 (53)

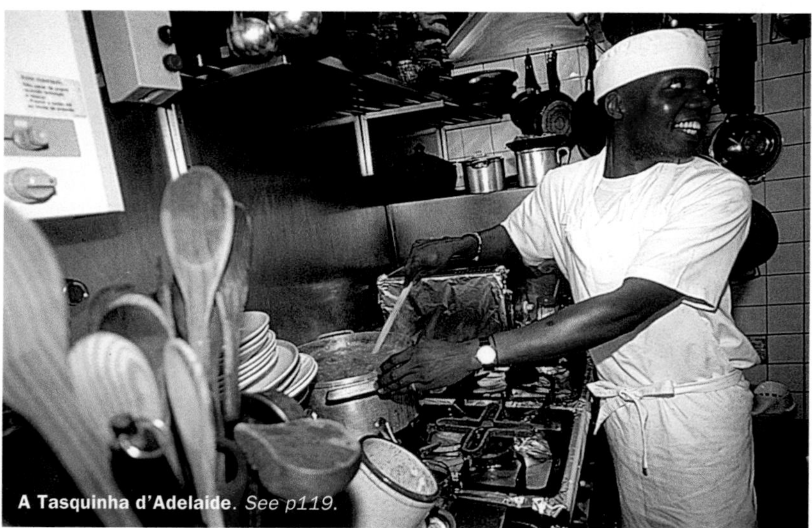

A Tasquinha d'Adelaide. *See p119.*

Green shoots

The traditional Lisbon menu yields little for the vegetarian besides omelettes and vegetable soup – and even *caldo verde* has pork *chouriço* bobbing in it as a matter of course. To make matters worse, the city's few vegetarian diners have lacked sparkle; most might as well offer a free hair shirt with every order.

Things are changing. Not only has the number of Italian chefs who know one end of an aubergine from the other increased – we particularly recommend **Mezzaluna** (*see p107*) – but that old standby, the curry house, has gone forth and multiplied. What's more, there are now several vegetarian restaurants that offer pleasurable, even sophisticated, dining.

The canteens remain, offering – it has to be said – unbeatable value, with mains from €3.25 and set menus from €5.50. In the Baixa, the downstairs diner at health food supermarket **Celeiro** (*see p143*) is the largest, but **Tao** (Rua dos Douradores 10, 21 885 0046, closed Sun) is a cheerier place that uses organic ingredients (vegans note: the fried tofu contains egg). One of its dining rooms has regular tables and chairs, the other, upstairs, low tables and floor cushions. **Yin Yang** (Rua dos Correeiros 14, 1st floor, 21 342 6551, closed Sat, Sun) is an established nearby alternative; there's a funkier newcomer a few streets over in the shape of **Megavega** (Rua dos Sapateiros 113, 21 346 8063, closed Sun), whose set menus include juices and desserts. The 'hot' main dish is kept on an inefficient stone slab so check if it needs microwaving before loading up with salads.

Chiado has several self-service lunch options that are only open for lunch Monday to Friday: the airy **Colmeia Vegan** (Rua Emenda 110, 2nd floor, 21 347 0500), the **Instituto Macrobiótico de Portugal** (Rua Anchieta 5, 2nd floor left, 21 324 2290) and, cheapest of all, the century-old vegan **Sociedade Portuguesa de Naturologia** (Rua do Alecrim, 38, 3rd floor, 21 346 3335).

In Estefânia, the vegan/macrobiotic restaurant and snack bar at **Espiral** (Praça Ilha do Faial 14A, 21 355 3990, closed Sun) has been joined by **Hare Krishna** (Rua Dona Estefânia 91, 21 314 0314, closed evenings, Sat, Sun), a religious centre that serves up a lacto-vegetarian feast for €5 (€4.50 students). In Campo Santana, **PSI** (Alameda Santo António dos Capuchos, 21 359 0573, closed Sun) is a pleasant place for lunch.

Away from these relative ghettos, the Portuguese love of soups means that food courts in shopping centres usually have soup and salad bars. Away from the shopping malls, good food can be found out at Parque das Nações at **Origens** (*see p124*), which has organic fare, though it's not meat free.

Genuine vegetarian dinner options are still scarce but no longer limited to one: the much-loved **Os Tibetanos** (*see p107*), which retains both à la carte and set menus. The stylish **Terra** (*see p111*) and **Oriente Chiado** (*see p107*), which claims to be Portugal's only 100 per cent vegan restaurant, have both opted for buffets. **Jardim dos Sentidos** (*see p107*) has a lunch buffet and limited à la carte menu, and a romantic garden. At Campo Pequeno, **Paladar Zen** (Avenida Barbosa du Bocage 107C, 21 795 0009, closed Sun) is a bright newcomer with a well-priced (€9) buffet that draws on both Asian and Mediterranean cuisine to challenge the entrenched local view of vegetarian eateries as places to do penance.

For more information on vegetarianism in Portugal, see www.e-macrobiotica.com (Instituto Macrobiótico), www.infonature.org (the more political Associação Vegetariana Portuguesa) and www.sejavegetariano.org (sparky animal rights organisation ANIMAL.

Located in a new residential development, Ban Thai rapidly made its mark, not least by highlighting Portugal's historical impact on Thai cuisine. Its mariners took chilli to Asia, and their wizard ways with yolks influenced Thai desserts. The starters are run of the mill but there's a good choice of main courses with ultra-fresh ingredients. Try steamed *robalo* or *Nua pad gra pao* (spicy mince). For dessert, as well as eggy confections there are some very Asian ones involving beans. At some point a waitress may pop on a headdress and dance. The place is no snip, but its weekday lunch deals (€10 and €8) are excellent value. Book for weekend dinners.

São Bento

African

Pastelaria Nascer do Sol

Rua Poço dos Negros 94, São Bento (96 658 9996). Tram 28. **Open** 11am-11pm daily. **Main courses** €5-€6. **No credit cards. Map** p246 K9 54

Eat, Drink, Shop

Despite the name, this is not a cake shop but rather a *tasca* that serves Angolan *moamba* and Cape Verdean *cachupa*, both stews – the first with chicken and okra, the second with maize, beans and meat – in helpings big enough for two. The gentle host, Senhor Ramos, makes all his customers feel very welcome, and he is willing to keep the kitchen open until midnight if necessary.

International

Merca-Tudo

Rua do Mercatudo 4, São Bento (21 396 9368). Tram 28. **Open** 8-11.30pm Mon-Sat. **Main courses** €7.50-€15. **Credit** AmEx, DC, MC, V. **Map** p246 K9 55

A cosy, candlelit warren whose boho atmosphere contrasts with the scruffy *tascas* and student bars of nearby Santos. Couscous and steak au poivre are on the menu along with a few Portuguese standards, and there's a good range of desserts.

Italian

A Galeria Gemelli

Rua de São Bento 334, São Bento (21 395 2552). Tram 28 then 5min walk/bus 6, 727, 773. **Open** 12.45-3pm, 8pm-midnight Tue-Fri; 8pm-midnight Sat. **Main courses** €13.50-€29.50. **Credit** MC, V. **Map** p246 K8 56

Up the road from parliament, this tiny, somewhat fussily decorated place is a favourite haunt of the current prime minister. Its Milanese chef, Augusto Gemelli, an exponent of 'creative Italian cuisine', usually greets guests personally, so if you haven't yet been able to order your sautéed porcini or foie gras and pear tortelloni with truffles, it's because he's busy in the kitchen. There are three tasting menus (€35, €45, €55), but you can eat well here for less. The place is good for vegetarians, but is not really suitable for children. There's free parking available up the road at the Clube Nacional Natação or down in Largo Vitorino Damásio.

Campo de Ourique

Portuguese

A Tasquinha d'Adelaide

Rua do Patrocínio 70-74 (21 396 2239). Tram 25, 28/bus 9. **Open** 12.30-3pm, 8.30pm-2am Mon-Sat. **Main courses** €18-€40. **Credit** AmEx, MC, V. **Map** p245 H8 57

Tucked away on a side street off the No.28 tram route, this 'little tavern' seats 24. So reserve and be punctual, as there's always competition to sample the culinary arts of Maria Adelaide Miranda, a painter-cook from remote Trás-os-Montes. From an open alcove in the dining room emerge hearty vegetable soups, roast leg of lamb and *pernil à patroa* (ham cooked the boss's way). There are tasty nibbles to tempt you while you wait. **Photo** *p117*.

Stop do Bairro

Rua Tenente Ferreira Durão 55A (21 388 8856). Tram 28 then 5min walk. **Open** noon-4pm, 7-11.30pm Tue-Sun. **Main courses** €10. **Credit** AmEx, DC, MC, V. **Map** p245 H7 58

Though famed for two decades for its fantastic food at low prices, Stop do Bairro remains unpretentious, its walls decked with slogans of the 'You don't have to be mad…' variety. The extensive menu takes in *bacalhau caras* (cheeks), *arroz de tamboril*, Azorean *polvo guisado* and, on Fridays, *cabidela de galinha*. Helpings are generous but hold out for a dessert; most are eggy and a challenge even to gluttons. The wine list is outstanding for this price bracket, starting with a drinkable house Lezíria. No booking so come early or wait your turn. **Photo** *p114*.

Lapa

Portuguese

Nariz de Vinho Tinto

Rua do Conde 75 (21 395 3035). Tram 25. **Open** 1-3pm, 8-11pm Tue-Fri; 8-11pm Sat, Sun. **Main courses** €12-€25. **Credit** AmEx, MC, V. **Map** p245 H9 59

The name means 'Red Wine Nose' – the restaurant's late founder, José Matos Cristovão, edited *Epicuro*, a cigar and wine lovers' magazine. His legacy is one of the finest wine lists in town, with something like 150 choices. The food's not bad, either. Guests, seated in two small dining rooms, choose from a menu that's full of game in season, and dishes like *bacalhau* baked with ham fat through the year.

Portuguese/International

Cipriani

Lapa Palace Hotel, Rua do Pau de Bandeira 4 (21 394 9494/www.lapapalace.com). Tram 25/bus 713. **Open** 12.30-3.30pm, 7.30-10.30pm daily. **Main courses** €20-€35. **Credit** AmEx, DC, MC, V. **Map** p245 H9 60

If you've got the cash, this place is worth every penny. It is in the Lapa Palace hotel (*see p48*) and Genoese chef Giorgio Damasio turns out impeccable seasonal food for impeccably turned-out tourists and upper-crust foodies. It's a mix of cordon bleu and posh Portuguese: foie gras with red wine; risotto mantecato with quail; and golden bream baked in salt and seaweed. The service is excellent and the river views are wonderful. **Photo** *p122*.

Clube dos Jornalistas

Rua das Trinas 129 R/C (21 397 7138/www.clubedosjornalistas.com). Tram 25/tram 28 then 10 min walk. **Open** noon-3pm, 7.30pm-midnight Mon-Sat. **Main courses** €10-€22. **Credit** AmEx, DC, MC, V. **Map** p245 J9 61

Based in a journalists' club in a lovely old house, this restaurant is now overseen by Leonard Guzman, the man behind La Moneda (*see p115* Yasmin) and other

Lisbon culinary experiments. The watchword is fusion, using seasonal ingredients. The charming garden is in use at lunchtimes and the atmosphere remains casual for such a well-connected place.

Brazilian

A Picanha

Rua das Janelas Verdes 96 (21 397 5401). Tram 25/bus 60, 713, 727. **Open** noon-3pm, 7.30-11.30pm Mon-Fri; 7.30pm-1am Sat, Sun. **Main courses** *Picanha* €13.50. **Credit** MC. **Map** p245 J10 62

If meat is murder, this is a canteen for serial killers. *Picanha* is a large lump of beef doused in garlic, grilled and hauled round tables where slices are shaved off on to plates. Here, the carving and gnashing of teeth is against a backdrop of antique *azulejos*. Great Caipirinhas too.

Ajuda

Portuguese

Restaurant Valle Flôr

Pestana Palace, Rua Jau 54, Alto de Santo Amaro (21 361 5600/fax 21 361 5601). Tram 18/bus 732. **Open** 12.30-3pm; 7-11pm daily. **Main courses** €18-€33. **Credit** AmEx, DC, MC, V. **Map** p244 E9 63

In the former palace of the Marquês Valle Flôr, now a deluxe hotel (*see p48*), this award-winning restaurant is run by Aimé Barroyer. A dynamic Frenchman, Barroyer has his own herb garden in the grounds and sources rare Portuguese ingredients from farms around the country. The food – Portuguese with a French-Italian twist – is prepared in kitchens directly beneath the frescoed dining room; a silent dumb-waiter brings up food-laden trolleys without a hint of the mayhem below. There's a tasting menu with four starters, five main courses and six desserts to choose from, including an award-winning rice pudding. A great place to spot dignitaries and visiting celebs.

Northern Lisbon

Portuguese

Na Ordem

Avenida Almirante Gago Coutinho 151, Airport (21 840 6117/96 136 8030). Bus 5, 21, 22, 91, 708. **Open** 12.30-3pm, 7.30-10pm Mon-Sat. **Set menus** *lunch* €30-€60; *dinner* €40-€60. **Credit** MC, V. **Map** p249 O1 64

Foodies who for years beat a path to Luís Suspiro's rural hideout near Cartaxo finally persuaded him to open a place in Lisbon in mid 2006. Many of his fans were doctors, and the restaurant is in the rather formal setting of the Ordem dos Médicos, near the airport, but all are welcome. Suspiro is an exponent of 'new Portuguese cuisine': dishes based on traditional originals, with modern techniques producing a sharper contrast of textures and tastes. His *bacalhau à bras*, for example, is with julienned vegetables and crunchy 'angel's hair' filaments of potato. Tremendous care is taken with the wines, of which there are hundreds, but Suspiro also draws on a myriad oils and vinegars. You can order à la carte service but set menus (including wine) are the norm.

Cervejarias

Ramiro

Avenida Almirante Reis 1H, Intendente (21 885 1024). Metro Intendente/tram 28. **Open** noon-1.30am Mon, Wed-Sun. **Main courses** €8-€20. **Credit** AmEx, MC, V. **Map** p246 M8 65

Senhor Ramiro is what lisboetas call a *cromo*, 'a card'. A native of Galícia in Spain, he set up this once tiny *marisqueira* in what was then a dodgy part of town. The fame of his sublime Spanish-style *gambas a ajillo* (prawns toasted in garlic and olive oil) spread, and soon Ramiro bought the shop next door, then the next and the next. Despite the extensions, you still have to queue, but service is rapid.

International

Basta Café Jardim

Rua Dona Estefânia 175, Estefânia (21 016 1134). Metro Saldanha. **Open** noon-11.30pm Tue-Sun. **Main courses** €8-€13.50. **No credit cards**. **Map** p249 M5 66

Creative cuisine in a setting that combines art deco and 1970s retro, Basta Café Jardim is run by the exotic pairing of Argentinian Josefina Cardeza and Serbian Milos Ivkovic. Suitably exotic flavours such as a Slavic beetroot soup and Thai chicken kebabs are served in a lovely wood-panelled room filled with contemporary furniture. And, yes, there is a word play in the restaurant's name: *basta* means 'enough' in Portuguese but 'garden' in Serbian: sure enough, out at the back there is an esplanade bar (open in winter with heaters) with park benches to lounge on.

Italian

Lucca

Travessa Henrique Cardoso 19B, Avenida da Roma (21 797 2687/1051/www.pizzerialucca.com). Metro Roma. **Open** noon-3.30pm, 7pm-1am Mon, Tue, Thur-Sun. **Main courses** €8-€12. **Credit** MC, V. **Map** p249 M3 67

In a city with few good Italian restaurants, Lucca's wood-fired oven is a sure thing. Add to that the generally good ingredients and friendly (if erratic) Brazilian staff, and you have a hit. The pasta is decent and there are meat dishes and salads, but the pizzas are tops: try the Lucca (ham, ricotta and rocket) or the Casanova, with porcini and cheese. For dessert, play safe with *panna cotta*. The two rooms fill up for dinner, so book ahead. It is also pretty noisy: more a neighbourhood eaterie than a place to impress a date. No relation to the trendier Luca (*see p105*).

Japanese

Assuka

Rua São Sebastião da Pedreira, Praça de Espanha (21 314 9345/www.assuka.com). Metro São Sebastião. **Open** noon-3pm, 7-11pm Mon-Sat. **Main courses** €10-€20. **Credit** AmEx, MC, V. **Map** p246 L6 68

A slick restaurant in a street full of cheap eateries hidden away behind the office buildings of Avenida António Augusto Aguiar. The menu roams far beyond sushi, with *sukiaki, yakiniku, lamen, gyoza* and, of course, tempura.

Osaka

Avenida Praia da Vitória 35-B, Saldanha (21 315 5210). Metro Saldanha. **Open** noon-3pm, 7pm-midnight daily. **Main courses** €8.50-€13.80. **Credit** MC, V. **Map** p249 M5 69

A large, unpretentious restaurant near the Praça do Duque de Saldanha, Osaka is good value at lunch, when menus including drink and coffee cost €11-€15. The fish is fresh and there's plenty of choice.

Eastern Lisbon

Portuguese

D'Avis

Rua do Grilo 96, Beato (21 868 1354/www.restaurantedavis.com). Bus 39, 718. **Open** 12.30-3.20pm, 7.30-10.30pm Mon-Sat. **Main courses** €7-€12.50. **No credit cards**.

It's in the back of beyond (albeit next to a splendid Manueline convent) but this rustic tavern attracts a stream of pilgrims for its authentic Alentejo regional specialities. These include *ensopada de borrego, cação frito com pimentão, pezinhos de porco de coentrada* (pork trotters with coriander), a slew of dishes involving *migas* (fried breadcrumbs – tastier than they sound) and lots of *bacalhau*. There's more cod (17 different dishes) a few doors down at the smarter but reasonably priced Casa do Bacalhau (No.54, 21 862 0007, closed Sun), which also has a vegetarian option.

Portuguese/International

Bica do Sapato

Avenida Infante Dom Henriques, Armazém B, Santa Apolónia (21 881 0320). Bus 6, 28, 81, 82, 90, 759. **Open** 8-11.30pm Mon; 12.30-3.30pm, 8-11.30pm Tue-Sat. **Main courses** €20-€35. **Credit** AmEx, DC, MC, V. **Map** p247 O9 70

Bica do Sapato is part owned by John Malkovich but you're more likely to spot one of his business partners, nightlife guru Manuel Reis and José Miranda – the latter often stands at the bar welcoming guests. The large space, dotted with designer furniture, is boxed off into a café-bar, the main restaurant and, upstairs, a sushi bar. The food in the restaurant is outstanding – from entrecôte to lobster, through crab ravioli in gazpacho sauce, to fillet of moonfish with oysters, spinach and baked tomato – as are the river views. The service veers from fine to faulty. Upstairs, the sushi is excellent.

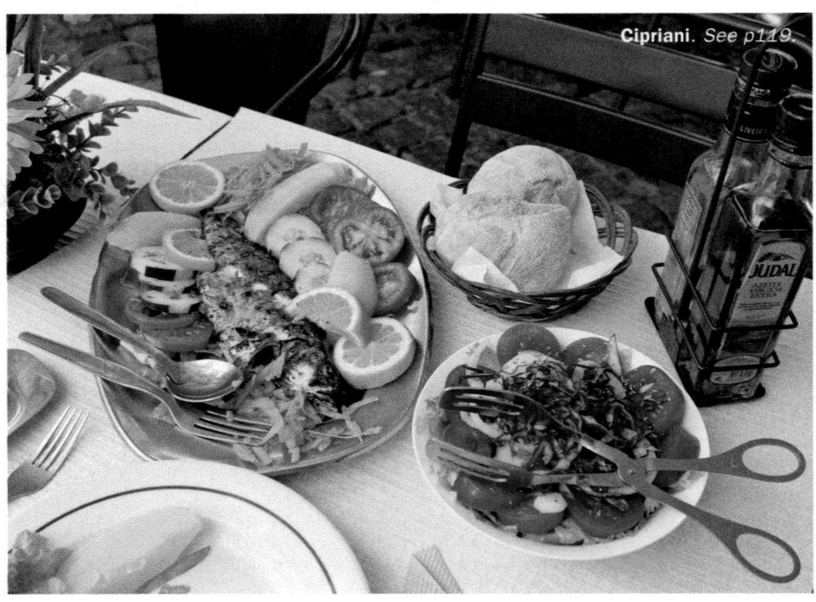

Cipriani. *See p119.*

Grape stuff

So you've picked your restaurant, scoffed the bread, fish paste and cheese left as an appetiser and chosen your dinner. Now – what to drink? Portugal may have a hard time persuading the international market that it is a reliable source of high-quality table wine, but visitors will find evidence to back up its case. Two decades of modernisation, in both wineries and vineyards, have had a mostly positive effect. As well as the producers listed below, the names of Portugal's four largest – Sogrape, José Maria da Fonseca, Caves Aliança and Companhia das Quintas – guarantee a minimum of quality.

RED WINES

It is a simplification – but a useful one – to say that Portuguese reds become more user-friendly as you go from north to south. From the northern Douro region (of port fame) come characterful and complex reds whose individuality rules out mass market appeal. There are many excellent wine-makers here, among them Kolheita de Ideias, Quinta de la Rosa, Quinta do Crasto and Quinta do Côtto. South of the Douro, the Dão, Bairrada and Beiras regions have much in common, but their wines are softer and slightly sweeter, thanks partly to more use of wood ageing. Bairrada is dominated by the baga grape variety, resulting in elegant, dry reds. Reliable producers there include Luís Pato and Quinta das Bágeiras; in the Dão, Dão Sul makes Quinta de Cabriz and other wines.

South of Coimbra, the Estremadura and Ribatejo regions used mainly to supply wine for blending and unthinking drinking. They still produce most by volume, but quality has taken a quantum leap: some of Portugal's fruitiest and friendliest reds are produced here, from indigenous and foreign grapes. Value for money is generally good, as there is no past to cash in on. Among the better wines are those from Casa Santos Lima and Quinta de Pancas in Estremadura, and Fiuza and Quinta do Casal Branco in Ribatejo.

Of the Lisbon region's once famous wine-growing areas, Colares and Carcavelos have faded. Bucelas, north of the city, now makes mainly white wine. South of Lisbon, the Setúbal peninsula offers both living history – in the form of old vines of the castelão (aka periquita) variety, yielding deep, velvety reds – and modernity. Palmela is a safe bet for warm, fruity reds at a good price. The cooperative at Pegões produces award-winning wines, as does JP.

Inland and south of Setúbal, the Alentejo has been Portugal's most successful region over the past decade. Once a source of easy-drinking reds – warm and sweetly fruity at best; thin, cooked and with overtones of manure at worst – it now produces wines from the great to the godawful. Value for money is hard to get, but in the higher price range there are some astonishing reds. Good use is made of most Portuguese grape varieties as well as foreign ones such as syrah and cabernet sauvignon. Look out for wines from Cortes de Cima, D'Avillez, Finagra (Esporão and others), Fundaçaõ Eugénio de Almeida, João Portugal Ramos and Tapada de Coelheiros.

The Algarve has a reputation for plonk. Demarcated in 1980 (before more deserving regions) to encourage local producers, there are still only a few making quality wines. One is Sir Cliff Richard, who proved that good wine can be made here. At a price.

WHITE WINES

More than any other Portuguese table wine, Vinho Verde (green wine), from the Minho in the far north, achieved global recognition in the latter half of the 20th century. Then excesses of sweetening and carbonisation, and the squeezing of yields and prices undid much of that achievement. As producers struggle to re-establish an identity for the wine, and make something that does not recall thin white wine mixed with soda water, drinkers can console themselves with one wine that has not lost its soul. Alvarinho, made from the grape of the same name in Melgaço and Monção, is not really Vinho Verde at all, given its fairly full body, straw colour and lack of fizz. It costs a lot, too.

The news from elsewhere is better. Portuguese whites have been transformed – from oxidised 'mature whites' and pale younger whites, to complex oak-aged and cleanly fruity ones. The changes began a couple of decades ago, and all regions now produce appealing whites. It is often the case with bottlings under one label that the red is dearer but the white is the better wine. And contrary to what pundits believed not so long ago, many of the best Portuguese whites now come from the hot plains of the Alentejo. Here at least, it is difficult to go wrong.

Italian

Casanova

Cais da Pedra à Bica do Sapato, Armazém B, Loja 7, Santa Apolónia (21 887 7532). Bus 6, 28, 81, 82, 90, 759. **Open** 6.30pm-1.30am Tue; 12.30pm-1.30am Wed-Sun. **Main courses** €10-€20. **Credit** AmEx, MC, V. **Map** p247 O9 71

An offshoot of Casa Nostra (*see p111*), Casanova quickly established itself as the place for pizza thanks to a huge wood-fired oven. They're all great, from a simple napoletana to the Casanova, laden with cherry tomatoes, rocket and mozzarella. (If you're a mozzarella fanatic, come on Friday night or Saturday, after the stuff arrives from Italy.) The rest is mostly predictable starters and pasta, with *panna cotta* and tiramisu for dessert. Diners catch waiters' attention by switching on a red bulb dangling above their table. No reservations, but tables are shared and the turnover is fast.

Parque das Nações

The many eating options in the Vasco da Gama shopping centre include a Portugália *cervejaria* with fine views. **Origens** is nearby, next to the Casino, which has three restaurants overseen by chef Fausto Airoldi, formerly of Bica do Sapato (*see p122*); the flagship, Pragma, has tasting menus from €60 and a vast wine list. The Parque das Nações itself also has lots of restaurants, including Italian-themed **La Rúcula** (Rossio dos Olivias, 21 892 2747), with decent pizzas and other mains from €9.

Portuguese

Origens

Alameda dos Oceanos Lote 1.02.1, 2A, Loja 1, Parque das Nações (restaurant 21 894 6166/shop 21 894 6167/www.origensbio.pt). Metro Oriente. **Open** *Restaurant* 12.30-3pm, 8-11pm Mon-Sat. *Esplanade* 11am-7pm Mon-Sat. **Main courses** €18-€26. **Credit** MC, V.

If your body is a temple, this is the place in which to worship at its altar. All the ingredients are organic (including the grapes that went into the wines on the very international list) and bursting with freshness. There are three vegetarian dishes but meat lovers are catered for too, as the restaurant serves the tenderest of steaks, served with fries or basmati rice and salad or sautéed vegetables (note that these cost extra). There are also other fish and meat options. It may seem a bit on the pricey side, but not only is everything delicious but it's presented with panache – chef Paulo Santos has worked with Vítor Sobral (now at Terreiro do Paço, *see p104*) and at Eleven (*see p105*) – while the service is informal and efficient. The restaurant also offers an €18 set lunch; the separate café section with esplanade serves pasta, hamburgers and steak from €6.

South of the river

There are many seafood restaurants near the Cacilhas ferry terminal, serving *caldeirada*, crab (*sapateiro*) and other scaly things. **As Colunas** (Rua Elias Garcia 51C, 21 499 0660, closed Thur) is a bustly place that also serves game.

Brazilian

Atira-te ao Rio

Cais do Ginjal 69-70, Cacilhas (21 275 1380). Ferry or boat taxi to Cacilhas from Cais do Sodré then 15min walk. **Open** 1-3pm, 8pm-midnight Tue-Sun. **Main courses** €10-€20. **Credit** AmEx.

The name means 'Throw yourself in the river' and it is right on the quay, so you get a great view of Lisbon. It's quite a trek to and from the ferry; ask about river taxis before leaving. Next door Ponto Final (21 276 0743), serves mainly Portuguese fare.

Cascais & Estoril

Portuguese

Porto de Santa Maria

Estrada do Guincho, Cascais (21 487 1036/0240/ www.portosantamaria.com). Train to Cascais then taxi. **Open** 12.15-3pm, 7-10.30pm Tue-Sun. **Main courses** €38.50-€55. **Credit** AmEx, DC, MC, V.

One of Portugal's most expensive restaurants and one of eight with a Michelin star (again) for 2007, this fish and seafood mecca is perched on the rocky Guincho coast, a 40-minute drive from Lisbon. The area's other Michelin-starred restaurant is Fortaleza do Guincho (21 487 0491, www.guinchotel.pt), in the hotel of the same name.

Chinese

Estoril Mandarin

Casino Estoril, Estoril (21 466 7270/www.casino estoril.com). Train to Estoril from Cais do Sodré. **Open** noon-3pm, 7.30-11pm Mon, Wed-Sun. **Main courses** €10-€150. **Credit** AmEx, DC, MC, V.

The best Chinese restaurant in the region, with fine food, decor and service.

International

La Villa

Praia do Tamariz 3, Estoril (21 468 0033). Train to Estoril from Cais do Sodré. **Open** 1-3.30pm, 8pm-midnight Tue-Fri, Sun. **Main courses** €30-€40. **Credit** AmEx, DC, MC, V.

One of the most fashionable places to eat on the Estoril coast. Downstairs, wonderful ocean views complement a sophisticated atmosphere, slick service and fine Mediterranean cuisine. Upstairs two Brazilian chefs meticulously prepare fine sushi and sashimi. The top-floor terrace overlooks Tamariz beach, and abuts a small modern art gallery.

Cafés

Come on in – the coffee's lovely.

Cerca Moura. *See p126.*

The Portuguese love their coffee. Most lisboetas tumble out of bed and into a coffee, usually a turbo-charged *bica* with a bag or two of sugar stirred in. Cafés ready to fuel this addiction are everywhere, ranging from workaday *pastelarias* (pastry shops) to *esplanadas* (outdoor seating decks) on the main avenues. But coffee's popularity is no recent phenomenon: Portugal, as colonial ruler of the world's largest producer of the stuff, has long had access to fine coffee.

In Lisbon, the growth of empire and the rise of the bourgeoisie were mirrored in the development of the Chiado district. The area's reputation as a hub for artistic and political brainstorming rests on two establishments: **Café A Brasileira**, which survives, and Café Marrare. 'Lisbon was the Chiado, and the Chiado was Café Marrare,' enthused one historian. Café A Brasileira's heyday was in the 1920s and '30s, when literary types such as Fernando Pessoa and José Pacheco could be found at one table, politicians at another, and actors from the Teatro da Trindade at a third.

That milieu was doomed long before the 1988 Chiado fire. Rossio's larger cafés had popular appeal and a stream of customers from the new railway station. In the 1940s, with the rest of Europe at war, Rossio's cafés flourished. However, a mere 20 years later most were gone. But as our listings show, there are signs of a revival of café culture in the Chiado, and overall Lisbon has more places to slurp coffee than ever.

A word of warning, though. If a café has an esplanade, beware: prices can more than double if you're outside. Standing at the counter is always cheapest. If you're wondering about where to pay, it's the *pré-pagamento* system: you go to the till first, pay and take the receipt to the serving counter.

Coffee beans are bought in four levels of quality; gold (highest), platinum, diamond and bar (lowest). The finest coffee will be freshly ground gold and it is worth asking staff which they are using. You'll taste the difference.

The best-known Portuguese pastry is the *pastel de nata*, or custard tart, which reaches its acme at **Antiga Confeitaria de Belém**. But there are many others, including *bolos de arroz*, or rice-flour cakes, *sonhos* ('dreams') – jam-free doughnuts, and *broas de mel*, honey-flavoured cornbread with a pleasant nutty taste but the consistency of lead shot.

The best Cafés

For lip-smacking lemonade
Pois, Café (*see p127*).

For organic ingredients
Royale Café (*see p128*).

For pastéis de nata
Antiga Confeitaria de Belém (*see p130*).

For views
Cerca Moura (*see p126*); Esplanada da Igreja da Graça (*see p127*).

To escape the 21st century
As Vicentinhas (*see p129*).

Baixa

Café Martinho da Arcada

Praça do Comércio 3 (21 887 9259). Metro Baixa-Chiado/tram 15, 18, 25, 28. **Open** 6.30am-11pm Mon-Sat. **Credit** AmEx, DC, MC, V. **Map** p251 M10 ❶

The café and its adjacent restaurant were one of poet Fernando Pessoa's favourite haunts (*see p78* **Walking Lisbon**). They are also worth a stop for their *pastéis de nata*, which you can eat at the wood-panelled counter or sitting at one of the marble-topped tables. But the esplanade is beset by exhaust fumes.

Castella do Paulo

Rua da Alfandega 120 (21 888 0019/www.castella.pt.vu). Tram 15, 18, 25. **Open** 7.30am-7.30pm Mon-Fri; noon-7.30pm Sat. **Credit** MC, V. **Map** p251 M10 ❷

This Japanese tea house makes a meal of the two countries' links – the Portuguese were the first Europeans to land in Japan. The Japanese cake from which it takes its name, served in delicate portions, was an adaptation of the giant Portuguese *pão de ló* (sponge). There are also bean cakes common to both countries and light Japanese-style meals.

Rossio

Café Nicola

Praça Dom Pedro IV (Rossio) 24 (21 346 0579). Metro Rossio/tram 12, 15. **Open** *Café* 8am-10pm Mon-Fri; 9am-10pm Sat; 10am-7pm Sun. *Restaurant* noon-10pm Mon-Sat. **Credit** AmEx, DC, MC, V. **Map** p250 L9 ❸

Nicola has been here since 1929, but occupies the site of an early 18th-century café where extemporising poet Manuel Maria Barbosa du Bocage held court (his statue is still toasted nightly) and which was briefly the headquarters of Napoleon's invading force. In the 20th century it was a centre for political intrigue, with police officers assigned to keep tabs on would-be agitators. Nicola emerged from a renovation a few years ago to its current marble, steel and glass splendour; the paintings are 1935 originals by Fernando Santos.

Other locations: Nicola Gourmet, Rua 1° de Dezembro 12, Rossio (21 342 9172).

Casa Suíça

Praça Dom Pedro IV (Rossio) 96 (21 321 4090). Metro Rossio/tram 12, 15. **Open** 7am-9pm daily. **Credit** MC, V. **Map** p250 M9 ❹

Suíça's extensive selection of sticky pastries is as good as ever, but there are also sandwiches, salads, yoghurts and shakes for the health-conscious. It has esplanades on Rossio and Praça da Figueira.

Confeitaria Nacional

Praça da Figueira 18B-C (21 342 4470/www.confeitarianacional.pt). Metro Rossio/tram 12, 15. **Open** 8am-8pm Mon-Sat. **Credit** AmEx, DC, MC, V. **Map** p250 M9 ❺

The plaque boasting 'over 100 years of existence' is itself an antique; Nacional was founded in 1829 and retains its glass cases and painted panelling. With fast, pleasant service, it's a good place to buy biscuits or cakes to take away. There is also a café.

Avenida da Liberdade & Marquês de Pombal

Bela Ipanema

Avenida da Liberdade 169 (21 357 2316). Metro Avenida. **Open** 7am-midnight Mon-Sat. **Credit** AmEx, DC, MC, V. **Map** p245 L8 ❻

The consummate snack bar: spacious counters, a large indoor seating space, and an *esplanada*. Juices, shakes and sundaes are a speciality, but there's also a huge selection of meals and snacks.

Confeitaria Marquês de Pombal

Avenida da Liberdade 244A-B (21 356 2362). Metro Marquês de Pombal. **Open** 7am-9.30pm Mon-Fri; 8am-5pm Sat. **Credit** AmEx, MC, V. **Map** p246 L7 ❼

A *pastelaria* on an industrial scale, packed at peak times. The ice-cream parlour is to the right as you enter; for the *pastelaria* head upstairs after taking a token from the woman at the till. The waiter takes your order and notes your number, and the bill awaits when you return to the till.

Parque Eduardo VIII

Linha d'Água

Rua Marquês de Fronteira, Jardim Amália Rodrigues (21 381 4327). Metro São Sebastião. **Open** 9am-midnight daily. **No credit cards**. **Map** p248 K5 ❽

At the very top of Parque Eduardo VII, this modern cafeteria by a circular pool is a haven of tranquillity. Fine salads, cakes and light meals are served inside to a cool musical soundtrack, while outside the accompaniment is the sound of water lapping beneath a boardwalk. Further down the eastern side of the park, Cafeteria Botequim do Rei (21 315 4611, closed Mon) has a pleasant esplanade.

East of Baixa

Near the entrance to the castle, luxury hotel Palácio Belmonte (*see p46*) houses Art Café, which serves fine foods from around Portugal against a backdrop of art exhibitions.

Alfama

Cerca Moura

Largo das Portas do Sol 4 (21 887 4859). Tram 28. **Open** 10am-2am daily. **Credit** AmEx, DC, MC, V. **Map** p251 N9 ❾

In summer the esplanade here is stiff with tourists gazing at the unrivalled view of Alfama. Despite the

Kick off your walking shoes and relax at **Pois, Café**.

crowds, it's ideal for a light snack as the kiosk serves toasties, baguettes and savoury snacks well into the night, weather permitting. On chilly days decamp to the cave-like bar built into the Moorish walls after which the place is named. **Photo** *p125.*

Pois, Café

Rua São João da Praça 93, Sé (21 886 2497). Tram 12, 28/bus 37. **Open** 11am-8pm Tue-Sun. **No credit cards**. **Map** p251 M10 ⑩

This Austrian-run café is a great place to lounge, reading the newspapers and magazines provided. The rustic decoration (or lack of it), mismatched furniture, and games and toys scattered about all add to the informal atmosphere in which sandwiches, salads, delicious cakes and fragrant Austrian lemonade are served. Various brunches too.

Graça

Esplanada da Igreja da Graça

Largo da Graça, Graça (no phone). Tram 28. **Open** *Winter* 11.30am-2am daily. *Summer* 11.30am-3am daily. **No credit cards**. **Map** p251 N9 ⑪

More a locals' hangout than Cerca Moura (*see p126*), this place fills up on sunny afternoons with people drawn to one of Lisbon's best views. Its toasted sandwiches and fresh lemonade are excellent, but service is variable, as is the music. A bica costs €1.

West of Baixa

Chiado

The Museu do Chiado (*see p162*) has a fine café, and a smart esplanade now operates out of the Teatro Nacional de São Carlos (*see p169*). Uphill in Largo do Carmo, several cafés and restaurants put tables out. If you need to check email, Cyber.bica (in the internet section of the Directory) is the best option.

Black Coffee

Rua Ivens 45 (tel/fax 21 347 4077). Metro Baixa-Chiado. **Open** 9am-midnight Mon-Thur; 9am-2am Fri; noon-2am Sat. **No credit cards**. **Map** p250 L9 ⑫

The menu is an undistinguished list of baguettes, salads and quiches, but the stylish coffee-and-cream decor shows this café has pretensions. After 8pm it morphs into a bar; on Fridays there's live Brazilian music from 10pm and on Saturdays a DJ.

Café A Brasileira

Rua Garrett 120 (21 346 9541). Metro Baixa-Chiado/tram 28. **Open** 8am-2am daily. **Credit** AmEx, V. **Map** p250 L9 ⑬

When A Brasileira opened in 1905, customers not only got a free *bica* when they bought a bag of beans, but the waiters were courteous. These days a coffee on the *esplanada* costs €1.30 and service is pretty off-hand. At the counter inside it's just €0.50 for a *bica* (€0.80 seated at a table) and you can gawp at the magnificent carved wood interior. At its 1920s peak, this place contributed greatly to the idea that while Coimbra studied and Oporto worked, Lisbon talked and made revolution. Nowadays intrigue has given way to tourists taking pictures by the statue of Fernando Pessoa (*see p78* **Walking Lisbon**).

Café dos Teatros

Rua António Maria Cardoso 58 (21 325 7658). Metro Baixa-Chiado/tram 28. **Open** 11am-2am daily. **Credit** AmEx, MC, V. **Map** p250 L10 ⓮

A café-restaurant-bar with a thespian bent thanks to the neighbouring playhouse. Good coffee and light meals, a stylish atmosphere and plenty of foreign newspapers to browse through.

Café no Chiado

Largo do Picadeiro 10-12 (21 346 0501/www.cafenochiado.pt). Metro Baixa-Chiado/tram 28. **Open** 10am-2am Mon-Thur; 10am-3am Fri, Sat. **Credit** MC, V. **Map** p250 L9 ⓯

Civilised yet informal, this café is great for settling down for an afternoon spent reading Portuguese and foreign newspapers. The *esplanada* has better coffee (and cheaper, at €1) than Café A Brasileira (*see p127*) and is more peaceful; even the trams rattling past provide a photo opportunity. Café no Chiado is a lunch favourite with media types, who can now tuck into prawn crêpes and English roast beef as well as Portuguese fare. Meals are also available out of hours. The owner is the Centro Nacional de Cultura, a non-state body that was a key cultural catalyst during the dictatorship; its library and free internet space are upstairs.

Pastelaria Bénard

Rua Garrett 104 (21 347 3133). Metro Baixa-Chiado/tram 28. **Open** 8am-11pm Mon-Sat. **Credit** AmEx, DC, MC, V. **Map** p250 L9 ⓰

Coffee and cakes of high quality are served here, in one of Lisbon's oldest tearooms, which is further evidenced by the tendency of the waiting staff to act as though they've seen it all before. You can also lunch, but as at neighbouring Café A Brasileira (*see p127*) prices all but triple if you sit outside.

Royale Café

Largo Rafael Bordalo Pinheiro 29 R/C E (21 346 9125/www.royalecafe.com). Metro Baixa-Chiado. **Open** 10am-midnight Mon-Sat; 10am-8pm Sun. **Credit** V. **Map** p250 L9 ⓱

A classy newcomer in a quiet square. Everything except the rye bread is made on the premises. Ingredients are organic or regional specialities such as *chouriço de cebola* (onion sausage) and *queijo da serra* (mountain cheese), the herbal teas are made from plants not bags, and there are old-fashioned tipples such as *quinado*, a fortified wine flavoured with quinine, and *licor de pinho* (pine), which they mix with orange, mint and cinnamon. The seasonal menu (chestnut soup in autumn, for example) has unusual combinations, such as a salad with rocket, pesto, dried tomatoes and chocolate. The newer St Germain Lounge Café opposite (No.18, 21 346 5212), stays open late on Fridays and Saturdays, serving cocktails and snacks to jazz and chill out.

SV Café

Rua do Capelo 20 (96 947 9871). Metro Baixa-Chiado/tram 28. **Open** 9.30am-12.30am Mon-Fri; noon-1am Sat. **No credit cards. Map** p250 L10 ⓲

This unassuming little place near the Teatro Nacional de São Carlos sells well priced, delectable savouries and light meals, plus great cakes.

Vertigo Café

Travessa do Carmo 4 (21 343 3112). Metro Baixa-Chiado. **Open** 10am-2am Mon-Sat; 10am-midnight Sun. **Credit** AmEx, DC, MC. **Map** p250 L9 ⓳

A cosy place to linger over a pot of exotic tea, snack on couscous, crêpes, cakes and bagels, or browse local or English-language newspapers. The stained glass and wood panelling give it a central European feel, and it's a favoured hangout of local bohos. Downstairs is a separate bar. For more teas, go round the corner to Chá do Carmo (Largo do Carmo 21).

Santa Catarina

Noobai

Miradouro do Adamastor (21 346 5014/www.noobaicafe.com). Metro Baixa-Chiado then 10min walk/tram 28. **Open** noon-midnight daily. **No credit cards. Map** p246 K9 ⓴

Right next to the Esplanada do Adamastor (*see p186*) and boasting the same sweeping river views, Noobai is set apart from the noisy scene that take over that *miradouro* as the day wears on. Its modish menu offers Mediterranean snacks such as tuna paste with capers, bruschettas, soups, salads, tarts and cakes, plus great Caipirinhas.

Bairro Alto & Príncipe Real

Cultura do Chá

Rua das Salgadeiras 38, Bairro Alto (21 343 0272). Metro Baixa-Chiado. **Open** 8am-9.30pm daily. **No credit cards. Map** p250 L9 ㉑

This tearoom in the trendy Bairro Alto looks as if it would be at home in Windsor. As well as a couple of dozen teas, it offers shakes, various kinds of hot chocolate and, of course, coffee. There are giant apple tarts, lemon meringue pies and chocolate cakes, and various quiches.

Esplanada do Jardim do Príncipe Real

Praça do Príncipe Real (96 231 1669/511 5851). Metro Rato/bus 58, 790. **Open** 8am-midnight daily. **No credit cards. Map** p250 K8 ㉒

Scruffy English teachers (the British Council is nearby) and geeky students abound at this popular meeting spot. There's some seating inside, but if you can,

Café etiquette

So you thought you could just walk in and order a coffee? How naïve. OK, you could say 'um café, por favor', but brace yourself for a tiny dose of a potent, bitter brew that, drunk neat, can disable tastebuds for hours. Anyway, it's a bit unimaginative just to ask for coffee when you can test the staff's patience while showing your appreciation of Portuguese culture.

For a milky coffee, served in a glass, ask for *um galão*, but add the words *da máquina* (from the machine) or the coffee may come from a tankful that's been standing around for an hour. The nearest thing to a cappuccino is *uma meia da leite* (half of milk). To make sure it's strong and hot, end the phrase with *da máquina com leite quente* (with hot milk).

Most locals don't bother with wimpy additions like milk. They opt for a *bica* (Lisbon waiters' slang – you order *um café* unless you're tacking on an adjective) or *um duplo* (double) if they're gasping, and offset the bitterness with sugar.

If a *bica* doesn't do it for you any more, try *uma italiana* – effectively, a thimbleful of hot coffee essence. Or get finicky and order *um café cheio/curto* (weaker/stronger). The faint-hearted order *um carioca*, a diluted *bica* (not to be confused with *um carioca de limão*, which is lemon rind in hot water). *Um abatanado* is still more diluted, and thus in a larger cup. For a different kind of boost, try *um café com cheirinho* – 'with a whiff' of *aguardente* (grape mash distillate). A decaf is *um descafeinado*.

The really tough customers refuse to accept a cup from on top of the coffee machine, where crockery is left to dry. If they want piping hot coffee but fret about burning their lips (don't you just hate that?), they order *uma bica escaldada numa chávena fria* ('scalded', in a cold cup).

To be a real pain in the neck, you could maybe even order *uma bica descafeinada escaldada pingada numa chávena fria*. But perhaps that really would be taking things just a little too far.

sit outside to take advantage of the great people-watching opportunities. The Praça do Príncipe Real is both a social centre for the local oldies and the heart of Lisbon's gay district.

Pão de Canela

Praça das Flores 27, Príncipe Real (21 397 2220). Metro Rato/bus 100. **Open** 7.30am-8pm daily. **Credit** MC, V. **Map** p246 K8 ㉓

A discreetly fashionable café in a cute square down from the Jardim do Príncipe Real, Pão de Canela has an *esplanada* blissfully free of traffic fumes. Tasty quiches and cakes too.

São Bento & beyond

Lapa

The café at the Museu de Arte Antiga (*see p84*) has tables in a lovely shady back garden.

O Chá da Lapa

Rua do Olival 8-10, Lapa (21 390 0888). Tram 25. **Open** 9am-7pm daily. **Credit** DC, MC, V. **Map** p246 K9 ㉔

'Tea of Lapa' is something of a misnomer, since the menu only stretches as far as Earl Grey and English Breakfast, but nevertheless the place is in the *salão de chá* tradition: genteel, with attentive staff and impeccably turned-out ladies. Quiches, biscuits and cakes are made on the premises.

Campo de Ourique

Lomar

Rua Tomás de Anunciação 72 (21 385 8417). Tram 25, 28. **Open** 7.30am-8pm Mon-Fri; 7.30am-5pm Sat. **No credit cards. Map** p245 H7 ㉕

A stylish neighbourhood *pastelaria* that attracts a mixture of local *tias* (literally aunts, but more or less 'ladies who lunch') and students who come in to natter over coffee and for the cakes and savouries all made on the premises. Can get a bit smoky.

Panificação Mecânica

Rua Silva Carvalho 209 (21 381 2260). Metro Rato then 10min walk/bus 58. **Open** 7am-8pm Mon-Fri; 7am-6pm Sat. **No credit cards. Map** p245 J7 ㉖

Chandeliers, tiles depicting ears of wheat, coloured enamel pillars, painted moulded ceilings and wall mirrors make this Lisbon's most over-the-top old *pastelaria*. It has been supplying the middle classes with top-notch bread and cakes for over a century, and now also sells cheeses and ice-cream.

Rato

As Vicentinhas

Rua do São Bento 700 (21 388 7040). Metro Rato. **Open** 3.30-7pm Tue-Sat. **No credit cards. Map** p246 K8 ㉗

This tearoom and religious knick-knack shop has functioned for three decades, and stepping from noisy

The best *pasteis* in Portugal at **Antiga Confeitaria de Belém**.

Rato into the hushed, whitewashed space is like entering another age. The tiny, genteel Vicentinhas – women dedicated to the 'promotion of Christian and cultural education' among the sick – talk and move at their own rhythm. There's no menu but the home-made cakes are displayed in all their glory.

Western waterfront

Esplanades are dotted between Cais do Sodré and Belém. They're much of a muchness but **Esplanada Doca de Santo** (21 396 3522), the first on your right, has nice thick shakes.

Cais do Sodré

Leitaria Caneças

Rua Bernardino da Costa 36, Cais do Sodré (21 342 3748). Metro Cais do Sodré/tram 15, 18. **Open** 6.30am-7.30pm Mon-Fri; 6.30am-12.30pm Sat. **No credit cards**. **Map** p250 L10 ㉘

This café is famous for bread and cakes, and popular with commuters getting their caffeine fix on their way from Cais do Sodré station. It passes a crucial test for a *pastelaria*: the ability to make *sonhos* that don't sit in your stomach for hours.

Belém

Antiga Confeitaria de Belém

Rua de Belém 84-92 (21 363 7423). Train to Belém from Cais do Sodré/tram 15. **Open** 8am-11pm daily. **Credit** MC, V. **Map** p244 C10 ㉙

It's virtually a crime in Portugal to walk past here without popping in for some of the famous *pastéis de Belém* – warm creamy tarts with puff pastry made according to a secret recipe. Only three bakers know it and even the likes of Jamie Oliver have failed to emulate the distinctive taste and texture. On an average weekday 10,000 *pasteis* are sold; at weekends the figure rises to over 20,000. Customers with time to spare scoff them two at a time in a warren of rooms lined with tiles depicting Belém in the early 17th century. Others take them away by the half-dozen in specially designed cardboard tubes.

Northern Lisbon

Café Mexicana

Avenida Guerra Junqueiro 30C, Praça de Londres (21 848 6117). Metro Alameda. **Open** 8am-midnight daily. **Credit** AmEx, DC, MC, V. **Map** p249 N5 ㉚

Mexicana is handy for a drink or meal after a visit to one of the nearby cinemas, as it serves food in the panelled 1960s dining room until closing time.

Magnolia Caffé

Largo do Campo Pequeno 2, Campo Pequeno (21 795 9852/www.magnoliacaffe.com). Metro Areeiro/Campo Pequeno. **Open** 8am-8pm Mon-Fri; 10am-8pm Sat, Sun. **Credit** MC, V (dining area only). **Map** p249 M4 ㉛

It may be a chain but Magnolia exudes contemporary style. Choose your snack at the counter or take a seat in the more formal dining area. Newspapers and magazines are on hand.

Other locations: Avenida de Roma 7 (21 847 1163); Praça dos Restauradores 58 (21 342 1270); Galerias Saldanha Residence, Loja 0.06, Avenida Fontes Pereira de Melo 42 E, Saldanha (21 357 0434).

Pastelaria Versailles

Avenida da República 15A, Saldanha (21 354 6340). Metro Saldanha. **Open** 7.30am-10pm daily. **Credit** AmEx, MC, V. **Map** p249 M5 ㉜

Great for afternoon tea or late-night hot chocolate surrounded by chandeliers, carved wooden display cases and stained glass. There is a huge selection of cakes, meringues and pastries.

Shops & Services

From dusty nooks to gleaming malls.

Back from the ashes. **Armazéns do Chiado**.

Wander the streets of Lisbon and you'll soon see that, unlike so many other cities, the capital still has traditional shops that have been plying their wares for decades. This is because local lease laws allow shopkeepers to pay tiny rents, thus offering some protection from the spread of the chain store. But, beginning with Amoreiras in 1987, shopping centres are encroaching on Lisbon, and it's not just suburbanites who flock to them.

However, a stroll around Chiado and Baixa, Lisbon's retail area since the late 18th century, doesn't suggest decline – even if older businesses are gradually disappearing. Rua da Conceição is still bursting at the seams with colourful haberdashers, some with art nouveau storefronts, offering buttons, ribbons, tassels, lace, sequins and feather boas as well as various alteration services. There are many excellent cobblers working in hallways amid piles of shoes. Herbalists sell miracle teas for every ailment and you can still get a shave at a barber.

Along with quaint, traditional shops come quaint traditions: a *volto já* (back soon) sign may or may not mean what it says, and most family businesses close for a month in summer.

Shopping in Lisbon is often a social occasion and nowhere is this more evident than in the Bairro Alto. Here, many boutiques open mid-afternoon and close in the early hours; bars sell clothes and even tiny shops have DJs.

Further afield, hop off tram 28 at well-to-do Campo de Ourique and you'll find the streets are lined not only with trees, but also with upmarket boutiques, children's clothes shops, and stores selling furnishings and household goods. In no other residential neighbourhood could one imagine, for example, a shop selling only items featuring cats (Gatos & Gatafunhos, Rua Coelho da Rocha 85B, 21 396 5442, www.gatosgatafunhos.com).

One-stop shopping

Department store

El Corte Inglés

Avenida António Augusto de Aguiar 31, Praça de Espanha (21 371 1711/www.elcorteingles.pt). Metro São Sebastião. **Open** 10am-10pm Mon-Thur; 10am-11.30pm Fri, Sat. **Credit** AmEx, MC, V. **Map** p248 K5.

Lisbon was without a major department store after the 1988 Chiado fire destroyed two – until the Spanish chain El Corte Inglés opened its Lisbon branch in 2001. It includes cinemas, restaurants and ample parking as well as departments from stationery to surfwear. The store has a more upmarket image in Portugal than in Spain, providing good service and a money-back guarantee.

Shopping centres

Extended families flock to these centres. Typically anchored by a hypermarket, they have a fair few chains not represented on the high street, with extended opening hours. The nearest thing to a mall downtown is the Armazéns do Chiado, one of the former grand department stores restored after the 1998 fire. Its anchor is Fnac (*see p133*) and its food court has great views. There is a cluster of medium-sized shopping centres around Picoas and Saldanha, two with cinemas. For something different, head for the hive of ethnic shops in the Centro Comercial Mouraria (**photo** *p135*) in the northeastern corner of Largo Martim Moniz.

Outlet shopping is out of town. **Campera** (Estrada Nacional 3, Carregado, 263 850 030, www.camper.pt) has 120 shops from Nike and Benetton to decent quality Portuguese labels such as Salsa and Cheyenne. There are four free shuttles a day from Gare do Oriente (30mins). South of the river in Alcochete, **Freeport** (21 234 3501, www.freeport.pt) claims to be Europe's largest designer outlet, with more than 200 shops and permanent 50 per cent discounts. TST buses 431 and 432 (30mins) serve it, at least hourly, also from Gare do Oriente.

All three malls listed below contain a Lusomundo multiplex cinema (*see p160*).

Amoreiras

Avenida Engenheiro Duarte Pacheco, Amoreiras (21 381 0240/www.amoreiras.com). Metro Rato then 15min walk/bus 48, 53, 58, 711, 718, 723. **Open** 10am-11pm daily. **Credit** varies. **Map** p245 J7.

Architect Tomás Taveira based the design for Portugal's first shopping centre on the Brazilian concept of many small entrances making it easy to get in. However, a maze-like layout and poor signage make it difficult to find your way out. Has the usual chains, plus a chapel.

Centro Colombo

Avenida Lusíada, Benfica (21 711 3600/www.colombo.pt). Metro Colégio Militar-Luz. **Open** 10am-midnight daily. **Credit** varies.

The self-declared largest mall in Iberia boasts a wealth of foreign and Portuguese chains, a health club, golf driving range, bowling alley and funfair. Wheelchairs and pushchairs are available free and there are kiddycars for rent. The nursery, chapel and a breakdown service are downstairs by the car park.

Centro Vasco da Gama

Avenida Dom João II, Parque das Nações (21 893 0600/www.centrovascodagama.pt). Metro Oriente. **Open** 10am-midnight daily. **Credit** varies.

A trip here teams up well with a visit to the attractions at the former Expo site, Parque das Nações. Stores are clustered by genre, under a glass roof over which water flows constantly, soothing shoppers' frayed nerves. When you're done, go up to the beer deck and gaze out at the Tagus.

Antiques & bric-a-brac

Antique and bric-a-brac shops are clustered in Rua de São Bento, Rua Dom Pedro V, Rua do Alecrim and around the Sé. There's a cluster of junk shops around the Feira de Ladra (*see p147*).

Antiguidades Dolls

Rua de São Bento 250-54, São Bento (21 397 8151). Metro Rato/tram 28. **Open** 10.30am-1.30pm, 3-7pm Mon-Fri; 11am-1pm, 3-7pm Sat. **Credit** AmEx, DC, MC, V. **Map** p246 K8.

As you've probably guessed from the name, this place sells old toys. But apart from the toys there's also Portuguese furniture from the 17th to 19th centuries and some Indo-Portuguese art. The opening hours can be a little on the erratic side.

Filmoedas

Rua da Madalena 189, Baixa (21 887 8317). Metro Rossio. **Open** 9.30am-1pm, 2-6.30pm Mon-Fri. Closed Aug. **No credit cards. Map** p247 M9.

A numismatist's delight, Filmoedas sells notes and coins, mainly from Portugal and the ex-colonies, including Mozambican curreny from 1914 and Portuguese coins dating back to Dom Manuel I and Dom Duarte I. Numismática Notafilia Diamantino at No.89 is also worth a look.

Galeria da Arcada

Rua Dom Pedro V 49, Porta A, Bairro Alto (21 346 8518). Bus 58, 790. **Open** 10am-1pm, 3-7pm Mon-Sat. **Credit** AmEx, DC, MC, V. **Map** p250 L8.

An impressive collection of 15th- to 19th-century religious carvings, primarily from Portugal, ranging from tiny crucifixes right up to a life-size depiction of the Annunciation.

Mayer

Rua do Loreto 18, Chiado (21 342 2881). Metro Baixa-Chiado/tram 28. **Open** 10am-1pm, 3-7pm Mon-Fri. **No credit cards. Map** p250 L9.

This small shop buys and sells jewellery, cameras and other oddities for the collector.

Haberdashers in Chiado. *See p131*.

Soares & Sousa

Rua da Madalena 80A, Baixa (21 886 9212). Metro Rossio/tram 12, 28. **Open** 9am-1pm, 3-7pm Mon-Fri. Closed Aug. **No credit cards**. **Map** p251 M9.

A tiny shop with a great range of military paraphernalia from around the world, although Portugal and its ex-colonies dominate.

Art supplies & stationery

Casa Varela

Rua da Rosa 321, Bairro Alto (21 342 8205). Bus 58, 790. **Open** 10am-1pm, 3-7pm Mon; 9.30am-1pm, 3-7pm Tue-Fri; 10am-1pm Sat. **No credit cards**. **Map** p250 L9.

A large collection of artists' supplies, including paints, pencils and drawing materials, brushes, paper and easels. If you can't find what you're after here, try Casa Ferreira down the road at No.185.

Other locations: Avenida de Madrid 28B, Areeiro (21 848 4396).

Papelaria Fernandes

Rua Áurea (Rua do Ouro) 145, Baixa (21 322 4830/ www.papelariafernandes.pt). Metro Baixa-Chiado. **Open** 9am-7pm Mon-Sat. **Credit** AmEx, MC, V. **Map** p250 L9.

This century-old retailer sells mainly office essentials, cards and wrapping paper, but it also has a decent range of art supplies and, coming right up to date, a copy centre upstairs. There's a specialised art branch in Campo de Ourique (Rua Silva Carvalho 145, 21 386 1913).

Other locations: throughout the city.

Bookshops & newsagents

BdMania

Rua das Flores 67, Chiado (21 346 1208/www.bd mania.pt). Metro Baixa-Chiado/tram 28. **Open** 10.30am-7.30pm Mon-Sat. **Credit** AmEx, MC, V. **Map** p250 L9.

BdMania imports comics from the USA, France, Spain and Belgium, with, for the avid collector, all the related merchandise (posters, models, books and T-shirts) that anyone could want.

Fnac

Armazéns do Chiado, Rua do Carmo 2, Chiado (21 322 1800/www.fnac.pt). Metro Baixa-Chiado/tram 28. **Open** 10am-10pm daily. **Credit** AmEx, DC, MC, V. **Map** p250 L9.

A very good range of Portuguese literature in translation, plus lots of books in English, French and Spanish. The music department has Portuguese, fado, Brazilian, African, jazz, classical and world music as well as pop and rock. There's also a well-stocked computer accessories department, camera and audio-visual equipment, a concert box office and a café with a programme of films and recitals.

Other locations: Centro Colombo (21 711 4200, *see p132*).

Ler Devagar

Rua da Barroca 59, Bairro Alto (21 347 0336/www. lerdevagar.com). Metro Baixa-Chiado. **Open** 6pm-midnight Wed; 6pm-2am Thur-Sat. **Credit** AmEx, MC, V. **Map** p250 L8.

'Read Slowly' has long been an important cultural centre, but its current accommodation, by the entrance to gallery-bar Zé dos Bois (*see p162*), means there's no space for now for its traditional menu of concerts, debates and exhibitions. The English section has political and social science as well as literature and the arts; the shop is strongest in French-language and Portuguese titles. The branch at the Cinemateca specialises in film. **Photo** *p136*.

Other locations: Cinemateca Portuguesa, Rua da Rosa 145, Bairro Alto.

Livraria Bertrand

Rua Garrett 73-5, Chiado (21 346 8646/www. bertrand.pt). Metro Baixa-Chiado/tram 28. **Open** 9am-8pm Mon-Thur; 9am-10pm Fri, Sat; 2-8pm Sun. **Credit** AmEx, DC, MC, V. **Map** p250 L9.

Founded in 1732, this is Portugal's oldest bookshop. Apart from local literature, it stocks a reasonable selection of English novels, as well as guidebooks and foreign magazines.

Other locations: throughout the city.

Livraria Britânica

Rua de São Marçal 83, Príncipe Real (21 342 8472). Metro Rato. **Open** 9.30am-7pm Mon-Fri; 9.30am-1pm Sat. **Credit** AmEx, MC, V. **Map** p246 K8.

An English-language bookshop that specialises in study books but also stocks an excellent range of novels, classics, children's books, bestsellers and recent releases. Will also order.

Livraria Buchholz

Rua Duque de Palmela 4, Avenida da Liberdade (21 317 0580/www.buchholz.pt). Metro Marquês de Pombal. **Open** 9am-9pm Mon-Sat. **Credit** AmEx, MC, V. **Map** p246 L7.

German-founded generalist bookstore covering everything from astronomy to sociology. There's also gay literature, classical and traditional music, and books in English and other languages.

Press & periodicals

Tabacaria Monaco

Praça Dom Pedro IV (Rossio) 21 (21 346 8191). Metro Rossio. **Open** 9am-7pm Mon-Fri; 9am-5pm Sat. **No credit cards**. **Map** p250/1 L9/M9.

A wide range of European and US newspapers and a fair number of foreign glossies.

Tema

Avenida da Liberdade 9 (21 342 0140). Metro Restauradores. **Open** 9am-9pm daily. **Credit** AmEx (Colombo branch only), MC, V. **Map** p250 L8.

A tunnel of a shop offering one of the city's best selections of foreign newspapers and magazines.

Other locations: Centro Colombo (21 716 6890; *see p132*).

Second-hand & antiquarian

Loja das Coleçcões

Rua da Misericórdia 111-17, Bairro Alto (21 346 3057). Metro Baixa-Chiado/tram 28. **Open** 10am-1pm, 2.30-7pm Mon-Fri; 10am-1pm Sat. **Credit** AmEx, MC, V. **Map** p250 L9.

The English-speaking owner specialises in old Portuguese comics and children's books. There are also other books, prints, old movie star photos, ancient postcards and old board games stacked up.

O Manuscrito Histórico

Calçada do Sacramento 50, Chiado (21 346 4283). Metro Baixa-Chiado/tram 28. **Open** 10am-1pm, 2-7.30pm Mon-Fri; 9am-1pm Sat. **No credit cards**. **Map** p 250 L9.

Old books, maps and prints dating from the 16th century. Specialises in European manuscripts.

Computers

Netcetera

Edifício Amoreiras Square, Rua Joshua Benolieil 1F, Amoreiras (21 384 9486/www.netcetera.pt). Metro Rato. **Open** 10am-1pm, 2-7pm. **Credit** DC, MC, V.

A certified Apple Centre that offers repairs and maintenance and has a good reputation. The company does Microsoft too, as well as web solutions, systems configuration and general consulting.

Suprides Computadores

Avenida 24 de Julho 78, Santos (21 380 2080/ 91 955 6580/96 200 4582/93 320 5200/www. suprides.com). Train to Santos from Cais do Sodré/tram 15, 18. **Open** 1-8pm Mon-Fri; 10am-1pm Sat. **No credit cards**. **Map** p245 H8.

A reputable computer supplier, recently moved to larger premises. English-speaking technicians offer PC repairs as well as hardware and accessories.

Costume hire

Guarda-Roupa Anahory

Rua da Madalena 85, 3rd floor, Baixa (21 887 2046). Metro Baixa-Chiado/tram 12, 28. **Open** 10am-1pm, 2-7pm Mon-Fri. Closed Aug. **No credit cards**. **Map** p251 M10.

You can rent formal wear, period costumes and carnival outfits (the shop is open on the Saturday before carnival) for about €75 a day. The full range is kept in a warehouse, so call ahead; if what you want is not in stock, staff will make it up, given notice.

Design & household goods

In any major shopping centre you'll find dozens of Portuguese and international chains full of ideas for jazzing up your home. There's an out-of-town IKEA too (Zona Industrial de Alfragide, Estrada Nacional 117, 21 470 5050). For second-hand furniture, look in *Ocasião*, a weekly with some 50 pages of classifieds. In general, while you may have to hunt for Portuguese-designed artefacts, there are plenty of shops that peddle imported ones. You could start in the **Santos Design District** (21 397 4183, www.santosdesigndistrict.com), a council-sponsored project with late openings (to 10pm) on the last Thursday of the month. There are also plenty of furniture shops in the middle of Avenida Almirante Reis.

For tasteful gift ideas, the state-run **Loja dos Museus** (21 347 8333) next door to the tourist office in Praça dos Restauradores has good quality replicas of exhibits from the country's museums (many of which also have shops).

Alma Lusa

Rua do São Bento 363 B/C, Rato (21 388 4094/ www.almalusa.com). Metro Rato. **Open** 11.30am-7.30pm Mon-Sat. **Credit** DC, MC, V. **Map** p246 K9.

At the top of a road lined with antique shops, 'Portuguese Soul' promotes the work of contemporary indigenous designers: snazzy items for home and personal use. There is also a branch in the Chiado, where upmarket rival Nosso Design (Rua Serpa Pinto 12A, 21 325 8960) is located as well.

Other locations: Rua do Almirante Pessanha 10, Chiado (21 343 2039).

Atlantis Crystal

Centro Colombo, Avenida Lusíada, Benfica (21 711 1054). Metro Colégio Militar-Luz. **Open** 10am-midnight daily. **Credit** AmEx, DC, MC, V.

Handmade Portuguese lead crystal, from copies of 18th-century goblets to modern glassware.

Other locations: throughout the city.

Cozinhomania

Rua Coelho da Rocha 41A, Campo de Ourique (21 396 2006). Tram 25, 28. **Open** 10.30am-7pm Mon-Sat. **Credit** AmEx, DC, MC, V. **Map** p245 H8.

Run by cooking fanatics, as the name suggests, this kitchen equipment store stocks design items and culinary gadgets of every imaginable kind. Its famed cookery courses, some which focus exclusively on desserts, open a window on to Portuguese cuisine.

Cutipol

Rua do Alecrim 113-15, Chiado (21 322 5075/www. cutipol.pt). Metro Baixa-Chiado/tram 28. **Open** 10am-2pm, 3-7pm Tue-Sat. **Credit** AmEx, MC, V. **Map** p250 L9.

Leading Portuguese cutlery maker, selling both machine-produced and gold-trimmed, handmade pieces, in stainless steel or silver. Also sells other household goods. The Cascais store is by the station.

Other locations: Alameda Duque de Palmela Loja 3, Cascais (21 483 8913).

Depósito da Marinha Grande

Rua de São Bento 418-26, São Bento (21 396 3234/ 3096). Tram 28 then 10min walk/bus 6, 727, 773. **Open** 9am-1pm, 3-7pm Mon-Fri; 9am-1pm Sat. **Credit** AmEx, MC, V. **Map** p246 K8.

Exotic jewellery and more at **Centro Comercial Mouraria**. *See p132.*

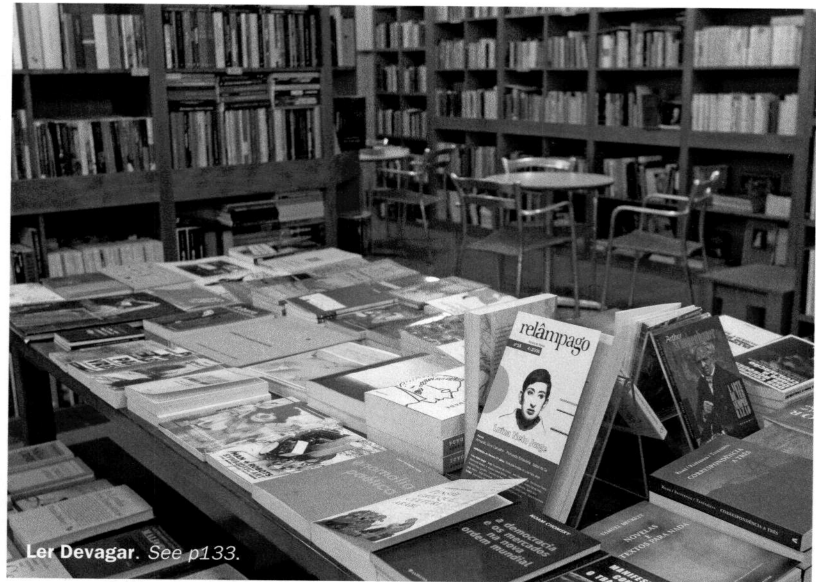

Ler Devagar. *See p133.*

Thousands of pieces of hand-blown glasswork in copies of old, unusual designs. Prices are reasonable, with large goblets selling for around €15. There's a sister shop down at No.234 (21 396 3234). **Photo** *p140.*
Other locations: Centro Colombo (21 716 3120; *see p132*).

Fábrica Features

Rua Garrett 83, 4th floor, Chiado (21 325 6765/ www.fabricafeatureslisboa.blogspot.com). Metro Baixa-Chiado. **Open** 10am-8pm Mon-Sat. **Credit** AmEx, DC, MC, V. **Map** p250/1 L9.
On the top floor of a large Benetton, this is one of only five spin-offs set up by the Italian company worldwide. It sells not only imported design but funky local artefacts, many using recycled materials. There's also an exhibition space with great views.

Interna Empório Casa

Rua Ivens 62, Chiado (21 340 5450). Metro Baixa-Chiado. **Open** 10.30am-7.30pm Mon-Sat. **Credit** MC, V. **Map** p246 K8.
One of Lisbon's longest established design stores, recently relocated from Príncipe Real. It carries kitchen gadgets, lamps, toys, office equipment and even food but disappointingly little of Portugal's excellent stainless steel cookware. For that, and less designer hype, head for a restaurant supplier such as Jotelar (Rua da Estrela 61, Estrela, 21 392 0560).

Izu Interiores

Rua Ivens 50, Chiado (21 347 6085/www-izu.pt). Metro Baixa-Chiado. **Open** 11am-3pm, 3.30-7pm Mon-Sat. **Credit** DC, MC, V.
The name of the store is something of a misnomer, as it sells more in the way of colourful knitwear and fair trade items than it does of household goods. Most of the stock is imported but if you look you'll be able to find some cool Portuguese jewellery and swinging Muu handbags.

Paris em Lisboa

Rua Garrett 77, Chiado (21 346 8885). Metro Baixa-Chiado. **Open** 10am-7pm Mon-Sat. **Credit** AmEx, DC, MC, V. **Map** p250/1 L9.
The name and façade are redolent of Portugal's 19th-century fixation with French style, but *senhoras bem* (posh ladies) still flock here today to stock up on towels and bed linen.

Pollux

Rua dos Fanqueiros 276, Baixa (21 881 1200/www.pollux.pt). Metro Rossio/tram 12, 15. **Open** 10am-7pm Mon-Sat. **Credit** AmEx, MC, V. **Map** p251 M10.
Nicknamed Pollux Bollocks by local expats, this nine-storey department store is jammed with things you never knew you needed – from crockery and kettles through orthopaedic pillows to camping gas.

Tom-Tom Shop

Rua do Século 4A-E & 19, Bairro Alto (21 347 9733). Metro Baixa-Chiado/tram 28. **Open** 11am-8pm Mon-Fri; 11am-7pm Sat. **Credit** AmEx, MC, V. **Map** p246 K9.
Stylish homeware, designer kitchenware and a good selection of lights, teapots, picture frames and door knobs. Lots of cheap gift possibilities.

Vista Alegre

Largo do Chiado 20-21, Chiado (21 346 1401/ www.vistaalegre.pt). Metro Baixa-Chiado/tram 28. **Open** 10am-7pm Mon-Sat. **Credit** AmEx, DC, MC, V. **Map** p250 L9.

Vista Alegre is the best-known Portuguese porcelain manufacturer, stocking a wide range of crockery, vases, plates and bowls. These include traditional designs, oriental-inspired styles and modern classics. Centro Colombo (*see p132*) houses one of many branches, as well as a Casa Alegre sister shop (21 716 4479) with trendier, cheaper lines. **Other locations**: throughout the city.

Dry cleaners & laundries

Most *lavandarias* offer both *limpeza a seco* (dry cleaning) and *roupa branca* (general laundry, often defined as only high-volume items). Dry cleaning costs between €2 and €5 per item; laundry around €2.50 per kilo. The ubiquitous **5 à Sec**, with branches around the city (in the Baixa there's one at Rua dos Correeiros 105-7), offers the usual services.

Lavandaria Salitre

Rua Nova de São Mamede 54, Rato (21 388 5328). Metro Rato. **Open** 10am-2pm Mon-Fri; 9am-1pm Sat. **No credit cards**. **Map** p250/1 M10.

General dry cleaning plus special treatment for curtains, tapestries and carpets; also washing and ironing of linen, and monthly ironing contracts. If you need a hem or anything more complicated, Dona Teresa in the branch round the corner at Rua de Salitre 171A (open 10am-2pm Mon-Fri) offers a reliable alterations service.

Lava Neve

Rua da Alegria 37-9, Avenida da Liberdade (21 346 6195). Metro Avenida. **Open** 10am-1pm, 3-7pm Mon-Fri; 9am-1pm Sat. **No credit cards**. **Map** p246 L8.

Both DIY or service washes cost €5.10 for a wash or €13.60 for wash and tumble dry, including detergent. Ironing and dry cleaning services are also offered.

Fashion

The Portuguese have long tended to dress conservatively, but things are taking a turn for the flamboyant. For club- and streetwear Bairro Alto is your best bet, though beware poor quality imports sold with a hefty mark-up. You'll find chains such as Zara and Mango throughout the city, but international label junkies should prowl Avenida da Liberdade. There's a Fashion Clinic (21 314 2828) in the Tivoli Forum shopping centre halfway up it. The same avenue showcases posher Portuguese brands such as the venerable **Rosa & Teixeira** (No.204, 21 311 0350), for men's suits, shirts and ties, and **Lanidor**. Chiado also has lots to offer. For local designers, *see p145* **After their own fashion**. For shoe shops, *see p139*.

Most Portuguese clothes stores retain seamstresses to do alterations (*arranjos*), so if something doesn't fit then you can be measured up, pay a small fee, and pick up the item a couple of days later. Some dry cleaners also do alterations, *see above*.

Agência 117

Rua do Norte 117, Bairro Alto (21 346 1270/ www.agencia117.com). Metro Baixa-Chiado/tram 28. **Open** 2pm-midnight Mon-Sat. **Credit** AmEx, MC, V. **Map** p250 N9.

Sneakers, sexy slip dresses, cut-off T-shirts and assorted 1970s-inspired clothes, plus a trendy hairdresser. Two doors down at No.113 and sharing an owner and opening hours, Fake (21 342 1578) sells Jean-Paul Gaultier gear, a range of sneakers and its own-label clothes, and doubles as a bar.

A Outra Face da Lua

Rua da Assunção 22, Baixa (21 886 3430/www. aoutrafacedalua.com). Metro Baixa-Chiado or Rossio/tram 12, 28. **Open** 10am-8pm Mon-Sat. **Credit** AmEx, MC, V. **Map** p250 L9.

Recycled and second-hand clothes, plus retro gear such as flower-power minis and wide-collared polyester shirts. The shop also stocks vintage wallpaper and other decorative objects, smoking paraphernalia, kitsch Portuguese tin toys and gadgets, and lots of different teas. Also a temporary tattoo service. **Other locations**: Calçada do Correio Velho 7, Sé (21 886 3186).

Eldorado

Rua do Norte 23-5, Bairro Alto (21 342 3935). Metro Baixa-Chiado/tram 28. **Open** 1-11pm Mon-Fri; 1pm-midnight Sat. **Credit** AmEx, MC, V. **Map** p250 L9.

One of Lisbon's first alternative clothes shops, selling new and second-hand retro gear, mostly from London. The stress is on the 1960s and 1970s, but there are also Adidas tops, leather jackets, hats and bags. There's a music section too. **Other locations**: Amoreiras (21 383 1836; *see p132*).

Gardénia

Rua Garrett 54, Chiado (21 342 1207/www.lojas-gardenia.pt). Metro Baixa-Chiado/tram 28. **Open** 9.30am-9.30pm Mon-Thur; 10am-10pm Fri, Sat; 1-8pm Sun. **Credit** AmEx, DC, MC, V. **Map** p250 L9.

The shoe selection is slightly less outrageous than it was, but with Donna Karan sneakers and Fluxá boots, Gardénia still draws the serious shoe fetishists. Sells some foreign clothing brands too. **Other locations**: Centro Vasco da Gama (21 896 0009; *see p132*).

Lanidor

Avenida da Liberdade 129B, Avenida da Liberdade (21 325 6735/www.lanidor.com). Metro Avenida. **Open** 10am-7.30pm Mon-Sat. **Credit** AmEx, DC, MC, V. **Map** p250/1 L8.

Port-able

Port is a cornerstone of Portuguese identity: one of the world's great wines and unique to Portugal. As a fortified, sweet wine perennially associated with elderly gentlemen it is not cool, but it has managed to transcend fashion and maintain a niche in world markets.

Lisbon does not produce port – the real stuff can only come from the Douro valley, fortified with *aguardente* by shippers based in Vila Nova de Gaia (across the river from Oporto), but the capital has plenty of shops that sell it. This is a guide to what to look for.

Port is traditionally divided into two broad categories: wood aged and bottle aged. The former is a feast of aromas: dried fruit, walnut shell, toast or burnt wood – you name it, you'll be able to sniff it. Bottle-aged port is deep and dark when young, with herbal and fruit aromas, gradually developing other flavours such as pepper, raisins and truffles as it ages.

Vintage port is the king of bottle-aged ports. It is wine from a single harvest, bottled after two or three years and then supposedly left to mature for at least a decade. In reality much hits the market soon after bottling, to be scooped up by eager consumers. Since this is the industry's top product it is important to maintain quality. Ultimately, the Port Wine Institute in Oporto is the guardian of this, but shippers make their own assessments before submitting a wine for certification. In the old days, when few shippers owned vineyards and most bought wine from farmers, it made sense to get together to discuss the quality of the harvest before each decided whether to declare the result as vintage. Today, when shippers own the best vineyards and are involved in all stages of production, such confabs look more like an exercise in controlling supply.

Many shippers also put out second-label vintages in years when they don't declare a normal vintage – 'declaring', if you like, their ability to make near vintage-quality wine every year. These are often called 'single quinta' wines, meaning they were made with grapes from a single estate rather than blended from several, as with a normal vintage.

Late-bottled vintage refers to wine from one year that has been kept in wood for between four and six years. If then bottled without filtration, it is known as a 'traditional' LBV and may compare well with a vintage. Filtered LBV can also be good.

With rare exceptions, 'vintage character port' is a labelling ploy – at best, it will be a good-quality ruby (*see below*). The opposite is true of **crusted port**: a blend of wines from several years, bottled young without filtration (hence the 'crust' or deposit that forms), it offers vintage-like qualities at a good price.

Wood-aged port has long been termed **tawny**, but most tawnies are now neither tawny in colour nor particularly interesting. They really need ten years in wood, but most have spent nowhere near that long. The right colour is sometimes achieved by blending red port with white, but that does nothing for flavour. Look for labels that describe the wine as 10, 20, 30, 40 or over 40 years old. These are legally binding (being the average age of wines in the blend), unlike terms such as fine, old, aged and reserve. If you baulk at the prices, you may be better off seeking out a ruby, which is an honestly young port.

Solar do Vinho do Porto

Rua de São Pedro de Alcântara 45, Bairro Alto (21 347 5707/www.ivp.pt). Metro Baixa-Chiado or Restauradores then 10min walk/bus 58, 790. **Open** 11am-midnight Mon-Fri; 2pm-midnight Sat. **Credit** AmEx, DC, MC, V. **Map** p250/1 L9.
A cool haven on the ground floor of the mid 18th-century São Pedro de Alcântara Palace. Waiters serve port by the glass from a menu of more than 200; you can also buy bottles.

Lanidor offers stylish and restrained women's fashion plus clothes for children and young teens. This is definitely one of the more up-market Portuguese brands, so you know what to expect in terms of both price and quality. Should you require a break from shopping the space also has a café restaurant, where you can get a reasonably priced lunch. There are Lanidor branches in all Lisbon's main shopping centres, or you can order online.
Other locations: throughout the city.

Mocho

Rua Almeida e Sousa 36A, Campo de Ourique (21 388 8346). Tram 25, 28. **Open** 9am-1pm, 3-7pm Mon-Fri; 10am-1pm Sat. **Credit** AmEx, DC, MC, V. **Map** p245 H7/J8.
Mocho is a neighbourhood boutique which sells women's ready to wear clothing. You'll find fashions ideal to wear to a business meeting or that little something more dressy ideal for a fancy dinner, and its own atelier can produce items to order.

Nunes Corrêa

Rua Augusta 250, Baixa (21 324 0930). Metro Baixa-Chiado/tram 28. **Open** 10am-7pm Mon-Sat. **Credit** AmEx, DC, MC, V. **Map** p251 M9.
This store's founder, Jacinto Nunes Corrêa, was tailor to the royal family in the late 19th century. It is one of several in the Baixa continuing the tradition of made-to-measure suits; delivery takes around a month. Ready-to-wear names such as Armani and Gant, sportswear and an exclusive range of shoes made by a sister company are available.

Oficina Mustra

Rua Rodrigues Sampaio 81, Avenida da Liberdade (91 251 7015). Metro Avenida. **Open** 10am-7pm Mon-Sat. **Credit** AmEx, DC, MC, V. **Map** p246 L7.
Off-the-peg and made-to-measure suits designed by a former creative director for an Italian clothing company with extensive experience in made to measure. Veríssimo Mustra sends designs to Naples where a team of tailors stitches them together using fine Italian and British fabrics. Accessories include scarves, bags and shoes.

Osklen

Rua do Carmo 9, Chiado (21 325 8844). Metro Baixa-Chiado. **Open** 10am-8pm Mon-Sat. **Credit** AmEx, DC, MC, V. **Map** p250/1 L9.
Hip Brazilian casual wear label that so far has European shops only here and in Italy. The chic, modern pieces aren't cheap, but can make you the best dressed bunny on the beach.

Rulys

Rua Nova do Almada 89-101, Chiado (21 342 0017/ www.rulys.pt). Metro Baixa-Chiado. **Open** 11am-8pm Mon-Fri; 10am-8pm Sat; 2-7pm Sun. **Credit** AmEx, MC, V. **Map** p250/1 L9/10.
This 'megastore' is the first Lisbon showcase for a Portuguese brand with an established presence up north. It has mid-priced casual clothing and accessories for men and women, designed with an eye to international trends (nothing too daring). A bit more quality and variety than Zara.

Jewellery & accessories

With three streets named after the trade (still appropriately so), the Baixa is the place to head for jewellery and silverware, as well as other accessories such as hats and gloves.

Araújos

Rua Áurea (Rua do Ouro) 261, Baixa (21 346 7810). Metro Rossio. **Open** 10am-1pm, 2.30-7pm Mon-Fri; 10am-1pm Sat. **Credit** AmEx, MC, V. **Map** 250 L9
An established jeweller with unusual gold and silver pieces, some of them copies of old designs.

Azevedo Rua

Praça Dom Pedro IV (Rossio) 69 & 72-3 (21 342 7511). Metro Rossio. **Open** 9.30am-7pm Mon-Fri; 9am-1pm Sat. **Credit** AmEx, MC, V. **Map** p250 L9.
Rossio used to be home to a whole community of hatters, though only this one, founded in 1886, now remains. Black, rabbitskin feltro hats (worn by Portuguese horsemen), or the style favoured by Fernando Pessoa, are stacked up to the ceiling in original wooden cabinets. There's also a large range of berets, Panama hats and bowlers.

Casa Batalha

Armazéns do Chiado, Rua do Carmo 2, Chiado (21 342 7313). Metro Baixa-Chiado/tram 28. **Open** 10am-10pm daily. **Credit** AmEx, DC, MC, V. **Map** p250 L9.
This family-run *bijutaria* (costume jeweller) offers a chic range of pieces, as well as hats, scarves and a colourful array of sequins and beads. There's also a facelift service for tired evening wear and handbags.
Other locations: Amoreiras (21 383 1891, *see p132*); Centro Colombo (21 716 3862, *see p132*); Galerias Saldanha, Avenida Fontes Pereira de Melo 42E, Saldanha (21 315 2079); Centro Vasco da Gama (21 895 5601, *see p132*).

Luvaria Ulisses

Rua do Carmo 87A, Chiado (21 342 0295). Metro Baixa-Chiado/tram 28. **Open** 10am-7pm Mon-Sat. **Credit** DC, MC, V. **Map** p250 L9.
Rows of drawers contain exquisite gloves indexed by size, colour and material, available in quarter sizes. There are leather, satin, lace, crocheted and sporting varieties, lined with fur, cashmere, cotton or silk. A pair of regular kidskin gloves costs from €50. They come with a simple guarantee: a free, unlimited repair service.

Ourivesaria Aliança

Rua Garrett 50, Chiado (21 342 3419). Metro Baixa-Chiado/tram 28. **Open** 3-7pm Mon; 11am-7pm Tue-Fri; 11am-1.30pm Sat. **No credit cards**. **Map** p 250 L9.
Worth a visit for the elaborate, gilded room, decorated in the style of Louis XV. There's a nice selection of silver trinkets, pendants, watches, cufflinks and pillboxes, some of them second-hand.

Pedra Dura

Edifício Monumental, Loja 7, Avenida Praia Vitória 71, Saldanha (21 315 2324/www.pedradura.net). Metro Saldanha. **Open** 10am-11pm Mon-Thur, Sun; 10am-midnight Fri, Sat. **Credit** AmEx, DC, MC, V. **Map** p249 M5.
Deservedly successful *bijutaria* whose unusual designs – some imported and many exclusive – stress fantasy rather than ostentation. Items are stashed in drawers, adding a sense of discovery. **Photo** *p142*.
Other locations: Centro Colombo (*see p132*); Cascais Villa, Avenida Marginal, Cascais (21 483 8610).

Shoes

Footwear is one of Portugal's traditional industries, and it shows in an abundance of shoe shops. Prices are competitive, but watch out for quality if they seem too cheap to be true.

Depósito da Marinha Grande. *See p134.*

Leading brands include **Charles** (www.charles.pt), with two branches on Rua Augusta (No.109 & No.275A). For a more funky approach, try **Gardénia** (*see p137*) or the Bairro Alto. If only Italian imports will do, try **Stivali** (Rua Castilho 71C, Marquês de Pombal, 21 386 0944).

Aerosoles

Rua do Carmo 79, Chiado (21 322 3670/www.aerosoles.eu). Metro Rossio/Baixa-Chiado. **Open** 10am-7.30pm Mon-Fri; 10am-7pm Sat. **Credit** AmEx, DC, MC, V. **Map** p250/1 L9.

Aerosoles manages the unusual feat of combining comfort with style. The company is one of the few Portuguese manufacturers to have built a brand abroad (though in the UK it has been limited by its contract supplying M&S).

Other locations: throughout the city.

Seaside

Largo Dom Pedro IV (Rossio) 57, Baixa (21 346 2072). Metro Rossio/Restauradores. **Open** 10am-8pm Mon-Fri; 10am-7.30pm Sat; 2-7pm Sun. **Credit** AmEx, MC, V. **Map** p250 M9.

At the cheaper end of the scale, this shop sells functional men's and women's styles on three floors. Most are made in Portugal (despite English- and Italian-sounding brand names) though some are from Spain.

Other locations: throughout the city.

Sneakers Delight

Rua do Norte 32, Bairro Alto (21 347 9976/www.sneakersdelight.pt). Metro Baixa-Chiado/tram 28. **Open** 1-11pm Mon-Thur; 1-11.30pm Fri, Sat. **Credit** AmEx, MC, V. **Map** p250 L9.

Specialises in, well, sneakers. After 7pm at weekends a DJ will help you test the boogiebility of the footwear on offer.

Other locations: Avenida Infante Dom Henrique, Armazém B, Santa Apolónia (21 882 2855).

Florists

Flores da Romeira Roma

Avenida de Roma 50C, Avenidas Novas (21 848 8289). Metro Roma. **Open** 8am-10pm Mon-Sat. **Credit** AmEx, DC, MC, V. **Map** p249 N4.

A veritable warehouse of cut flowers and potted plants. Credit cards can only be used in the shop; for telephone orders, payment by cash or cheque will be collected first. Helpful staff speak English, are with Interflora and deliver until 11pm seven days a week.

Horto do Campo Grande

Campo Grande 171, Avenidas Novas (21 782 6660/www.hortodocampogrande.com). Metro Campo Grande. **Open** 9am-7pm daily. **Credit** V. **Map** p248 L1.

An enormous garden centre selling all manner of flora, from bonsai trees to 7m-high (23ft) palms and giant cacti. The florist here does Interflora and the centre offers gardening services and plant rental.

Food & drink

There's a *mercearia* (grocer) on every other corner and any number of *padarias* (bakeries) and *talhos* (butchers). At the other extreme are the hypermarkets, successfully luring away ever more customers. For tips on buying port, *see p138* **Port-able**.

Bread & cakes

Look out for *pastelarias* (cake shops) bearing the words *fábrico próprio* – made on the premises. Biscuits are often sold by the kilo and all *pastelarias* will box up your purchases *para levar* (to take away). See also Antiga Confeitaria de Belém (*see p130*), which offers what are generally held to be the city's best *pastéis de nata* (custard tarts).

Panificação do Chiado

Calçada do Sacramento 26, Chiado (21 342 4044/ www.panificacaodochiado.pt). Metro Baixa-Chiado. **Open** 7am-7pm Mon-Fri; 8am-7pm Sat. **No credit cards**. **Map** p250 L9.

A bakery founded in 1917 that's bang up to date: as well an array of traditional Portuguese breads and cakes, it now churns out pita, oregano bread, focacia and bagels. The bread recipe used specially for the late dictator Salazar was recently dusted off.

Foreign delis

Despite the huge range of goods stocked by hypermarkets, there are products they don't have. For a concentration of delis, try Centro Comercial Mouraria (Largo Martin Moniz), a warren of ethnic shops and cafés.

GB Store

Avenida Gago Coutinho Lote 4, São João do Estoril (21 466 2453). Train to São João do Estoril from Cais do Sodré. **Open** 9am-7pm Mon-Fri; 10am-6pm Sat. **Credit** AmEx, MC.

Minimarket selling exclusively UK imports, much frequented by homesick expats stocking up on Shreddies, PG Tips and Club biscuits. For Christmas puds, stuffing mix and Christmas crackers, get your order in before mid November.

Portuguese delis

Charcutaria Brasil

Rua Alexandre Herculano 90, Rato (21 388 5644). Metro Rato. **Open** 7am-9pm Mon-Fri; 7am-2pm Sat. **Credit** V. **Map** p246 K7.

Wines, cheeses, ham, sausages and other local deli produce. A takeaway counter features spit-roasted chickens and typical dishes. During the hunting season you may see hares and pheasants, complete with fur or feathers.

Charcutaria Moy

Rua Dom Pedro V 111, Príncipe Real (21 346 7011). Metro Rato/bus 58, 790. **Open** 10am-8pm Mon-Thur; 10am-9pm Fri, Sat; 10am-5pm Sun. **No credit cards**. **Map** p250/1 L8.

A pricey delicatessen stocking French and Italian luxury foods, as well as good quality local products.

Manteigaria Silva

Rua Dom Antão de Almada 1C-D, Baixa (21 342 4905). Metro Rossio. **Open** 9am-7pm Mon-Sat. **Credit** AmEx, MC, V. **Map** p251 M9.

The Portuguese have been eating *bacalhau* (salt cod) for centuries. It's sold dried and salted, and the smelly, kite-shaped cod carcasses are stacked up whole ready for chopping to order. Alternatively, you can buy *caras* (faces) and *línguas* (tongues). The shop also stocks canned fish and has a cheese and *presunto* (cured ham) counter.

Manuel Tavares

Rua da Betesga 1A-B, Baixa (21 342 4209). Metro Rossio. **Open** 9.30am-7.30pm Mon-Sat. **Credit** AmEx, DC, MC, V. **Map** p251 M9.

A vast range of *chouriço* (sausage) including *morçelas* (black pudding) and *chouriço doce* (with honey and almonds). Also *presunto*, smoked pig's tongues, Portuguese cheese, dried fruit, *bacalhau* and port.

Martins & Costa

Rua Alexandre Herculano 34, Marquês de Pombal (21 314 1617). Metro Marquês de Pombal. **Open** 9am-7pm Mon-Fri; 9am-1pm Sat. **Credit** MC, V. **Map** p246 L7.

A mouth-watering range of Portuguese and foreign gourmet treats: smelly cheeses, smoked meat and fish, wines, pastries and cakes that are cooked on the premises. Imported goods include Marmite, mint sauce and specialist teas – none of 'em cheap.

Supermarkets & hypermarkets

Lisbon's hypermarkets are usually housed in shopping centres: Continente, Pão de Açucar/ Jumbo or Carrefour, all much the same in price and selection. Stand-alone supermarket Pingo

Open wide the drawers of delight at **Pedra Dura**. *See p139*.

Doce has numerous downtown branches, as does the more limited but better value Minipreço. The El Corte Inglés department store (*see p131*) has a posher supermarket and vast gourmet section in the basement.

Mercado Praça da Figueira

Praça da Figueira 10B, Rossio (21 886 7464). Metro Rossio. **Open** 8.30am-8pm Mon-Fri; 8.30am-7pm Sat. **Credit** AmEx, MC, V. **Map** p250/1 M9.

A narrow entrance lined with fruit displays opens out into a small supermarket. It's an atmospheric place to shop, with original Pombaline arches and beams, and lined with *azulejos* (added later).

Tea & coffee

A Carioca

Rua da Misericórdia 9, Chiado (21 346 9567/21 342 0377). Metro Baixa-Chiado/tram 28. **Open** 9am-7pm Mon-Fri; 9am-1pm Sat. **No credit cards.** **Map** p250 L9.

Everything from cheap coffee at €1.80 per kilo to specialist beans costing up to €19 per kilo. Staff make up blends on request and grind them to suit your coffee-maker; they're also happy to let you taste other products. Established since 1936.

Casa Pereira

Rua Garrett 38, Chiado (21 342 6694). Metro Baixa-Chiado/tram 28. **Open** 9am-1pm, 3-7pm Mon, Sat; 9am-7pm Tue-Fri. **No credit cards.** **Map** p250 L9.

Old, established shop selling imported coffee from Timor, Brazil and other ex-colonies. These days it also has imported tea, biscuits and chocolates.

Vegetarian & health food

Ambiência (21 456 0477, www.ambiencia.pt) delivers baskets of organic food throughout the region. Food from organic shop **Origens** comes via the no menu service (21 381 3939/93 381 3939, www.no-menu.com).

BioCoop

Rua Salgueiro Maia 14, Figo Maduro, Prior Velho (21 941 0479/www.biocoop.coop). Bus 5, 25, 45, 81. **Open** 11am-8pm Tue-Fri; 8am-2pm Sat. **No credit cards.**

Lisbon's only proper organic market is by the entrance to a military airfield, on the city's municipal limits. It has plenty of treats if you arrive early from Thursday to Saturday. (There is no fresh bread or meat, and less fresh produce in general, on Tuesday and Wednesday.) If you bus it, ask the driver to set you down by Figo Maduro. If you go by taxi, be prepared to map-read.

Celeiro Dieta

Rua 1° de Dezembro 65, Baixa (21 030 60 30). Metro Rossio. **Open** 8.30am-8pm Mon-Fri; 8.30am-7pm Sat. **Credit** AmEx, MC, V. **Map** p250 L9

Health food chain selling vegan products, cereals, beans, pulses, vitamins, herbal cures and vitamin supplements. There's also a decent selection of health-giving breads and organic vegetables (these mainly imported), a range of books upstairs, and a self-service restaurant in the basement.

Other locations: throughout the city.

Wine & alcohol

Wine, port and Madeira are the obvious reasons to head for a *garrafeira* (drinks shop). There are also excellent fortified muscat wines, particularly Moscatel de Setúbal. Local liqueurs include Licor Beirão (with herbs), Amêndoa Amarga (with bitter almond) and *ginjinha* (with morello cherries, *see p191* **Cherry aid**). There are also stronger options such as *aguardente* (wine distillate, or brandy in other words) and *bagaçeira* (Portugal's *grappa*, distilled from the skins and stems of grapes). Portuguese absinthe is a misnomer: it contains neither the legendary ingredients such as wormwood nor the alcohol level (68 per cent) of the stuff Baudelaire drank. For a guide to buying port, *see p138* **Port-able**.

Adivinho

Travessa do Almada 24, Sé (21 886 0419). Tram 12, 28/bus 37. **Open** 11am-8pm Mon-Sat. **Credit** AmEx, DC, MC, V. **Map** p250/1 M10.

A large shop in a restored Pombaline building opened in 2004 by a French couple – she from a wine-producing family, he an economist. It covers all Portugal's regions, and there are free tastings, plus more serious paid seminars. They ship abroad.

Garrafeira de Campo de Ourique

Rua Tomás da Anunciação 29A, Campo de Ourique (21 397 3494). Tram 28. **Open** 9am-7.30pm Mon-Fri; 9am-1pm, 3-7.30pm Sat. **Credit** AmEx, MC, V. **Map** p245 N9.

One of Lisbon's best shops in terms of variety, especially for ports and spirits. Browsing is enjoyable, but ask if you can't find what you want – there is stock hidden elsewhere.

Garrafeira Nacional

Rua de Santa Justa 18-24, Baixa (21 887 9080). Metro Baixa-Chiado/tram 12, 28. **Open** 9.30am-7.30pm Mon-Fri; 9am-1pm Sat. **Credit** AmEx, DC, MC, V. **Map** p251 M9.

Over 4,000 different Portuguese wines and ports (plus the country's largest range of malt whiskies). There's also a selection of crystallised fruit. Staff are helpful and shipping can be arranged. **Photo** *p146*.

Napoleão

Rua dos Fanqueiros 70, Baixa (21 887 2042/www.napoleao.co.pt). Metro Baixa-Chiado/tram 12, 28. **Open** 9.30am-8pm Mon-Sat. **Credit** AmEx, MC, V. **Map** p251 M10.

Multilingual staff help you choose from the wide range of Portuguese wines and ports, which can be shipped. To add to the experience, there's a Roman ruin visible through a glass floor.

Other locations: throughout the city.

Handicrafts

Azulejos (*see* *p32* **Lisbon's got the blues**) the beautiful blue tiles that you see decorating many of the city's buildings, are some of the most popular Lisbon souvenirs. There's plenty of poor quality tourist tat in the shops but a little care (and this guide) will ensure that you take home some of the fine hand-painted, contemporary and antique tiles that are available. There are also distinctive regional ceramics and pottery, textiles from linen tablecloths to woollen blankets, and *bordado* (embroidery) – the most expensive of which comes from Madeira and, if genuine, carries a seal guaranteeing authenticity.

A Arte da Terra

Rua Augusto Rosa 40, Sé (21 274 5975/www.aartedaterra.pt). Tram 12, 28/bus 37. **Open** 10am-8pm Tue-Sat. **Credit** AmEx, DC, MV, V. **Map** p251 M10.
Displayed in stone mangers in the 12th-century former stables of the Sé cathedral is an immense variety of handicrafts and other *típico* products. Linen, embroidery, rustic clothing, fado and folk CDs, toys and pottery – including dozens of traditional figurines of the city's favourite son, Santo António. In fact, why go anywhere else? You could easily get all your souvenirs right here.

Loja Portugal Rural

Rua Saraiva de Carvalho 216-20, Campo de Ourique (21 395 8889). Tram 25, 28/bus 9. **Open** 10am-8pm Mon-Sat. **No credit cards**. **Map** p245 H8.
A large shop devoted to promoting regional products, stocking ceramics, metalwork and other decorative creations, as well as handcrafted wooden toys, rag dolls, clogs, woollen jackets and rugs. It also has an excellent delicatessen.

Santos Ofícios Artesanatos

Rua da Madalena 87, Baixa (21 887 2031/www.santosoficios-artesanato.pt). Metro Rossio/tram 28. **Open** 10am-8pm Mon-Sat. **Credit** AmEx, MC, V. **Map** p251 M10.
A cut above the usual tacky tourist shops, stocking a fine selection of handmade blankets, rugs, toys, pottery, clothes and baskets. The newer Nós por Cá down the road at No.76 (21 886 2631) has a funkier take on things, with unusual tile designs and bags made of coffee packets sewn together.

Tiles

Ratton

Rua Academia das Ciências 2C, São Bento (21 346 0948). Tram 28. **Open** 10am-1.30pm, 3-7pm Mon-Fri. **No credit cards**. **Map** p246 K9.
Contemporary designs, in collaboration with Portuguese and foreign artists, including Júlio Pomar and Paula Rego. The gallery has some temporary exhibits but most designs are in catalogues; reproductions cost €45-€50 per tile.

Sant'Anna

Rua do Alecrim 95, Chiado (21 342 2537/www.fabrica-santanna.com). Metro Baixa-Chiado/tram 28. **Open** 9.30am-7pm Mon-Fri; 10am-2pm Sat. **Credit** AmEx, DC, MC, V. **Map** p250 L10.
Sant'Anna has been producing handmade tiles since 1741 and sells copies of designs dating from the 17th and 18th centuries. It's worth dropping in if you're about to retile your bathroom or kitchen. They're happy to manufacture to order and ship abroad.
Other locations: Factory showroom, Calçada da Boa-Hora 96, Ajuda (21 363 8292).

Solar

Rua Dom Pedro V 68-70, Bairro Alto (21 346 5522). Bus 58, 790. **Open** 10am-7pm Mon-Fri; 10am-1pm Sat. **Credit** AmEx. **Map** p246 L8.
An incredible collection of over half a million antique *azulejos* from the 15th to 19th centuries, displayed chronologically. They come mainly from old palaces, churches and houses.

Viúva Lamego

Largo do Intendente 25, Martim Moniz (21 885 2408/www.viuvalamego.com). Metro Intendente. **Open** 10am-7pm Mon-Fri; 10am-2pm Sat. **Credit** AmEx, DC, MC, V. **Map** p246 M8.
In Lisbon's seediest neighbourhood – a once pretty square that is now a scuzzy red-light district – this shop has been in business since 1849. Its tiles now cover many of Lisbon's Metro stations (*see* *p32* **Lisbon's got the blues**). Most of the large selection of hand-painted tiles are copies of old designs but new ones can be made to order and shipped worldwide.
Other locations: Calçada do Sacramento 29, Chiado (21 346 9692).

Health & beauty

Cosmetics & perfumes

Perfumes & Companhia

Edifício Grandela, Rua do Carmo 42C, Chiado (21 347 9552). Metro Baixa-Chiado/tram 28. **Open** 10am-7.30pm Mon-Sat. **Credit** AmEx, DC, MC, V. **Map** p250 L9.
A great range of upmarket perfumes and cosmetics from the major French houses. Free testers mean you could come out smelling like a tart's handbag.
Other locations: throughout the city.

Hairdressers & barbers

Most *cabeleireiros* (hairdressers) will give a decent man's trim for €8. Some also offer a cut, shave, manicure, pedicure and shoeshine. Upscale ones such as **Elvira Guedes** (Edifício Castilho, Loja 15, Rua Castilho 39, Marquês de Pombal, 21 353 3278) are now offering massages and aromatherapy as well. African salons and specialist shops cluster in the south-east corner of Largo Martim Moniz and in the Centro Comercial Mouraria, at its northern end.

After their own fashion

Portuguese fashion design has a short history, although northern manufacturers have long made the clothing and shoes that has then gone on to be marketed by the better-known international labels. Local pioneer Ana Salazar launched her own-label collection as recently as the early 1980s, though she was making fashion statements long before. During the last years of the Salazar regime, she was jazzing things up with clothes imported from London and sold in her shop, Maçã. In the 1970s it was one of the 'in' places for cool, revolutionary threads. And then, towards the end of the 1980s the Bairro Alto nightlife scene made the place a magnet for young designers. As some became established they moved to neighbouring, posher Chiado: the distinction is largely intact today.

It's only in the past 15 years or so that a real local fashion industry has grown up, with design schools opening and regular catwalk events featuring rising talent in addition to some of the top names in Portuguese design. Regular shows in Lisbon and Oporto as well as, more occasionally, São Paulo, New York and Paris, see the participation of the names listed below, and the likes of Anabela Baldaque, Luís Buchinho, Paulo Cravo and Nuno Baltazar, Nuno Gama, Maria Gambina and Miguel Vieira. To browse the latest collections of those listed here, and many others, see www.modalisboa.pt (click on designers.pt) or, alternatively, www.portugalfashion.com.

Ana Salazar

Rua do Carmo 87, Chiado (21 347 2289/ www.anasalazar.pt). Metro Baixa-Chiado. **Open** 10am-7pm Mon-Sat. **Credit** AmEx, MC, V. **Map** p250/1 L9.

Collections for men and women: suits, jackets and dresses with unusual flourishes and finishing touches. The shop also has shoes, handbags, belts and other accessories.

Other locations: Avenida de Roma 16, Roma (21 848 6799).

Fátima Lopes

Rua da Atalaia 36, Bairro Alto (21 324 0540/ www.fatima-lopes.com). Metro Baixa-Chiado/ tram 28. **Open** 10am-1.30pm, 2-8pm Mon-Fri; noon-2.30pm, 3.30-8pm Sat. **Credit** AmEx, MC, V. **Map** p250/1 L9.

Mens- and womenswear to catch the eye: bold colours and figure-hugging leather loom large. Their extrovert Madeiran-born designer lives upstairs.

Other locations: Avenida de Roma 44 D/E, Campo Pequeno (21 849 5986).

José António Tenente

Travessa do Carmo 8, Chiado (21 342 2560). Metro Baixa-Chiado/tram 28. **Open** 10.30am-1.30pm, 2.30-7.30pm Tue-Sat. **Credit** AmEx, DC, MC, V. **Map** p250/1 L9.

This established designer produces men's and women's suits, cotton shirts, shoes, bags and other accessories along more conservative lines than most Bairro Alto boutiques. This store is an outlet, carrying items from past collections; for the current collection visit the Picoas store.

Other locations: Picoas Plaza, Rua Tomás Ribeiro 65, Saldanha (21 315 1404); Atelier, Avenida do Ultramar 13C, Cascais (21 482 7220).

la

Rua da Atalaia 96, Bairro Alto (21 346 1815). Metro Baixa-Chiado/tram 28. **Open** 2-8pm Mon-Wed; 2-10pm Thur-Sat. **Credit** AmEx, MC, V. **Map** p250/1 L9.

Distinctive, colourful womenswear by Portuguese designer Lena Aires.

Lidija Kolovrat

Rua do Salitre 169, Rato (21 387 4536). Metro Rato. **Open** 9am-7pm Mon-Fri. **Credit** AmEx, MC, V. **Map** p246 K7/8.

Art meets fashion in this 'space' run by Bosnian Croat designer Lidija Kolovrat. The price tags on her creations are reasonable; whether you'd walk down the street in them is another matter.

Manuel Alves & José Manuel Gonçalves

Rua Serpa Pinto 15B, Chiado (21 346 0690/ www.alvesgoncalves.com). Metro Baixa-Chiado/tram 28. **Open** 10.30am-7.30pm Tue-Sat. **Credit** AmEx, MC, V. **Map** p250/1 L9.

Among the earliest of the Bairro Alto designers, this pair now produce haute couture for men and women and ready-to-wear for women. The latter – flowing skirts and little black numbers with chic suits, shoes and accessories – is sold in this Chiado shop. The atelier (Rua das Flores 105 1º, 21 347 5137) is by appointment.

Garrafeira Nacional. *See p143.*

Barbearia Campos

Largo do Chiado 4, Chiado (21 342 8476). Metro Baixa-Chiado/tram 28. **Open** 10am-2pm, 4-7pm Mon-Thur; 9am-2pm, 4-7pm Fri; 9am-1pm Sat. **No credit cards**. **Map** p250 L9.

Opened over a century ago, this barber has changed little since. The original marble counters hold porcelain sinks and a crudely erected boiler provides hot water. There's an intriguing collection of old brushes, scissors and bottles that look as though they should be in a museum. A shave is €6.50, a men's cut €9.

Facto

Rua do Norte 42, Bairro Alto (21 347 8821/ www.factohair.com). Metro Baixa-Chiado/tram 28. **Open** 11.30am-8.30pm Mon-Sat. **No credit cards**. **Map** p250 L9.

Take one butcher's shop with flagstone floor, some restored barber's chairs and a dynamic London duo – they occasionally DJ at local bars out of hours – and you get Facto. Book ahead. The newer store by the river is larger but also busy.

Other locations: Avenida Infante D Henrique, Armazém B, Loja 9, Santa Apolónia (21 882 2898/ 96 870 42 36).

WIP – Work In Progress

Rua da Bica Duarte Belo 47-9, Bica (21 346 1486/ www.hairport.info). Metro Baixa-Chiado/tram 28. **Open** 11am-9.30pm Mon-Fri; 11.30am-8pm Sat. **Credit** MC, V. **Map** p250 L9.

A cool hairdresser with multinational staff and trendy background tunes. A place for a radical restyle.

Spas

There are large spas at several leading hotels, including the **Four Seasons Hotel Ritz** (*see p41*) and the **Pestana Palace** (*see p48*).

H2omen

Rua do Viriato 11A, Saldanha (21 315 7096/www. h2omem.com). Metro Picoas. **Open** 9am-10pm Mon-Fri, 10am-9pm Sat. **Credit** DC, MC, V. **Map** p246 L6.

No entry for women at Lisbon's only men's spa, which offers everything from a shave and haircut to detox. Minimalist design, flickering candles and ambient music soothe the savage businessman. The house speciality, an hour's worth of aromatic massages, costs €70; the dry (waterbed) hydromassage is a relative snip at €20 for half an hour.

Le Spa

Rua Silva Carvalho 234B, Amoreiras (21 385 0252/ www.lespa.info). Tram 28. **Open** 10am-8.30pm Mon-Fri; 10am-7pm Sat, Sun. **No credit cards**. **Map** p245 J7/8.

This serene day spa has massages and treatments for body and face, hands and feet that engage all five senses. Most are from Asia: shiatsu, ayurvedic and Indian head massage, Thai yoga, tui na and reflexology. Packages include one for mother and daughter; a day here with five treatments plus a light meal will set you back €305.

Herbalists

Sweet-smelling *ervanárias* still thrive, with customers discussing their ailments in hushed tones with the shopkeeper. Herbs come in 100-gram (3.5-ounce) bags and are then made into a tea. There's an enormous variety, used to cure everything from alcoholism to haemorrhoids. The packaging gives away what's being offered. A large green eye means the herbs will ward off jealousy; wads of banknotes signify money.

Ervanária Eufémia Neves Almeida

Praça da Figueira 6, Baixa (21 346 8855). Metro Rossio. **Open** 10am-7pm Mon-Fri; 10am-1pm Sat. Closed late Aug. **No credit cards**. **Map** p250 M9.

Established more than 150 years ago, this herbalist is located under a staircase and sells local and imported medicinal herbs, diet products and sticks of Brazilian incense that promise to bring their hopeful burner luck, happiness or true love.

Key-cutting

Chaves do Areeiro

Praça Francisco Sá Carneiro (Areeiro) 10D-E, Avenidas Novas (21 845 3010/www.chavesareeiro. pt). Metro Areeiro. **Open** 9am-7pm Mon-Fri; 9am-1pm Sat. **Credit** V. **Map** p249 N4.

Lisbon's most reputable key-cutting chain. The emergency door-opening service is available during opening hours, so if you're locked out in the evening try the one in the Centro Colombo (21 716 9009, *see p132*), which is open until midnight.

Other locations: throughout the city.

Markets

Feira da Ladra

Campo de Santa Clara, São Vicente. Tram 28 to Igreja de São Vicente. **Open** approx 6am-4pm Tue, Sat. **No credit cards**. **Map** p247 N9.
A famous flea market with a large proportion of junk, often at inflated prices. Haggling is a must. Pitches are mostly laid out on the ground, with more permanent shops around the perimeter where you can pick up decent semi-antique furniture.

Feira das Colecções

Mercado da Ribeira, first floor, Avenida 24 de Julho, Cais do Sodré (21 031 2600/1/www.espacoribeira.pt). Metro Cais do Sodré. **Open** 9am-1pm Sun.
No credit cards. **Map** p246 K10.
Almost 100 collector-traders set up stalls displaying stamps, books, cards, watches and other objects of desire at this weekly fair on the top floor of a big old market hall.

Feira de Cascais

Praça de Touros, Avenida Pedro Álvares Cabral, Cascais. Train to Cascais from Cais do Sodré, then BusCas. **Open** 8am-7pm on 1st & 3rd Sun of mth.
No credit cards.
This twice-monthly market is one of the region's biggest, selling everything from eucalyptus cuttings to three-piece suites. Mostly, it's clothes and linen: faux-label shirts and dubious Levi's, but also seconds of the real thing at reasonable prices. Come early or at lunch if you get claustrophobic in crowds.

Feira de Productos de Agricultura Biológica

Praça do Príncipe Real (21 782 5400). Metro Rato/ bus 58, 773, 790. **Open** 9am-3pm Sat. **No credit cards**. **Map** p250/1 K8.
Small weekly open-air organic food market frequented by expats and trendy locals.

Mercado do Campo de Ourique

Rua Francisco Metrass/Rua Coelho da Rocha, Campo de Ourique (21 396 2272). Tram 25, 28. **Open** 7am-2pm Mon-Sat. **No credit cards**. **Map** p245 H8.
This market hall offers a wide range of fruit, vegetables, flowers, salted cod and meat. Fresh fish is available Tuesday to Saturday.

Mercado Praça de Espanha

Metro Praça de Espanha. **Open** 9am-7pm Mon-Sat.
No credit cards. **Map** p248 K4.
Mainly watches, plastic sunglasses, car stereos and the like, looking as if they fell off the back of a lorry, displayed to the background beat from competing CD stalls. The market is housed in a large shed on the northern side of a busy roundabout.

Music

Fnac (*see p133*) also has an extensive collection of classical, popular, world, fado and folk. The Feira da Ladra (*see p147*) has some interesting stalls. There's also a three-day Feira do Disco on the ground floor of the Gare do Oriente in mid October.

Café da Música Diapasão

Avenida João XXI 45A, Avenidas Novas (21 843 7710). Metro Areeiro. **Open** 8.30am-11pm Mon-Sat.
No credit cards. **Map** p249 M4/N4.
Diapasão has long been one of Lisbon's best-loved music stores, selling a wide range of instruments and accessories. It's been forced to branch out, and while still catering to musicians now also serves sushi, snacks and salads to all comers. The cheap draft beer (€0.90) and Caipirinhas (€3.50) slip down easily when there's live music (6-8pm Tue, & Thu).

Carbono

Rua do Telhal 6B, Avenida da Liberdade (21 342 3757). Metro Avenida. **Open** 11am-7pm Mon-Sat.
No credit cards. **Map** p246 L8.
Alternative discoteca stocking local and international releases – new and second-hand – and lots of vinyl. A good source of information about new artists and projects.

Discolecção

Calçada do Duque 17, Rossio (21 347 1486). Metro Rossio. **Open** 1-8pm Mon-Fri; 11am-2pm Sat. Closed 1st 2wks Aug. **No credit cards**.
Map p250 L9.
Second-hand vinyl spanning decades, with lots more stored in a garage – ask if you're looking for something in particular. Fluent English spoken.

Discoteca Amália

Rua Áurea (Rua do Ouro) 272, Baixa (21 342 0939). Metro Baixa-Chiado. **Open** 9.30am-1pm, 3-7pm Mon-Fri; 9.30am-1pm, 3-5pm Sat. **Credit** AmEx, MC, V. **Map** p250 L9.
A specialist in fado and other traditional music, with plenty of classics from Amália and her ilk, as well as contemporary artists.
Other locations: van on Rua do Carmo, Chiado (21 347 0276).

Embassy Sound

Rua da Atalaia 17, Bairro Alto (21 347 8017). Metro Baixa-Chiado. **Open** 2-9pm Mon-Sat.
No credit cards. **Map** p250/1 L9.
Embassy Sound is a new store dedicated to reggae, roots and dub, with classics from the 1960s to the '90s plus new releases and vinyl remixes direct from Jamaica and elsewhere.

Trem Azul

Rua do Alecrim 21, Chiado (21 342 3141/www.cleanfeed-records.com). Metro Baixa-Chiado/Cais do Sodré. **Open** 10am-7.30pm Mon-Sat. **Credit** MC, V.
Map p250/1 L9/10.
Hidden away down some steps below street level is Lisbon's only specialised jazz music store. The shop is linked with Clean Feed Records (www-cleanfeed-records.com), a young Portuguese label with international reach, and it hosts regular concerts for Lisbon's jazz aficionados.

Valentim de Carvalho

Centro Cultural de Belém, Praça do Império, Belém (21 362 4815/www.valentim.pt). Tram 15/train to Belém from Cais do Sodré. **Open** 10am-9pm daily. **Credit** AmEx, MC, V. **Map** p244 B10.

The Portuguese music retailer – run separately from the record label of the same name – has struggled to compete with Fnac and is concentrating resources on small outlets in shopping centres. It stocks a good selection of pop, rock, dance, classical, jazz, Brazilian and African music.

Other locations: throughout the city.

Violino

Calçada do Sacramento 48, Chiado (21 346 9355). Metro Baixa-Chiado/tram 28. **Open** 9am-1pm, 3-7pm Mon-Fri; 9am-1pm Sat. **Credit** AmEx, MC, V. **Map** p250 L9.

An instrument shop that sells Portuguese guitars, along with Chinese violins and modern electric instruments, plus strings. Staff also do repairs.

Opticians & sunglasses

GIL Oculista

Rua da Prata, 138-40, Baixa (21 887 9829). Metro Baixa-Chiado/tram 12, 28. **Open** 9.30am-7pm Mon-Fri; 9.30am-1pm Sat. **Credit** AmEx, MC, V. **Map** p250 M9.

Established in 1865, this shop offers personal service and a decent range of glasses and sunglasses.

Multiópticas

Rua do Carmo 102, Chiado (21 323 4500/www.multiopticas.pt). Metro Baixa-Chiado. **Open** 9am-7.30pm Mon-Fri; 9am-7pm Sat. **Credit** AmEx, DC, MC, V. **Map** p250 L9.

Modern, efficient chain with a large range of frames and one-hour delivery. The spin-off chain, Sun Planet, specialises in sunglasses.

Other locations: throughout the city.

Photography

Colorfoto

Rua Visconde de Santarém 75C, Saldanha (21 312 9490). Metro Saldanha. **Open** 9.30am-7.30pm Mon-Fri. **Credit** AmEx. **Map** p248 M5.

Specialises in professional supplies: films, repairs, cameras and other equipment. There's a developing service too, and this branch sells second-hand cameras. The Alvalade branch is open on Saturdays.

Other locations: Praça de Alvalade 2D, Alvalade (21 793 2475).

Embaixada Lomográfica de Lisboa

Rua da Atalaia 31, Bairro Alto (21 342 1075/www.lomografiaportugal.com). Metro Baixa-Chiado. **Open** 2-9pm Mon-Sat. **Credit** MC, V. **Map** p250/1 L9.

This active 'Lomo Embassy' makes clear that the ultra-snappy camera has hit Lisbon hard. There's a wide range of funky designs on offer, and competitions, events and exhibitions occur regularly.

Foto Sport

Rua Augusta 249, Baixa (21 346 3333/www.fotosport.pt). Metro Baixa-Chiado/tram 28. **Open** 9am-7pm Mon-Fri; 10am-7pm Sat. **Credit** AmEx, MC, V. **Map** p250 M9.

Sells film, cameras and albums and offers same-day developing and framing services.

Other locations: throughout the city.

Repairs

Household

Europ Assistance

Avenida Columbano Bordalo Pinheiro 75, 10th floor, Praça de Espanha (21 388 6282/www.europ-assistance.pt). Metro Rato. **Open** 9am-6pm Mon-Fri. **Credit** MC, V. **Map** p245 J8.

Basically, an insurance arrangement. This Europe-wide organisation offers, for an annual subscription of €75, assorted 24-hour household services: plumbers, electricians, glaziers, locksmiths and carpenters. It also offers policies for medical services and travel, which can be obtained from their UK office (01444 442365, www.europ-assistance.co.uk).

Luggage repairs

Casa Forra

Poço do Borratém 32, Baixa (21 888 2734). Metro Rossio. **Open** 9am-1pm, 2-7pm Mon-Fri; 9am-1pm Sat. **No credit cards**. **Map** p251 M9.

Downstairs is every kind of shoe and luggage accessory – take a ticket, wait for your number to come up and you'll be served. Upstairs, at the back, staff will repair or modify leather goods.

Shoeshines & repairs

There are loads of old cobblers who'll mend your shoes, and an army of shoeshiners clustered round Rossio and busy street corners. A shoeshine costs about €3, though there's nothing to stop you giving more.

Engraxadoria do Chiado

Rua Garrett 47, Chiado (21 346 1757). Metro Baixa-Chiado/tram 28. **Open** 8.30am-7pm Mon-Fri. Closed Aug. **No credit cards**. **Map** p250 L9.

Busy shoeshine place, complete with red-leather chairs, antique ashtrays and magazines.

Toys

Hospital das Bonecas

Praça da Figueira 7, Baixa (21 342 8574). Metro Rossio. **Open** 10am-7pm Mon-Fri; 10am-1pm Sat. **No credit cards**. **Map** p250 M9.

Surgery at this 'dolls' hospital takes place upstairs. In the ground-floor shop you can update your dolls' wardrobe. Portuguese ragdolls, porcelain dolls and a selection of Barbies are for sale.

Arts & Entertainment

Features

Praça de Touros do Campo Pequeno. *See p200.*

Festivals & Events

The party line.

Festas are held throughout the year – mostly to celebrate saints' days – and many lisboetas are close enough to their rural roots to keep track of goings-on in their ancestral village. Though religious in origin, festas generally involve drinking, listening to bad music, setting off firecrackers and eating greasy doughnuts, *see p152* **Their idea of fun**.

Spring

Spring brings **Easter**: Portugal is a Catholic country, so this means more than chocolate eggs. **Holy Week** processions take place around the country, the biggest and most solemn in Braga in the north. Easter Sunday also heralds the start of the bullfighting season (*see p200* **No death in the afternoon**). Film festival **IndieLisboa** (*see p160*) takes place in late April, and **Super Bock Super Rock**, in late May, kicks off the music fests (*see p180*).

Moda Lisboa

Venue varies (21 321 3000/www.modalisboa.pt). **Date** mid Mar & mid Oct.

A twice-yearly fashion show, at which Portuguese designers have their stuff strutted. For more on local designers, *see p145* **After their own fashion**.

Lisbon Half Marathon

21 441 3182/www.maratonaclubedeportugal.com. **Date** late Mar.

Starting south of the Ponte 25 de Abril and ending at the Mosteiro dos Jerónimos, this course is a fast one, and several world record times have been set here. The upper limit is 35,000 participants; the event claims to be the world's biggest at this distance.

Senhor dos Passos

Igreja da Graça (21 887 3943). Tram 28. **Date** second Sun in Lent.

A figure of a bleeding Christ is carried on a litter of violets around one of Lisbon's seven hills, starting and ending at the Igreja da Graça, in a tradition some five centuries old. It is very solemn, but attended by leading socialites, thus making it one of the few religious processions to appear in gossip magazines.

25 April

Information: Associação 25 de Abril (21 324 1420).

A national holiday marking the anniversary of the bloodless 1974 coup that ended decades of dictatorship. Official speeches are made and nostalgic lefties parade on Avenida da Liberdade. Few other people mark the anniversary these days.

Estoril Open

Estádio Nacional, Complexo Desportivo do Jamor, 1495 Cruz Quebrada (800 211 010/www.estorilopen.net). Train to Algés from Cais do Sodré, then bus 76. **Tickets** *Day* €5-€30. *Week* €75-€90; €3 under-18s Mon-Fri; all except Centre Court free under-15s, over-64s. Qualifying stages free. **Date** late Apr-early May.

Portugal's most important tennis tournament takes place around Easter, usually attracting some lesser known international names as it's the first ATP tournament of the season on clay in Europe.

Semana Académica de Lisboa/Queima das Fitas

21 847 6277/www.academicadelisboa.pt. **Date** May.

Portuguese students pin coloured ribbons to their gowns corresponding to their faculty. When the academic year ends they bless them, stage a *queima das fitas* (burning of the ribbons) and get riotously drunk. The partying lasts for days and features gigs by leading Portuguese bands, which in Lisbon take place at Parque Tejo, beyond Parque das Nações. At the oldest university, in Coimbra, the whole week-long event is called Queima das Fitas. For events nationwide, see http://queimas-pt.blogspot.com.

Feira do Livro

Parque Eduardo VII (21 843 5180). Metro Marquês de Pombal. **Date** May/June.

Book fair with open-air stalls selling discounted and second-hand books, plus rare and signed volumes. Mostly Portuguese, but there's usually also a stall or two with English-language stuff.

Summer

June and July are the peak period for tourism, and the city council organises free concerts and other events, especially during the Festas dos Santos Populares (*see p152* **Their idea of fun**). In August, most locals head for the Algarve, making this a good time to explore a now half-empty capital – and, given the heat, the region's own fine beaches (*see p207*). In northern Portugal, August festivals abound, drawing *saudade*-stricken emigrants.

Troia International Film Festival (Festroia)

Forum Luísa Todi, Avenida Luísa Todi 61, Setúbal (information 265 525 908/265 534 059/www.festroia.pt). Train from Entrecampos to Setúbal/bus from Praça de Espanha. **Date** late May-early June.

Long held in Setúbal, this festival is in its 23rd year in 2007. It focuses on countries whose output of features is no more than a score a year, but also organises tributes and competitions.

Festas dos Santos Populares

See p152 **Their idea of fun**. **Date** June.

Festival de Sintra

Centro Cultural Olga de Cadaval, Praça Dr Francisco Sá Carneiro, Sintra (21 910 7110/box office 21 910 7118/www.ccolgacadaval.pt) or Sintra tourist office (see p216). Train to Sintra from Roma-Areeiro, Entrecampos or Sete Rios. **Date** June-July.

Classical music and ballet dominate the roster in this annual event, which has been going for over four decades. Some take place in romantic settings such as Sintra's Palácio Nacional and Palácio da Pena (*see p214*), or the Palácio Nacional de Queluz (*see p216*).

Estoril Jazz

Auditório Parque Palmela, Estoril (21 466 3813/fax 21 467 2280). Train to Monte Estoril from Cais do Sodré. **Date** 1st weekend July.

One of Portugal's oldest jazz festivals, attracting familiar faces from the jazz world.

Festival Internacional de Teatro

Teatro Municipal de Almada, Avenida Professor Egas Moniz, Almada (21 273 9360/21 275 2175/ www.ctalmada.pt). **Tickets** €5-€25; €3.75-€18.75 concessions. **Date** July.

Organised by the Companhia de Teatro de Almada, Portugal's largest theatre festival has attracted thousands of spectators since the 1974 Revolution, and spawned myriad groups. Drama and dance from Portuguese and foreign groups (these are subtitled in Portuguese if necessary) is staged at venues north and south of the river, including the CCB (*see p161*).

Festa do Mar

Baía de Cascais. Information Cascais tourist office (see p214). Train from Cais do Sodré to Cascais. **Date** late July.

The Festival of the Sea, organised by the Cascais fishermen's association, includes a parade of traditional boats, fado singing, fireworks and the procession of Nossa Senhora dos Navegantes (Our Lady of the Seafarers).

Festival Sudoeste

Herdade da Casa Branca, Zambujeira do Mar (www.musicanocoracao.pt). **Tickets** day €40; 4 days €70 (incl camping). **Date** early Aug.

Portugal's biggest music event takes place on the Alentejo coast, a couple of hours' drive south of Lisbon. For more on music festivals, *see p180*.

Jazz em Agosto

Centro de Arte Moderna José de Azeredo Perdigão, Rua Dr Nicolau Bettencourt, Praça de Espanha (21 782 3483/3474/Fundação Gulbenkian 21 782 3627/www.musica.gulbenkian.pt/jazz). Metro São Sebastião. **Tickets** €10-€20. **Date** early Aug.

International and local artists – including some quite big names in experimental jazz – perform at the Gulbenkian Foundation (*see p96*).

Festa do Avante. *See p152.*

Their idea of fun

The **Festas dos Santos Populares** is not one party but a whole month of them during which 'the people's saints' – António, João and Pedro – have their days. These are the excuse for some pretty unusual ideas of fun. Lisbon favourite Santo António is patron of lovers, and in the run-up to his day on 13 June, secret admirers hand over pots of basil with corny poems attached to a paper carnation. In Oporto's big rave-up on 23 June, in honour of São João, complete strangers hit you over the head with giant plastic hammers or shove bunches of giant garlic under your nose.

In Lisbon, the afternoon of 12 June sees the wedding of the Noivos de Santo António, in which 13 lucky pairs of *noivos* (fiancés) get married with all expenses paid by the city council. That evening a colourful parade, the Marchas Populares, inches down the Avenida de Liberdade; each *bairro* contributes a group dressed in themed costumes that performs a song written for the competition. There is only limited tiered seating, and the pavements are crowded; to get a proper look at the groups, you could instead attend one of the pre-competition showcases held some ten days earlier at the Pavilhão Atlântico (*see p177*). That gives you a sense not only of how much work goes into the enterprise but of the fierce rivalries involved: the mood in the arena when Alfama, Castelo and Mouraria are in action recalls a football derby – and fists have been known to fly.

After the Marchas on the night of 12 June lisboetas hold an *arraial*, street party, serving sardines and sangria to allcomers; in Alfama you may have to queue to sit down and it is packed until sunrise. Other *bairros populares* such as Madragoa can be just as much fun, with more elbow room.

The following afternoon – Santo António's day itself, an official local holiday – there is a procession from the Igreja de Santo António to the Sé cathedral. Although the two are a stone's throw apart, the procession takes at least two hours to snake around Alfama. Afterwards, the saint's devotees linger, placing a mountain of candles around a statue of him.

That's not the end of it, though. Throughout June *arraiais* are held in the city's *bairros* on a staggered timetable, and the council puts on lots of free shows downtown, in Monsanto or in Belém.

For further information, see www.egeac.pt or pick up a leaflet in tourist offices, hotels and cafés.

Autumn

As Lisbon fills up again, cultural life revives. As well as the annual events listed below, there's the biennial **Luzboa** (www.luzboa.com), a festival of contemporary visual and performance art that literally casts a new light on urban spaces. The next is in September 2008, its theme Lisbon's waterfront.

Mid October every year brings another **Moda Lisboa** (*see p150*) and Portugal's motorcycling **Grand Prix**, held in Estoril (*see p199*). The **Doclisboa** documentary fest (*see p160*) takes place in late October, the **Arte Lisboa** fair (*see p161*) in mid November.

Outside Lisbon, **Mafra**'s music festival (*see p169*) runs from October into early November. The latter is a good time for chocaholics to visit Óbidos for the **chocolate festival**; *see p218*.

Festa do Avante

Quinta da Amora, Seixa (21 781 3800/www.pcp.pt). Ferry from Cais do Sodré to Cacilhas then bus to Festa. **Tickets** 3 days €17.50 (€25 on the day). **Date** 1st weekend in Sept.

They don't get many votes, but the Communists know how to organise a party. Cross the river for a three-day extravaganza featuring rock, roots and even classical music, plus food and drink from around Portugal. Tickets from the Lisbon party's offices at Avenida da Liberdade 170. **Photo** *p151*.

Festival de Cinema Gay e Lésbico de Lisboa

Venues vary (91 843 3536/www.lisbonfilmfest.org). **Date** last 2wks in Sept.

With over 100 films and support from the British Council and Goethe-Institut as well as the city council, this is perhaps Europe's largest gay film festival.

Festa da Nossa Senhora do Cabo

Santuário da Nossa Senhora do Cabo, Cabo Espichel (21 268 0565). **Date** last weekend in Sept.

Fishermen gather at a sanctuary atop Cabo Espichel (*see p218*) to pray for a good year. There's a mass and procession of the image of the Virigin on Sunday.

Navaratri Festival

Comunidade Hindú de Portugal, Alameda Mahatma Gandhi, Lumiar (21 757 6524/www.comunidade hindu.org). Metro Campo Grande then bus 78. **Admission** €2/day. **Date** late Sept/early Oct.

This annual festival of Lisbon's Hindu community lasts nine days and features traditional dancing, songs and music. All are welcome.

Republic Day

Date 5 Oct.

On the anniversary of the 1910 declaration of the Republic, a national holiday, Lisbon's mayor makes a speech from the balcony of the Câmara Municipal (city hall) from which that declaration was made. It's on Praça do Município, next to Praça do Comércio.

Festa do Chiado

Information Centro Nacional de Cultura (21 346 6722/www.cnc.pt). Metro Baixa-Chiado/tram 28. **Date** late Oct.

A week of concerts, exhibitions, open-air book stalls, free guided tours and conferences.

Seixal Jazz

Various venues, Seixal (21 227 6700/www.cm-seixal.pt/seixaljazz) or Turismo (21 227 5732/tickets 21 097 6103). Ferry from Cais do Sodré to Seixal/TST bus from Praça de Espanha. **Tickets** €10; €7.50 concessions. **Date** last wk Oct-1st wk Nov (next 2007).

This festival (now held biennially) south of the river attracts good musicians who are not household names.

Dia de Todos os Santos/ Dia dos Mortos

Date 1 Nov.

Florists come out in force for the 'Day of the Dead', selling chrysanthemums at the gates of cemeteries as families leave flowers and candles on graves.

São Martinho

Date 11 Nov.

It's traditional to hold a roasted chestnut party (*Magusto*) to celebrate the opening of the first barrels of *água pé* (new wine). Some restaurants and fado houses observe the tradition, but in these days of strict hygiene regulations, *água pé* is no longer freely sold. The equally traditional *jeropiga*, a sugary fortified wine, is easier to find.

Winter

The **Música em São Roque** festival (*see p169*) runs from November to January. In December, the council organises classical **Concertos de Natal** in Lisbon churches.

Lisbon Marathon

21 361 6160/21 386 1811/www.lisbon-marathon.com. **Date** late Nov/early Dec.

Lisbon's big race is less scenic than the Half Marathon, but avoids hills in order to attract record chasers. It goes twice round a course that starts in Praça do Comércio, going along the river to Belém, back and up to Praça do Chile, and returning via Santa Apolónia. A half marathon and fun run are usually also organised.

Dia da Restauração da Independência

Castelo de São Jorge (21 880 0620). Information Real Associação de Lisboa (21 342 9782/8115). Tram 12, 28/bus 37. **Date** 1 Dec.

On the eve of this public holiday celebrating Portugal's 1640 liberation from the Spanish, Dom Duarte Pio – the man who would be king if the country weren't a republic – holds the Jantar dos Conjurados (Conspirators' Dinner). They meet at the castle and then go for dinner at a restaurant. Some of his would-be subjects gather to watch, or buy tickets for the feast (sometimes available on the door).

Natal (Christmas)

From late November onwards, the Baixa, Chiado and Avenida da Liberdade are decked out in light displays. Parish churches try to outdo one another with the best moss-covered cribs. Bakeries stock up with *bolo rei* or 'king cake', a large fruit bun, traditionally with a bean hidden in it. Whoever gets the bean (and breaks a tooth) will have a year's luck but is then supposed to buy the cake next time round. Christmas dinner, of *bacalhau*, on the evening of 24 December, is followed by the opening of presents and midnight mass. On the 25th, people are once more out and about and many cafés are open.

New Year

Seen in with fireworks and usually a concert by a leading Portuguese artist at Praça do Comercio or Parque das Nações. Otherwise no big deal.

Carnaval

Date Feb (start of Lent).

Children dress up for parties but this religious festival is not otherwise much celebrated in Lisbon. Torres Vedras, a 40-minute bus ride north, has floats, music and masked revellers. South of the river, Montijo and Sesimbra (*see p218*) have jolly parades.

Children

Child-friendly as ever and a growing number of organised activities.

The Portuguese love children but until recently there wasn't actually much in Lisbon for youngsters to do. However, bits of Expo 98 remain and families flock to what is now known as **Parque das Nações**. Here you'll find the **Oceanário** as well as an interactive science museum at the **Pavilhão do Conhecimento**. Both are great for children and parents might appreciate the educational side. Less instructive but just as much fun are the **Teleférico** (cable car), mini train, water sports activities, playgrounds and bikes for hire. If you plan on visiting several attractions, the Cartão do Parque (€16.50; €8.50 under-13s; free under-fours) gets you into the main ones and includes discounts on food and some services. North of the former Expo site, the green lawns of the **Parque de Tejo** hug the river, offering close-up views of estuary birds and more bang for your bike – great for burning off excess energy. On that note, it's worth remembering that just getting about Lisbon can be pretty exhausting. Streets are cobbled and hilly, so pushing prams is not easy and little feet will soon get tired. However, the transport system is efficient, reliable, well priced and accessible if walking isn't your thing. And there are always the beaches: free, nearby and a whole lot more fun than museums. *See pp207-12.*

If the sun gets too much or the weather is lousy, the shopping chateau **Centro Colombo** (*see p132*) has an array of amusement arcades and multiscreen cinemas, as well as a Funcenter (21 711 3700, open noon-1am daily). This has a rollercoaster, karting track, virtual reality simulators, bumper cars and a 24-lane bowling alley. It's loud, brash and full of bright lights and cheap food; children love it.

Generally speaking, you'll have nothing to worry about at dinner time as children are welcome and restaurants usually try to cater for everyone's needs. If you eat on an esplanade, such as those in Belém, the kids can run off their meals while you digest yours. Be sensible, not nervous: Portugal does not have a history of children disappearing from the streets and locals confidently let theirs run amok.

As for indoor activities, the **Centro Cultural de Belém** often stages shows for children and both it and the **Gulbenkian Foundation** have departments that stage shows and workshops for kids all year round (*see p161*). Several museums have summer courses; the **Museu Do Traje** (*see p95*) has those aged six to 12 learning theatrical expression, yoga and hip hop, and gardening in the magical Parque Monteiro-Mor.

The **Museu da Marioneta** (*see p90*) hosts shows and workshops for various ages, including mask-making and shadow puppets. Of children's theatre troupes, the best-established is **Teatro Infantil de Lisboa** (21 886 05 03/715 40 57, www.til-tl.pt), which adapts well-known fables for all ages, with audience participation. **Chapitô** (*see p187*) has courses for kids, from cookery to circus arts, while the **União Budista Portuguesa** (213 634 363/93 320 4213) has yoga classes for under-12s and over-12s on alternate Sundays.

For listings information, look in the 'Públicozinho' section at the back of Saturday's *Público*. You can also find this information in the Putos section at http://lazer.publico.clix.pt. Also worth a look is the city council's *Agenda Cultural*, a monthly calendar available at most tourist sites and hotels, which lists events that may be of interest to children. During June's Festas (*see p152*), there's a plethora of special events for kids, while in August and September Ciência Viva (808 200 205, www.cienciaviva.pt) organises free science-related activities, from peering through telescopes to visiting hydroelectric dams. The regional tourist board at www.atl-turismolisboa.pt also has suggestions for families.

Transport

Buses: free under-fives, then full fare.
Trains: free under-fives; half-price under-11s; full fare 12 and over. If your child looks older than their years, it's best to carry a form of ID.
Metro: free under-fives, then full fare.
Taxis are plentiful in Lisbon. Seatbelts are not obligatory in the back but are recommended, particularly as taxi drivers have a tendency to speak over their shoulder while driving!

Childminding

If you are staying in one of the bigger hotels, babysitting services will be provided. The smaller ones will try and accommodate you if they don't provide an official service.

Oceanário. *See p156.*

Clube dos Traquinas
21 757 5399 /96 607 2593/96 604 9436/ www.clubedostraquinas.com. **No credit cards.**
Provides professional babysitters for the Lisbon, Cascais and Sintra areas at €11 per hour (€13.90 after 11pm), with better-value daily, weekend and monthly rates. Reliable service.

Sightseeing

One of the best ways to see Lisbon's sights is the 90-minute **Circuito das Colinas** tour, a comfortable journey over the city's seven hills on a refurbished tram, with a useful English commentary: a good way to tackle the daunting topography. Though not cheap, it is reasonable value compared with Carris's open-top bus tours. There is also a two-hour **Tagus boat trip**, which offers panoramic views with a refreshing breeze; the ordinary commuter ferry is an obvious budget alternative.

Slogging up to the **Castelo de São Jorge** (*see p72*) is a memorable experience, worth the trip for the bird's-eye view of the city, although entrance to the castle is no longer free. Those who don't fancy the climb can take trams 12 or 28 or, all the way to the top, bus 37.

To the west, the **Torre de Belém** (*see p86*) riverbank has plenty of greensward. Across the road, the **Mosteiro dos Jerónimos** (*see p86*) has an enchanting medieval feel to it. Out of town, **Sintra**, **Estoril** and **Cascais** are great for children tired of the city, *see pp213-218.*

Carris Tour
96 629 8558/www.carris.pt. **Departures** *Tagus Tour* Nov-Feb hourly 11.15am-4.15pm daily. Mar-Oct half-hourly 10.15am-5.15pm daily. July-Sept half-hourly 9.15am-5.15pm, then hourly to 8.15pm daily. *Olisipo Tour* Nov-Feb 11.30am, 1.30pm, 3.30pm daily. Mar-Oct hourly 10.30am-5.30pm daily. **Tickets** €14; €7 4-10s; free under-4s. **No credit cards.**
Open-topped buses, operating on a hop on-hop off basis and with English commentary, set off from the north side of Praça do Comércio on two different Lisbon circuits (1hr 45mins each). One takes in the centre and Belém, the other loops past the Zoo and out to Parque das Nações.

Circuito das Colinas
96 629 8558/www.carris.pt. **Departures** *Oct-May* 10am, 10.30am, 11am, noon, 1pm, 1.30pm, then half-hourly 3-6pm daily. *June-Sept* half-hourly 10am-7pm daily. **Tickets** €17; €8.50 4-10s; free under-4s. **No credit cards.**
The distinctive red tram sets off from the same spot in Praça do Comércio as the buses on its circuito das colinas, or 'hills circuit'. Fun, but definitely on the expensive side for a large family.

Cruzeiros no Tejo
21 322 4000/www.transtejo.pt. **Departures** *Apr-Oct* 3pm daily. Closed Nov-Mar. **Tickets** €20; €10 6-12s; free under-6s. **No credit cards.**
The Transtejo ferry company offers guided trips that leave from Terreiro do Paço wharf and take around two hours to complete. There's a cafeteria service on board to stave off starvation.

Jardim Zoológico.

Museums & zoos

Centro Artístico Infantil

Centro de Arte Moderna (CAMJAP), Rua Dr Nicolau de Bettencourt, Praça de Espanha (21 782 3477/ www.camjap.gulbenkian.org). Metro Praça de Espanha. **Open** 10am-12.30pm, 3-5pm Mon-Fri. **Admission** free. **Map** p248 K4.

In the garden of the Gulbenkian Foundation, this centre has toys, musical instruments and painting facilities. The theme of the interactive exhibitions changes every few months.

Centro de Pedagogia e Animação

Centro Cultural Belém, Praça do Império, Belém (workshops 21 361 2899/8/box office 21 361 2444/ www.ccb.pt). Train from Cais do Sodré to Belém/ tram 15/bus 28, 714, 727, 751. **Open** 11am-1pm, 3-6pm Mon-Fri. **Box office** 1-7.30pm. **Admission** €2, weekend shows usually €3. **Credit** AmEx, DC, MC, V. **Map** p244 B10.

This cultural complex has plenty of activities aimed at children: theatre, music and dance performances, workshops and exhibitions.

Jardim Zoológico de Lisboa

Estrada de Benfica 158-60, Sete Rios (21 723 2910/ www.zoolisboa.pt). Metro Jardim Zoológico. **Open** *May-Sept* 10am-8pm daily (last entrance 6.45pm). *Oct-Apr* 10am-6pm daily (last entrance 4.45pm). **Admission** €12.50; €9.50 3-11s; free under-3s. **No credit cards**. **Map** p244 J3.

Lisbon's zoo accommodates a wide variety of species from almost every continent. It also has a botanical garden, cafés and an amusement park, and a mini-train to take the strain on hot days. The Museu das Crianças (21 390 9412/397 6007, www.museudascriancas.eu), a play area with trained helpers that organises drawing, painting, papier mâché and printing workshops for children aged four to 12, is also moving in soon.

Oceanário

Esplanada Dom Carlos I, Parque das Nações (21 891 7002/www.oceanario.pt). Metro Oriente. **Open** *Summer* 10am-7pm daily. *Winter* 10am-6pm daily. **Admission** €10.50; €5.25 4-12s; €25 family; free under-3s. **Credit** AmEx, DC, MC, V.

The Oceanarium, at the former Expo site, is one of Europe's largest aquariums, with 8,000 fish, birds and mammals in rooms and tanks that represent the earth's oceans. At the core is the huge Atlantic tank, containing sharks and rays, but children are just as likely to appreciate the penguins, otters and jellyfish that live elsewhere in the aquarium. It's a terrific day out – or night if you book the popular Sleeping with the Sharks package (€60 per person). The Oceanarium also organises Saturday morning concerts for under-fours (€25) and its Nautical Centre (21 891 8532) gives kids a chance to mess about in boats in the sheltered Doca dos Olivais. **Photo** *p155*.

Pavilhão de Conhecimento

Alameda dos Oceanos, Parque das Nações (21 891 7100/www.pavconhecimento.pt). Metro Oriente. **Open** 10am-6pm Tue-Fri; 11am-7pm Sat, Sun. **Admission** €6; €3 7-17s; €2.50 3-6s; free under-2s; family €13. **Credit** AmEx, V.

The Pavilion of Knowledge, an interactive science and technology centre also at the Expo 98 site, features changing exhibitions that make for an excellent mix of fun and learning. **Photo** *p157*.

Planetário Calouste Gulbenkian

Praça do Império, Belém (21 362 0002/http:// planetario.online.pt). Train from Cais do Sodré to Belém/tram 15/bus 28, 714, 727, 751. **Sessions** *July-Sept* 11am, 2.30pm, 4pm Wed, Thur; 3.30pm Sat, Sun. *Oct-June* 4pm Thur; 3.30pm Sat; 11am, 3.30pm Sun. **Admission** €4; €2 under-18s, students. Free to all Sun 11am. **No credit cards**. **Map** p244 B9.

The 330-seater planetarium is a real buzz for children. After a revamp, it should soon have sessions in English at weekends; but phone to check. Next door, the Museu da Marinha might interest the nautically minded youngster.

Quinta Pedagógica dos Olivais

Rua Cidade Lobito, Olivais Sul (21 855 0930). Metro Olivais. **Open** *Oct-Apr* 10am-5.30pm Sat, Sun. *May-Sept* 10am-6pm Sat, Sun. **Admission** free.

This council-run city farm houses a wide range of animals, some of them Portuguese breeds, and also offers in-house workshops on various rural pursuits (make sure you book in advance) such as bread-making and traditional embroidery.

Parks

Parque das Nações

Parque das Nações (21 891 9333/www.parquedas nacoes.pt). Metro Oriente. **Open** *Playgrounds* 24hrs daily. *Tejo Bike* Summer 10am-8pm daily. Winter 11am-6pm daily. *Cable car* Oct-May 11am-7pm Mon-Fri; 10am-8pm Sat, Sun. June-Sept 11am-8pm Mon-Fri; 10am-9pm Sat, Sun. **Admission** *Playgrounds* free. **Tickets** *Cable car* one way €3.50, round trip €5.50; €1.80 5-14s, round trip €3; free under-5s. **Credit** AmEx, V.

The former Expo site has two main play areas: the Music Playground, at Passeio dos Tágides, near the Vasco da Gama Tower, where young visitors can try different musical instruments; and, beyond it, the Parque do Tejo Playground, which has a climbing wall and rope pyramid. There are several landscaped open spaces nearby. The Parque das Nações also has a half-mile cable car ride, bike hire (from €2; €1.50 child) and a mini train; the latter two start by the booth in front of the Vasco da Gama shopping centre, which has maps and information.

Parque Eduardo VII

Metro Marquês de Pombal/Parque. **Open** 24hrs daily. **Admission** free. **Map** p246 K6.

Plenty of greenery, a small playground, plus two greenhouses to explore. There are two esplanades with a view of Lisbon; the one at the top, the Linha d'Água has an esplanade and a shallow pool that is irresistible to toddlers – and dogs.

Parque Florestal de Monsanto

Espaço Monsanto, Estrada do Barcal, Monte das Perdizes (21 817 0200/1/www.cm-lisboa.pt/monsanto). Metro Jardim Zoológico then bus 70/bus 24/bus 723, 727, 732. **Open** *Espaço Monsanto* Winter 9.30am-5pm Tue-Fri; 9.30am-5pm Sat; 2-5pm Sun. Summer 9.30am-5pm Tue-Sat; 2-5pm Sun. *Playgrounds* Oct-Mar 9am-6pm daily. Apr-Sept 9am-8pm daily. Summer 9am-8pm Tue-Sun. **Admission** free.

Lisbon's green lung, Monsanto Forest Park was long seen as a haunt of drug dealers and prostitutes but is gaining in popularity thanks to municipal investment and open-air events. A good thing too: it boasts 306km (190 miles) of trails and several playgrounds. The largest and most popular is the hilltop Parque Recreativo do Alto da Serafina, a large adventure park near the Aqueduto. It has a leafy picnic area, a driving circuit for children, climbing wall, boats and restaurant – and marvellous views. On the east side of the forest, the revamped Parque Infantil de Alvito offers three safe play areas for different ages. To the southwest, the Parque Recreativo dos Moinhos de Santana has lawns, a lake and waterfall, play area and two old windmills. For exhibitions and information on the forest, visit the Espaço Monsanto, near the adventure park at Mata de São Domingos.

Sports

Older children can take advantage of those deep ocean rollers by learning how to surf. The **Portuguese Surfing Federation** lists recommended schools with English-speaking instructors at www.surfingportugal.com. On the beaches west of Lisbon, we would pick out the **Carcavelos Surf School** (96 613 1203/96 285 0497, www.windsurfcafe.pt) or **Surf in S Pedro** (91 636 2559), on a beach that is good for beginners. Further afield, beyond Sintra, there is the **Academia Surfada** in Ericeira (261 866 162) or, south of the river, the **Caparica Surf School** (21 291 9078) and **Escola Oficial de Surf** (93 630 0139). All offer courses of several hours and hire out wetsuits and boards.

For sailing courses, as well as other sports activities, *see pp197-203*. In Cascais, there is also the **Watersport Centre** run out of John David's beachside café (21 483 0455), near the station. It has waterskiing and windsurfing gear, and pedalos at reasonable prices.

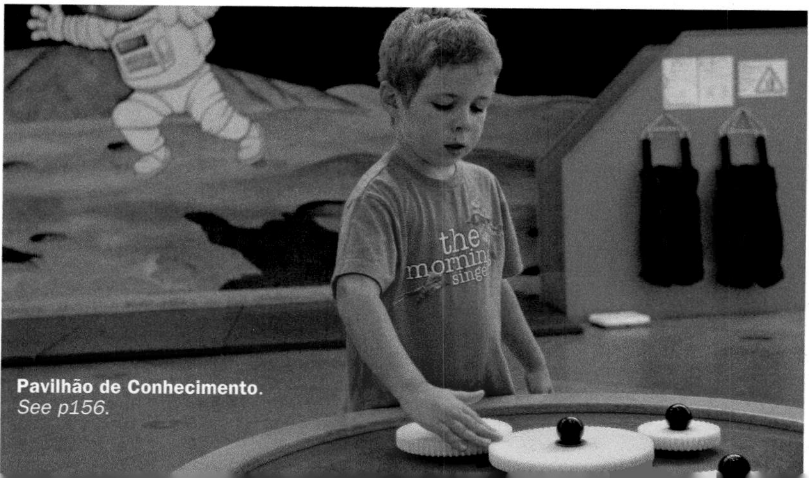

Pavilhão de Conhecimento.
See p156.

Film

Film-going has revived, even if film-making hasn't.

If, rather than Hollywood's flash and crash, you like your films slow and meditative, Portuguese cinema could be for you. Local auteurs explore colour and space, while disappearing down the narrative culs-de-sac of a character's *saudade*. This does not make for box office hits, though. Portugal is the European country with both the highest proportion (40-50 per cent) of output exhibited in leading festivals abroad and the lowest share of the domestic box office (less than one per cent).

Lisbon has always been the heart of the industry. In 1922 businessman Raul de Caldevilla bought the Quinta das Conchas estate in Lumiar with plans to build a film city, and after the Estado Novo regime was installed in 1928, propaganda chief António Ferro oversaw the creation of Cinelândia, housing the Tobis film laboratories and the Lisboa Filme studios. The buildings survive today, dwarfed by high-rise flats.

After the fall of Salazar the Cinema Novo group was established by the Centro Português de Cinema with help from the Gulbenkian Foundation, while the government created the Instituto Português de Cinema. These twin approaches remain. The 'commercial' school, spearheaded by directors such as Joaquim Leitão, António Pedro Vasconcelos and Leonel Vieira, targets the domestic market. But since the Revolution, Portuguese cinema has been dominated by the auteur tradition, which lives a mainly hand-to-mouth existence.

State funding tripled under the Socialists from 1995, but the budget of national film institute, ICAM, subsequently suffered sharp cuts. Yet great optimism was stoked by box office hits such as Joaquim Leitão's *Tentação* (Temptation) and sponsorship from private broadcaster SIC. But as the economy slowed, advertising revenues dwindled, and home-grown and Brazilian *telenovelas* dominated the small screen. Their influence was evident in the SIC-sponsored *O Crime de Padre Amaro* – a steamy 2005 adaptation of Eça de Queiroz's novel that lagged behind the Mexican-made one by several years but broke domestic box office records for a Portuguese movie. Marco Martins' directorial debut in the same year, *Alice* – about a father's obsessive search for his daughter – did well with a very different approach: recalling, as one critic put it, that everyday life exists.

Both went on general release in the Hollywood-dominated multiplexes that have taken over the role of the old picture palaces on the Avenida da Liberdade. The **São Jorge** at No.175 (21 310 3400) was bought by the council a few years ago – with one of Lisbon's largest screens, spacious reception areas and a balcony overlooking the avenue, it is a good central venue for festivals – but is no longer in continuous use. **Fórum Lisboa** (Avenida da Roma 14, 21 842 0900) is another council owned auditorium. But for regular programming, fans of European and independent US film should look to **King**, **Quarteto** and **Monumental**.

In July and August King and Quarteto re-run films from the past year, and in August there's open-air cinema at Inatel's stadium (*see p203*). **Optimus Open Air** is in September, with blockbusters projected on to what is claimed to be the world's largest screen (400 square metres/4,300 square feet) at the riverside Doca dos Santos (information/reservations 707 234 234) amid restaurants, pouffes and free popcorn.

At the municipal Videoteca de Lisboa (Largo do Calvário 2, Alcântara, 21 361 0220), there is a large collection of videos to watch for free on the premises, though only after you've paid €1.26 to join (take a passport or ID). Foreign cultural institutes, including the British Council (*see p231*) also have video libraries; the Institut Franco-Português (Avenida Luís Bivar 91, 21 311 1400, www.ifp-lisboa.com) is alone in having 35mm equipment and regular screenings. Spain's Instituto Cervantes (Rua Sta. Marta 43, 21 310 50 20, http://lisboa.cervantes.es) and Germany's Goethe-Institut (Campo dos Martíres da Pátria 37, 21 882 4510, www.goethe.de/lisboa) also run mini-festivals, while Fnac (*see p133*) has the odd free screening.

SCREENING INFORMATION

All Lisbon's big shopping centres have cinemas. Other screens are tucked away in odd corners of the city, so a map will come in handy. Listings can be found in newspapers, magazines such as *Visão*, or online at www.cinecartaz.publico.pt. Online credit card booking is available for Lusomundo cinemas at www.cinemas-pt.sapo.pt and for King, Monumental, Millennium Alvaláxia and Nimas (Avenida 5 de Outubro 42B, 21 357 4362) – a one-screen affair that shows French movies – at www.medeiafilmes.pt (full-price tickets only). You can buy tickets for

The old man and the screen

Portugal's marginal geographical and cultural position and its film industry's benign 'institutionalisation' have led to highly personal, often eccentric, results. The likes of Wim Wenders and Aki Kaurismaki have described it as one of the last bastions of ambitious European art film.

Nobody embodies this more clearly than **Manoel de Oliveira**, who turned 98 in 2006 yet still turns out at least one elegant, if difficult, feature a year. The only active director whose career began in the silent era, Oliveira is a Jesuit-educated former racing driver who ran in the fast lane as a young man. However, his style is characterised by silences and slow camera movements. Watching his films is like entering a church: removed from the hubbub, we find echoing pauses and formal tableaux.

Oliveira's work has always split opinions. His 1931 debut, *Douro, Faina Fluvial*, a silent about the river that runs through his native Oporto, outraged critics at home but won praise abroad. His first feature, *Aniki-Bóbó* (1942), was also dismissed, but this magical tale of the city's urchins is now among his best-loved works.

Difficulties in obtaining financing under the dictatorship prompted a lengthy career break; he only made his third feature film in 1972, at the age of 63. But he was just getting started. After the Revolution he became the unofficial standard-bearer of Portuguese cinema and was 'discovered' by French and Italian critics through the 1978 *Amor de Perdição* (Love of Perdition).

By the 1990s he was working with leading actors such as the late Marcello Mastroianni, who in his last film role played Oliveira as... an ageing film director, in the 1997 *Viagem ao Princípio do Mundo* (Journey to the Beginning of the World). Marcello's daughter, Chiara, starred in *A Carta* (The Letter), which won the Jury Prize at Cannes in 1999.

In recent years Oliveira has been prolific, and in 2004 the Venice jury awarded him a second Honorary Golden Lion.

the larger complexes over the phone, or reserve, in which case you pick them up 30 minutes before. Films are subtitled rather than dubbed, except for indigenous films and children's animations – though even here there are sessions with the original version ('VO'). Lisbon cinemas change programmes on Thursday.

Cinemas

Cinemateca Portuguesa/ Museu de Cinema

Rua Barata Salgueiro 39, Marquês de Pombal (21 359 6262/recorded information 21 359 6266/www.cinemateca.pt). Metro Marquês de Pombal. **Open** *Box office* 2.30-3.30pm, 6-10pm. *Exhibitions* 12.30pm-12.30am Mon-Sat. **Tickets** *Films* €2.50; €2 concessions. *Museum* free. **No credit cards. Map** p244 L7.

Lisbon's equivalent of London's National Film Theatre was recently revamped, and now has a café-bistro, bookshop and space for exhibitions in a new atrium (note the columns, made of film reels stacked on top of one another). Two screens show as many as five films a day, as part of retrospectives of classics from world cinema, and in July and August there are screenings on the upstairs patio, too. Only members may reserve, and there may be queues for rare or popular classics. The Cinemateca has had the legal status of a museum since cinephile Dr Felix Ribeiro persuaded the government to found it in 1948. The archive, in his former home, contains 19,000 books and 1,500 other publications in European languages, plus posters and other items from Portuguese cinema. To visit the library (*biblioteca*), take a passport or ID and seek out the helpful, English-speaking librarians in the old building.

King

Avenida Frei Miguel Contreiras 52A, Avenida de Roma (21 848 0808). Metro Roma. **Open** *Box office* 1-10.30pm daily. *Last show* 10pm. **Tickets** €5; €4 Mon & concessions. **No credit cards. Map** p249 L7

The best of European cinema, plus local films, on three screens. There's a minimalist café and a bookshop that was Lisbon's best for film-related material, but is now reopening under new management.

Lusomundo Amoreiras

Avenida Engenheiro Duarte Pacheco, Amoreiras (bookings/reservations 707 246 362). Bus 48, 53, 58, 74, 83, 711, 718, 723. **Open** *Box office* noon-12.35am Mon-Sat; 10.30am-12.35am Sun. *Phone bookings* 11am-11pm daily. *Last show* 12.30am. **Tickets** €5.20; €4 Mon & concessions. Reservations €0.25. **Credit** (phone only) AmEx, MC, V. **Map** p245 J7.

Tickets are bought from a single booth, but the ten screens are scattered around the shopping centre, so look for the overhead signs. There are well-equipped Lusomundo multiplexes in two other Lisbon shopping centres, each with ten screens and identical prices, box office hours and phone number.

Other locations: Centro Colombo (*see p132*); Centro Vasco da Gama (*see p132*).

Millenium Alvaláxia

Estádio José Alvalade, Campo Grande (21 754 90 00). Metro Campo Grande. **Open** *Box office* noon-1am daily. *Last show* 12.30am. **Tickets** €5.20; €4.20 before 3pm & concessions. **No credit cards**.

Dominating the rather bare Alvaláxia shopping centre in Sporting's stadium complex, this cinema has 16 screens, one of which has Lisbon's only digital system. There's a restaurant, café and two bars. Irritatingly, there is sometimes just one queue for either popcorn or tickets.

Monumental/Saldanha Residence

Edifício Monumental, Avenida Praia Vitória 71/ Saldanha Residence, Avenida Fontes Pereira de Melo, Saldanha (21 314 2223). Metro Saldanha. **Open** *Box office* 11am-12.30am daily. *Last show* 12.30am. **Tickets** €5; €4 concessions; €3.50 Mon. **No credit cards**. **Map** p249 M5.

Eight screens showing leading independent films and European art-house fare, split between two shopping centres a hundred yards apart. (Both box offices sell tickets for all films.) The cinemas have excellent sound and vision, and the highest audiences per screen in Lisbon. There's a fine café and bar at the Monumental, offering a range of Belgian beers and food.

Quarteto

Rua Flores do Lima 1, Avenidas Novas (21 797 1378). Metro Roma or Entrecampos. **Open** *Box office* 2pm-12.30am daily. *Last show* 10pm. **Tickets** €4.50; €3.50 Mon & concessions. **No credit cards. Map** p249 M3.

A key independent cinema showing US and European films, its walls plastered with posters from cult films. Also has a small bar and sells indie video titles. No reservations.

Twin Towers

Galerias Twin Towers, Rua de Campolide 351C, Sete Rios/Praça de Espanha (21 724 231/2). Bus 5, 701. **Open** *Box office* 12.30pm-12.35am daily. *Last show* 12.30am. **Tickets** €5; €3.75 Mon & concessions. **No credit cards**. **Map** p248 J5.

Located in the basement of the Twin Towers mall, there are five excellent screens – claimed by owner Filmitalus to be Portugal's finest.

UCI Cinemas

El Corte Inglés, Avenida António Augusto Aguiar 31, Praça de Espanha (Phone bookings 707 232 221). Metro São Sebastião. **Open** *Box office* 1.30pm-12.35am daily. *Phone bookings* 9am-midnight. *Last show* 12.30am. **Tickets** *Box office* €5.40; €4.50 concessions. *Phone bookings* €6.40. **No credit cards**. **Map** p248 L5

A 14-screen multiplex. Major releases are shown on more than one screen allowing staggered times, and the VIP seats are super comfortable.

Festivals & events

IndieLisboa (21 315 83 99, www.indielisboa.com) is a festival of independent film with national and international competitions, held over ten days in late April. Three years old in 2006, it has been a massive success, drawing tens of thousands of spectators to the São Jorge to see 300 or so films from around the world. In recent years, the same outfit has organised a showcase for Portuguese short films in June.

Festroia (265 525 908/265 553 4059, www.festroia.pt) is the only international generalist event of its size in the region, and attracts some big foreign names for its juries. Held around June in Setúbal, it focuses on the work of countries with an annual production of fewer than 21 feature films. *See also p150.*

Lisbon Village Festival (707 200 583, http://lisbon.villagefestival.net), a relatively new showcase for digital film, is also in June.

The **Festival de Cinema Gay e Lésbico** (21 395 5447, www.lisbonfilmfest.org), held in late September at the Quarteto and elsewhere, comprises more than 100 films.

The **Festa do Cinema Francês** (www.festadocinemafrances.com) opens in Lisbon in early October, sometimes in the presence of a French star, before touring nationwide. In 2006 it screened 32 films at the IFP, São Jorge and Cinemateca.

The **Festival Internacional de Cinema Documental de Lisboa** (21 882 1446, www.doclisboa.org), known to its friends as **DocLisboa**, is another relative newcomer. Over ten days in October some 100 films are shown at Culturgest (*see p161*). There are eight sections, three of them competitive, complemented by directors' workshops and talks.

Galleries

Lisbon has an edge, plus major modern and contemporary collections.

Portugal's art scene has worked hard to recover from the four decades it spent in the international wilderness under the Salazar dictatorship. When the 1974 Revolution ended the isolation there was a flurry of activity. But while some contemporary artists still have a real edge, 'international' trends have tended to take over.

Now the emphasis is on multimedia, installation and video art, which are not easy to sell. **Arte Lisboa** (www.artelisboa.fil.pt), held every November since 2000 at the Feira Internacional de Lisboa (21 892 1500, www.fil.pt) in Parque das Nações, is helping.

The Portuguese artists best known abroad are Pedro Cabrita Reis, Julião Sarmento and Paula Rego. Reis (b. Lisbon 1956) uses a vast range of materials, often drawn from architecture and construction, for installations that are often site-specific. Sarmento (b. Lisbon 1948) makes huge paintings, sculptures and video installations, frequently hinging on secrecy and voyeurism. Paula Rego (b. Lisbon 1935), the most widely acclaimed, studied art at the Slade in London and settled there in 1976. Her pictures are filled with allusions to Portuguese culture.

Lisbon's major institutions – the **CCB** in Belém and **Culturgest** in central Lisbon – host mainly contemporary art as well as meetings, debates and forums. The CCB also housed the excellent Museu de Design until it recently moved out to make room for José Berardo's vast modern art collection.

Lisbon hasn't got an art district; commercial galleries are located where rent is affordable and there is a stream of passers-by. Opening hours are often casual, so call ahead. Sometimes several galleries hold openings on the same Saturday afternoon – a traditional time for gallery hopping – offering a good opportunity for people watching. Another is auctions organised by Leiria e Nascimento (21 362 1765/21 361 8146/7/8, www.lnleiloes.pt) at the Tapada da Ajuda, a former royal hunting lodge. For information on what's on, see Saturday's edition of *Público* or its Guia do Lazer website http://lazer.publico.clix.pt or the free monthly *Agenda Cultural*, found in cafés and tourist offices. The galleries section of its website, www.lisboacultural.com, has a useful map for each entry. For visitors with Portuguese, *Flirt* is a handy monthly freebie while the quarterly *A Bíblia* has an impressive roster of contributors.

Exhibition spaces

Casa da Cerca – Centro de Arte Contemporanea

Rua da Cerca 2, Almada (21 272 4950/www.m-almada.pt). Ferry to Cacilhas from Cais do Sodré then bus 101. **Open** 10am-6pm Tue-Fri; 1-6pm Sat, Sun. **Admission** free.

This handsome baroque palace south of the river, boasting a commanding cliff-top view, occasionally host exhibitions of contemporary Portuguese work.

Casa Fernando Pessoa

Rua Coelho da Rocha 16, Campo de Ourique (21 391 3270/7). Tram 25, 28/bus 9, 74. **Open** 10am-6pm Mon-Wed, Fri; 1-8pm Thur. **Admission** free. **Map** p245 H8.

This little museum dedicated to the Lisbon poet Fernando Pessoa has two rooms for art shows. It's a stimulating environment, with poetry readings and a pleasant restaurant.

Centro Cultural de Belém (CCB)

Praça do Império, Belém (21 361 2400/www.ccb.pt). Tram 15/train from Cais do Sodré/bus 27, 28, 714, 727, 729, 751. **Open** 10am-7pm Tue-Sun (last entry 6.15pm). **Admission** €2-€5; half-price concessions. **Credit** AmEx, MC, V. **Map** p245 B10.

Pale and stark, and offset by the beauty of the 16th-century Mosteiro dos Jerónimos, this grandiose and culturally vital building opened in 1993. Its Centro de Exposições is the best public art space in town, much of it now taken over by the Berardo collection (*see p163* **Money talks... and walks**). There are also several cafés, a restaurant and a bookshop.

Centro de Arte Moderna José de Azeredeo Perdigão

Fundação Calouste Gulbenkian, Rua Dr Nicolau Bettencourt, Praça de Espanha (21 782 3474/www.gulbenkian.pt). Metro São Sebastião. **Open** 10am-6pm Tue-Sun. **Admission** €3 (€5 with main museum); free under-7s, students, over-64s. Free for all Sun. **Credit** MC, V. **Map** p248 K4.

Part of the extraordinary Gulbenkian complex (*see p170* **Fifty years of Mr Five Percent's legacy**), the CAMJAP is a fine modernist building set in a lovely park, with a canteen and bookshop. Its collection is an excellent foil to the Old Masters adorning the main museum (*see p96*), comprising Portuguese works from the last 100 years. Modernism is represented by key artists, such as surrealists António Pedro and António Dacosta. It has interesting exhibitions, and also features weekend guided visits, talks and activities for children.

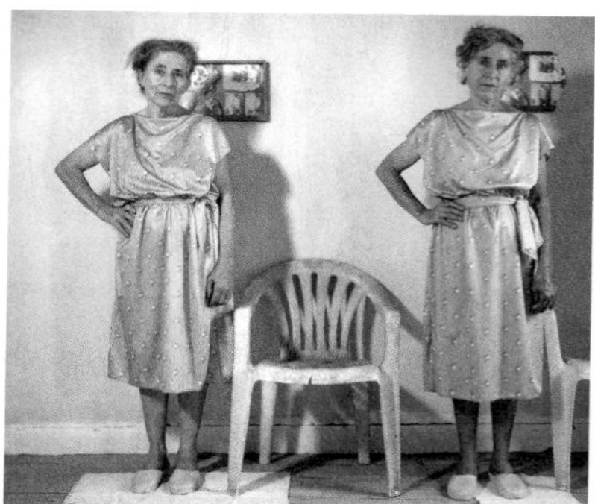

A picture of happiness at **Módulo.**

Culturgest

Edifício Caixa Geral de Depósitos, Rua Arco do Cego 1, Campo Pequeno (21 790 5155/www.culturgest.pt). Metro Campo Pequeno. **Open** 11am-7pm Mon, Wed-Fri (last entry 6.30pm); 2-8pm Sat, Sun (last entry 7.30pm). **Admission** €2; €1.20-€1.40 concessions; free under-17s. **Credit** MC, V. **Map** p249 M4.

Housed in Portugal's biggest building, the headquarters of sponsor bank Caixa Geral, this foundation is more avant-garde than the CCB in its programming. For exhibitions there are free audio guides, and guided visits at 5pm on Sundays.

Museu do Chiado

Rua Serpa Pinto 4, Chiado (21 343 2148/www.museudochiado-ipmuseus.pt). Metro Baixa-Chiado/tram 28. **Open** 10am-6pm Tue-Sun. **Admission** €3; €1.50 concessions; free under-15s. Free for all Sun to 2pm. **No credit cards. Map** p250 L10.

Founded in 1911, this state-run museum re-opened in 1994 after a hiatus following the 1988 Chiado fire with a cool, modernist redesign by French architect Jean-Michel Wilmotte. The permanent collection delineates a century-and-a-half of Portuguese art, from romanticism through naturalism to neo-realism, surrealism and abstractionism. There are frequent exhibitions, and a pleasant café and patio.

Pavilhão Branco

Museu da Cidade, Campo Grande 245, Campo Grande (21 751 3200). Metro Campo Grande. **Open** 10am-1pm, 2-6pm Tue-Sun. **Admission** free. **Map** p248 L1.

In the gardens of the Museu da Cidade (*see p94*), the modern White Pavilion and its black twin are among Lisbon's most interesting spaces, mainly hosting shows by established Portuguese artists.

Sociedade Nacional de Belas Artes

Rue Barata Salgueiro 36, Marquês de Pombal (21 313 8510/www.snba.pt). Metro Marquês de Pombal. **Open** 2-8pm Mon-Sat. **Admission** free. **Map** p246 L7.

Three exhibition spaces run by artists for artists – many began careers here; it also runs competitions.

Commercial galleries

Galeria 111

Campo Grande 113, Alvalade (21 797 7418/www.galeria111.pt). Metro Campo Grande. **Open** 10am-7pm Mon-Sat. **No credit cards. Map** p248 L2.

This high-profile gallery was founded before the 1974 Revolution with a huge stock of work by Paula Rego, Alexandre Pomar and António Dacosta, and other contemporary artists. There is a fine collection of prints and drawings, plus a bookshop.

Galeria Diferença

Rua São Filipe Néri, 42CV, Rato (21 383 2193/www.triplov.com/galeria_diferenca). Metro Rato. **Open** 3-8pm Tue-Sat. **No credit cards. Map** p246 K7.

Small, friendly gallery showcasing work known and unknown. It was launched by artists in 1979 with the aim of providing studio space and publishing the odd book, as well as exhibiting.

Galeria Graça.Brandão

Rua dos Caetanos 26, Bairro Alto (21 346 9183/4/www.galeriagracabrandao.com). Metro Baixa-Ciado. **Open** 10am-8pm Tue-Sat. **No credit cards. Map** p250 L9.

This recently opened branch of a successful Oporto operation shows high-quality art from Portuguese-speaking countries, with an emphasis on Brazil.

Galeria Luís Serpa

Rua Tenente Raúl Cascais 1B, Príncipe Real (21 397 7794/www.galerialuisserpa.com). Metro Rato. **Open** 3-7.30pm Tue-Sat. **No credit cards. Map** p246 K8.

This gallery has exhibited many high-profile artists (mainly of Portuguese and Brazilian extraction). Although it's less cutting edge now, the gallery still regularly shows exceptional pieces.

Galeria São Mamede

Rua Escola Politécnica 161-75, Rato (21 397 3255/www.saomamede.com). Metro Rato. **Open** 10.30am-1pm, 3-7.30pm Tue-Sat. **Credit** V. **Map** p246 K8.

One of Lisbon's oldest galleries, concentrating on rising contemporary Portuguese artists working in painting, design, sculpture and ceramics.

Galeria Zé dos Bois

Rua da Barroca 59, Bairro Alto (21 343 0205/www.zedosbois.org). Metro Baixa-Chiado. **Open** 5-11pm Tue-Sat. **No credit cards. Map** p250 L9.

This collective has promoted new artists in non-conventional areas such as radical multimedia and body arts since it sprang up in 1994. There's a lively bar (*see p184*) and a space for live music.

Other locations: Negócio, Rua de O Século 9 (Porta 5); Tercenas, Travessa de José António Pereira 19.

Módulo – Centro Difusor de Arte

Calçada dos Mestres 34A-B, Campolide (21 388 5570). Bus 2. **Open** 3-8pm Mon-Sat. **No credit cards. Map** p245 J6.

Módulo's 'art diffusion centre' is one of Lisbon's most interesting exhibition spaces, balancing new trends with international artists of repute.

Money talks... and walks

When France's ambassador to Portugal presented José 'Joe' Berardo with the insignia of a Chevalier de la Légion d'Honneur, it was a sign that things were getting interesting.

The knighthood for the Portuguese millionaire had been decreed by President Jacques Chirac for services to art. Many pieces from Berardo's vast collection of modern art have been shown in France over the years. But there was also a competitive edge to the proceedings: the French followed up the decoration with the offer of a permanent home for Berardo's collection.

The magnate, a native of Madeira who made his fortune in South Africa's mines but who now lives in Portugal, had been talking to Portuguese officials for years about creating a museum in Lisbon. The bulk of his collection, which comprises works by 550 artists representing dozens of modern movements, was languishing in the CCB's vaults. Only a small proportion was on show at the Sintra Museu de Arte Moderna (*pictured*), a former casino in the damp hill town. Berardo took a hard line: he'd provide the art; the state must provide the building.

Broad agreement was reached at the end of 2005 – the deadline set by Berardo – after Prime Minister José Sócrates stepped in. The accord was signed the following April at a ceremony that Sócrates said represented 'the end of ten years of incomprehensible hesitations'. The Museu Colecção Berardo was to house 863 of Berardo's estimated 4,000 artworks in what he said could be 'the world's most visited museum'. He expressed relief that he would not have to move abroad, adding mischievously: 'I can't even speak French.'

Critics deplored the state's picking up the bill for maintaining a private collection and questioned the ten-year deadline set for it to buy the treasures to ensure they stay for good. But António Mega Ferreira, the CCB's chairman, called for everyone to 'dream big together' and create 'the world's best cultural centre'.

Meanwhile, a rival has emerged with the opening near Cascais of a showcase for what its owners claim is the world's most important collection of late-20th-century and early 21st-century art. In an unlikely setting, by a Makro cash and carry (useful if asking for directions) is the 1,860 square-metre (20,000 square-foot) warehouse of the Ellipse Foundation.

Comprising hundreds of works by seminal artists active since the 1970s, others in mid-career, and emerging artists from around the world, the collection was formed as an investment by banker João Rendeiro, but is now being shown in tranches.

While Ellipse has so far kept a low profile, its contemporary panache together with the encyclopaedic modernity of 'The Berardo' could prove irresistible to art lovers.

Sintra Museu de Arte Moderna.

Ellipse Foundation

Rua das Fisgas, Pedro Furado, Alcoitão, Cascais (21 469 1806/ www.ellipsefoundation.com). Train from Cais do Sodré to Estoril/ Cascais then bus 406. **Open** During exhibitions 10am-6pm Fri-Sun. **Admission** free.

Sintra Museu de Arte Moderna

Avenida Heliodoro Salgado, Sintra (21 924 8170). Train to Portela de Sintra from Sete Rios. **Open** 10am-6pm Tue-Sun. **Admission** €3; €1.50 concessions; free under-10s. Free for all Sun to 2pm. **Credit** AmEx, MC, V.

Gay & Lesbian

Forget the fetish – Lisbon's scene is laid-back and loveable.

Portugal has come a long way since the 1974 Revolution and, although traditional family values prevail outside the big cities, live-and-let-live attitudes have spread to this south-western corner of Europe. With a balmy climate, charming locals and rich nightlife you have the makings of a great destination.

Although a recent poll found that fewer than one-third of Portuguese questioned approved of the idea of a law to establish gay civil partnership, you'll find a warm welcome in a city where mixed bars and clubs often offer the best evening out, reflecting the easy way in which differing groups socialise together. If you prefer exclusively gay places, there's also plenty of choice. Women are welcome in all of Lisbon's gay bars and clubs.

Gay and lesbian movements are not politically radical but the Pride event, which takes place in mid June, is growing and is now held in a prominent downtown location in Praça da Figueira; the **Festival de Cinema Gay e Lésbico** (*see p160*) celebrated its tenth anniversary in September 2006; and politicians are talking about the idea of giving legal recognition to same-sex partnerships. Still, you won't find much, if anything, in the way of themed or fetish bars, and public displays of affection between gay couples are not common. Instead, make the most of the laid-back atmosphere and the attractive and friendly residents, who are always eager to welcome foreign visitors and make sure they experience the best of what Lisbon has to offer.

Nights out don't really get going until after 11pm. Barring one or two places, venues are located in the adjoining areas of Príncipe Real – where you'll find a couple of clubs and the older-established gay bars – and the eternally trendy Bairro Alto. Here **Portas Largas** (*see p184*) remains a popular place to start an evening out, but even busier these days is the crossroads where **Sétimo Céu**, **Side** (for both, *see p166*) and several other bars are located. In warm weather, a predominantly gay crowd mingles and parties in the streets outside the bars until they close at 2am. Only after that hour do the clubs start to fill, here and down by the river.

For more information on what's going on, www.portugalgay.pt is a user friendly and informative site about gay activities throughout Portugal, in English, French, Spanish and German. For the Pride event, see www.portugalpride.org. But to be really well informed, talk to bar staff in Portas Largas, Side or **Bar 106** (*see p165*). For lesbians, http://lesboa.blogspot.com is a newcomer that flags events, albeit in Portuguese. For organisations offering advice and information, see our Directory.

Where to stay

As well as the following gay hotels, we recommend the **Pensão Londres** (*see p47*) in Bairro Alto, **Residencial Alegria** (*see p43*), **Pensão Globo** (*see p47*) and **York House** (*see p51*). The newer **Pensão Luar** (*see p48*) is a welcoming lesbian/mixed place.

Hotel Anjo Azul

Rua Luz Soriano 75, Bairro Alto, 1200-246 (tel/fax 21 347 8069/www.cb2web.com/anjoazul). Metro Baixa-Chiado/tram 28/bus 92. **Rates** €40-€50 single; €50-€75 double. **Credit** AmEx, MC, V. **Map** p250 K9.

Lisbon's most renowned gay hotel is excellent value for money, being clean, friendly and well situated on a quiet street (where celebrated poet Fernando Pessoa also lived) in the Bairro Alto. It has 20 rooms over four floors, some with bathrooms and even jacuzzi, decorated in a simple yet comfortable style. Check it all out on the excellent website. Each floor has two communal bathrooms.

Internet (dataport). TV (DVD).

Pousada dos Anjos

Rua dos Anjos 31, Anjos, 1150 (21 357 2759/www.pousadadosanjos.com). Metro Intendente. **Rates** €20-€25 single; €25-€30 double (without toilet), €35-€50 (with toilet); €35-€45 triple (without toilet), €45-€60 (with toilet); €55-€70 quadruple; €60-€75 suite. **Credit** MC, V. **Map** p246 M7.

This gay hotel is run by the owner of Portas Largas (*see p184*). The restored home of an 18th-century countess, it has 32 rooms ranging from singles to suites. There is also a garden in the back, especially pleasant in summer, when parties are held there. The only drawback is that the hotel is not within walking distance of Bairro Alto. If you'll be wanting breakfast (€5), let reception know when you check in.

Internet (dataport). TV (cable).

Nightlife

The city's gay bars are split between the fashionable Bairro Alto quarter and nearby Príncipe Real where you'll find the more

Max. *See p166.*

traditional gay bars and a couple of dance clubs. **Baliza** (*see p185*) in Bica is also very gay friendly. At all of the following venues there is no admission charge unless stated. After drinks in the Bairro Alto, people tend to peel off either to gay venues like **Trumps** (*see p166*) and **Finalmente** (*see below*) in Príncipe Real or to big dance clubs such as **Kremlin** (*see p188*) or **Lux** (*see p182*), where the far end of the left-hand bar downstairs is a gay area. **Frágil** (*see p184*) is a halfway house in the Bairro Alto for many on their way down to the riverside clubs.

Água no Bico

Rua de São Marcal 170, Príncipe Real (21 347 2830). Metro Rato/bus 58, 790. **Open** 9pm-2am daily. **No credit cards**. **Map** p246 K8.

A cosy and relaxed bar that is situated between Bric-a-Bar and Bar 106. Água no Bico tends to attract an older crowd. Has internet access.

Bar 106

Rua da São Marçal 106, Príncipe Real (21 342 7373/96 634 4860/www.bar106.com). Metro Rato/ bus 58, 790. **Open** 9pm-2am daily. **No credit cards**. **Map** p246 K8.

This stylish modern bar with a fun, friendly atmosphere hosts regular themed events including a 'Screw Party' (not what you might think!) on Fridays and a message party on Sundays. José will fill you in on what's hot and what's not on the gay scene. There's a daily happy hour (9-11.30pm).

Bric-a-Bar

Rua Cecílio de Sousa 84, Príncipe Real (21 342 8971). Metro Rato/bus 58, 92, 790. **Open** midnight-3am Wed, Thur, Sun; midnight-4am Fri, Sat. **No credit cards**. **Map** p246 K8.

On most nights the atmosphere here is more cruisy than the Lisbon average, largely because it's the only venue that plays porn videos and has a dark room – tucked up on the third floor. Amélia, who minds the door, might look like your grandmother but don't let this put you off. Bric-a-Bar, the oldest gay bar in Lisbon, was allowed to exist in the dark days of dictatorship and Amélia must have seen it all.

Finalmente

Rua da Palmeira 33, Príncipe Real (21 347 9923). Metro Rato/bus 58, 92, 790. **Open** 11pm-6am daily. **Admission** €5 (incl drink). **Credit** V. **Map** p250 K8.

The kitsch drag show here, which starts around 2am, is a Lisbon institution, and the place is packed at weekends. After the acts, it's dark, clubby and cruisy, and the younger clients on the raised dance floor are almost as entertaining as the drag show itself.

Heróis

Calçada do Sacramento 14, Chiado (21 342 0077). Metro Baixa-Chiado/tram 28/bus 92. **Open** noon-2am daily. **No credit cards**. **Map** p250 L6.

Favoured by the young and the seriously fashionable, this modern bar/restaurant is a ten-minute walk from the centre of the Bairro Alto. Gays tend to show up after 9pm for a drink.

Purex.

Max

Rua de São Marçal 15, Príncipe Real (21 395 2726). Metro Rato/bus 58, 92, 790. **Open** 9pm-2am daily. **No credit cards. Map** p246 K8.

There's always something going on at Max: from Drag Show Sunday to Strip Show Thursday and in between a message party on Mondays. The place is dimly lit and gets packed at weekends, especially when they bring out the tiny portable stage used for the shows. The clientele is generally older and it's an ideal spot for a chat and a drink before moving on to one of the nearby clubs. You can't miss the lilac-coloured paint outside, covering the ground floor. Happy hour 9-11.30pm daily. **Photo** *p165.*

Memorial

Rua Gustavo Matos Sequeira 42A, Príncipe Real (21 390 7147). Metro Rato/bus 58, 92, 790. **Open** 10pm-4am Tue-Sun. **No credit cards. Map** p246 K8.

Memorial is one of the oldest lesbian bar-clubs in Lisbon, with music for all tastes. There are occasional drag shows as well as a Sunday afternoon matinée (4-8pm), where there's plenty of slow music played for dancing cheek to cheek.

Primas

Rua da Atalaia 154-6, Bairro Alto (21 342 5925). Metro Baixa-Chiado/tram 28/bus 92. **Open** 10pm-4am Mon-Sat. **No credit cards. Map** p251 L9.

You can't get simpler than this tavern with its two pool tables and, remarkably, a jukebox. The owners are three cousins, all women, who run a very unpretentious place with beer and sandwiches on offer, and who know the scene, making it quietly popular with Lisbon's lesbians.

Purex

Rua das Salgadeiras 28, Bairro Alto (96 348 8641). Metro Baixa-Chiado/tram 28/bus 92. **Open** 11pm-4am Tue-Sun. **No credit cards. Map** p250 L9.

Trendy lesbian/mixed bar. Look for the orange doors as there's no sign. Busy at weekends when a DJ provides the latest sounds.

Sétimo Céu

Travessa da Espera 54, Bairro Alto (no phone). Metro Baixa-Chiado/tram 28/bus 92. **Open** 10pm-2am daily. **No credit cards. Map** p250 L9.

A busy and fashionable bar with a DJ. In warm weather the crowd spills out on to the street and mixes with the clientele from Side next door and Clube da Esquina (*see p183*) round the corner, in a street party with something for every taste.

Side

Rua da Barroca 33-5, Bairro Alto (no phone). Metro Baixa-Chiado/tram 28/bus 92. **Open** 10pm-2am daily. **No credit cards. Map** p250 L9.

Light, bright and crowded in the evenings with a young, well-heeled crowd tucking into delicious, if a mite dear, sandwiches and salads, Side's biggest drawback is the lack of elbow room. But the staff are friendly and chat happily as they take care of every detail. This trendy café bar has the same owners as Sétimo Céu (*see above*), and thus makes a good place to pick up tips on gay goings on. It's also a good place to begin your night out, or you could try Clube da Esquina opposite.

Trumps

Rua Imprensa Nacional 104B, Príncipe Real (21 397 1059). Metro Rato/bus 58, 92, 790. **Open** midnight-6am Fri, Sat. **Admission** €10 (incl drinks). **Credit** V. **Map** p246 K8.

Two dance floors and three bars makes Trumps Lisbon's biggest gay club, with techno and house in the main space and pop and Brazilian music elsewhere. It gets busy from 2am after the Bairro Alto bars close, and has regular shows with drag and scantily clad go-go boys. In summer it opens some Sundays for foam parties.

Further out

Mister Gay

Quinta da Silveira, Monte de Caparica (96 258 6803). **Open** midnight-6am Fri, Sat. **Admission** €8. **No credit cards**.
Across the river from Lisbon off the Via Rápida, the main road to the beach at Caparica, this huge club with a provincial feel is in a converted warehouse, and hosts drag and strip shows. It's a popular venue for lesbians, though it attracts a really diverse crowd. Things don't really get going until 2am when the music is mostly techno and house. Even with wheels, getting there is complicated (although there is a map on the relevant page of http://portugal-gay.pt/guide). If you are taking a taxi, you can cut costs by first catching a train over the river to Pragal from Campolide, Entrecampos or Sete Rios.

Cafés & restaurants

Almost all restaurants in Bairro Alto and Príncipe Real are gay-friendly, though some more so than others. There are no exclusively gay restaurants in Lisbon, although **Heróis** (*see p165*), a bar that also serves food, is gayer than most. We recommend **Baralto** (Rua Diário de Notícias 31, 21 342 6739); **Pap' Açorda** (*see p109*); and **Sinal Vermelho** (Rua das Gáveas 89, 21 343 1281). Most local cafés are friendly too. **Café A Brasileira** (*see p125*) gets particularly cruisy in the early evening.

Mar a Dentro Café

Rua do Alecrim 35, Chiado (21 346 9158) Metro Chiado or Cais do Sodré. **Open** 10am-11pm Mon-Fri; 2pm-1am Sat. **No credit cards**. **Map** p250 L10.
This ultra-modern café located between the Bairro Alto and Cais do Sodré station is gay owned and run. Mar a Dentro is a good place to stop for lunch or early evening drinks, and it offers salads and light meals as well as cocktails. It also has free wireless internet access.

Saunas

Lisbon's saunas get a bad rap from some visitors, who see them as scruffy in comparison with facilities elsewhere in Europe.

Sertório Sauna Club

Calçada da Patriarcal 34, Príncipe Real (21 347 0335). Metro Rato. **Open** 3pm-8am Mon-Sat; 3pm-midnight Sun. **Admission** €11. **No credit cards**. **Map** p246 K8.
Lots of space and lots of cabins. This sauna boasts sauna, steam room, jacuzzi, dark rooms, videos, a bar and a gym. It really gets going when the bars and clubs start closing nearby. The owner runs another similarly-priced sauna, Viriato, on the other side of the Avenida da Liberdade on Rua do Telhal (No.4B, 21 342 9436, open 1am-2pm daily).

Spartakus

Largo de Trindade Coelho 2, Bairro Alto (no phone). Metro Baixa-Chiado. **Open** 3pm-9am daily. **Admission** €11. **No credit cards**. **Map** p250 L9.
A slightly scruffy sauna over three floors in Bairro Alto that gets busy at weekends after the bars close. It has a sauna and steam room, jacuzzi, bar and videos. Condoms are supplied.

Cruising

Cruising in Lisbon is usually limited to parks, both day and night, and beaches. Be on the alert for muggers and the occasional police patrols.

As far as the parks go, things have quietened down of late. The central Parque Eduardo VII and Jardim do Príncipe Real have been tidied up and new lighting has been installed, so activity has reduced. Due to the proximity of gay bars and clubs there is still some cruising, though, especially at weekends. Most of the wooded areas have been cleared at Cidade Universitária (University Campus) in Campo Grande so the area is really only used for car cruising now.

All is not lost, though, as there's still plenty of activity on the Caparica coast (*see p210*) south of the river. The beaches at mini-train stops 17, 18 and 19 are nude and gay beaches. If you arrive in the day during the summer and want to cruise head to the dunes. At night, all year round, there's car cruising in the access roads and parking areas.

Cruise control at **Jardim do Príncipe Real**.

Music: Classical & Opera

Port and circumstance.

Festival Internacional de Música de Mafra.

Portuguese composers are not a particularly well-known bunch. But the country has strong musical traditions, underpinned by royal patronage in previous centuries. Its early repertoire has been rediscovered, and a browse through the CD racks will uncover some excellent recordings of works by Dom Dinis, the medieval troubadour king and patron of the arts, early Renaissance composers such as Pedro de Escobar, or later ones such as Manuel Cardoso and João Rebelo. Modern musicians of renown have also tackled the 'colossal baroque' *Te Deum* of António Teixeira, the virtuoso harpsichord sonatas of Carlos Seixas and the rococo elegance of Sousa Carvalho.

Royal patronage was exemplified by Dom João IV's music library, which was famous throughout Europe, but that was lost in the 1755 earthquake. Patronage continued with his successors, however, with Dom João V sending Portuguese composers to Italy to study and bringing Domenico Scarlatti to Lisbon to teach. Composers such as Domingos Bomtempo (1775-1842), Viana da Mota (1868-1948), a pupil of Liszt, and the innovative Luís de Freitas Branco (1890-1955) were the fruits of these efforts.

Contemporary Portuguese performers who have made an impact internationally include pianists Maria João Pires, Artur Pizarro, Pedro Burmester and António Rosado, as well as the Portuguese-born soprano Jennifer Smith. Many concerts in Lisbon take place in churches, monasteries and palaces, while summer festivals attract international artists.

The **Orquestra Gulbenkian** is Portugal's oldest; as in other Lisbon formations, foreign musicians are well represented, creating a cosmopolitan atmosphere backstage. The state-run **Orquestra Sinfónica Portuguesa** is based at the Teatro Nacional de São Carlos but also plays at the CCB and around Portugal. Its repertoire includes major symphonic and operatic works but it has had a somewhat unsettled existence since its creation in 1993. Italian Giovanni Andreoli was appointed resident conductor in 2006.

Lisbon's third orchestra, the **Orquestra Metropolitana de Lisboa** (21 361 7325, www.oml.pt) was founded in 1992 and is run by a consortium of sponsors. It plays hundreds of concerts annually – not just orchestral but also solo performances and chamber music at unusual venues. After a period of upheaval, it is now led by Álvaro Cassuto, who is keen on experimenting (for example with fado). In 2006/7 an OML season ticket was introduced (€150 for 30 concerts) as well as a Cartão Orquestra (€75) that comes with ten tickets and access to some rehearsals.

TICKETS & INFORMATION

Newspapers have daily listings for the most prestigious venues. *Público* has a cultural supplement on Fridays and *Expresso* on Saturdays. *Agenda Cultural,* available from tourist offices, many hotels and online at www.lisboacultural.pt, is also handy.

For some shows you can buy tickets at Multibanco (ATM) cash machines, but in general people pick them up at the venue, often after reserving by phone. Tickets may also be bought for a fee at ABEP, Agência de Bilhetes Alvalade and Fnac (*see p133*) or by phone or online with Ticket Line (21 003 6300/707 234 234, 11am-8pm Mon-Fri, 1-8pm Sat, Sun, www.ticketline.pt) or Plateia (21 434 6304, 11am-1pm, 2-6pm Mon-Fri, www.plateia.iol.pt). With the latter two you may buy online, using Visa or Mastercard. You then pick your tickets up at the venue or, with Ticket Line, at their offices (Avenida Elias Garcia 137-3°, 217 803 670/1, 11am-7pm Mon-Fri) near Campo Pequeno.

ABEP

Praça dos Restauradores, Restauradores (21 342 5360). Metro Restauradores. **Open** 9am-9pm Mon-Sat. **No credit cards. Map** p250 L8.

Agência de Bilhetes Alvalade

Alvalade Shopping, Praça de Alvalade 6B, Alvalade (21 795 5859). Metro Alvalade. **Open** 11am-9.30pm Mon-Sat; 12.30-8.30pm Sun. **No credit cards. Map** p249 M2.

Venues

As well as those listed, the Centro Cultural de Belém (*see p161*) hosts classical concerts on a regular basis: its Grande Auditório (tickets from €7; half-price under-31s) has fine acoustics for large-scale works and opera, while the Pequeno Auditório is more intimate. A tiny rehearsing room is used for alternative music. The CCB had to suspend the 2007 Festa da Música, its biggest annual event, for budgetary reasons, but its one-day Festa de Primavera, in late March, does include free concerts. At Culturgest (*see p161*), the Grande Auditório (tickets €15-€20) has a capacity of 618 and reasonable acoustics, and is used for contemporary music. It has no capacity for symphonic works. The Teatro da Trindade (*see p193*) now stages some light operas, while the Pavilhão Atlântico (*see p177*) is used for musical spectaculars.

Coliseu dos Recreios

Rua das Portas de Santo Antão 96, Baixa (21 324 0585/www.coliseulisboa.com). Metro Restauradores or Rossio. **Open** *Box office* 1-7.30pm Mon-Sat or until 30mins after start of performance. **Tickets** €10-€75. **No credit cards. Map** p250 L8.

Lisbon's coliseum was completed in 1890 and stages everything from circus through rock concerts to classic operas. Acoustics vary; try the left side.

Teatro Camões

Passeio de Neptuno, Parque das Nações (21 892 3470/7). Metro Oriente. **Open** *Box office* 2-7pm Tue-Sat, or until 30mins after start of performance. **Tickets** €5-€35. **Credit** AmEx, DC, MC, V.

Built for Expo 98, this big blue glass and metal cube seats 890 amid state-of-the-art acoustics. It is home to the Companhia Nacional do Bailado (*see p195*).

Teatro Nacional de São Carlos

Rua Serpa Pinto 9, Chiado (21 325 3045/www.saocarlos.pt). Metro Baixa-Chiado/tram 28. **Open** *Box office* 1-7pm Mon-Fri. **Tickets** prices vary. **Credit** AmEx, MC, V. **Map** p250 L10.

A grand 18th-century opera house inspired by La Scala, with a rococo interior, excellent acoustics and good visibility. Despite years of underinvestment in opera, and perennial budget problems, its Italian director Paolo Pinamonti has fostered native excellence and used his contacts to produce well-balanced seasons full of surprises.

Festivals

The Festival de Sintra (mid June-July, *see p151*) is a highlight for classical buffs, with concerts by international artists, often in beautiful settings. Almada has a Mês da Música in October, embracing classical to fado. In December look out for Lisbon city council's Concertos de Natal.

Festival Internacional de Orgão de Lisboa

Tickets & information Juventude Musical Portuguesa, Avenida da Liberdade 13 2°, 1250 (21 357 3131/www.jmp.pt/festival). **Admission** free. **Date** Sept-Oct.

Free organ concerts that take place in half-a-dozen Lisbon churches over a fortnight. It attracts foreign organists who are big noises in the field, but Portuguese musicians get a look in too.

Música Viva

Tickets & information 21 457 5068/www.misomusic.com. **Tickets** €10; €5 under 31s. **Children's concerts** €2. **Date** late Sept-late Oct.

A series of experimental music concerts (including several world premières) in venues from the Gulbenkian to Mosteiro dos Jerónimos, and an important forum for musical creativity.

Festival Internacional de Música de Mafra

See p152 (261 817 550/261 811 947). **Tickets** €5-€8. **Date** Oct-early Nov.

Held over a series of weekends at Mafra palace (*see p217*), this innovative festival focuses on baroque and contemporary music. The basilica is used as a spectacular setting for some concerts. The first 30 people to turn up at the box office with a ticket get a guided visit to the palace.

Música em São Roque

Largo Trindade Coelho, Bairro Alto (21 323 5380). Metro Baixa-Chiado/tram 28. **Tickets** €2.50-€5. **Date** Nov-Jan.

Two or three concerts per week, some in the lavish 16th-century Igreja de São Roque – a perfect backdrop for *música antiga* – some in the adjoining museum. Tickets are sold on the door.

Fifty years of Mr Five Per Cent's legacy

The Gulbenkian Foundation's status as Lisbon's most important cultural institution is unchallenged and, perhaps, unchallengeable. On turning 50, it marked the milestone with a string of events running through to mid 2007: simultaneously paying homage to its founder, highlighting its own contribution to society, and indicating its future course.

Calouste Gulbenkian was born in Istanbul in 1869, into a family of Armenian traders. He made his money in oil, his deal-making earning him the nickname 'Mr Five Per Cent'.

Gulbenkian is said to have begun his collection in his teens, after picking up some coins in a bazaar. By the time he died in 1955, it was one of the most valuable in private hands, and unrivalled in Europe for Islamic and oriental art. He left it all to a foundation – which later built the **Museu Calouste Gulbenkian** (*see p96*) – and endowed it with his fortune.

Over the decades the Gulbenkian has filled a considerable gap in Portugal left by feeble state funding. It runs the **Centro de Arte Moderna** (*see p161*), provides grants to students, publishes arts-related material and runs a specialist central library and nationwide network that puts the state's efforts to shame. Its funds are not limitless, but in the field of music in particular the foundation remains unrivalled.

Founded as a chamber group in 1962, the Gulbenkian Orchestra developed its own distinctive sound, although with 60 players it falls short of symphonic dimensions. While its size makes it flexible, and its repertoire is vast, the end result depends upon the inspiration provided by the conductor. In 2002 American Lawrence Foster took over as resident maestro. Guest conductors are also a feature of the October to May seasons; one of the current crop, Portuguese emigrée Joana Carneiro, director of the Los Angeles Philharmonic, is the first woman to conduct the Gulbenkian.

The foundation's concert series – for which combined tickets are available – brings major world orchestras, chamber groups and soloists to the Grande Auditório and other spaces, including the outdoor amphitheatre, as well as to other Lisbon venues.

The 100-strong Gulbenkian Choir, founded two years after the orchestra and under the baton of Michel Corboz since 1969, has won plaudits in recent years for its work with Frans Brüggen's Orchestra of the 18th Century.

Fundação Calouste Gulbenkian

Avenida de Berna 45A, Praça de Espanha (21 782 3000/tickets 21 782 3700/3030/ www.musica.gulbenkian.pt). Metro São Sebastião. **Open** *Box office* 10am-7pm Mon-Fri; 10am-5.30pm Sat (to 7pm if concert); 10am-7pm on Sun if concert. **Tickets** €5-€60; 30% discount concessions. **Credit** AmEx, MC, V. **Map** p248 K4.

Music: Fado

Fated to make a comeback.

Clube de Fado. *See p173.*

It might surprise you to learn that Lisbon has a highly developed musical genre of its own, but once you've heard fado's tuneful melancholy it is indissociable from its home town. These days the style is back in fashion and can be heard in a growing number of venues, from buttoned up restaurants to shabby *tascas*. Wherever you choose to listen to fado, it's fair to say that you don't really know Lisbon until you have done so.

Fado means 'fate' and is often regarded as an expression of the supposed national trait of fatalism. Whatever the truth of this, many songs, whether performed by men or women, do touch upon betrayal, jealousy and disappointed love. Fado is also linked with the notion of *saudade*: longing for something impossible to attain (*see p14* **Wish you were here, wish I were there**). However, fado can be upbeat in tone. In the more informal venues, audiences tend to be less reverential and may interrupt the singer with repartee. Another lighter touch is the *desgarrada*, a conversation in song, where singers challenge each other, often with caustic remarks. The spontaneity of this varies.

In fado, conveying sentiment is more important than technical perfection (singers in *tascas* may be a little harsh on the ear). The *fadista* is accompanied by a *guitarra*, a 12-string Portuguese guitar, and a *viola*, an acoustic Spanish guitar. The *guitarra* is shaped like a mandolin and its strings are arranged in pairs, producing a resonant sound that at times highlights the singer's melody and at others plays solo, while the *viola* provides a rhythmic accompaniment to them both. *Guitarra* players may pursue careers of their own, making music that requires no vocal accompaniment. The supreme example of this is Carlos Paredes.

The origins of fado are the subject of bitter debate. One Brazilian academic aggrieved Portuguese sensibilities by claiming that it was introduced from Brazil in the first half of the 19th century; the earliest known reference to fado, in 1883, described it as incorporating a sensual dance, prompting some to link it with samba. Others see fado as a legacy of the Moors, due to similarities with North African singing styles. Most agree that it owes something to the troubadour tradition of medieval Provence. (This is more obvious with Coimbra fado, a quite different musical form performed by male university students or alumni.)

In the mid 1800s fado was associated with Lisbon low life, and was performed in the seedy taverns of working-class *bairros*, notably Alfama and Mouraria, where legendary *fadista* Maria Severa Onofriana – known as 'A Severa' – lived and loved until her death at the age of just 26. But it was taken up by members of the aristocracy such as the Marquês de Marialva, hence the word *marialvismo*, the romantic attraction felt by the upper classes for the pastimes of their social inferiors. This was the first in a series of transformations that took fado beyond its humble origins. Another was the interest of intellectuals in the 20th century; as poets began to write lyrics for fado, they made it more sophisticated.

Radio, the gramophone and then television helped fado became a truly national music – as did the efforts of the Salazar regime, which mythologised it as an element of national identity. (The first ever Portuguese talkie was Leitão de Barros's *A Severa*, based on the popular 1901 drama by Júlio Dantas that had built on existing myth.) However, this could perhaps not have happened without Amália. Born in 1920 to a poor family and possessed of a uniquely expressive voice ('I don't sing fado – it sings in me,' she said) Amália Rodrigues became fado's biggest ever star, taking it from the taverns to the stage, the recording studio and the screen in *Capas Negras*, a film that broke national box office records in 1947. She was the first *fadista* to gain international recognition, singing at the Paris Olympia and appearing on Broadway.

Amália, and fado itself, fell out of favour after the 1974 Revolution but has since been fully rehabilitated (*see p175* **Talkin' 'bout my geração**). When Amália died in 1999, she was mourned by the nation (campaigning was suspended for the general election due a few days later) and her remains were subsequently transferred to the Panteão Nacional de Santa Engracia (*see p72*). In retrospect, her passing can be seen to have marked the end of an era. While most of the fado sung in Lisbon restaurants is in the tradition she embodied, and female *fadista*s are still often measured against her, today's vibrant scene has taken a step away from that tradition, to renew it.

Venues

Fado needs the right setting to work its magic and the convention is to stop talking during the performance. There are always several singers, so don't worry if you don't like the first. In posher *casas de fado* (fado houses) – restaurants where professional musicians perform – the standard of music is invariably good, but remember that people who sing (sometimes every day) for a living can get a little jaded. This doesn't happen in the taverns specialising in *fado vadio* (vagabond fado), where a more laid-back attitude prevails and anyone may get up and sing. Another difference is that, while admission to *fado vadio* places is invariably free, restaurants require customers to dine (at prices higher than equivalent eateries) or to stump up a *consumo mínimo* (minimum consumption). On less busy nights, they may allow you to come in later and nurse a drink; do check first. Average dinner prices given below are of set menus where these exist, but they are not obligatory. In general, restaurant kitchens close around midnight – but when the *casa de fado* itself closes will depend on how much business there is. In touristy

Tasca do Chico. *See p174.*

places, there is some folk dancing on offer; this is usually wound up at about 10pm, to get to the more serious business of fado.

In summer there are other opportunities to listen in, with the council laying on fado on the 28 tram on June evenings, and the odd open-air fado shows. The Mercado da Ribeira (*see p147*) also hosts concerts.

Casas de fado

Adega Machado

Rua do Norte 91, Bairro Alto (21 322 4640). Metro Baixa-Chiado/tram 28. **Open** 8pm-3am Tue-Sun. *Fado & folk dancing* 9.15pm. *Fado* only from 11pm. **Admission** minimum spend €16. **Dinner average** €30. **Credit** AmEx, DC, MC, V. **Map** p250 L9.
A folksy place dating from 1931, with oil lamps, checked tablecloths, black-and-white photos of Amália, and lots of handclapping. Its large size attracts tour groups (for which it puts on some very un-Lisbon folk dancing), yet it retains its atmosphere. Presiding is Filipe de Araújo Machado, grandson of the founder; house star is Marina Rosa.

A Parreirinha de Alfama

Beco do Espírito Santo 1, Alfama (21 886 8209). Tram 18, 25/bus 9, 28, 35, 81, 82, 90, 746, 759, 794. **Open** 8pm-after midnight. *Fado* from 9.30pm. **Admission** dinner only until 11pm, average €30; after 11pm minimum spend €10. **Credit** AmEx, DC, MC, V. **Map** p251 N10.
This low-ceilinged, atmospheric restaurant in an alley off the Largo do Chafariz de Dentro is owned by fado legend Argentina Santos. She doesn't sing every night, but monitors the quality (of both singing and audience) from a seat near the door.

Bacalhau de Molho

Beco dos Armazéns do Linho 1, Alfama (21 886 3767/www.casadelinhares.com). Tram 18, 25 then 5min walk/bus 9, 28, 35, 81, 82, 90, 746, 759, 794. **Open** 8pm-midnight daily. *Fado* from 9pm. **Admission** minimum spend €20. **Dinner average** €45. **Credit** AmEx, DC, MC, V.
Four singers a night perform in this cosy restaurant. As the name suggests, it has *bacalhau* aplenty, so you can kill two *típico* experiences with one stone.

Clube de Fado

Rua São João da Praça 92-4, Alfama (21 885 2704/ 21 888 2694/www.clube-de-fado.com). Tram 28. **Open** 8pm-2am daily. *Fado* 9.30pm. **Admission** dinner only until 11.30pm; after 11.30pm €15 (includes drink), €20 (two drinks). **Dinner average** €45. **Credit** AmEx, MC, V. **Map** p251 M10.
Owned by *guitarrista* Mário Pacheco, this club attracts his friends, who may get up and do a turn, and features sessions by leading traditional *fadistas*. It has a lovely atmosphere, with stone columns and arches dividing the room into nooks. **Photo** *p171*.

Mesa de Frades

Rua dos Remédios 139, Alfama (91 702 9436). Tram 18, 25/bus 9, 28, 35, 81, 82, 90, 746, 759, 794. **Open** 8pm-2am daily. *Fado* from 10.30pm. **Dinner average** €25. **Credit** MC, V. **Map** p245 J9.
This *azulejo*-lined former chapel of the Quinta da Dona Rosa, a palace built by Dom João V for one of his lovers, is owned by *guitarra* player Pedro de

Castro. Its roster includes Pedro Moutinho (Fridays) and Cidália Moreira (Saturdays), but you never know who might roll up in the wee hours: Moutinho's brother Camané, perhaps, or their other *fadista* brother, Hélder. Twice a week the thrilling Carminho sings (Mondays she shares with flautist Rao Kyao, Wednesdays are hers alone). The food is Portuguese, prettified: *bacalhau com natas* with parmesan and the like. Booking is a must.

O Faia

Rua da Barroca 54-6, Bairro Alto (21 342 6742). Metro Baixa-Chiado/tram 28. **Open** 8pm-2am Mon-Sat. *Fado* 9.30pm. **Admission** minimum spend €17.50. **Dinner average** €45. **Credit** AmEx, DC, MC, V. **Map** p250 L9.

Upmarket and slightly antiseptic venue but an excellent place to hear good-quality *fadistas*. They include Anita Guerreiro, who had a successful career in *revista* (music hall) before focusing on fado, and António Rocha, known for his classic style.

O Forcado

Rua da Rosa 219-21, Bairro Alto (21 346 8579). Metro Baixa-Chiado, then 10min walk/bus 58, 790. **Open** 7.30pm-1am daily. *Fado & folk dancing* 9-11pm. *Fado* only 11pm-1am. **Admission** minimum spend €15. **Dinner** set menu €27. **Credit** AmEx, DC, MC, V. **Map** p250 L9.

A cavernous place that caters to tour groups, offering both fado and folk dancing. It works on a shift system so is not somewhere to spend an entire evening, but its size means it attracts some of the better performers of both Lisbon and Coimbra fado.

O Timpanas

Rua Gilberto Rola 24, Alcântara (21 390 6655/ www.timpanas.pt). Bus 60, 713, 727, 773. **Open** 8.30pm-2am Mon, Wed-Sun. *Fado & folk dancing* 9pm. *Fado* only from 10pm. **Admission** minimum spend €20. **Credit** MC, V. **Map** p245 G9.

Off the beaten tourist track in Alcântara, near the leafy Tapada das Necessidades park, this fado joint has both fado and folk dancing. The food is decent, if not sophisticated.

Senhor Vinho

Rua do Meio à Lapa 18, Lapa (21 397 2681/www.restsrvinho.com). Tram 25. **Open** 8pm-2am Mon-Sat. *Fado* 9.30pm. **Admission** minimum spend €23. **Dinner average** €45. **Credit** AmEx, DC, MC, V. **Map** p245 J9.

This Lisbon classic has helped launch countless fadistas, including Mariza and Camané (*see p175* **Talkin' 'bout my geração**). Look out for sweet-voiced Carlos Macedo (who also plays *guitarra*), Maria Dilar, António Zambujo (who adds Spanish guitar to his singing talents) and Aldina Duarte (Camané's ex). The restaurant is owned by the grande dame of fado, Maria da Fé, who sings towards the end of the evening. To hear Coimbra fado, come on Friday or Saturday, for Dr Machado Soares. The food is good, booking essential.

Velho Páteo de Santana

Rua Dr Almeida Amaral 6, Campo Santana (21 314 1063/4/www.velhopateodesantana.com). Elevador do Lavra then 10min walk/bus 30, 723, 759, 790. **Open** 8pm-2am Tue-Sun. *Fado* 9pm. **Admission** minimum spend €20 **Dinner average** €40. **Credit** AmEx, MC, V. **Map** p246 M7.

A newish venue aimed at groups but not too impersonal, as the space is split between two rooms and a patio. The all-in menu is reasonably priced and there are house specialities. From the Baixa, take the funicular near the Coliseu, head left and then skirt Campo dos Martíres da Pátria; the restaurant is opposite the Hospital dos Capuchos.

Fado vadio

With fado vadio the *consumo mínimo* business does not apply, so for the uninitiated or impecunious it's a good place to start. Just don't expect quality food or quality singing – or any singing, for that matter; phone ahead to check there is fado on any given evening.

In Alfama, **A Fermentação** (Largo São Rafael 1, 91 707 9290, fado 8pm-midnight Thur) is a gallery, restaurant and *fado vadio* venue in one tiny space. A cobblestone's throw away is the busy **Baiuca** (Rua de São Miguel 20, 21 886 7284, fado 8pm-1am Mon, Thur-Sun), opened in 1998 by a former bank clerk and run by his two friendly daughters. You must order a meal but are unlikely to pay more than €17 a head. *Fadista*s from other restaurants often drop in.

Up in Graça is the ultra-local **O Jaime** (Rua da Graça 91, 21 888 1560, fado 4-8pm Sat, Sun & holidays), where you can tuck into a hearty lunch before fado sessions. During them emotion runs high, with dramatic pauses punctuated only by the rumble of a passing tram. Here, as across town at the better known **Tasca do Chico** (Rua Diário de Notícias 39, 21 343 1040, fado 8pm-1am Wed & Fri, pictured p172), you can just poke your head in the door. In fact, that may be all you can do; to get a seat, arrive early. Near Saldanha, **A Tasca do Careca** (Rua Engenheiro Vieira da Silva 2A, 21 357 5265, fado 8pm-2am Sat) – 'Baldie's tavern' – is a legendary venue that Mísia likes to visit now and again to stay grounded.

A plethora of neighbourhood clubs also hold periodic sessions. You'll stick out but this is as authentic as it gets. The **Grupo Excursionista Vai Tu** (Rua da Bica Duarte Belo 6-8, 21 346 0848) is a fun place where a host of *fadistas* come for dinner and to sing at Sunday evening get togethers (one or two a month in winter). The **Grupo Desportivo de Mouraria** (Travessa do Nazaré 21, no phone) is in fado's heartland. For details of its next Sunday session, call its president, João Pedro, on 96 251 8547; to book call Toni on 91 877 8405.

Talkin' 'bout my geração

After the 1974 Revolution fado withered as many Portuguese distanced themselves from a style that was tainted by its associations with the dictatorship. The left, and intellectuals in particular, turned to the unimpeachably plebeian folk, which enjoyed a huge revival.

The peerless Amália Rodrigues, whose career had been promoted by the Salazar regime and who had personal links with some of its leading figures, was shunted into a ghetto. She and other *fadistas* of her generation such as Alfredo Marceneiro soldiered on, as did the younger Carlos do Carmo, João Braga and Nuno de Cãmara Pereira. The flame was kept burning in the clubs of Alfama, Mouraria and other *bairros históricos*, and in some upper-class circles where family gatherings ended with members doing a turn. There were also competitions such as the televised Grande Noite de Fado. But fado remained deeply unfashionable.

It was only in the 1990s, when a handful of youngsters started to make it big abroad, that the nation as a whole sat up and took notice. Madredeus led the way; though the group did not perform fado their image was clearly influenced by the tradition. They were followed by Dulce Pontes, who ranged across a spectrum of styles but covered some of the songs Amália was best known for, albeit in a less melodramatic style. Though one of Portugal's most popular recording artists, there were times when Pontes was doing better abroad, particularly in the Netherlands. The Dutch have also taken to Cristina Branco, who has only very recently been embraced by her compatriots.

Mísia, now one of fado's best-known names, began her career in Spain. That, plus her modern visual style and her mixing of fado with other influences, earned her opprobrium from purists. The younger Mariza, currently the biggest star abroad, won plaudits there before her star quality was fully recognised at home. In the UK and elsewhere, she collected awards; in Portugal, conservatives turned their noses up at the packaging, while failing to appreciate the quality of the contents. Despite her punky image and experience with blues and jazz, Mariza shows great respect for the fado tradition, as befits someone who grew up in Mouraria (though born in Mozambique).

Contrasting with Mariza's style is the more formal Kátia Guerreiro, a qualified doctor who, like Oporto native Mísia, is not from Lisbon (she lived in the Azores until she was 18) but grew up listening to fado recordings. She's one of several *fadistas* who have performed at London's annual Gulbenkian-sponsored Atlantic Waves Festival.

The city council belatedly recognised the need to cherish Lisbon's most highly developed art form with the inauguration in 1998 of the **Casa do Fado e da Guitarra Portuguesa** in Alfama. The museum has regular themed exhibitions, a documentation centre, an auditorium seating 90 and a shop selling CDs and fado paraphernalia. The attached school runs courses in Portuguese guitar and Spanish guitar for fado, as well as seminars for songwriters and workshops for *fadistas*. It is pleased to accept motivated foreigners. There's also a café attached that functions as a *casa de fado* on Thursday, Friday and Saturday nights.

The fado renewal is gathering momentum, leaving youngsters free to develop their own style. Watch out for talents such as Hélder Moutinho, Maria Ana Bobone, Ana Sofia Varela and Mafalda Arnauth. Fado has even crossed over into the rock world, with the most classical of young male *fadistas*, Camané, performing at festivals as lead vocalist for Portuguese supergroup Humanos. At times, he looked startled to be there singing to such huge crowds.

It is female *fadistas* that are most in fashion, however. The latest young talent is Raquel Tavares, a native who in 2006 released her first recording at the age of 21, with a 15-year career already behind her. Her limpid style shows that, like others of her generation, she sees no need to resort to the excesses that were once a trap for *fadistas* trying to lay the ghost of Amália.

Casa do Fado e da Guitarra Portuguesa

Largo do Chafariz de Dentro 1, Alfama (museum 21 882 3470/café 21 886 0219/ www.egeac.pt/casadofado). Tram 18, 25/bus 9, 28, 35, 81, 82, 90, 746, 759, 794. **Open** *Museum* 10am-1pm, 2-6pm Tue-Sun (last entry 5.30pm). *Library* 2-6pm Tue-Fri. *School* 2-8pm Tue-Fri. *Café* 10am-1am Tue-Sun (fado 9.30pm Thur-Sat). **Admission** *Museum* €3; €1.50 concessions; free under-7s. Free for all Sun to 2pm. **Fado dinner** €23 (food only); after 11pm €10 minimum spend. **Credit** MC, V.

Music: Rock, Roots & Jazz

Lisbon has more places than ever to hear live music.

Keep your ears open as you walk around town and you'll realise that you're in a very diverse musical environment. A balmy climate and tolerant attitude mean that pop and samba, fado and Cape Verdean mornas, chilly northern European techno and feisty local rap all spill on to the beaches of Caparica and the streets of Bairro Alto and Santos.

There's little tradition of teenage wannabes playing bars in the hope of hitting the big time, but there are places with in-house bands. As for touring famous acts, Portugal used to be off the edge of the world, but they now turn up regularly, particularly for festivals. Some performers are passionately embraced by locals and return frequently; this has happened with artists as diverse as David Byrne and Massive Attack. The staging of the 2005 MTV Europe Awards in Lisbon brought more recognition, even if there was little contact with locals.

TICKETS & INFORMATION

Dailies Público and *Diário de Notícias* have music sections with listings, and a showbiz magazine on Fridays. Online, the Música section of http://lazer.publico.clix.pt is pretty comprehensive. Tickets can be obtained from agencies ABEP and Agência Alvalade (for both, *see p169*) and also Fnac (*see p133*) – whose cafés often showcase local talent – or Ticketline (21 003 6300, www.ticketline.pt). In general, tickets have risen sharply in price but are still cheap compared with much of Europe.

Fonoteca

Edifício Monumental, Loja 17, Praça Duque de Saldanha, Saldanha (21 353 6231/2/www.cm-lisboa.pt/fonoteca). Metro Saldanha. **Open** 10am-7pm Tue-Sat. **Admission** free. **Map** p248 L5.

Tucked into the basement of a shopping centre, the Fonoteca record library has 20,000 CDs in its collection you can listen to on the premises, plus books, DVDs and magazines. It has resident musicologists and hosts irregular talks and intimate performances.

Rock & pop

Initial impressions of Portuguese popular music may be negative. *Pimba*, cheesy local pop, is the tip of an iceberg that reaches right down into rural Portugal, where bands play boom-bang-a-bang music at summer fairs. It wasn't until the mid 1990s that Pedro Abrunhosa, who went on to record his Portuguese funk in Prince's Paisley Park studios, breathed some life into the scene. It has since diversified considerably, but remains fairly derivative. The debate continues between those who think that only English sounds 'right'– oblivious to the naffness that can result – and those who let rip in their native tongue. Current media darlings the Gift are in the former camp, the older Clã – fronted by the versatile Manuela Azevedo – in the latter. Dance music has taken some of the sting out of the issue but it's refreshing to see Da Weasel headline festivals with their uniquely Portuguese hip hop.

Rapper Boss AC is popular with a younger crowd, as is ska and reggae – though the local scene has produced nothing of global interest. But in other musical areas, more exploratory collectives are gaining exposure, including deadpan spaghetti western duo Dead Combo. Such performers also benefit from the recent emergence of venues willing to provide a stage (or just a corner) for something other than tired covers. There is also an increasing overlap between clubs and live venues, so take a look at our Nightlife chapter as well.

Concerts at major venues usually start at 9pm, but doors open an hour earlier. At smaller, alternative venues shows start at 10pm or later.

Major venues

Lisbon football club Sporting's stadium (*see p198*) hosts the occasional big concert by U2 and the like, and a number of Lisbon concert halls are used for rock as well as classical music: the Coliseu dos Recreios (*see p169*); Culturgest (*see p161*), whose programming leans towards jazz and sounds from around the world; and the Centro Cultural de Belém (*see p161*). The CCB's main auditorium makes audiences feel they should be on their best behaviour, but there are more relaxed free concerts at 7pm most weekdays in the terrace bar. Paradise Garage (*see p191*) is an atmospheric place for metal and indie.

Aula Magna

Alameda da Universidade, Cidade Universitária (21 011 3406). Metro Cidade Universitária. **Tickets** €20-€30. **No credit cards. Map** p248 L2.

With its wide, steeply banked seating area, this university amphitheatre does not really lend itself to rock concerts, but can pull them off given the right act.

Casino Lisboa

Alameda dos Oceanos, Parque das Nações (21 466 7700/www.casinolisboa.pt). Metro Oriente. **Open** 3pm-3am Mon-Thur, Sun; 4pm-4am Fri, Sat. *Live music* 9.30pm, 11.30pm. **Admission** €15-€35. **Credit** AmEx, DC, MC, V.

This slick new glass complex contains several restaurants and bars, hundreds of slot machines and a 634-seat auditorium with the latest equipment. It regularly stages concerts by leading Portuguese and foreign jazz and other artists.

Pavilhão Atlântico

Rossio dos Olivais, Parque das Nações (21 891 8409/ www.pavilhaoatlantico.pt). Metro Oriente. **Tickets** €20-€50. **No credit cards.**

Built for Expo 98 to an impressive design by Regino Cruz, this UFO-shaped arena by the river is Lisbon's premier indoor rock venue, albeit not always the most atmospheric. It kicked off with a legendary show by Massive Attack and since then has hosted the likes of Bob Dylan, Alanis Morissette, Eric Clapton and Madonna.

Live music bars

As well as the venues listed below, the Hard Rock Café (Avenida da Liberdade 2, 21 324 5280, www.hardrock.com) has bands twice weekly (11pm-1am Mon & Sun). Hennessy's (Rua Cais do Sodré 32, 21 343 1064), a large 'Irish pub' down by the river, has live music from 11pm every night, none of it Irish. At other bars, nights may vary, so it's best to check.

Musicais

Passeio do Oriente, Doca do Jardim do Tabaco, Avenida Infante Dom Henrique Pavilhão A/B, Santa Apolónia (93 758 3698/www.passeioriente.com/ pomusicais.htm). Bus 9, 28, 35, 81, 82, 90, 746, 759, 794. **Open** *Summer* noon-3am Mon-Thur, Sun; noon-4am Fri, Sat. *Winter* noon-midnight Mon-Thur, Sun; noon-3am Fri, Sat. *Live music* 11.30pm some days. **Admission** free. **Credit** MC, V. **Map** p247 O9.

A sprawling, hotel lobby-like space with riverside esplanade and Brazilian restaurant attached. There's live music (Portuguese and Anglo-US covers, or Brazilian sounds) on some Wednesdays, Fridays and Saturdays. On Sunday local bands may get a look in.

O Sítio do Cefalópode

Largo do Contador-Mor 4B, Castelo (91 643 9577/ www.cefalopode.com). Tram 12, 28. **Open** 10pm-2am Mon-Thur, Sun; 10pm-4am Fri, Sat. *Live music* from 11.30pm. **Admission** free or €5 (includes one drink). **No credit cards. Map** p251 M9.

Opened in October 2005 and already a magnet for music lovers, with everything from Brazilian *choro* to experimental jazz. The owners are enthusiastic and well connected, and leading Portuguese and promising foreign musicians can be heard here. The cellar space is tiny so if you want to avoid sitting on the stairs, turn up early but bring reading matter with you as the shows start late.

Refúgio das Freiras

Avenida Dom Carlos I 57, Loja 2, Santos (no phone). Tram 25/tram 28, then 5mins walk/bus 6, 49. **Open** 11pm-4am daily. *Live music* from 12.30am Thur-Sat. **Admission** free. **No credit cards. Map** p246 K10.

The 'Nuns' Refuge' is a grizzled bar in Santos that purveys rock covers and cheap beer to an eager, mainly student audience. The house shot is Pastel de Nata (custard tart).

Rock in Chiado Café

Rua Paiva de Andrade 7-13, off Largo do Chiado, Chiado (21 346 4859/www.rockinchiado.com). Metro Baixa-Chiado. **Open** 4pm-3am daily. *Live music* from 11.30pm Tue-Sun. **Admission** free. **Credit** MC, V. **Map** p250 L9.

This new 100-seat café-restaurant attracts a varied crowd with its programming: karaoke on Mondays, *fado vadio* on Tuesdays, goth on Wednesdays, reggae on Thursdays, tributes and covers on Fridays and Saturdays, and Brazilian on Sundays.

Templários

Rua Flores do Lima 8A, Entre Campos (21 797 0177/ http://templarios.blog.pt). Metro Roma/Entrecampos. **Open** 10.30pm-2am Mon-Thur; 10.30pm-3am Fri, Sat. *Live music* from 12.30am Mon-Sat. **Admission** free. **Credit** AmEx, MC, V. **Map** p248 M3.

A bar where punters of all ages knock back beer and Caipirinhas while listening to Portuguese and international standards, as well as the odd original set. Reservations are guaranteed only until 11.30pm.

Folk

It was a song by José Afonso on the radio that cued the 1974 Revolution, and folk had great importance in defining a new Portuguese identity during that period. Singers such as Sérgio Godinho, Fausto and Vitorino have repopularised traditional songs from the Alentejo, while Júlio Pereira and bagpipers Gaiteros de Lisboa base their work on traditional music. But folk's popularity has faded in recent years as fado's has soared.

Among Portuguese artists known abroad, only Madredeus (haunting or vapid, depending on your taste) are global stars, but talented singers such as Dulce Pontes and Cristina Branco have made a name for themselves (*see p175* **Talkin' 'bout my geração**). Many draw on both folk and fado traditions, as do the funky Donna Maria, who have done well mixing electro with traditional instruments.

A side **Ondajazz**. *See p181*.

Anos Sessenta

Largo do Terreirinho 21, Mouraria (21 887 3444). Metro Martim Moniz. **Open** 6-8pm, 10pm-4am Tue-Sat. *Live music* 11pm-3am Tue-Sat. **Admission** free. **Credit** DC, MC, V. **Map** p251 M9.

The nostalgic name ('The Sixties') reflects both much of the music on offer and the ambience created by the regular patrons: typically middle-aged civil servants and professionals. Mainly soloists and duos perform on African, folk and Brazilian evenings.

Inda a noite é uma criança

Praça das Flores 8, São Bento (21 396 3545). Metro Rato then 10min walk/bus 773. **Open** 10.30pm-4am Mon-Sat. *Live music* midnight-2.30am Mon-Sat. **Admission** free. **Credit** V. **Map** p246 K8.

'The night is but a child' is the bar's name, but most of its regulars are between 30 and 50. Guitar soloists or duos play Portuguese folk from the past 30 years in a friendly, intimate atmosphere.

O'Gilins

Rua dos Remolares 8, Cais do Sodré (21 342 1899). Metro Cais do Sodré/tram 15, 18, 25. **Open** 11am-2pm daily. *Live music* 11pm Thur-Sat; 11pm some Wed. **Admission** free. **No credit cards**.

Low-key Irish pub that offers the now obligatory ingredients of Guinness (always), Sky Sports (occasionally) and Celtic music (three days a week), as well as hearty Irish breakfasts until 6pm on Sundays. It attracts a mix of Portuguese and expats.

RibeirArte Bar Café

Mercado da Ribeira, piso superior, Avenida 24 de Julho, Cais do Sodré (21 031 2605/0/http://espaco ribeira.pt/cantinho.html). **Open** noon-3pm Mon; noon-3am Tue-Sat; 1-8pm Sun. *Live music* 11pm Thur-Sat. **Credit** AmEx, MC, V. **Map** p250 K/L 10.

On the top floor of an old market, this 85-seater bar has live Brazilian music on Thursday and 'Portuguese music' – basically folk – on Friday and Saturday.

African

In recent years Lisbon has built a reputation as a place to hear African music. The most established locally based artists are Cape Verdeans Dany Silva and Tito Paris, but youngsters go more for Lura, also from Cape Verde, or Hélder – known as Rei do Kuduro for his mastery of this electronic mix of ragga and Angolan *kizomba*. Sara Tavares is rare in breaking through to a mass audience.

Music from Portugal's former African colonies can be heard on state radio station RDP África (101.5 FM); you could also make a lunchtime visit to the Associação Cabo Verde (*see p26* **Ethnic Lisbon**). As well as the places listed below, A Lontra (*see p192*) is currently hosting live bands on Thursdays, mainly from Cape Verde, Angola or Guinea Bissau. Restaurante Marina (Rua dos Poiais de São Bento 79, 96 512 5531), a tiny place in São Bento, has just started with Cape Verdean guitar and vocals on Fridays and Saturdays from 10pm. Anos Sessenta (*see above*) also has African evenings.

B.leza

Largo Conde Barão 50, Santos (21 394 0146/93 461 4921/http://blogdibleza.blogspot.com). Tram 15, 18, 25. **Open** 11.30pm-4.30am Tue-Sun. *Live music* 11.30pm Tue-Sat. **Admission** €5-€6 Tue-Thur, Sun; €10 Fri, Sat. **No credit cards**. **Map** p246 K9.

Housed in a crumbling 16th-century mansion, this club named after a late great Cape Verdean guitarist plays a key role in projecting his country's music abroad. On Tuesdays and Wednesdays there are various urban sounds, but Thursdays to Saturdays are reserved for the house band. There's a strong boy-meets-girl feel to the dancefloor on these nights, and unaccompanied women wishing to remain so may get a little too much attention. Sundays often feature rap, reggae or DJs, attracting a younger crowd. A hearty African dinner can be had for a few euros.

Casa da Morna

Rua Rodrigues Faria 21, Alcântara (21 364 63 99/ 96 640 8656). Train from Cais do Sodré to Alcântara Mar/tram 15, 18. **Open** 8pm-2am Mon-Sat. *Live music* 8.30pm Mon-Sat. **Admission** dinner average €20. **Credit** MC, V.

Alcântara, once Lisbon's techno heartland, has now become its African nightlife mecca, with Luanda (*see p192*) pulling in the younger generation and now veteran Cape Verdean musician Tito Paris opening this restaurant in the same street.

Enclave

Rua do Sol ao Rato 71A, Rato (21 388 8738). Metro Rato. **Open** *Restaurant* 8.30pm-4am Mon, Wed-Sun. *Live music* 9.30pm Mon, Wed-Sun. *Live music & disco* 12.30-4am Fri, Sat. **Admission** *Disco* minimum spend €10 Fri, Sat. **No credit cards**. **Map** p245 J7.

Cape Verdean singer Bana founded Enclave in the 1970s and it became a Lisbon fixture. Tito Paris is now the resident performer. There's live music upstairs in the restaurant until midnight and then on Friday and Saturday downstairs in the disco, where it can get very crowded.

Brazilian

Both Caipirinhas and recorded Brazilian music are consumed in quantity in Lisbon bars, but community centre Casa do Brasil (Rua São Pedro de Alcântara 63-1D, 21 347 1580, www.casadobrasil.info) is as authentic as it gets, with live *forró* on Fridays from 10pm until 2am. The mood is informal and floor space at a premium. The more generic Casa de América Latina (Avenida 24 de Julho 118B, 21 395 5309) has MPB (*música popular brasileira*) covers from 11pm on Fridays and samba on Saturdays. In summer, at Parque das Nações, the riverside Passeio do Oriente (Rua da Pimenta 51, 21 895

6147) has Brazilian music every lunchtime, on Friday and Saturday nights, and on weekend afternoons. Rock in Chiado (*see p177*) has live Brazilian music on Sundays, Restaurante Marina (*see p179*) on Thursdays from 10pm, and Anos Sessenta (*see p179*) some nights.

Armazém F

Rua da Cintura, Armazém 65, Cais do Gás, Santos (21 322 0160/www.armazemf.com). Metro Cais do Sodré, then 10min walk. **Open** 7pm-12.30am Mon-Thur, Sun; 7pm-4am Fri, Sat. *Live music* 9-11.30pm Tue-Sun; 9pm & 11.30pm Fri, Sat. **Credit** AmEx, DC, MC, V.

In this cavernous riverside warehouse, guitar and vocals provide a mellow soundtrack for dinner in the upstairs grill. On Friday and Saturday the tempo moves up a notch around midnight with live *forró*, *axé* music or samba, followed by DJs. Also themed parties (samba or Brazilian country) some Sundays.

Ar Puro

Rua da Atalaia 108, Bairro Alto (91 241 2988/96 495 1385). Bus 58, 790. **Open** 8pm-2am daily. *Live music* 10pm daily. **No credit cards**. **Map** p250/1 L9.

'Pure Air' is a friendly bar with guitar and vocal sounds, an unusual range of home-flavoured *cachaças*, and an even more unusual no-smoking policy. If you need a fag break you can take your drink outside and hear perfectly well as the place is tiny.

Chafarica

Calçada de São Vicente 79-81, São Vicente (21 886 7449). Tram 28. **Open** 10pm-3am Mon-Thur; 10pm-4am Fri, Sat. *Live music* 11.30pm-3am Mon-Thur; 11.30pm-4am Fri, Sat. **Admission** €5 Fri, Sat. **No credit cards**. **Map** p251 N9.

A cosy bar where regulars sip well-mixed Caipirinhas. Resident musicians play melodic standards during the week and more up-tempo fare at weekends, when dancers pack the place out.

Other venues

Up by the castle, Santiago Alquimista (Rua de Santiago 19, 21 888 4503/91 851 2114, www.santiagoalquimista.com) is an elegant space with a balcony on three sides overlooking a low stage and bar area that hosts indie bands local and foreign, DJ parties, stand-up comedy or theatre (admission from €5), usually from 10pm. Round the corner at Bartô, underneath restaurant-bar Chapitô (*see p187*), you'll find jazz and world music as well as poetry. The wash-tank stage in what was once the laundry of a women's prison is cramped but has good acoustics.

In Graça, the venerable workers' club Voz do Operário (Rua da Voz do Operário 13, 21 886 2155, www.vozoperario.pt) has live music in its bar on Fridays and Saturdays from 11pm, with the emphasis on folk.

At the bottom of Alfama, Bacalheiro (Rua dos Bacalhoeiros 125, 2nd floor, 21 886 4891) is an offbeat club with a symbolic €1 membership that has live music most Saturdays at 8pm and 10pm, and an acoustic 'experience' on Sunday from 7.30pm. By the riverside, in the same dockside complex as Musicais (*see p177*), Club Lua (96 195 0490/1, www.clublua.com) is a fair sized, split-level venue run by trance heads who organise live music shows, often reggae and dub, as well as parties and arty events.

Over in Santos, dance music haven Mini-Mercado (*see p189*) often has live bands – sorry, collectives. Meanwhile ZDB (*see p185*) is a centre for experimental music, with a couple of live shows a week. Also in Santos, the bar above Teatro Cinearte (*see p194*) has tango and other live music some nights (see http://bar-a-barraca.blogspot.com).

Festivals

The season starts in late May, with **Super Bock Super Rock**, held by the eponymous brewer (www.superbock.pt) on a stretch of asphalt on the eastern waterfront. It invariably has an impressive line-up with selected Portuguese acts. The biennial **Rock in Rio Lisboa** (http://rockinrio-lisboa.sapo.pt; next in 2008) is a slicker rival held at the Parque de Belavista. It favours established stars such as Sting and Portuguese rockers Xutos e Pontapés. There's also a dance tent.

High summer brings open air bashes by the river. Look out for the dance music oriented **Hype** in June, the reggae-rich **Summer Sessions** in early July, and the indie hip **Lisbon Soundz** later that month. On the second, sponsor TMN (21 791 4400, www.tmn.pt) has information; the others are run by Portugal's leading promoter, Música no Coração (21 315 6554, www.musicanocoracao.pt). Its **Cool Jazz Fest** (www.cooljazzfest.pt), in mid to late July, brings commercial jazz, hip hop and Brazilian musicians to venues in Oeiras, Mafra and Cascais.

Late July is also the time for Portugal's leading 'world music' event, **Festival Musicais do Mundo** (269 630 665, www.fmm.com.pt), a couple of hours south of Lisbon in the port city of Sines. Musicians come from the world over to play in a friendly vibe.

The biggest event, **Festival Sudoeste**, takes place further down the coast at Zambujeira do Mar, in early August. Now into its second decade, it packs an unrivalled range of music into four litter strewn days (*see p151*).

Back in the Lisbon area, in early September the communist **Festa do Avante** (*see p152*) runs the gamut of styles on a site south of the river. In November the downtown **Número Festival** (96 681 6785, www.numero-projecta.com) organises musical happenings.

Hot and cool

Lisbon is a jazz city. Here, music is played in the kind of smoke-filled bars and cellars where Charlie Parker and Billie Holiday would have felt at home. Of these clubs none is more redolent of that era than **Hot Clube de Portugal**. Founded in 1948, Hot Clube is one of Europe's oldest venues. Louis Armstrong and Count Basie played it in the early days, and touring foreigners still turn up. But Hot Clube doesn't trade on its past and today mainly showcases talented young locals. Artists play two sets a night, at 11pm and 12.30am. Later on big names sometimes drop by to jam after gigs elsewhere. In 1991 the Hot Clube founded Portugal's first jazz school (Escola de Jazz Luís Vilas Boas, 21 361 9740), which now has 80 or so students doing a three-year course, and has ties with two US universities. Several other schools have since sprung up, including the Escola Jazz de Barreiro (Rua Dr Eusébio Leão 11, Barreiro, 21 207 3116, 91 495 9132, www.escolajazzbarreiro.com.pt), a 40-minute journey south of Lisbon. It has its own jazz club, the be jazz café (93 324 4400), with jam sessions on Thursdays and Saturdays from 11pm and a couple of concerts a week.

Lisbon has two other two established venues: the smoky **Catacumbas Jazz Bar**, which has jam sessions on Mondays from 11pm, live jazz every other Thursday, and an open piano policy; and **Speakeasy**, a bar-restaurant owned by a son of fado singer Carlos do Carmo. It caters to both the Cascais jet set and jazz purists: the latter often come midweek, leaving the rest of the time to blues and funk fans. The aficionado should book a front table in order to avoid background chatter.

These two venues have recently been joined by the spacious **Ondajazz** in Alfama and the poky **Cefalópode** (*see p177*) up near the castle. The former's midweek programming has a strongly African feel, but includes plenty of jazz. Admission is free, or sometimes €5 or €10; on Friday nights there's a buffet with jam session. Cefalópode is still more varied, and often has crossover or experimental jazz music.

Over near the Bairro Alto, **A Bicaense** (*see p186*) has live jazz from 11pm on Wednesdays. There are also weekly concerts, sometimes very experimental, at music store Trem Azul (Rua do Alecrim 21A, 21 342 3141). This is the only shop in Lisbon devoted to jazz and is linked to Clean Feed Records, a label set up in 2001 to add some colour to what its founders saw as a 'grey' local scene. It has made dozens of recordings by Portuguese and little exposed foreign artists.

The Centro Cultural de Belém (*see p161*) hosts big-name concerts and, speaking of big-name concerts, what trip south would be complete without a trip to a summer festival to hear world-class jazz in balmy open-air settings. The most famous is Estoril Jazz (*see p151*), with more than two decades of landmark concerts behind it. Jazz em Agosto (*see p151*) is held on summer evenings in an amphitheatre in the Gulbenkian's lovely gardens. The Teatro Municipal de São Luíz (*see p194*) hosts the odd concert in its airy Winter Garden, as well as a mini-festival every spring. In July the Goethe-Institut has twice-weekly concerts in its Jazz im Goethe Garten (JiGG) event. Finally, there's Seixal Jazz (*see p153*), beyond the city limits.

For the latest club, concert and festival listings visit www.jazzportugal.ua.pt .

Catacumbas Jazz Bar

Travessa Água da Flor 43, Bairro Alto (21 346 3969). Metro Baixo Chiado. **Open** 10pm-4am Mon-Sat. **Admission** free. **No credit cards. Map** p250 L9.

Hot Clube de Portugal

Praça da Alegria 39, Restauradores (21 346 7369/www.hcp.pt). Metro Avenida. **Open** 10pm-2am Tue-Sat. **Admission** €7-€10. **No credit cards. Map** p246 L8.

Ondajazz

Arco de Jesus 7, Alfama (21 887 3064/91 918 48 00/67/www.ondajazz.com). Tram 18, 25/bus 9, 28, 35, 81, 82, 90, 746, 759, 794. **Open** 9pm-2am Tue-Thur, 9pm-3am Fri, Sat. *Live music* 11pm. **Admission** free-€10. **No credit cards. Photo** *p178.*

Speakeasy

Cais das Oficinas, Armazém 115, Rocha Conde d'Obidos, Alcântara (21 390 9166/91 230 2908/www.speakeasy-bar.com). Train to Santos from Cais do Sodré then 5min walk/ tram 15, 18/bus 14, 28, 32, 43. **Open** 8pm-3am Mon-Wed; 8pm-4am Thur-Sat. **Admission** free. Credit AmEx, DC, MC, V.

Nightlife

Ease your way through the night.

Lisbon is an outdoors city and that applies to its nightlife. At the weekend it can seem like every partygoer in the country has come to town. But even when people are milling around the alleys of Bairro Alto or sitting in a 3am traffic jam, the atmosphere remains happy.

There are clubs too, of course, though in this city the dividing line between bars and clubs is fine. (If you're lucky, you may not even have to pay to dance the night away; for all places listed below, admission is free unless otherwise stated. Where an admission price is listed that full amount goes towards your drinks bill.) The bar-club symbiosis is partly how Lisbon earned its justified fame as a non-stop party: you can go out on a Friday night and return home on Monday without interrupting the fun for longer than it takes to catch a cab along the river. In general, the scene is best in summer, when everything gets going later and by the time you resurface, the sun is up and the buses running.

While there are many good nights to be had, few clubs have a consistent music policy. The scene belongs to the crews that make it – the Nylon label, Journeys, Sonic, Raska, Dubdelight, infiltration – but it's **Lux**, the premier nightspot, that gets most of the attention. Still, other clubs can be interesting. Several showcase decent DJs and plenty generate a good atmosphere that makes up for more mediocre talent.

There is also a year-round supply of one-off parties in myriad locations, from secluded restaurants through empty warehouses to bars on the Caparica coast. Look out as well for Yes Mi Selecta (ragga/dancehall), Nuno Forte (drum 'n' bass), Dinis (disco-drum 'n' bass) and the Cooltrain Crew.

In terms of neighbourhoods, formerly studenty Santos has been losing ground, with youngsters now piling into the Bairro Alto at weekends. There, despite the limitations resulting from it being a residential area, there are also signs of the arrival in force of *betos* – the Portuguese equivalent of sloanes. Lovers of cutting-edge sounds seem to be heading in the other direction. In Santos, the discerning **Left** has been joined by **Mini-Mercado**.

In fact, nightlife is no longer restricted to just two or three areas. The bar in the bucolic garden of Basta Café Jardim (*see p121*) is an oasis, with the theatre upstairs pulling in more punters. And even Alfama offers more than just fado. For bars here and elsewhere whose main fare is live music, see the music chapters.

Chiado, though not a nightlife area, has several cafés that make good places to meet up for an evening out. Bar-restaurant Heróis (*see p165*) is worth a mention: it is part of the gay scene but all enjoy the loungey atmosphere.

African dancehalls are dotted around town, inhabiting their own parallel nightlife universe. But it's in regular clubs and at parties that the happening 'African' sound – actually a Lisbon sound since it could only emerge here – looms large. Electronic or progressive kuduro is a breakbeat/hip hop makeover of the Angolan rhythm of the same name, Buraka Som Sistema its leading exponents.

For all the latest, pick up *Dance Club* magazine or snag flyers from record shops Supafly (Rua da Barroca 15, 21 347 8325) in the Bairro Alto or Flur (Avenida Infante Dom Henrique, Armazém B Loja 4, Cais da Pedra, 21 882 1101), near Lux. For general info on what's on, visit http://lecool.com (click on 'lisboa' and then 'Leia …').

Bairro Alto

The Bairro Alto was for two centuries an area of whorehouses and fado. By the mid 1990s the area teemed with more bars than anyone could handle in one night. Here we've listed a small selection of institutions, old favourites and new arrivals. Some gay-run places, such as Purex (*see p166*), are actually fairly mixed, and worth checking out. For music oriented bars in Bairro Alto see the music chapters.

For a civilised start to the night, an aperitif or a post-prandial drink, you could do worse than visit the Solar do Vinho do Porto (*see p138* **Port-able**). Unfortunately, the Elevador da Glória, opposite, is out of action as work on a rail tunnel drags on. So don't get off the Metro at Restauradores unless you're prepared to walk up a steep slope. Baixa-Chiado (or the No.28 tram) is the best station for Bairro Alto venues with door numbers under 200 (that is, nearer the river); for higher numbers, it's more of a haul, although you can catch buses 58 or 790 up Rua da Misericórdia. Alternatively, start from Rato Metro, which is further away. The No.92 bus, which goes via the Bairro Alto to Príncipe Real, only sets off from Praça do Comércio half-hourly (via Cais do Sodré), with the last bus at 11pm.

Bars

Arroz Doce

Rua da Atalaia 117A-21 (no phone). Metro Baixa-Chiado/tram 28. **Open** 6pm-4am Mon-Sat. **No credit cards. Map** p250 L9.

A favourite of young bohos who come for two reasons: a (locally) legendary drink and a passionate fado singer. Pontapé na Cona, the 'kick in the pussy', is the drink and its contents remain, perhaps thankfully, something of a mystery. Delivering just as much of a kick for the regulars – when she can be persuaded – is Tia Alice, a fado singer of real zeal.

B'Artis

Rua do Diário de Notícias 95-7 (21 342 4795). Metro Baixa-Chiado/tram 28. **Open** 9pm-4am daily. **No credit cards. Map** p250 L9.

A cosy, smoky, jazz-driven bar signposted by a red light, B'Artis is filled with wooden furniture, stone-topped tables, old posters, figurines and glass-fronted bookcases. It can be hard to get a table after midnight but there are stools and standing room at the back. An atmospheric place, although staff can get testy on busy nights.

BedRoom

Rua do Norte 86 (no phone). Metro Baixa-Chiado. **Open** 10pm-3am Wed-Sat. **No credit cards. Map** p250/1 L9.

Cinco Lounge. *See p185.*

This large music-driven bar is something of a foreign body in the Bairro Alto given its somewhat snobbish door policy (requiring minimum age and class status at the doorman's discretion). The concept is in the name: old beds in plush red, and retro wallpaper, making for an ambience geared to flirting. Music ranges from '80s and '90s (Wednesdays) to funk, house and hip hop. On Thursdays local star DJ Xana Guerra spins discs, on Fridays it's dubster Félix da Cat and on Saturdays there's an in-house duo. BedRoom attracts *betos* (sloanes) who come to see and be seen. Velvet (No.121, 96 130 8317, open 10.30pm-4am Tue-Sat) is less self-consciously exclusive.

Café Diário

Rua do Diário de Notícias 3 (no phone). Metro Baixa-Chiado/tram 28. **Open** 9.30pm-4am Mon-Thur; 10pm-4am Fri, Sat. **No credit cards. Map** p250 L9.

Café Diário is a small single-room bar painted in blocks of lively colour. It's a quiet place to meet friends, and early evenings are popular with older couples and professionals. Busier nights see the place fired up by danceable African and Brazilian imports.

Café Suave

Rua do Diário de Notícias 4-6 (21 324 0337). Metro Baixa-Chiado/tram 28. **Open** 10pm-2am daily. **No credit cards. Map** p250 L9.

Now in its red period (after spells in orange and lime green), this bar is no longer hip, but remains a popular summer drinking spot thanks to its unpretentious atmosphere and friendly staff. At weekends the street between it and Café Diário heaves with people.

Capela

Rua da Atalaia 45 (no phone). Metro Baixa-Chiado/tram 28. **Open** 10pm-4am daily. **No credit cards. Map** p250 L9.

With a bar in front and a few tables out the back, this small, atmospheric bar can get overcrowded and smoky at weekends. It is often even more packed after 2am, when other bars close and everybody who isn't going clubbing piles in to continue the party. Capela is not nearly so fashionable as it was but still has a good line in experimental electro.

Clandestino

Rua da Barroca 99 (21 346 81 94). Metro Baixa-Chiado/tram 28. **Open** 10pm-4am Mon-Sat. **No credit cards. Map** p250 L9.

After years as the only late bar in the area, serving up rock and alternative music, Clandestino is a Bairro Alto legend. The walls are covered with graffiti – you're welcome to write your own thoughts if you can find a space. Snacks served until late.

Clube da Esquina

Rua da Barroca 30-32 (93 866 1134). Metro Baixa-Chiado/tram 28. **Open** 4pm-2am daily. **No credit cards. Map** p250 L9.

A groovy, welcoming bar decorated with antique radios that's a bit of a squeeze on busy weekends, with a small counter and a few sociable tables. Although one owner is a hip hop scenester, it's a chilled-out assortment of beats, reggae, rare groove, funk, house, electro and dub that draws a diverse and amiable mix. It has changing painting or photography exhibitions. As the night wears on, the street fills with revellers.

Estádio

Rua São Pedro de Alcântara 11 (21 342 2716). Metro Baixa-Chiado/tram 28. **Open** 1pm-2am daily. Closed Aug. **No credit cards. Map** p250 L9.

There's no name outside but you can recognise this bar by the paintings of Roman-style stadiums – *estádios* – around the walls. It's a pleasingly scruffy place with rudimentary snacks, a snowy television and the tackiest jukebox in Lisbon, in which a diet of fado is lightened by the odd 1970s pop tune. Young bohos mix with garrulous old geezers around formica-topped tables, served by a famously gruff old waiter who is a sweetie at heart. A perennial meeting point for foreign students living in Lisbon.

Janela da Atalaia

Rua da Atalaia 158-60 (21 346 5988). Metro Baixa-Chiado/tram 28. **Open** 7pm-4am Mon-Sat. **No credit cards. Map** p250 L9.

A cosy place, with world music to soothe your tired senses. Live music on Wednesday starts at 11pm (Brazilian is a regular, fado appears occasionally). There are sandwiches and light snacks to eat and if you don't feel like going inside, staff sell cheap beer at the window.

Keops

Rua da Rosa 157 (no phone). Metro Baixa-Chiado/tram 28. **Open** *Winter* 10.30pm-4am Tue-Sat. *Summer* 10.30pm-4am Mon-Sat. **No credit cards. Map** p250 L9.

A Bairro Alto old-timer that has been pulling in the crowds for over a decade. Though Keops recently changed hands, you can still dance at the rear of the bar to Latin rhythms, house or '80s tunes.

Lisbona Bar

Rua da Atalaia 196-8 (21 347 1412). Metro Baixa-Chiado/tram 28. **Open** 1pm-2am Mon-Sat. **Credit** AmEx, MC, V. **Map** p250 L9.

An unpretentious bar at the unfashionable end of Rua da Atalaia, used by locals who see cheap beer and a friendly vibe as more important than in-crowd cred. The black-and-white tiling is covered in graffiti – add your own.

Majong

Rua da Atalaia 3-5 (21 342 1039). Metro Baixa-Chiado/tram 28. **Open** 7pm-4am daily. **No credit cards. Map** p250 L9.

Majong, a busy corner watering hole, is a key Bairro Alto bar, with thoughtful decor and balanced lighting, although the giant screen showing videos and Chinese movies can be overly dominating if you're trying to hold a conversation. Discs are spun by house DJs Audioholic and Anti-Mix – the latter Majong's owner, João Lee, who has never learned how to mix.

The best decor in town at **Pavilhão Chinês**. *See p186.*

It is favoured by the self-consciously avant-garde, among them some mean table football players. After 11pm it can get absurdly crowded.

Maria Caxuxa

Rua da Barroca 12 (96 503 9094). Metro Baixa-Chiado. **Open** 7pm-2am Mon-Sat. **No credit cards. Map** p250/1 L9.

The phrase *do tempo da Maria Caxuxa* means very old, but this café-bar in a former cake factory (the old ovens and other original gear remain) packs in the really young. DJs spin lounge music during the week, when it's an ideal place to relax. At weekends they up the tempo with dub and house, and happy drinkers spill out into the street.

Mexe Café

Rua da Trombeta 2A (no phone). Metro Baixa-Chiado/tram 28. **Open** 10pm-4am daily. **No credit cards. Map** p250 L9.

A hectic scene-y bar, with a different DJ every day. The dub, electro, house and Detroit can create a loud, unhinged and edgy atmosphere.

Mezcal

Travessa Água da Flor 20 (21 343 1863). Metro Baixa Chiado/tram 28. **Open** 10pm-4am daily. **No credit cards. Map** p250 L9.

Don't be misled by the kids hanging around outside, lured by the cheap takeaway beer; this bar is ideal for tequila fans. The tacos are not the real thing but not far off, and they improve whenever a Mexican takes over in the kitchen. The music is mainly Mexican.

Páginas Tantas

Rua do Diário de Notícias 85-7 (21 346 5495). Metro Baixa Chiado/tram 28. **Open** 9pm-4am daily. **No credit cards. Map** p250 L9.

A spacious bar that is a good post-prandial destination if you want to wind down rather than rage, since trad jazz is played at talkable volume. It's supposedly a journalists' hangout – hence the name 'so many pages' – but attracts all types. It can get quite smoky, so stick to the lower area if that bothers you.

Portas Largas

Rua da Atalaia 103-5 (no phone). Metro Baixa-Chiado/tram 28. **Open** 8pm-3.30am Mon-Sat. **No credit cards. Map** p250 L9.

Its location in the centre of the Bairro Alto and opposite Frágil (*see p185*) make this place a real hub, and on summer nights the street outside is packed. Owned and run by gay people, it's quite mixed, particularly early on. The decor is unchanged from when it was a scruffy *tasca* before the in-crowd's arrival; same marble tables, same peanut-littered floor and same fado blasting away until 11pm or so. When not full it's quite dull. Excellent Caipirinhas.

Clubs

Frágil and ZDB have seen many rivals come and go, but Bairro Alto's clubbing potential is limited by the fact that it is a residential area.

Frágil

Rua da Atalaia 128 (tel/fax 21 346 9578). Metro Baixa-Chiado/tram 28/bus 92. **Open** *Winter* 11.30pm-4am Thur-Sat. *Summer* 11.30pm-4am Mon-Sat. **Admission** free-€5. **No credit cards. Map** p250 L9.

In the 1980s and early '90s this was the fashionable club. Under its original owner, Manuel Reis (now at Lux), Frágil launched the Bairro Alto as the nightlife district it is today. A small place to carry such a big reputation, these days it has a more subdued existence: a weekend favourite for a frenetic gay scene, otherwise just another club with no particular crowd.

ZDB

Rua da Barroca 59 (office 21 343 0205/ www.zedosbois.org). Metro Baixa-Chiado/tram 28/bus 92. **Open** Concerts/DJ sets usually 10pm-2am Thur-Sat. **Admission** €5-€10. **No credit cards. Map** p250/1 L9.

An unpretentious arts space (*see p162*) that draws a hip crowd with low-fi sensibilities. There's lots of live music but also DJs; look out for the resident Trash Converters (electro-fied chart pop). Crap acoustics are made up for by fairly priced beer and a lively atmosphere. It's best to call or check the website in advance, as opening days and times vary.

Príncipe Real & São Bento

Príncipe Real is essentially an extension of Bairro Alto, with fewer bars and a greater gay focus (*see p165*). São Bento, with an established African community, has **A Lontra**, with live music club B.leza (*see p179*) not far away.

Bars

Cinco Lounge

Rua Ruben António Leitão 17A, Príncipe Real (21 342 4033/www.cincolounge.com). Metro Rato then 15min walk/bus 773. **Open** 6pm-2am Mon-Sat. **Credit** AmEx.

Lisbon's first New York-style cocktail bar is a colourful haven in a bit of a nightlife no-man's-land. Brits David and Julie have built up a loyal clientele, who come to lounge on low sofas and savour some of the 100 drinks on offer: from classic Martinis through fruity mocktails to the divine Lemon Pie. Food is limited to *tostas*, but over the road at no.2A, the laid-back café-bar Alquimia (21 017 0018) serves meals until 10pm and snacks until midnight. **Photo** *p183*.

Enoteca-Chafariz do Vinho

Chafariz da Mãe d'Água, below Príncipe Real (21 342 2079/www.chafarizdovinho.com). Metro Rato. **Open** 6pm-2am Tue-Sun. **Credit** MC, V. **Map** p246 L8.

Owned by João Paulo Martins, Portugal's most influential wine writer, this is Lisbon's only wine bar worthy of the name. Housed in a former water reservoir that is a national monument, with a terrace on the steps outside, it's the best place in town to taste wine from around the world, some sold by the glass.

Pavilhão Chinês

Rua Dom Pedro V 89, Príncipe Real (21 342 4729). Metro Baixa-Chiado/tram 28. **Open** 6pm-2am Mon-Sat; 9pm-2am Sun. **Credit** AmEx, MC, V. **Map** p250 L8.

Undoubtedly Lisbon's best bar decor, courtesy of Luís Pinto Coelho. The network of rooms is lined with floor-to-ceiling glass cases stuffed with toy battleships, eastern European army officers' hats and other grim ornaments. This museum of kitsch is not cheap, but worth a look. The back room is an atmospheric setting for a frame of pool. **Photo** *p184.*

Clubs

Incógnito Bar

Rua dos Poiais de São Bento 37, São Bento (21 390 8755/www.incognitobar.com). Tram 28. **Open** 11pm-4am Wed-Sat. **Admission** free-€10 (incl drinks). **Credit** AmEx, MC, V. **Map** p246 K9.

An established 'alternative dance-bar', Incógnito offers a discerning mix from across the indie-rock-dance spectrum at weekends, with dance-oriented DJs during the week. A decent small venue, the somewhat aimless crowd it attracts is its main drawback. Still, it covers all ages, and is low on posers. Doorman D'Artagnan is a card.

Santa Catarina & Bica

Places here are also really part of the Bairro Alto scene. The Esplanada do Adamastor, with its simple café (21 343 0582, open 11am-2am daily) and fine views of the river, has a laid-back vibe and fills up on warm nights. Noobai (*see p128*), next door, is more secluded. At the bottom of Bica is Bar Belo da Bica (*see p192*).

Bars

A Bicaense

Rua da Bica de Duarte Belo 42, Bica (21 015 6040). Metro Baixa-Chiado/tram 28/bus 92. **Open** 7pm-2am Tue-Sat. **No credit cards**. **Map** p250 L9.

A large converted *tasca* that is cool, unpretentious and best enjoyed away from the rush and push of weekends. One room has a long bar with stools for perching and a few tables, the other a small bar, comfy chairs and space to dance. Fine sounds – dub, electro, funk, and reggae from resident DJs, plus live jazz on Wednesdays (from 11pm) – indomitable staff, and a large range of spirits attract a creative crowd.

Baliza

Rua da Bica de Duarte Belo 51A, Bica (21 347 8719). Metro Baixa-Chiado/tram 28. **Open** 6pm-2am Mon-Sat. **No credit cards**. **Map** p250 L9.

Once an old-style football *tasca* – its name means 'goal' – this tiny café-bar is peaceful by day and bubbly at night. Friendly staff, wild-berry vodkas, excellent *tostas* and a flirtatious gay/straight clientele all add to the irresistible mix.

Souk

Rua Marechal Saldanha 6, Santa Catarina (21 346 5859/96 235 0524). Metro Baixa-Chiado. **Open** 11pm-4am Mon-Sat. **No credit cards**. **Map** p250/1 K9.

A bar-cum-gallery-cum-theatre (with two spaces for experimental art and shows), Souk has DJs and occasional live music. It attracts a young crowd, particularly for the regular electronic dub and reggae sessions, with local crews such as the Positronics.

Alfama, Sé, Castelo & Graça

Although this side of town has congenial spots for an aperitivo before dinner or an *aguardente* to wind up the night – such as Cerca Moura (*see p126*) and the Esplanada da Igreja da Graça (*see p127*) – it never had a scene as such. But live music places have sprung up in recent years including bars Ondajazz and Cefalópode (for both *see p181* **Hot and cool**), and busy venue Santiago Alquimista (*see p180*).

Bars

Caxin

Costa do Castelo 22, Castelo (21 888 0263). Metro Rossio/tram 12, 28/bus 37. **Open** 9.30pm-2am Mon-Thur; 9.30pm-4am Fri, Sat. **No credit cards**. **Map** p251 M9.

Super **Mini-Mercado**. *See p188.*

A Moroccan-style bar with appropriately low-slung tables, dim lighting, water pipes for hire and a reasonable taste in music – North African drifting into Sting. Smoke what you will; your oxygen intake will be more of a problem, since it does tend to get a bit on the fuggy side in here.

Chapitô

Costa do Castelo 7, Castelo (21 885 5550). Tram 12, 28/bus 37. **Open** *Bar* 10pm-2am Tue-Sun. *Restaurant* 7.30pm-2am Mon-Fri; noon-2am Sat, Sun. **No credit cards. Map** p251 M9.

A bar and restaurant attached to the Chapitô circus school. Visitors can enjoy one of the best views in Lisbon while tucking into an international menu. A separately run basement bar, Bartô, has exhibitions and occasional live music.

Costa do Castelo – Bar das Imagens

Calçada Marquês de Tancos 1, Castelo (21 888 4636). Tram 12, 28/bus 37 then 10min walk. **Open** 11am-2am Tue-Sat; 3-11pm Sun. **Credit** MC, V. **Map** p251 M9.

Bar des Imagens is a well run place, with a decent range of spirits, excellent ice-creams and blankets against the cold. The bar also scores points for its terrace, which looks out over the Baixa. A perfect place to sit at sunset and enjoy a dubby soundtrack, from turntables parked outside.

Tejo Bar

Beco do Vigário 1A, Alfama (91 464 5705). Tram 28/bus 12, 34. **Open** 10pm-2am daily. **No credit cards.**

An alternative, informal place with a handful of tables with low seats and shelves bearing books and board games. Its Brazilian owner, nicknamed Mané do Café, is an amateur artist, novelist and poet, and presides over daily readings. Anyone may strum the house guitar (don't applaud, though – patrons rub their hands together to minimise noise). The bar has many regulars – who help themselves to drinks, noting down what they've taken – but is also a magnet for students and musicians. Mané is incapable of throwing people out, so the place often closes after 5am.

Cais do Sodré

During the Salazar years, the harbour area was the only place visiting foreigners could find late drinking and lowlife. The lowlife remains in and around Rua Nova de Carvalho, where prostitutes solicit on the street and seedy sex bars are named after distant port cities. Many retain their tacky '70s decor, although Texas has now been transformed into **MusicBox**. Europa at No.18 Rua Nova do Carvalho (21 342 1848) has also had a makeover and has initiated DJ sets. O'Gilins (*see p179*) is Lisbon's only Irish bar, with regular live music. If South America is more to your taste there are live Brazilian sounds at Armazém F (*see p180*).

Bars

British Bar

Rua Bernardino Costa 52 (21 342 2367). Metro Cais do Sodré/tram 15, 18, 25. **Open** 8am-midnight Mon-Thur; 8am-2am Fri, Sat. **No credit cards. Map** p250 L10.

With a long bar and wooden floor, the British Bar is designed like an English pub, but you'll rarely find a native of the isles anywhere in sight. A classic Lisbon establishment, it has carried on in its own dignified way since 1919, offering a great selection of aperitifs and a digestif of its own. It also has a famous clock that marks out the time with Swiss precision, only in reverse.

Lounge

Rua da Moeda 1 (no phone). Metro Cais do Sodré/tram 15, 18, 25. **Open** 10pm-4am Tue-Sun. **No credit cards. Map** p246 K9.

Lounge, a roomy Bairro Alto-style bar, has moderate prices, an unkempt and youngish crowd and interesting musical events. On regular nights, decent DJs spin an underground mix of electro and minimal techno, and there is the occasional themed party.

Meninos do Rio

Rua da Cintura, Armazém 225 (no phone). Metro Cais do Sodré then 10min walk/tram 15, 18. **Open** *May-Sept* noon-2am daily.

An unremarkable dockside terrace a short walk west from Cais do Sodré that has been the in place for after-dinner drinks of late. It is thick with *betos* (Portuguese sloanes); the palm trees and balmy riverside situation are a saving grace. Indoors, Sushi Rio (21 322 0070) serves regular and fusion sushi daily until around midnight, and has enviable river views and a balcony open all year, thanks to heaters.

Pump House

Rua da Moeda 1 (21 397 2059). Metro Cais do Sodré. **Open** 11pm-2am Mon-Thur, Sun; noon-4am Fri, Sat. **No credit cards. Map** p246 K10.

Large wood-panelled pub run in no-nonsense fashion by a British-Portuguese couple. It has a pool table and dartboard and is a safe bet if you don't want to miss live footie. Food is decent though limited to sandwiches, chilli con carne and the like. As well as karaoke nights there's a quiz on Sunday that attracts English teachers, stray sailors and tourists.

Clubs

Jamaica

Rua Nova de Carvalho 8 (21 342 1859). Metro Cais do Sodré/tram 15, 18. **Open** midnight-6am Tue-Sat. **Admission** free-€6 (incl drink). **No credit cards. Map** p246 L10.

In a notorious red-light zone and yet still going for some 35 years, Jamaica is a world unto itself. The DJs paddle in nostalgia (from Iggy Pop to the Waterboys) but they know their stuff and unfailingly get the mixed crowd moving.

MusicBox
Rua Nova do Carvalho 24 (21 343 0107/96 022 4320/www.musicboxlisboa.com). Metro Cais do Sodré. **Open** 10pm-4am Wed, Thur; 10pm-6am Fri, Sat. **Admission** €6-€10 (€3 drink included). **No credit cards**. **Map** p246 L10.
Scruffy old Texas became MusicBox at the end of 2006. Since then the contacts built up over the years by owner Alexandre Cortez (bass player for innovative veterans Rádio Macau and former partner in the legendary Lisbon music venue Johnny Guitar) has allowed him to snare some impressive local acts. DJ sets (some with VJs) and concerts are varied, from rock through dance to dubstep.

Santos & Avenida 24 de Julho

Younger than the Bairro Alto, older than the Docas, the scene in Santos and along the Avenida 24 de Julho opened up in part for one obvious reason: cars can drive along here whereas in the Bairro Alto there's no parking at all. As a result cruising the Avenida has become a popular nocturnal pastime. The area bristles with bars, though few we would actively recommend. In fact, sometimes the best way to enjoy a night down here is simply to drink a few beers at a fast-food van and watch the world sweep by.

Bars

Estado Líquido
Largo de Santos 5A, Santos (tel/fax 21 395 5820/ www.estadoliquido.com). Tram 15, 18, 25, 28. **Open** 8pm-2am Mon-Wed, Sun; 8pm-3am Thur; 8pm-4am Fri, Sat. **No credit cards**. **Map** p245 J10.
A laid-back bar where DJs such as local favourites Anthony Millard of infiltration (who spins Detroit sounds) and Mike Stellar (specialising in anything from bossa to deep grooves) supply chilled dance music. On Sundays it moves down another notch with lounge nights. The bar has a sushi lounge attached (21 397 2022), which also delivers.

Left
Largo Vitorino Damásio 3F, Santos (21 395 1227/www.leftbar.blogspot.com). Tram 15, 18, 25. **Open** 10pm-4am Tue-Sat; 10pm-2am Sun. **No credit cards**. **Map** p245 J10.
The warm red glow and fine music of this narrow disco-café-bar attract a bohemian crowd with an excellent spread of ages. It's a good place to come around midnight for a drink and to listen to a different DJ every night, although it does tend to fill up later on if there's a big name at the desk.

Mini-Mercado
Avenida Dom Carlos I 67, Santos (96 045 1198/96 656 9576/www.clubemercado.blogspot.com). Metro Cais do Sodré/tram 15, 18, 25. **Open** 10pm-4am Tue-Sat. **No credit cards**. **Map** p246 K9/10.

Op Art Café. *See p190.*

Late night food for thought

Lisbon's thriving nightlife scene long ago created a demand for late-night eats. More recently there have also been calls for some late-night culture too.

Along Avenida 24 de Julho and opposite Lux on Avenida Dom Infante Henrique, trailers sell hamburgers, *bifanas* (braised pork steaks), and Portuguese supper staples *caldo verde* (cabbage soup) and *pão chouriço* (sausage bread). And if you leave your club only at first light, you can sup a hot chocolate at the Mercado da Ribeira (*see p147*).

For something more formal, Café no Chiado (*see p128*) serves light meals out of hours; while Galeto (Avenida da República 14, Saldanha, 21 356 0269; open 7pm-3am daily) is a fab 1960s snack-bar with an encyclopaedic menu and a wooden counter that loops back and forth across the panelled room. Snob (Rua do Século 178, Príncipe Real, 21 395 2911; open 6pm-2am daily) is known as a journos' and politicos' hangout but is actually more frequented by people who go to see if they can spot journalists and politicians; it has late-night steak. The similar Café de São Bento (Rua de São Bento 212, open 12.30-7pm Mon-Thur; 2.30pm-2am Fri & Sat), opposite parliament, targets a similar niche. Neither is cheap, and for steak La Pararrucha (*see p110*) is better value, also attracts the odd celebrity, and is itself open reasonably late. For budget food in São Bento, visit the unmarked Cape Verdean canteen known as Cachupa upstairs at Rua Poço dos Negros 73 (no phone); it's open all night from 3am at weekends but can get a bit heavy. Downtown, Solmar (*see p105*) serves snacks until the early hours.

You can feed your mind until late with an art exhibition at ZDB (*see p185*) or a bit of browsing at Ler Devagar ('slow reading', *see p133*) – both currently in the same building. If it's poetry you're after, you could also drop by the newer Da Mariquinhas (Rua dos Cordoeiros 8, Largo de Santo Antoninho, 96 000 5360; open noon-midnight Wed-Sun), which boasts 'rare books, strong alcohol and polyglot staff'.

The new, more compact location for Clube Mercado, a Bairro Alto venue that until the end of 2006 was Lisbon's most happening venue. It retains its watchword 'Eat More Fruit!!' and an impressive roster of DJs, but now has no space for bands – although live events elsewhere are promised. Hardcore kuduro, dub and electro funk rule the turntables, tempered with drum 'n' bass, hip hop and soul. **Photo** *p186*.

Pérola de Santos

Calçada Ribeiro Santos 25, Santos (21 390 0024). Metro Cais do Sodré/tram 18, 15. **Open** 10pm-4am Tue-Sun. **No credit cards**. **Map** p245 J10.

A pleasant bar on a lively corner that's unusually relaxed for the area. It attracts plenty of students with cheap drinks and the fact that some of the city's most popular clubs are only a short walk away.

Clubs

Kapital

Avenida 24 de Julho 68, Santos (21 395 7101/www.kapital.pt). Metro Cais do Sodré/tram 15, 18. **Open** 11pm-6am Thur-Sat. **Admission** free-€10. **Credit** AmEx, MC, V. **Map** p245 J10.

The absolute antithesis of the Bairro Alto. Kapital, a three-tiered vision in white, is essentially a hang-out for young rich kids and poorer aspirational types, but there are usually also a few students trying to negotiate the doormen's arbitrary criteria. A Lisbon institution, with little else to recommend it.

Kremlin

Rua das Escadinhas da Praia 5, Santos (21 395 7101/www.kremlin-k.com). Metro Cais do Sodré/tram 15, 18. **Open** midnight-6am Fri, Sat. **Admission** free-€10. **Credit** AmEx, MC, V. **Map** p245 J10.

Once the most intense scene in town, these days the music (house on two dance floors) is lighter and the crowd more restrained, but Kremlin retains much of its character – which always included a fairly charged atmosphere. Doormen have a notoriously short fuse. There was also a shooting a few years ago, but nothing to do with the club so don't be put off.

Docas & Alcântara

Docas, a veritable shopping mall of docklands nightlife, has been slowly losing custom, although the opening of cavernous house and chill-out venue Buddha Lx (Gare Marítima de Alcântara, 21 395 0555, open 9pm-4am Wed-Sun) shows there's life in the old docks yet. Meanwhile, the more authentic Alcântara is doing better, not least by becoming something of a centre for African music.

Bars

by me

Edifício Alcântara Rio, Rua Fradesso Silveira, Bloco V, Loja 6, Alcântara (21 363 0067). Tram 15, 18. **Open** 6pm-2am Tue-Sat. **Credit** MC, V. **Map** p245 G9.

Lisbon's best club. **Lux**. *See p192.*

This modish bar on the ground floor of a new estate in Alcântara makes for a calm (if not quiet) stop between clubs. Sit on cushions on the floor or choose from a range of seating in various styles and colours. It attracts well-heeled, laid-back clubbers.

Clubs

Alcântara Club

Rua da Cozinha Económica 11, Alcântara (no phone/ www.alcantara-club.com). Tram 15, 18. **Open** 1-8am Wed-Sun. **Admission** €6-€12 (incl drinks). **Credit** MC, V.

Not to be confused with the old Alcântara Mar, the distinction is not helped by the fact that this place just happens to occupy part of the older club's premises. Its house nights aren't as trippy either, but have a charmingly innocent sparkle. On Fridays and Saturdays the club often stays open until after 10am. W (21 363 6840, www.wdisco.com), in the same building but with its entrance round the corner, opens only Wednesday (Ladies' Night) and Sunday, when it hosts sessions from other clubs' PRs, so music and atmosphere depend on the event.

Belém Bar Café

Avenida Brasilia, Pavilhão Poente, Belém (21 362 4232/www.belembarcafe.com). Train to Belém from Cais do Sodré/tram 15. **Open** *Bar* 11pm-2am Tue; 11pm-3am Wed, Thur; 11pm-5am Fri, Sat. *Restaurant* 12.30-3pm, 8pm-midnight Tue-Fri; 8pm-midnight Sat. **Admission** from €5. **Credit** AmEx, DC, MC, V. **Map** p244 A10.

BBC is a self-consciously fashionable place that attracts carfuls of women that turn up hoping to catch a glimpse of its owner, model-turned-actor Paulo Pires. Though styled a lounge bar, BBC is far from anything you might call casual; you'll be asked to pay a silly admission price if the place is busy and they don't like your look. Don't even bother coming in trainers. During the day and evening the place operates as an unexceptional restaurant, albeit with a fine view of the Tagus. It is well beyond Alcântara, but if driving from town, take the flyover (signs to Torre de Belém) to the river side of the railway.

Op Art Café

Doca de Santo Amaro, Docas (21 395 6787/ www.opartcafe.com). Tram 15, 18. **Open** 12.30pm-4am Tue-Thur, Sun; noon-5am Fri, Sat. **Credit** AmEx, MC, V.

A riverside café/restaurant/club, Op Art could easily be an aquarium, but even without its in-your-face architecture it would stand out from the identikit bars of Docas. It's a mostly party crowd that gathers in the early hours, but the music rocks. Op Art is still a top spot for electro lovers, with Fridays and Saturdays devoted to it (after 2am); during the week jazz and chill out dominate. The dockside location makes for a lovely summer venue. **Photo** *p188.*

Paradise Garage

Rua João Oliveira Miguéis 38-48, Alcântara (no phone/www.paradisegarage.com). Tram 15, 18. **Open** 11.30pm-4am Thur-Sat. *After-hours* 8am-4pm Sat, Sun. **Admission** varies. **Credit** MC, V.

Sound, crowd and music vary enormously at this club-cum-live venue, where DJs rarely drive too hard. On Saturdays 'ClubGarage' nights are followed by after-hours sessions from Dubdelight, when it's always deep house.

Amoreiras & Rato

Bars

Procópio

Alto de São Francisco 21A, Amoreiras (21 385 2851). Metro Rato. **Open** 6pm-3am Mon-Fri; 9pm-3am Sat. **Credit** MC, V. **Map** p246 K7.

An older version of Pavilhão Chinês (*see p186*), run by designer Pinto Coelho's ex-wife Alice. Pricey, but nonetheless it's worth seeing for its quite extraordinary Wild-West-saloon-meets-musty-museum feel. Procópio is just off Rua João Penha, in the old Amoreiras neighbourhood (south of the shopping centre of that name). Ring the bell to get in.

Northern Lisbon

Saldanha now boasts a garden-bar at Basta Café Jardim (*see p121*), as well as venerable late snack bar Galeto (*see p189* **Late night food for thought**).

Bars

Boulevard Concept

Rua Praia da Vitória 35, Saldanha (21 315 0593/91 660 4067/www.boulevard-chilloutconcept.com). Metro Saldanha. **Open** 10am-2am Mon-Fri; noon-2am Sat, Sun. **Credit** DC, MC, V.

Boulevard is a colourful place that has the declared aim of being the sort of venue one might find on 'a great boulevard in a world metropolis'. Despite the somewhat kitschy result, it is a hit with local kids. Perhaps that success is due in part to there being few local alternatives and the thoughtful provision of wireless internet. Staff serve beer, pizzas, pasta, baguettes, burgers and *tostas*. After 9pm the music switches from chill out to dance music.

Just Be

Avenida Frei Miguel Contreiras 54B, Roma (21 849 4503). Metro Roma. **Open** 9pm-midnight daily. **No credit cards**. **Map** p249 N3/4.

With the Teatro Maria Matos next door and the King Triplex cinema round the corner, this low-fi bar is a welcome arrival in an area otherwise pretty much bereft of places to socialise. Sip a cocktail to the sound of chill out music as you lounge on a sofa.

Santa Apolónia

Off the road from Praça do Comércio, the riverside Jardim do Tabaco complex houses Musicais (*see p177*) and live venue Club Lua (*see p180*) among others.

Cherry aid

Could this be the world's most localised drinking phenomenon? Around the north-eastern end of Rossio are a few tiny bars that survive almost entirely by selling a drink you won't spot in Lisbon's trendier venues: a sticky cherry liqueur called *ginjinha*. Opening early and closing at midnight, these bars never lack custom – partly because they're in one of the most touristy parts of Lisbon, and partly because *ginjinha*, which many older folks still make at home, reminds sentimental Portuguese of their grandmothers.

The biggest-selling brand is Ginja Sem Rival, which comes with or without whole cherries. But Ginja Espinheira, showcased in A Ginjinha at Largo de São Domingos 8 (open 7am-midnight daily), makes for stiff competition. A fixture since 1840, this bar also serves home-made lemonade and Eduardino, a herbal liqueur.

A few yards away, at Rua das Portas de Santo Antão 7, another minuscule place with an ancient frontage (open 9am-midnight daily) serves Ginja Sem Rival and Eduardino, as well as *aguardente* and port. Further up, at No.61, is Ginginha Popular (open 7am-midnight daily). There are also *ginjinha* bars at Travessa da Ribeira 24 near Cais do Sodré, and at Largo de Trindade Coelho 17 in Bairro Alto.

There are some attractive bottles of the stuff. The best presented is Ginja Sem Rival with cherries, but the finest is Ginginha de Alcobaça, a lighter-coloured, less alcoholic tipple sold in a conical bottle. After a few *ginjinhas* you might start thinking one of these would make a lovely souvenir. But face facts: back home it'll only gather dust at the back of the drinks cabinet. Try it in Rossio, where it belongs.

Find Africa in Lisbon at **Mussulo**

Clubs

Lux

Avenida Infante Dom Henrique, Amazém A, Cais da Pedra a Santa Apolónia (21 882 0890/www.luxfragil.com). Bus 6, 28, 8, 82, 90, 759. **Open** 10pm-6am Tue-Sat. **Admission** €12 (includes €12 drinks). **Credit** AmEx, DC, MC, V. **Map** p247 O9.

Lisbon's best club: two dance floors (one loungey, one sweaty) and a roof terrace overlooking the river. As the hip furniture indicates, it is very much a see-and-be-seen place rather than one of unabated hedonism. But the crowd is friendly enough, and the measures Lisbon-large. House and guest DJs offer everything from electro beats through hip hop to the odd burst of '80s music. Thursdays are popular with locals keen on catching known leftfield names; on Saturdays the place is mobbed by out of towners. Lux's programme – which includes live bands as well as big international DJs – and its catch-all social role remain unrivalled. Exude photogenic importance at the door if you arrive after 2am. **Photo** *p190.*

African Clubs

African clubs move to their own night-time beat. As well as the following, there's live music at B.Leza, Casa da Morna and Enclave (for all, *see p179*). South of the river in Caparica, the beach crowd stays on for kizomba and pop at Ondeando (Praia da Vila 26, 21 290 5499).

A Lontra

Rua de São Bento 157, São Bento (21 004 6409). Bus 6, 49/tram 28 then 10min walk. **Open** 11.30pm-6am Tue-Thur, Sun; 11.30pm-7am Fri, Sat. **Admission** free Tue-Thur, Sun; €10 for men/free for women Fri; €20 for men/€4 for women Sat. **Credit** MC, V. **Map** p246 K9.

A venerable disco with a funky vibe and intimate dance floor. There's live African music on Thursdays and the occasional DJ set with dub, techno and kuduro, but regular nights offer a pretty cheesy mix of kizomba and funaná. Admission is at the doorman's whim.

Bar Belo da Bica

Rua da Bica Duarte Belo 23, Bica (96 424 8454/91 812 8832/http://barbelodabica.blogspot.com). Metro Baixa-Chiado/tram 28. **Open** 8pm-2.30am Tue-Sat. **No credit cards**.

Opened in mid 2006, this friendly bar halfway along Bica has live music from 9pm, Wednesdays to Fridays – usually from Cape Verde, though it aims to feature performers from all Portuguese speaking countries – and a DJ spinning African sounds on Saturdays. Despite the bar's tiny size, expect to dance.

ComVento Club

Calçada Marquês de Abrantes 38A, Santos (91 727 8464/96 501 3900/www.comventoclub.com). Tram 25. **Open** 11pm-6am Fri, Sat. **Admission** €6 for women; €12 for men (incl drinks). **No credit cards**. **Map** p p245 J9.

Two distinct areas: one focussing on hip hop, the other downstairs (featuring the elegant arches of the former convent that gives the venue its punning name) for new African sounds. Apart from the two regular nights, there are periodic R&B, soul and themed parties, plus bands.

Luanda

Travessa Teixeira Júnior 6, Alcântara (21 362 4459/96 560 2142/www.discoluanda.com). Tram 15, 18. **Open** *Winter* 11pm-6am Thur-Sat; *Summer* 11pm-6am Wed-Sun. **Admission** €6 women (incl drink); €12 men (incl 2 drinks). **Credit** AmEx, DC, MC, V.

It is partly the success of Luanda that has drawn other African enterprises to Alcântara, where techno once reigned. The club attracts a young, laid-back crowd for Friday and Saturday nights' kizomba and zouk; Thursday is Ladies' Night. The place was briefly infamous in 2000 when someone tossed a tear gas canister on to a packed dance floor.

Mussulo

Rua Sousa Martins 5D, Estefânia (21 355 6872). Metro Picoas. **Open** 11pm-6am Wed-Sun. **Admission** from €7. **No credit cards**. **Map** p246 L6.

Long the throbbing heart of Lisbon's African club scene, drawing a diverse crowd of all ages. Mainly lusophone zouk and Luandan kuduro are on offer, though they throw in a bit of Brazilian music now and then. Sunday nights are legendary. Wednesday is Ladies' Night, Friday students'. No trainers.

Performing Arts

Creativity in adversity – and the audiences are finally there.

Gilded glory: **Teatro da Trindade**.

The end of the millennium was a difficult time for the performing arts in Lisbon. The politically engaged audiences of the 1970s – when 'the Revolution arrived on stage before it arrived in the streets', as one critic put it – were a distant memory, while government budget crises prompted deep cuts in funding.

Somehow, both the theatre and dance scenes remained vibrant, artistically if not financially. And audiences have finally been won over – or rather forged, since theatre-going is not a firmly rooted tradition. As in the visual arts (*see p161*) Lisbon's relative isolation has spawned both hackneyed pretension and shining originality. But there's now plenty of choice: state and independent companies abound, offering ballet and Gil Vicente (the 16th-century father of Portuguese drama), Strindberg and street theatre.

State funding remains dominant – and limited, so even critically acclaimed shows may run for just a few days. But the growing commercial sector, led by **Teatro Villaret** (Avenida Fontes Pereira de Melo 30A, 21 353 8687), has at least given more people a taste for theatre. Feisty independents such as Artistas Unidos (*see p196* **Don't help the homeless**) do valuable work. And Lisbon is fertile ground for physical theatre, which generates inventive shows accessible to non-Portuguese speakers, by companies such as **Chapitô**, **Meridional** and **Sensurround**.

TICKETS AND INFORMATION

Newspaper listings cover the big theatres and some independents; for other sources, *see p168*. The rest can be gleaned from poster spotting, leaflet gathering and word of mouth. Shows are usually at 9.30pm from Wednesday or Thursday to Saturday; there may be a Sunday matinée. It's best to call to check. Whatever a box office's normal hours, on performance days it is invariably open at least for the hour before showtime. Most Lisbon theatre-goers buy at the theatre, often after reserving by phone, but agencies such as the ABEP booth in Praça dos Restauradores, Fnac, Ticket Line and the virtual agency Plateia, have tickets for big shows. *See p168*.

Establishment theatres

With Lisbon's largest auditorium, another medium-sized one and a studio theatre, all with machinery, the **Centro Cultural de Belém** (*see p161*) has the best facilities. Its programme encompasses national and foreign groups, offering everything from puppet theatre to Pina Bausch. **Culturgest** (*see p161*), founded in 1993, usually has more adventurous theatre and dance programming. The **Coliseu** (*see p169*) hosts visiting circuses and ballet companies, the **Pavilhão Atlântico** (*see p177*) musical and ice spectaculars.

Teatro da Trindade

Rua Nova Trindade 9, Bairro Alto (21 342 3200/ box office 21 342 000/http://teatrotrindade.inatel.pt). Metro Baixa-Chiado. **Open** *Box office* 2-6pm Tue; 2-8pm Wed-Sat; 1-4.30pm Sun. **Tickets** €8-€15. **Credit** AmEx, DC, MC, V. **Map** p250 L9.

A 19th-century gilded jewel that specialises in high profile one-off shows and new plays with a strong political theme. The theatre is now striking out in a fresh musical direction, bringing light opera to the masses. There's also a studio theatre and a smoky basement bar that offers music and comedy.

Teatro Maria Vitória

Parque Mayer, Avenida da Liberdade (21 346 1740). Metro Avenida. **Open** *Box office* 1-9.30pm daily. **Tickets** €12.50-€25. **No credit cards**. **Map** p246 L8.

The only theatre not to have gone dark in Parque Mayer, Lisbon's old theatreland and home to *revista*, the music hall that provided an escape valve under Salazar. It stages two shows a night with a trademark mix of slapstick, glittery camp and mild satire.

Teatro Municipal de São Luíz

Rua António Maria Cardoso 40, Chiado (21 325 7640/box office 21 325 7650/www.teatrosaoluiz.egeac.pt). Metro Baixa-Chiado. **Open** *Box office* 1-7pm daily. **Tickets** Main auditorium €8-€30; from €5 concessions. **No credit cards**. **Map** p250 L10.

Another council-run establishment, whose 1,000-seat main auditorium stages everything from world music to theatre. The glass-walled Jardim de Inverno (Winter Garden) hosts talks and concerts, including a mini jazz festival in early April. There's a studio theatre downstairs too.

Teatro Municipal Maria Matos

Avenida Miguel Frei Contreiras 52, Avenida de Roma (21 843 8800/box office 21 843 8801/www.teatromariamatos.egeac.pt). Metro Roma. **Open** *Box office* 3-10pm Tue, 3pm-midnight Wed-Sun. **Tickets** €15; €7.50-€10 concessions. **No credit cards**. **Map** p249 N3.

This council-owned 500-seat theatre is now run by leading actor Diogo Infante. It hosts productions by selected companies, as well as jazz and other concerts. The upstairs café has a small stage, magazines and ambient music.

Teatro Nacional Dona Maria II

Praça Dom Pedro IV, Rossio (21 325 0800/box office 21 325 0835/www.teatro-dmaria.pt). Metro Rossio. **Open** *Box office* 1-10pm Tue-Sat, 1-7pm Sun. **Tickets** €7.50-€20; €5.25-€14 concessions; half-price Thur. **No credit cards**. **Map** p250 M9.

Inaugurated in 1846, this national theatre for many years failed to maintain and update a serious classical repertoire. But after a series of budget crises, it seems stable under its current artistic director Carlos Fragateiro. The 320-seat Sala Garrett (named after the founder) and 52-seat studio stage in-house productions, some in partnership with independents, and periodically host foreign groups. There are workshops for children, Lisbon's only thespian bookshop and a café with great cakes. A few tickets are sold on the day (1-3pm) at €5.

Alternative theatres

Casa d'Os Dias da Água

Rua Dona Estefânia 175, Estefânia (21 357 4094/box office 21 314 0352/www.sensurround.pt). Metro Saldanha. **Open** *Box office* 1hr before performance; phone bookings 10am-8.30pm Mon-Thur; 10am-6pm Fri, Sat. **Tickets** €10; €7.50 concessions. **No credit cards**. **Map** p246 M6.

In a lovely old mansion, above trendy restaurant Basta (*see p121*), this space is run by Sensurround, the vehicle for inventive actress-director Lúcia Sigalho. It hosts everything from exhibitions of applied arts to dance and debates.

Chapitô

Costa do Castelo 1-7, Castelo (21 885 5550/www.chapito.org). Tram 12, 28/bus 37. **Open** *Box office* 2hrs before performance; phone bookings 10am-8pm daily. **Tickets** *Children's shows* €5. *Other shows* €10. **No credit cards**. **Map** p251M9.

This venue has a unique atmosphere, with students from the circus school and tourists rubbing shoulders on a restaurant patio that has fabulous views. It's home to the Companhia do Chapitô, a troupe known for its inspired comic physical theatre, overseen by London-based director John Mowat.

Espaço da Mitra

Rua do Açucar 64, Poço do Bispo (21 868 9246/www.teatromeridional.net). Bus 28, 718, 755. **Open** *Box office* 2hrs before performance; phone bookings 9am-7pm Mon-Sat. **Tickets** €12; €8 concessions. **No credit cards**.

A converted warehouse in eastern Lisbon is the base of Teatro Meridional, a Portuguese-Spanish group the focuses on comic and physical drama. It often stages works by African authors. Shows at 10pm.

Estrela Hall

Rua Saraiva de Carvalho, Estrela (21 396 1946/www.lisbonplayers.com.pt). Tram 28 then 10min walk/bus 9. **Open** *Box office* varies with performance time; book by leaving message. **Tickets** €10. **No credit cards**. **Map** p245 J8.

Home to the Lisbon Players, a long established group (since 1947) that performs regularly in English. The focus is on the classics, but musicals get a look in. The hall is also used by Tagus Theatre, a more professional outfit that tours Portugal and Britain.

Teatro Aberto

Praça de Espanha (21 388 0086/box office 21 388 0089/www.teatroaberto.com). Metro São Sebastião/Praça de Espanha. **Open** *Box office* 2-10pm Mon-Sat; 2-7pm Sun. **Tickets** €15; €10 concessions. **No credit cards**. **Map** p248 K4.

Now housed in a modern building with two plush auditoriums (one with 400 seats, the other half that), theatre company O Novo Grupo is the successor of the cutting-edge 1970s Grupo 4. Under João Lourenço and his partner, playwright and Germanist Vera San Payo de Lemos, its repertoire is slanted towards heavyweights such as Brecht.

Teatro Cinearte

Largo dos Santos 2, Santos (21 396 5360/5275/www.abarraca.pt). Tram 15, 25/tram 28 then 10min walk/train to Santos from Cais do Sodré. **Open** 1hr 30mins before performance. **Tickets** €12.50; €10 concessions. **No credit cards**. **Map** p245 J10.

The showcase for A Barraca, a group founded 30 years ago and led by Maria do Céu Guerra, one of a handful of established women directors. It stages productions of modern Portuguese and European classics. There are two auditoriums, and the upstairs café-bar (www.bar-a-barraca.blogspot.com) has an offbeat programme of concerts, poetry and stand-up comedy, as well as workshops for children.

Teatro da Comuna

Praça de Espanha (21 722 1770/6/www.comuna teatropesquisa.pt). Metro Praça de Espanha. **Open** *Box office* 8-9.30pm on performance days; phone bookings 10am-7.30pm Mon-Sat. **Tickets** prices vary. **No credit cards. Map** p248 K4.

Resident company Communa – Teatro de Pesquisa (Theatre of Research) has a history of experimentation dating from the mid '70s, but today the theatre plays host to both mainstream and alternative pieces. Four performance spaces, including one for comedy.

Teatro da Cornucópia

Rua Tenente Raul Cascais 1A, Rato (21 396 1515/ www.teatro-cornucopia.pt). Metro Rato. **Open** *Box office* 2.30-9.30pm Tue-Sat; 2-4pm Sun. **Tickets** €13; €6.50 concessions. **No credit cards. Map** p246 K8.

Tucked away in a quiet corner of Príncipe Real is this well-equipped theatre with a 135-seat auditorium where the respected Teatro do Bairro Alto group serves up challenging productions. In charge is Luís Miguel Cintra, a fine actor much used by veteran film director Manoel de Oliveira.

Teatro Politeama

Rua das Portas de Santo Antão 109, Rossio (21 324 5500/box office 21 324 504/16/www.teatro politeama.net). Metro Rossio. **Open** *Box office* 4.30-8pm Mon-Fri. **Tickets** €10-€30. **No credit cards. Map** p250 L8.

This 700-seat theatre puts on slick musicals and cabaret-style *revistas*, materminded by *empresario* Filipe La Feria. The latest long-running production is *Música no Coração* (Sound of Music).

Teatro Taborda

Costa do Castelo 75, Castelo (21 885 4190/www. egeac.pt/taborda). Tram 12, 28/bus 37. **Open** *Box office* 2pm-midnight Tue-Sun. **Tickets** €8; €2-€5.50 concessions. **No credit cards. Map** p247 M9.

A council-owned theatre with spectacular views from the restaurant terrace out back. There's a late 19th-century auditorium with 150 seats, a small room for low-budget performances and an exhibition space.

Dance

Classical ballet has a short history in Portugal, with the **Companhia Nacional de Bailado** (21 347 4048/9, www.cnb.pt) only set up in 1977. It is based at the Teatro Luís de Camões (*see p169*), which is currently branching out, with shows and workshops for all ages.

A generation of choreographers was nurtured at the Ballet Gulbenkian – for 40 years Portugal's strongest contemporary dance company. So when the Fundação Gulbenkian in 2005 announced plans to wind it up, reactions ranged from shock to anger. In fact, the thinking behind the decision underscored the vitality of Portuguese dance: it was felt that resources could be better used to fund independents.

Away from the big institutions, Lisbon's community is good at collaborating, with **Forum Dança** (21 342 8985, www.forum danca.pt), **Vo'arte** (*see p196*, Lugar à Dança), **CEM** (21 887 1917/1763, ww.c-e-m.org) and **Alkantara** (*see p196*) offering festivals, workshops and information. Few companies have their own performance space, but most tour regularly abroad. The **Companhia Portuguesa de Bailado Contemporâneo** (21 394 1000/0460, www.cpbc.pt), founded in 1998 by Gulbenkian veteran Vasco Wellencamp, is among the more accessible. **Olga Roriz** and her eponymous company (21 848 2318, www.olgaroriz.com) tackle provocative social, political or religious themes. João Fiadeiro's **RE.AL** company (www.re-al.org, 21 390 9255) collaborates with other groups such as **Artistas Unidos** (*see p196* **Don't help the homeless**), freely mixing in text and drama. Vera Mantero, seen by many as Portugal's most important choreographer, heads **O Rumo do Fumo** (21 343 1647, www.orumodofumo.com). Her work is playful but can seem hermetic. **Clara Andermatt** and the company that bears her name (21 347 0333) do interesting work with Cape Verdean artists. Also well known abroad is **Rui Horta**, another Gulbenkian product who has tried his hand in areas from film to circus, and now runs a dance research centre (266 899 856/7, www. oespacodotempo.pt) in the Alentejo.

If you want to dance, there's a plethora of courses advertised in *Agenda Cultural*, for example at Chapitô (*see p194*). There are also periodic open dances (tango, samba and so on) at the Teatro Municipal de São Luíz (*see p194*), while the CCB runs tea dances one weekend a month. CEM (*see above*) workshops are also open to amateurs, while the Escola Superior de Dança (21 324 4774, www.esd.ipl.pt) has summer courses.

Theatre & dance festivals

The **Festival de Sintra** (*see p151*), from mid June to July, is the highlight of the year for ballet fans, regularly attracting major foreign companies. **Festival Internacional de Teatro** (*see p151*), in July, is Portugal's biggest theatrical orgy and now includes dance too. There is also a smaller **Mostra de Teatro de Almada** (21 272 4735, box office 21 272 4927/20) in February, at local venues. The

A Sul international dance festival, organised in September by the Algarve's Fundo no Fundo (289 824 783, http://nofundodofundo.com.sapo.pt), includes some shows in Lisbon.

Alkantara Festival

21 315 2267/www.alkantara.pt. **Date** June.

This multi-disciplinary festival replaced Danças na Cidade in 2006, after a four-year hiatus. Alkantara, the name of a Lisbon neighbourhood, means bridge in Arabic. The stress is on links between artists, cultures (particularly Mediterranean) and art forms.

BaixAnima

Information: Lisbon City Council tourist department (21 358 8591). **Date** July-Sept.

Street theatre, circus and music are laid on by the council from 5pm on weekends and holidays in Rua Augusta, Rua Garrett, and Rua Portas de Santo Antão. There are similar shows around Christmas.

Lugar à Dança

21 393 2410/www.voarte.com. **Date** June-July.

Started by the Vo'arte dance collective for Expo 98, this festival offers a mix of movement and street entertainment in urban spaces.

Quinzena da Dança de Almada

21 258 3175/www.cdanca-almada.pt. **Date** Oct-Nov.

Contemporary dance festival staged annually since 1993, largely showcasing Portuguese groups. The events take place mostly in Almada.

Don't help the homeless

Many of Lisbon's myriad homeless theatre and dance groups exist largely in their artistic director's imagination. One genuinely constant presence is **Artistas Unidos**, founded in 1996 by the fine actor Jorge Silva Melo, though he only occasionally appears on stage. Despite being both professional and adventurous, Artistas Unidos has no performance space to call its own – partly, it seems, because of neglect on the part of the city council.

Artistas Unidos spent two-and-a-half productive years in A Capital, a former newspaper building in the Bairro Alto, staging works by leading authors such as Sarah Kane and Jon Fosse, as well as a string of Pinter plays. Productions were often Portuguese premieres (30 in all); the group has provided an invaluable service by publishing many of the translated texts made for its productions.

In August 2002 the council closed A Capital down, 'alleging' (the group's word) that it was unsafe, but promising to renovate it. The group moved to the Taborda for what it hoped would be a temporary stay. There followed more premieres, including works by the Presnyakov Brothers, who attended the opening night of a memorable *Terrorism*. Meanwhile A Capital remained derelict despite petitions and protests from local supporters and leading figures in international theatre. The group says that the council declines to answer its letters.

Some city officials may be aware of the quality of Artistas Unidos' work, but the fact that it is political in the broadest sense counts against it. Making a virtue out of necessity, the group secures funding from a wider range of institutions than is common in Lisbon, including foreign embassies.

After moving out of the Taborda in mid 2005, the group has performed at the Centro Cultural de Belém and other Lisbon theatres and toured nationwide. It is currently using the chapel of a former women's prison in Graça, the Convento das Mónicas. From its offices near Campo Santana (Rua da Bempostinha 19B, 21 370 0120, 96 196 0281, www.artistasunidos.pt), Silva Melo continues to draw on a large roster of actors, as well as entering into interesting collaborations with artists from other areas, such as choreographer João Fiadeiro.

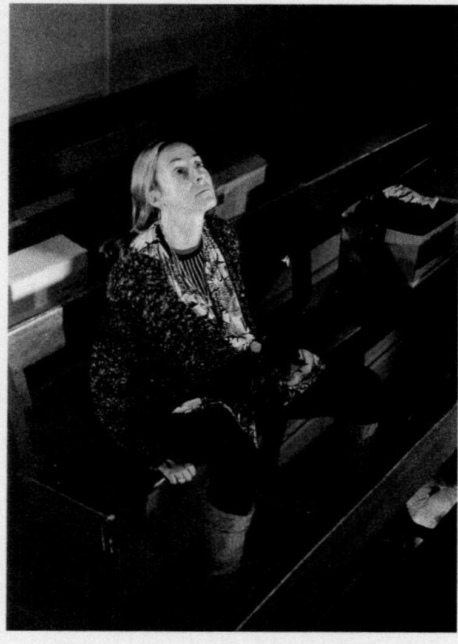

Sport & Fitness

Another three F's: football, football, football.

Bridge of thighs. The Lisbon **Half Marathon**. *See p198.*

No one could claim that the Portuguese are as successful at sport as, say, the Australians, but that's not due to lack of passion. A shortage of money bears much of the blame, coupled with an exclusive focus on soccer. Even here though, there have been few triumphs, although Benfica won the European Cup in 1961 and 1962, and FC Porto in 1987 and again in 2004. The national team came third in the 1966 World Cup, beating reigning champions Brazil on the way, and did well to finish third at Euro 2000, beaten by eventual winners France. After making a pig's ear of the 2002 World Cup, the remnants of the Golden Generation redeemed themselves by reaching the final of Euro 2004, which turned into a huge party as the final was held in Portugal. Coach Luis Felipe Scolari, though Brazilian, drummed up national pride; more than a few of the flags draped on houses then at his request were still there when the 2006 World Cup came round. His squad once more performed well and reached the semi-finals – knocking out England again in the process.

In contrast to the high profile of the national team, the domestic league is a dull three-way fight between Benfica, Porto and Sporting. (Boavista's 2001 win was a blip.)

There is growing interest in other sports such as basketball (thanks to Ticha Penicheiro's spectacular US career), volleyball (mainly the beach variety) and athletics. Since marathon runner Carlos Lopes won Portugal's first Olympic gold in 1984, Portugal has produced a string of fine runners, including Rosa Mota, Fernanda Ribeiro and António Pinto. The stress on stamina events persists: today's crop includes heptathlete Naide Gomes and Vanessa Fernandes, current world triathlon number one.

TICKETS

For events and venues check sports dailies *A Bola*, *Record* and *O Jogo*. Agencies ABEP and Agência Alvalade sell tickets for major events. For both, *see p169*. Both Lisbon's big football clubs sell tickets online (often with extra fees) and from machines at the stadium.

Spectator sports

Athletics

There are several road races during the year to watch or take part in. The biggest is the Half Marathon (*see p150;* pictured *p197*) in late March (there's another in September), but it's the Lisbon Marathon (*see p153*), in December, that attracts the leading athletes.

Dressage

The Sociedade Hípica Portuguesa, founded in 1910, organises the annual Concurso Internacional de Saltos de Obstáculos, including a Nations Cup with foreign teams held in late May at the Hipódromo do Campo Grande. The other annual event is the three-day Festival Internacional do Cavalo Puro Sangue Lusitano. This is held each June at the Hipódromo and with some 300 horses and riders participating, it is the biggest showcase for the Lusitano breed. For riding schools, *see p201*.

Associação Portuguesa de Criadores do Cavalo Puro Sangue Lusitano

Rua Sebastião José de Carvalho e Melo 157, 1D, Cascais (21 354 1684/1688/www.cavalo-lusitano.com). Train from Cais do Sodré. **Map** p246 L7.

Sociedade Hípica Portuguesa

Hipódromo do Campo Grande, Campo Grande (21 781 7410/www.shp-portugal.com). Metro Campo Grande. **Map** p248 L2.

Football

Although the Portuguese are football mad – it's the main topic of conversation in bars and the three top-selling dailies are devoted to the sport – attendances at matches are generally poor since most people can't afford tickets. FC Porto's dominance has also put a dampener on things for fans of the capital's two big clubs. The season runs from late August until the May/June Cup Final at the Estádio Nacional. Tickets can be bought there or at the Federação Portuguesa de Futebol (21 325 2700/2789, www.fpf.pt).

Clube de Futebol Os Belenenses

Estádio do Restelo, Avenida do Restelo (21 301 0461/7881/www.osbelenenses.com). Bus 28, 714, 751. **Tickets** €7-€15. **No credit cards**. **Map** p244 B9.

Belenenses won the title in 1946, one of only two clubs to break the Benfica-Sporting-Porto triumvirate. The stadium has fine river views and is uphill from Belém, so a match can make for a good end to a day's sightseeing, though atmosphere may be lacking.

Sport Lisboa e Benefica. *See p199.*

Clube de Futebol Estrela da Amadora

Estádio José Gomes, Avenida Dom José I, Reboleira, Amadora (21 499 9110/ www.cfeamadora.net). Train to Amadora from Roma-Areeiro, Entrecampos or Sete Rios. **Tickets** €10-€30. **No credit cards**.

A young (1932) and small club in the populous suburban town of Amadora.

Estádio Nacional-Jamor

Complexo Desportivo do Jamor, Praça da Maratona, Cruz Quebrada (21 419 7212/21 414 6030). Train to Algés from Cais do Sodré then bus 76 to Faculdade de Motricidade Humana. **Open** *Complex* 8am-8pm daily. **Admission** varies. **No credit cards**.

Opened in 1944, the national stadium has 50,000 seats which are filled only for the end-of-season Taça de Portugal final in May or June; it is also used as the training ground for the national team and for athletics. To visit, take the A5 towards Cascais; the pylons rise majestically above the firs and eucalyptus of the surrounding park.

Sporting Club de Portugal

Estádio José Alvalade Século XXI, Rua Fernando da Fonseca, Campo Grande (21 751 6000/707 204 4444/www.sporting.pt). Metro Campo Grande. **Tickets** €30-€155. **Credit** MC, V.

Sporting won the league in 2000 after an 18-year drought but, like Lisbon rivals Benfica, are now back to playing second fiddle to the northern giant Porto. The ground, built in time for Euro 2004, has been dubbed 'the bathroom' by Benfica fans because of its external tiling. The compact shape makes for a good atmosphere but don't tell Benfica fans we said that.

Sport Lisboa e Benfica

Estádio da Luz, Avenida General Norton de Matos, Estrada da Lu (21 721 9500/box office 707 200 100/www.slbenfica.pt). Metro Alto dos Moinhos/ Colégio Militar-Luz. **Tickets** *Portuguese league* €20-€55; €10-€18 concessions. *European competitions* €25-€75. **Credit** MC, V.
This imposing bowl of 65,000 red seats in four tiers hosted the final of Euro 2004. It hews to the concept of the original Luz: red arches and a half-translucent roof letting in natural light (although the 'Stadium of light' moniker comes from the neighbourhood, Luz). Yet it is a truly 21st-century complex, with nine panoramic restaurants (reservations 21 712 5180, open noon-midnight Mon-Sat, noon-5pm Sun), a health club, a Benfica museum – and Eusébio's statue, which had presided over four decades of decline at the original main entrance. The new stadium lifted club pride after years of poor results, helping Benfica to its 2003/4 league title. The pre-match ritual, in which an eagle swoops above the crowd to land on a handler's glove, makes it worth arriving early. **Photo** *p198.*

Motor sport

At least until 2008 the Dakar Rally (formerly known as Paris-Dakar) is to start in Lisbon. It includes one full stage in Portugal – from Belém to Portimão in the Algarve – and another straddling the border with Spain, before the whole circus crosses to North Africa on its way to the Senegalese capital. For more, see www.dakar.com.

Circuito do Estoril

Avenida Alfredo César Torres, Alcabideche (21 460 9500/www.circuito-estoril.pt). Train to Estoril from Cais do Sodré, then bus 418, 456/ticket-holders' shuttle from Casino. By car: A5, Estoril exit, then follow signs. **Open** *Box office* 9am-7pm daily. **Tickets** varies; MotoGP €10-€70; €10 11-14s; under-11s free. **Credit** DC, MC, V.
The Autódromo Fernanda Pires da Silva, as it is officially known, was dropped from the Formula 1 racing calendar a decade ago, a debacle that led to the state taking over control. The track has since been upgraded to make good those safety failings, but there's no sign of it being reinstated on the Formula 1 calendar. In the absence of the four wheeled circus the big international event now is the motorcycling Grand Prix, in mid October, but there are also A1, FIA Touring Car, truck and drag races, and a classic car show in early October.

Roller hockey

Known in some countries as rink hockey, *hóquei em patins* (on skates) is second only to football among spectator sports. Portugal's men rank among the best; Portugal has won 15 world titles, most recently in 2003. The season runs September to June; games are on weekend afternoons and evenings.

Clube Desportivo de Paço d'Arcos

Pavilhão Gimnodesportivo, Avenida Bonneville Franco, Paço d'Arcos (21 443 2238/http:// cdpa.com.sapo.pt). Train to Paço d'Arcos from Cais do Sodré. **Tickets** €10. **No credit cards.**
The best arena, and a crowd that creates an intense atmosphere making life tough for opponents. Still, they haven't won the league in decades.

Tennis

The Estoril Open (*see p150*) is one of Portugal's few regular international sports events of any consequence. It's a good place to spot up-and-coming Spaniards.

Participation sports

If you're staying for a while, the Lisbon Casuals (21 457 4684, www.lisboncasuals.net) is a sociable multi-sports club based in the grounds of St Julian's School in Carcavelos, with football, cricket, baseball, field hockey (men's and mixed), tennis and badminton.

Bowling

Funcenter Colombo

Centro Colombo, Loja A206, Avenida Lusíada, Benfica (21 711 3700). Metro Colégio Militar-Luz. **Open** Bowling noon-1am Mon-Thur; noon-2am Fri; 11am-2am Sat; 11am-1am Sun. **Admission** (incl shoes) from €3 per game (10 rolls); from €3.75 after 8pm. **Credit** AmEx, MC, V.
Ten-pin bowling with 24 alleys in the Colombo shopping centre (*see p132*). At night there is 'extreme bowling', played in near darkness with fluorescent balls, accompanied by loud music.

Fishing

A licence from the Direcção-Geral – or from fishing shops at a couple of days' notice – is in theory needed for fishing in Portugal's rivers, though few people bother. Sea angling was always free, but there are plans to bring in a licence, along with some bag limits, in 2007. Along the coast from Oeiras to Cascais and up to Cabo da Roca you can catch grey mullet, sea bream, squid and sea bass. The River Tagus is improving after years of pollution and grey mullet are returning to its waters. The Federação Portuguesa de Pesca Desportiva (21 314 0177, 936 525 852, www.fppd.pt) runs championships and can provide advice. For boat trips, try Tuttamania (*see p202*).

Casa Diana

Rua Pascoal de Melo 62D, Estefânia (21 355 4063/21 319 2940). Metro Arroios. **Open** 9am-1pm, 3-7pm Mon-Fri; 9am-1pm Sat. **No credit cards. Map** p246 M6.

No death in the afternoon

To aficionados bullfighting is definitely not sport, except in the Shakespearean sense of 'fun'. It may not be your idea of fun (or the bull's), but many Portuguese are passionate about a tradition that, as they are quick to point out, goes back more than 2,000 years. A huge subculture has grown up around it, linked with a rural world that is losing its influence in society and intertwined with notions of class in complex ways. Does that remind you of anything?

British campaigners against fox hunting were, indeed, among those who were represented at the small but noisy protest outside Lisbon's 19th-century Praça de Touros when it finally reopened in May 2006 after a seven-year hiatus.

Trying to ignore the protest was the cream of a certain segment of Portuguese society. Their reactions to the shouted slogans were fierce – 'I respect their views: why the hell can't they respect mine?' – and also recalled the lament of Britain's hunt followers: 'They just don't understand country ways. We're the animal-lovers.'

Indeed, in Portugal, unlike Spain, it is illegal to kill the bull in the ring (although it is butchered afterwards). Although classic Portuguese *touradas* might have disappointed Hemingway, they are still bloody affairs. The spectacle starts with a rider in 18th-century costume, mounted on an elegant Lusitano horse, sticking small spears into the bull to irk it. Then the *forcados* enter the ring – half-a-dozen unarmed catchers on foot who wrestle the bull after enticing it to charge. For many, these amateurs are the real heroes, even if the bulls' horns are tipped.

Bullfighting no longer has the mass appeal it did before the advent of TV, though there are towns, such as Montijo (Praça de Touros, 21 231 0632), south of the Tagus, where it is a big deal. The reopening of a revamped bullring in Lisbon might be seen as heralding a revival. Most agencies sold tickets for the 2006 season, but at least one gave up after a barrage of protest emails. And whereas for a century the arena was used pretty well only for bullfights, after the €50 million (£34 million) overhaul – which added a shopping centre and Lisbon's largest car park – today it is only viable if hired out for other events.

Visitors who want more action could visit Vila Franca de Xira (tourist office 263 285 605, www.cm-vfxira.pt), 20 minutes north, where fighting bulls and Lusitano horses are bred. It has a full season of events, capped by an October fair with lashings of music, food and drink, and a Pamplona style running of the bulls.

Praça de Touros do Campo Pequeno

Avenida da República (21 799 8450/box office 21 782 0575). Metro Campo Pequeno. **Open** *Box office* 11am-7pm Mon-Fri; 2-7pm Sat, Sun or until performance starts. **Bullfights** *Easter-Sept* 10pm Thur. **Admission** *Bullfights* €15-€75. **No credit cards. Map** p249 M4.

At this well-stocked fishing shop staff are always on hand to help with advice and supplies.

Direcção-Geral das Florestas

Avenida João Crisóstomo 26-8, Saldanha (21 312 4800). Metro Saldanha. **Open** 9.30am-4pm Mon-Fri. **No credit cards. Map** p248 L5.

This Agriculture Ministry office issues the required river-fishing licences: €1.58 for a borough, €4.09 for a regional and €7.60 for a national one. Under-14s need none if accompanied by an adult.

Fitness

The law requires a certificate of physical health but many gyms will allow you to sign a waiver.

Academia Life Club

Rua Cintura do Porto, Armazém J, Santos (21 395 6428). Tram 15, 18. Metro Cais do Sodré. **Open** 7am-11pm Mon-Fri; 9am-8pm Sat; 9am-6pm Sun. **Admission** Day pass €20. **Credit** DC, MC, V.

Lisbon's first modern gym offers aerobics, step and powerstep, a sauna and Turkish bath, weights and cardiofitness training. Access from the tram route is via the walkway over Santos rail station.

Clube VII

Parque Eduardo VII, Marquês de Pombal (21 384 8300/808 277 288/www.clubvii.com). Metro Marquês de Pombal. **Open** 7am-10.30pm Mon-Fri, 9am-9pm Sat, 10am-6pm Sun. **Admission** Passes: day €34, week €120, month €188. **Credit** AmEx, DC, MC, V.

The place you're most likely to find yourself on the treadmill next to a top businessman. Classes range from bodypump and spinning to yoga, and there are personal trainers on hand. There's a 25m (82ft) pool, covered tennis courts and a squash court.

Solinca Health & Fitness Club

Centro Colombo, Loja A201, Avenida Lusíada (21 012 9670). Metro Colégio Militar-Luz. **Open** 7am-10pm Mon-Fri; 9am-8pm Sat, Sun. **Admission** Day pass €20. **Credit** AmEx, MC, V.

Three-storey gym at the Colombo centre. Offers squash, aerobics and hydroaerobics, hydrotherapy, massages, solarium, step, sauna, Turkish bath, weights, cardiofitness and a 25m (82ft) pool.

Other locations: Centro Vasco da Gama (21 893 0706; *see p132*)

Golf

Golf remains a minority sport in Portugal, although golfing tourists in their thousands flock to the Algarve. Portugal hosts three important tournaments on the European circuit: the Portuguese, Madeira and Estoril Opens. In 2005 it hosted the World Cup for the first time. If you're driving from Lisbon to any of the clubs below, start by taking the A5 towards Cascais.

Golfe do Estoril

Avenida da República, Estoril (21 468 0176). Train to Estoril from Cais do Sodré, then bus 406/411. **Open** 7.30am-8pm daily. **Green fee** €57. **Credit** AmEx, MC, V.

Jean Gassiat designed the first nine holes in 1929, and the rest were completed by Mackenzie Ross; the 16th is said to be the best in Portugal. Unfortunately, the A5 now slices through the course. This 18-hole par-69 course is for members only at weekends, when non-members can still use the nine-hole par-34 course (€25). If you're driving, leave the A5 at Estoril; you'll see the clubhouse a few hundred yards along the Sintra road.

Lisbon Sports Club

Casal da Carregueira, Belas (21 431 0077). Train from Sete Rios to Queluz-Belas. **Open** 8am-7pm daily. **Green fee** €45; €60 weekends. **Credit** AmEx, MC, V.

A tricky 18-hole (par 69) course crossed by the River Jamor north of Queluz. This is the second oldest golf club in Portugal, founded in 1922 by British expats. To drive, take the A5 as far as Monsanto and then the IC19 towards Sintra; at Queluz, take the EN117 to Belas and beyond. Further on is a resort, Belas Club de Campo (www.belasgolf.com, 21 962 6640), with another two courses.

Oitavos Golf

Quinta da Marinha, Casa da Quinta 25, Cascais (21 486 0600/www.quintadamarinha-oitavosgolfe.pt). Train to Cascais from Cais do Sodré then bus 425 (Mon-Fri)/bus 405 then 10min walk. **Open** 8am-8pm daily (but members only from 9.30am Sat, Sun). **Green fee** €150; €115 weekends. **Credit** AmEx, DC, MC, V.

A new (2001) par-71 course laid out by American golf architect Arthur Hills among pine woods and reforested dunes within sight of the ocean, with an ultra-stylish clubhouse. Lying within the Sintra-Cascais Natural Park, it contains environmentally protected areas. Practice facilities include a 300m (984ft) driving range and two putting greens.

Quinta da Penha Longa

Quinta da Penha Longa, Estrada da Lagoa Azul, Linhó, Sintra (21 924 9031/00/www.penhalonga.com). Train to Cascais from Cais do Sodré, then bus 403 to Malveira. **Open** *Winter* 7.30am-7.30pm daily. *Summer* 7.30am-9pm daily. **Green fee** €90; €120 weekends. **Credit** AmEx, DC, MC, V.

Arguably the best 18-hole (par-72) course in the area, designed by Robert Trent Jones Jr, near the Sintra hills, with glimpses of the Atlantic coast. There is a smaller adjacent nine-hole course costing €33 (€45 at weekends). There's no public transport but you could get a taxi in Malveira. To drive, exit the A5 at Estoril, take the EN9 towards Sintra and turn left at the sign for Lagoa Azul; the course is a little further on.

Riding

Around the Cascais coast area there are various places to have riding lessons, and riding trips are available around the Sintra hills or Guincho.

Centro Hípico da Costa do Estoril

Avenida da Charneca 186, Cascais (21 487 2064/96 503 7024/www.centrohipicocostaestoril.com). Train to Cascais from Cais do Sodré then bus 403 to Charneca. **Open** *June-Sept* 9am-1pm, 4-8pm Tue-Sun. *Oct-May* 10am-1pm, 3-7pm Tue-Sun. **Lessons** €16/hr-€21/hr; €130-€165 for 10 lessons. **Rides** €26/hr; €220 for 10. **No credit cards**.

This centre outside Cascais offers rides in the Cascais-Guincho area and the Sintra hills, as well as lessons from beginner to competitive level in dressage and show jumping. By car, it's two minutes from the end of the A5: take the Malveira road and then turn left for Charneca; the Centro is on your right.

Escola de Equitação do Centro Hípico da Quinta da Marinha

Quinta da Marinha, Casa 25, Areia, Cascais (91 813 9434/www.quintadamarinha-centrohipico.pt). Bus 404, 415. **Open** *Winter* 9am-1pm, 3-7pm daily. *Summer* 9am-1pm, 4-8pm daily. **Lessons** €20/hr; €140 for 8 lessons. **No credit cards**.

Surfing.

Part of a riding and breeding mega-complex with 400 horses, on one of Portugal's most exclusive estates. It offers guided rides in the Cascais-Sintra region, with monthly deals available.

Sailing

Despite the proximity of so much blue water, no club in the Lisbon area hires out sailing boats. As well as the listings below, in Cascais there's the municipal Escola de Actividades Naúticas e Canoagem (21 482 5581). For more information on sailing in Portugal, contact the Belém-based Federação Portuguesa de Vela (21 365 8500, www.fpvela.pt).

Associação Naval de Lisboa

Doca de Belém, Belém (21 361 9480/www.anl.pt). Train to Belém from Cais de Sodré. **Map** p244 C10.

Year-round courses (practice and theory) for sailors with some experience as well as for beginners. The latter include several for children, in either Optimists or dinghies. The Clube Naval (21 363 0061) next door also has courses in sailing (it has disabled-adapted boats), canoeing and rowing.

Clube Naval de Cascais

Esplanada Dom Luís Filipe, Marina de Cascais, Cascais (21 483 0125/www.cncascais.com). Train to Cascais from Cais do Sodré, then bus BusCas to Jardim Marechal Carmona.

A plethora of courses are on offer at this club in Cascais marina.

Tuttamania

Marina de Cascais, Loja 127, Cascais (21 483 3083/93 876 9224/93 484 3636/www.tuttamania.com). Train to Cascais from Cais do Sodré, then BusCas to Jardim Marechal Carmona. **Lessons** from €250/eight 4hr lessons.

Private company in Cascais offering lessons as well as sailing or motorboat trips (with skipper). Hiring a boat for up to six costs from €225 for half-a-day (including drinks); you may go as far as Guincho.

Squash

Courts are scarce. Lisboa Racket Centre (*see p203*), Clube VII and Solinca (for both, *see p201*) also each have one.

Ginásio Flete

Rua Aprigio Mafra 23, Alvalade (21 840 9074). Metro Alvalade/bus 31, 45, 83, 750. **Open** 8.30am-2pm, 3-11pm Mon-Fri; 10am-2pm Sat. **Admission** €14/hr. **No credit cards. Map** p249 N1.

Three squash courts, though in poor condition.

Squash Olaias

Olaias Clube, Rua Robalo Gouveia, Olaias (21 840 7130/reservations 21 847 3742). Metro Olaias. **Open** 10am-midnight Mon-Thur; 10am-11pm Fri; 10am-9pm Sat; 10am-3pm Sun. **Admission** €12/hr except weekdays 6-8pm (€18/hr). **No credit cards.**

Four courts where national squad members train. To play at peak times you must book in advance. The complex also has tennis courts, a gym and two pools.

Surfing

The most obvious port of call is Carcavelos (*see p208* and below), where the best waves are in early autumn or spring. It's a beach break with shifting peaks, with no nasty reefs, so is good for beginners. But its local nickname, 'muddy waters', points to perennial pollution problems. Speaking of locals, it's best to leave them to it in 'the zone' at the eastern end of the beach, which gets the best of the waves. Those with a more dainty disposition might prefer the Caparica coast (*see p210*). Again, it's good for beginners, with mellow, shifting peaks (rights and lefts) and (except in high summer) room for all. You could start at São João de Caparica (*see p211*), which has beach bars where bedraggled beginners can recover. Elsewhere, there's Guincho (*see p209*), whose fierce waves are only for the brave, and Praia Grande (*see p209*) on the Sintra coast, which hosts national and international championships.

If you're shopping for equipment, staff at the Ericeira Surf Shop (21 716 7605) in Centro Colombo (*see p132*) know their stuff. For lessons, *see p157* or check out www.100surf.pt – which also has information on tides and equipment hire.

Linha de Onda

Rua Sacadura Cabral 197B, São Pedro do Estoril (291 437 9313/91 994 5490/www.linhadeonda.com). Train from Cais do Sodré to São Pedro do Estoril. **Lessons** €25; €95/five; €170/ten. **No credit cards**.

Surf 'training centre' offering board and wetsuit hire and lessons for all ages by certified instructors (prices include equipment). In winter these usually take place in Carcavelos, in summer in Guincho. They also organise 'tours' and camps further afield.

Swimming

In winter city pools get crowded and times for anything other than lessons are generally limited, so check first for *natação livre* (free swimming). As with gyms, you may be asked for a doctor's note. In summer things are quieter as locals decamp to the beach; some pools close in August. For more information see the Beaches chapter.

Non-members may use Inatel's Parque de Jogos 1° de Maio (*see below*), including the pool (open 7am-10.30pm Mon-Fri; 9am-8pm Sat & Sun; admission €0.53 plus €4.24/45mins; €4.84/45mins after 6pm). The complex of which Squash Olaias (*see p202*) forms a part has two pools. The only Olympic-sized pool in the region is near the Estádio Nacional (*see p198*; 21 415 6400), but you must join (€33.60) to use it.

Ateneu Comércial de Lisboa

Rua das Portas de Santo Antão 110, Baixa (21 324 6060/www.ateneulisboa.pt). Metro Restauradores. **Open** 7.30am-12.30pm, 1.30-5pm Mon, Wed, Fri; 7.30-10am, 1.30-5pm Tue, Thur; 9.30am-12.30pm Sat. Closed Aug. **Admission** €5; €29/10 visits. **No credit cards**. **Map** p250 M9.

The Ateneu was founded in a former aristocratic residence in 1880, as a sort of society for Lisbon shop assistants. The decaying building provides a roof for everything from chess to acupuncture, but non-members may only swim. The 25m (82ft) top-floor pool is a 1930s period piece, but it's under glass and the chlorine fumes can be strong on hot days.

Piscina da Penha de França

Calçada do Poço dos Mouros 2, Penha de França (21 816 1750). Metro Arroios/bus 107. **Open** 8am-8pm Mon-Fri; 9am-8pm Sat, Sun. **Admission** €1.52 (€1.99 after 7pm). **No credit cards**. **Map** p247 N6.

Municipally run, indoor, heated, 25m (82ft) pool plus a solarium, open in summer. There are classes, but you can just swim any time.

Tennis

The most central covered facilities are at Clube VII (*see p201*). There are two tatty municipal hard courts in the northern part of the Jardim do Campo Grande (9am-7pm daily, €1.40/hr); book at the adjoining café (21 759 0934). Call ahead if you want to play after 5.30pm.

Centro de Ténis de Monsanto

Parque Florestal de Monsanto (21 363 8073/21 364 8741). Bus 24. **Open** 8.30am-9pm daily (changing rooms to 8pm). **Admission** €6.50-€11.50/hr; lighting €4/hr extra. **No credit cards**.

This municipal complex in Monsanto forest has 15 courts, from covered and uncovered clay and synthetic grass (most floodlit) to cheaper fast courts. Non-members can't book but may call an hour ahead to see how the land lies. Overlooking the courts are a café and restaurant (21 364 6302; closed Mon, dinner Sun), specialising in grilled fish and meat.

Clube de Ténis do Jamor

Complexo Desportivo do Jamor, Praça da Maratona, Cruz Quebrada (21 414 6041). Train to Algés from Cais do Sodré then bus 76. **Open** 8am-10pm Mon-Sat; 8am-8pm Sun. **Admission** *Uncovered court* €5/hr. *Covered court* €5.60/hr. *Floodlit court* €10/hr. **No credit cards**.

The venue for the Estoril Open (*see p150*), this suburban club boasts 34 clay courts (ten floodlit and two covered), plus six fast ones, two mini-tennis courts and three marked practice walls.

Lisboa Racket Centre

Rua Alferes Malheiro, Alvalade (21 846 0232). Bus 31, 44, 45, 83, 750. **Open** 8am-10pm Mon-Fri; 9am-8pm Sat, Sun. **Admission** €5/hr per person; €8/hr per person after dusk. **No credit cards**. **Map** p249 01.

Located in a small park, this friendly club has nine courts (seven floodlit) making it the best in-town option. It also has a gym, sauna, pool and restaurant.

Parque de Jogos 1º de Maio

Avenida Rio de Janeiro, Alvalade (21 845 3470/www.inatel.pt). **Open** 7am-10.45pm Mon-Fri; 7.30am-10.45pm Sat, Sun. Closed Aug. **Admission** €0.53 plus €7/hr (€12 after 6pm). **No credit cards**. **Map** p249 N2/3.

This sports complex owned by workers institute Inatel has three outdoor hard-surface courts, with floodlights, open till late. But take note: they lock up at 11pm. The booth is closed on Sunday, so for that you must book and pay in advance.

See page 215

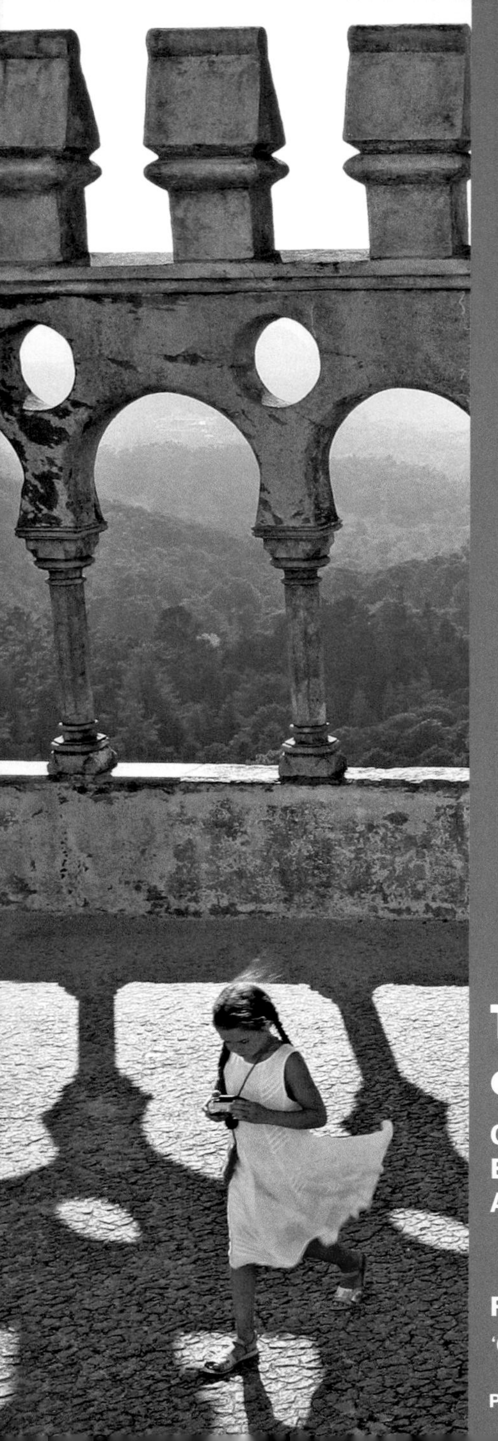

Trips Out of Town

Features

Pálacio da Pena. *See p215.*

Getting Started

The best ways to hit the road – or rails – and get out of the city.

By bus

For long distances, coaches are quicker and cheaper than rail. The main hub is **Terminal Rodoviário de Lisboa** (Praça Marechal Humberto Delgado, Rua das Laranjeiras, 21 358 1460, information 808 224 488/21 358 1466, ticket office open 6am-1am). It's behind Sete Rios rail station; from the platform of Jardim Zoológico Metro station, follow signs to Terminal de Autocarros but in the rail station, ignore signs for (local) buses and turn left. Through the glass doors, steps lead to an escalator up to the terminal.

Rede Expresso (www.rede-expressos.pt) and **Eva** (www.eva-bus.com) are the two main operators. Both have concessions. You can buy tickets at the terminal, online or at agencies such as Terra Nova Viagens e Turismo at Praça Francisco Sá Carneiro (Areeiro) 12 (21 843 7980), Cruzeiro (Rua do Alecrim 7, 21 322 1000) and Abreu branches including Avenida da Liberdade 160 (21 323 0200) and Praça Duque da Terceira 20 (Cais do Sodré, 21 324 2450).

Greater Lisbon is served by regional companies; with these, fares are cheaper if you buy double tickets in advance (*pré-comprados*), validated on board. **Mafrense** (261 816 152, www.mafrense.pt) has buses to Mafra and Ericeira from Campo Grande bus station, where it has a booth (21 758 2212); **Vimeca** (21 435 7472) to Queluz. South of the river is the domain of **Transportes Sul do Tejo** (21 042 7072/0, www.tsuldotejo.pt); its Lisbon base is Praça de Espanha (21 726 4415, booth closed Sat pm, Sun).

Scotturb (21 469 9127, 21 468 2298, www.scotturb.com) covers the Cascais-Sintra region. Its one-day pass, at €8.50, is worth it if you plan several trips; for €12 you get train travel to and from Lisbon too. Timetables and discounted tickets can be had from its counters at Cascais bus station (beneath Cascaisvila shopping centre, open 7.30am-7.30pm Mon-Fri; 9.30am-1.30pm, 2.30-6.30pm Sat & Sun) and opposite Sintra rail station (21 923 0381, open 9am-12.30pm, 2-6pm Mon-Fri; 9am-1pm, 2-6pm Sat & Sun).

By car

Portugal's road network has improved but the country's insanely cavalier motorists haven't. Signposts are often lacking, so find a good map.

For routes east and south to anywhere other than Caparica and Sesimbra, use the Ponte Vasco da Gama; the Ponte 25 de Abril can get congested. From the Praça Marquês de Pombal, head north-east up Avenida Fontes Pereira de Melo, following signs for the airport and then for the A12/Ponte Vasco da Gama.

For the north, start as above but follow signs for the A1 E80 (IP1). *See also p223.*

By train

The Lisbon–Oporto route is the best service run by national rail company **CP** (21 318 5990, www.cp.pt). Trains depart from Santa Apolónia (Avenida Infante Dom Henrique, open 6am-midnight daily) which is not on the Metro but served by myriad buses. You can also board at Lisboa-Oriente (Avenida de Berlim, 1998, open 5.30am-11.45pm daily), which is on the red Metro line. For rail information, call 808 208 208 or freephone 800 200 904 (7am-11pm daily).

For the Algarve and parts of the Alentejo, journey times have been slashed by trains using the line under the Ponte 25 de Abril. Services start at Oriente and stop at Entrecampos.

The same bridge is used by **Fertagus** (797 127 127, www.fertagus.pt) trains towards Setúbal from Roma-Areeiro, stopping at Entrecampos, Sete Rios (both on the Metro) and Campolide before crossing to Pragal, where you can catch a bus to Caparica.

For Sintra, so long as Rossio is closed for structural repairs, you can board at Roma-Areeiro, Entrecampos or Sete Rios. Some services start further east, at Oriente. For Mafra and Óbidos, set out from Entrecampos.

Cais do Sodré (freephone 800 203 067) is the terminal for the line to Cascais and the beaches of the Estoril coast. If you plan to tour the Cascais-Sintra region, consider buying a €12 one-day rail and bus pass.

Long-distance tickets should be bought in advance at the station (where special Alfa vending machines accept credit cards) or at Multibanco (ATM) machines (the receipt serves as your ticket). For suburban trips, five-day tickets and ten-trip tickets are available from machines. Under-14s travel half-price; under-fives go free. On long-distance services, you can usually take bikes for free. On suburban lines, bikes are free at weekends, otherwise €1.50.

Beaches

All that ... and a beach holiday too.

Hey, **Guincho**, fancy a beach all to yourself? *See p209.*

Think of Portuguese beaches and the mind automatically turns southward, to the Algarve. But, let's be honest, what else can you do there apart from play golf? Come to Lisbon and you can combine sunbathing and sightseeing, beach combing and bar hopping. There are sheltered coves on the Estoril coast all the way to wild and windswept Guincho. Across the Tagus, Caparica is the gateway to miles of dune-backed sands, served by bars catering to distinct groups of lisboetas. Further south are more isolated beaches. The Blue Flag foundation okayed 45 beaches in the Lisbon district in 2006, but water quality varies, particularly on the Estoril coast. For an update, visit www.blueflag.org/blueflag. (Note that if a beach isn't listed, it may be because it has no lifeguard.)

Portugal is an important port of call for leading surfers and windsurfers, *see p203.* While the waters between Lisbon and Cascais are fairly sheltered, take care elsewhere; there are several drownings each year. Note the colour of the flag flying on the beach: if it's red, limit yourself to paddling. Only during the bathing season (June-mid Sept) are lifeguards on duty on designated beaches. Note also the ocean's chill, particularly north of Lisbon. Surfers should pack their wetsuits.

Lisbon to Cascais

Catch the Cascais train from Cais do Sodré and you can be lying on your towel in 45 minutes. The further down the line you go, the more resort-like the surroundings. When travelling to smaller stations, buy a return or keep coins handy, since counters may close as early as 4.30pm and then tickets are available only from machines. The return journey offers fine views of Lisbon at sunset.

At Estoril and on some other beaches sunshades and sunloungers can be rented for €4 to €10 per item. A continuous promenade runs between São João do Estoril and Cascais; bars and restaurants with esplanades abound, some with shower facilities. Between Estoril and Cascais there is also fitness equipment at regular intervals.

Carcavelos

Oeiras has a Piscina Oceânica (21 446 2550, open June-Sept), a fun seawater pool, that posts water quality daily. But only past the São Julião da Barra headland would you want to plunge into the sea. There are several working-class districts along this stretch, perhaps explaining why investment in the Praia de Carcavelos has been inadequate – although there are plans to change that. A good thing too: its broad sands are unmatched along this coast, despite the lack of a blue flag in 2006. It is packed in summer, attracting hordes of local youngsters. There are also volleyball nets, and the beach is popular with surfers all year round. At the Windsurf Café (21 457 8965), you can rent kayaks or book lessons with top local experts in surfing, bodyboard and kite-surfing (the last of these only in winter). Angel's Bar (21 457 0611, www.angelsbar.com) offers lessons, and is a big beach tennis centre. It has four internet PCs (from €1.50) and a webcam so you can check the surf from your hotel. Carcavelos is one of two beaches in the Lisbon area (the other is Adraga, *see p209*) with free *tiralôs*, a chair-cum-beach vehicle to help disabled people into the water (call 91 220 8118, 21 482 5272, June-mid Sept, 9.30am-6pm daily). At the eastern end of Carcavelos, craggy rocks mark off a middle-class hangout. The larger of two bars here, Bar Moinho (21 458 0194, closed Wed), has deckchairs and chillout music, and stays open until 2am.

Parede

The peeling promenade might not exude the elegance of Estoril or Cascais, but this sheltered patch of sand is quieter than both and good for bathing (it has a blue flag). Older Portuguese flock here for the high iodine content in the waters – supposedly efficacious against rheumatism.

Westward from Parede shelves of rock reach out into the sea, creating pools where waves break low. Further on, Praia das Avencas, reached on foot via a subway, is served year round by cosy Bar das Avencas (21 457 2717, closed Tue).

São Pedro do Estoril

An attractive beach, little frequented by tourists, but crowded on summer weekends. A narrow strip of sand slips into clear waters where slabs of rock create shades of blue and green. This explains the popularity of São Pedro with divers, but makes for a dodgy dip at low tide. If you're driving from Lisbon, go round the roundabout to get on to the beach side and enter the clifftop car park. Down below is the secluded Praia de Bafureira, which has bars that are popular with local youngsters.

São João do Estoril

Two beaches, linked by a promenade. Praia da Poça is a 'locals' beach that offers respite from crowds and is excellent for windsurfing. At the western end is a large seawater pool; at the other, Bar Atlantis is good for watching sunsets. Prettier and quieter Azarujinha beach is round the headland towards Lisbon.

Estoril

The narrow strand at Tamariz beach, next to Estoril station, is occupied by a mix of tourists and locals and the promenade is filled with the tables of adjoining bars and restaurants (some doubling as noisy nightspots). If you want the seclusion of a private pool, the Piscinas de Tamariz (open June-mid Sept, 10am-7pm daily, from €8, concessions after 2pm) keep the mob at bay. Along the promenade towards Cascais is Bar Jonas (closed Wed), where you can sip sangria and listen to ambient music, and beyond it another beach with its own station (Monte Estoril). At the Cascais end, Escotiha Bar tempts Brits with fish and chips. Further on is a seawater pool; take care as the waves lap over with some force.

Cascais

The first Cascais beach is a frisbee throw from the train station: Praia da Conceição, separated by a strip of sand from Praia da Duquesa. John David's Café (21 483 0455/4268), at the east end of the beach by the station, panders to Anglo-Saxon palates, while the attached Cascais Watersport Centre offers waterskiing, windsurfing or pedal boats. Like other bars, it has showers, changing rooms and sunbeds for hire. Beyond Hotel Albatroz (*see p55*) is tiny Praia da Rainha. In front of Praça do 5 de Outubro, Praia da Ribeira is bigger but geared to fishing.

Where to eat

At Carcavelos, **A Pastorinha** (21 457 1892, main courses €18-€35, closed Tue) is a good fish restaurant. **Sun 7 Bar** (21 458 6575), on the same beach, serves up chicken and fajitas. **Alcatruz**, a funky clifftop shack between São Pedro and São João, serves snacks and drinks until the wee hours. At São João, **Peixe na Linha** (Praia da Bafureira, 21 468 5388, closed Mon, main courses €12.50-€25) has a varied menu and giddy sea views. For Estoril and Cascais, *see p213.*

Getting there

By car

The A5 toll motorway, which is well signposted around Praça de Espanha and Praça Marquês de Pombal, closes in on the coast around Estoril. The N6 'Marginal' hugs the coastline, but is prone to traffic.

By train

Trains leave Cais do Sodré every 15-30mins, stopping at the destinations above (Cascais 30mins, fare €1.55). Trains run as late as 1.30am both ways. Beware: some do not stop at every destination, some finish at Oeiras. The furthest you'll have to walk to a beach is 10mins, at Carcavelos.

Guincho & the Sintra coast

The sea crashes into the rocks with a new violence beyond Cascais. Boca do Inferno (*see p213*) marks the change. At Guincho, cliffs give way to a great bank of sand, ringed by heath and woodland. Further north, the Sintra hills end in the cliffs of Cabo da Roca (*see p215*). Beyond here the beaches are smaller, tucked between dramatic headlands and linked by clifftop trails as far north as Magoito.

Guincho

Six km (four miles) from Cascais, the open sands of Praia Grande do Guincho stretch back, forming dunes that reach up the hillside beyond the main road. To the north, the Sintra hills form a craggy horizon, and fresh pine scents mix with the salty ocean tang. Dismissed in the 1940s by *Life* magazine as a beach with no future, Guincho is now a prime destination. But take heed. A breeze in Cascais probably means it is blowing a gale here. Bathers should also be wary of powerful waves and currents; note there are no lifeguards in the middle of the beach.

Guincho is among Europe's top spots for windsurfing, but not for beginners. It can offer good surfing, but mainly early and late when the wind dies down. At the southern end, Aerial Wind & Surf (21 467 4327, www.aerial-pt.com) offers lessons and rents equipment. Estalagem do Muchaxo (*see p57*), a hotel built around an old fort, has an excellent restaurant and its own sheltered seawater pool (open mid May-Sept, non-guests €11 Mon-Fri, €14.50 Sat & Sun). Just to the south are two smaller, more sheltered beaches, with showers. There's another saltwater pool here (open mid May-mid Oct), attached to the restaurant João Padeiro.

At the opposite, northern end (or a 20min walk on from where the 405 bus turns inland; turn left after the picnic site), Bar do Guincho draws watersports enthusiasts. The restaurant has a decent menu (main courses €9.50-€15, closed Mon) and is cosy in winter. You can rent kite- and windsurf equipment from Brisas e Ventanias (91 954 2366, 96 255 4490); it also offers courses. To reach tiny, sheltered Praia do Abano follow the track past Bar do Guincho car park for another 1.3km (one mile). **Photo** *p207*.

Azenhas do Mar

This picturesque village clings to a headland north of Praia das Maçãs – there's a 2km (1 mile) marked footpath between the two. Open-air cafés (one in a Moorish watermill) and a restaurant with picture windows overlook a minute beach. Steps lead down to a rock-cut seawater pool refilled by the tide (free). The pool above the restaurant charges €10 a day.

Praia da Adraga

A road winds downhill from Almoçageme to a near-perfect beach wedged between tall cliffs. At one end, an arch has formed through the rocks and at low tide, you can discover a string of caves. A beachfront bar and restaurant complete the picture. Adraga is 15km (nine miles) north of Guincho, signposted off the Sintra road. Public transport is limited (buses to Almoçageme, then a 20min walk), although a clifftop trail does link it with Praia Grande (*see below*). The narrow road down to the beach can get congested. Adraga, like Carcavelos (*see p208*), has *tiralôs* to transport disabled people to the spot of their choice (21 923 8500, mid June-mid Sept 10am-1pm, 3-7pm Mon-Fri, Sun). Access from the parking lot has ramps for wheelchairs.

Praia das Maçãs

A medium-sized family beach by a village with lots of seafood restaurants. It has changing rooms and showers, plus municipal sports facilities and a swimming pool nearby. If you're using public transport, the tram ride down the leafy Sintra hills and through the village of Colares, with its ancient vineyards, is fun. Friday is best as locals mob it at weekends.

Praia Grande

Signposted from the Sintra road north of Adraga, this beach is less secluded than its neighbour, with several restaurants. At the northern end, Hotel Arribas (21 928 9050) boasts an Olympic-sized pool (mid June-Sept, €6.50 Mon-Fri, €9.50 Sat & Sun). Surf competitions are held here. The southern end attracts a younger, sporty crowd. A track leads to Praia Pequena, a smaller beach accessible from below at low tide. Near Bar do Fundo, 338 steps lead to clifftop trails running north and south.

Where to eat

Fish restaurants dot the coast road near Guincho, so you can divide your attention between the sunset and the seafood. **Mestre Zé** (21 487 0275, main courses €15-€35) and **João Padeiro** (21 485 7141, main courses €17.50-€35) are both good places to stop. The posher **Porto de Santa Maria** (*see p124*) is on the same road.

There's no shortage of places to eat at Praia das Maçãs, but with the better restaurants, it's best to book in summer. Near the bus stop, **Búzio** (Avenida Eugéne Levy 56, 21 929 2172, main courses €9-€19.50) has a loyal local clientele. Another friendly place, with a beach view, is **O Loureiro** (21 929 2442, main courses €8-€22), not to be confused with the snackbar of the same name. It has everything from grilled *carapau* (horse mackerel) to roast kid. **Neptuno** (21 929 1222, main courses €9.50-€16) is on the beach and glass-fronted, ensuring a fine view.

Azenhas do Mar (21 928 0739, main courses €13.50-€18), in the village of the same name, is renowned for its seafood and location – it feels as though the waves are set to come crashing on to your plate – so it's best to book.

Getting there

By bicycle

It's a long climb over the Sintra foothills but cycling from Cascais to Guincho is easy, and there's a superb track (20-30mins). BiCas (Bicycles of Cascais, 21 460

Caparica.

6250) are lent for free from three strategically located booths – one right by the train station (Apr-Sept 8am-7pm daily, Oct-Mar 9am-4pm Mon-Fri, 9am-5pm Sat & Sun, last pick-up 1hr before closing). You'll need a passport or ID card; under-16s with parents only.

By bus

A taxi (21 466 0101, 21 465 9500) to Guincho should cost no more than €7. But buses 405 and 415 leave Cascais roughly every hour and are reliable. For sea views on the outward journey, take the 405 (the bus stops at the restaurants and sights we mention); ditto for the 415 on the return leg. The fare is €2.45; for tips on cheaper travel, *see p206*.

For beaches north of Guincho, it makes sense to catch a bus from Portela de Sintra or Sintra rail stations. The 403 to Almoçageme starts at the latter; others at the former. You can either catch the 433 to Portela from Sintra station, or walk to the nearest stop (turn right out of Sintra station and walk for 10mins, turning right after the precinct). From here the 439 goes to Almoçageme, the 441 to Praia Grande, Praia das Maçãs and Azenhas do Mar. The 440 also goes to Azenhas. One-way fares are €2.45.

By car

For Guincho, take the Estrada do Guincho coast road out of Cascais, or the inland route through Birre and Areia villages. For beaches further north, take the N247 from Guincho.

By tram

From June to September, the tram to Praia das Maçãs leaves roughly hourly (9.30am-5.25pm Fri-Sun; tickets €1-€2) from a stop equidistant from Sintra and Portela de Sintra rail stations. From the former, turn right out of the station and walk for 10mins. The terminus is after the museum; buses also stop opposite.

The Caparica coast

The Caparica coast begins near the mouth of the River Tagus, where a huge maritime grain silo dominates Trafaria village. Although it is one enormous strand, each stretch has its own feel, with the tone set by beach bars.

South from Caparica town, dunes rise up a short distance from the sea and beyond them thickets of green reach inland to the base of a tree-crowned sandstone cliff. In spring this area is a sea of yellow flowers. The density of the beach population fluctuates with the popularity of the bars which are spaced along the dunes and reached by wooden walkways from the mini-train stops and car parks. Many have showers and first aid posts. Some have music and dancing; most are closed out of season.

Caparica

Not for those seeking sophistication or seclusion. Main access to the beach is via the busy Rua dos Pescadores, near where Lisbon buses unload. The approach is a jumble of restaurants and stalls, before you reach the Transpraia, a small open-air train that stops at beaches all the way to Fonte da Telha.

Fonte da Telha

The Transpraia train line ends just before the village. The beach is busy here, with live music bars such as Cabana (21 297 7711) pulling in younger customers. Its diving centre functions year round. A walk up to the wooded hilltop (where buses to and from the Cacilhas ferries stop) yields wonderful views and access to clifftop paths.

Praia da Mata

The true beauty of this coast reveals itself around Praia da Mata (train stop 8). This area tends to be busy, as it is the closest point to town where you can enjoy the beauty of the landscape with nothing more than an occasional bar blocking the view. Bar Praia has a reasonably priced downstairs restaurant serving fish and meat dishes.

Praia da Nova Vaga to Fonte da Telha

The sands are less crowded from Praia da Nova Vaga (stop 16), a favourite with kitesurfers. Tartaruga Bar is on hand with juices and snacks. After Praia da Bela Vista (stop 17) the beach bars disappear. The final 3km (two-mile) stretch to Fonte da Telha is a male nudist domain and the site for much gay cruising – the dunes are very active, though the beach is fairly quiet. But there are peaceful spots on the fringes and things get mixed again soon after stop 19.

Praia da Riviera to Praia do Rei

This stretch attracts a younger, more middle-class crowd with wheels. At Praia da Riviera (stop 9) an eponymous restaurant offers grilled fish in cramped surroundings, but it's fresh and cheaper than Queen's Beach Club at stop 10. Between the two is Bar Casa do Sol, with a surf school (96 602 5252, www.essencia-surf.pt) attached. At Praia do Castelo (stop 11), where volleyball nets dot the beach in summer, bars serve fish, salads, shots and cocktails. The Cabana do Pescador, by stop 12, is a rather more serious eaterie. Beachside Delmare (96 905 3404) stays open until the early hours.

Praia do Rei to Praia da Sereia

At Praia do Rei (stop 13) another eponymous restaurant offers good fish and seafood. Hula Hula bar attracts a younger crowd, serving all the salads, juices and cocktails you'd expect. On Praia da Morena (stop 14) Borda D'Água tends to draw an older middle-class crowd, thanks to discreetly placed sun loungers. At Praia da Sereia (stop 15), a blue-flag beach, Bar Waikiki (21 296 2129) is where young poseurs hang out. During the day drinks are served to sun loungers on the beach.

Praia Nova

The first stretches are a rag-bag of wooden beach huts and bars. There are families entrenched in the sands, but this area is also thick with local children. At train stop 5, Bar Golfinho is a popular hangout, with a stoned surfy feel and live bands on summer evenings.

São João de Caparica

Liked by the Portuguese but relatively unknown to tourists, this beach is backed by campsites and has a large shaded car park. There are several bars, some of which serve snacks and meals, and a crèche. This spot is also highly regarded by surfers and windsurfers, although the currents nearer the northern end can be treacherous.

Where to eat

If you opt for Trafaria as your ferry port, this untouristy fishing village is an excellent place to lunch. Caparica has several good seafood restaurants on the promenade, notably the bustly **O Barbas** (Praia da Vila 26, 21 290

0163, main courses €7.50-€16, closed late Sept). The esplanade is quieter.

At Transpraia train stop 12, fish restaurant **Cabana do Pescador** (Praia do Pescador, 21 296 2152, main courses €7.50-€15) attracts lunch crowds even in winter.

In Fonte da Telha, **O Camões** (Avenida 1° de Maio, Lote 94, 21 296 3865, main courses €7-€14, closed Thur) is a local standard that serves fish caught by the owners. Further on, **Beira Mar** (Rua 1° de Maio C-105, 21 297 2636/91 931 2526, main courses €10-€17) is trendier, with a beach-facing terrace. **Inéditu's Bar** (91 724 0460) has good hamburgers for €2.

Getting there

By boat

Catch a boat from Cais do Sodré to Cacilhas and then a 135 bus to Costa de Caparica (30mins) The ferry costs €0.72, the bus €2.45 (you can buy cheaper double tickets at the booth, which also has timetables). The last bus back is usually at 8pm; if you miss it you can catch one to Praça de Espanha. The last ferry back is at 2am.

An alternative is the ferry from Belém to Trafaria (every 30min/1hr). From there the 129 takes you to Caparica (30mins, fare €1.64); or hop off at São João when you see the sign 'Praias'. The last boat from Trafaria is at 11pm.

In Caparica, the little Transpraia train awaits (21 290 0529, June-Sept, some spring weekends). It scoots between the dunes: ring the bell to get off; stops are numbered. There are two zones; the most you'll pay is €2.10 single and €4 return, and there are concessions. The last train back leaves Fonte da Telha at 7pm.

There is also the 130 bus, running parallel to the coast from Caparica as far as the dirt track that leads to Praia do Rei/Morena/da Sereia (look out for the blue signs) and then turning inland. The stops are a 5-15min walk from the beaches.

To go direct to Fonte da Telha from Cacilhas, catch the 127 bus (50 mins, then a 15min walk). The last bus back is after 11.30pm.

By bus

TST's 153 service leaves Praça de Espanha at roughly hourly intervals, dropping you off 40mins later in Praça da Liberdade, next to Caparica market, a 5min walk from the mini-train (*see p210*). The last bus back (from round the corner) is at midnight.

Alternatives are the 161, which starts from Praça do Areeiro, with a stop at Campo Pequeno and, on summer weekends (June-mid Sept), Carris bus 75 from Campo Grande Metro (fare €3.30 return).

By car

You can get from Lisbon to anywhere on the Caparica coast in less than an hour, provided you avoid rush hour. Follow signs to Caparica. From there the coast road gives access to 12km (7.5 miles) of beaches as far as Fonte da Telha. These are signposted off the road down dusty tracks; each has parking. On summer weekends the traffic back to town can be horrendous.

By train

Fertagus trains towards Coina and Setubal leave Roma-Areeiro at 20-30min intervals, stopping at Entrecampos, Sete Rios and Campolide. After the bridge comes Pragal, where you get off and catch a bus to Caparica. The train takes 17mins from Roma (fare €1.50), the bus a further 25mins (fare €2.45). Buses run well after the last train from Pragal, at 12.57am.

Lagoa de Albufeira & Meco

South of Fonte da Telha only the first tiny stretch of beach is accessible by car. Walking this way you are unlikely to see a soul other than an occasional misanthropic nudist. The isolation increases the further you go, until you near Albufeira lagoon and then Meco. Here, the sea seems bluer, the shrubbery greener and the air fresher.

Lagoa de Albufeira

A tree-lined lagoon winds inland, cut off from the sea by a sandbar. The constant breeze and smooth waters make it ideal to try windsurfing; Escola de Windsurf Lagoa de Albufeira (21 268 4527) can help out. There are two restaurants on the beach, and another simple restaurant and a café by the lake.

Meco

A kilometre or so south of Lagoa de Albufeira, a big sandstone rock marks Praia Moinho de Baixo. Here you'll find a good seafood restaurant and, thanks to the road link with Meco village, more people. The stretch beyond is nudist. Don't be alarmed if mud-caked natives sway into view; water trickling down the cliffside forms a clay that makes an ideal all-over mud pack. Walking around the headland at low tide gets you to Praia das Bicas, where there is another restaurant and a clifftop campsite. Meco has more bars and restaurants, plus trendy shops.

Where to eat

O Peralta (21 268 3696, main courses €8-€20), at the turning for the main beach, is a Meco institution – although not cheap. In the village, **Mequinhu's** (Rua do Comércio 20, 21 268 3648, €9-€18) is a cheaper alternative.

Getting there

By bus

Day-tripping here by public transport is challenging. Set off early, with a timetable. TST buses run to Sesimbra from Praça de Espanha or Cacilhas. Get off at Santana; around 4 buses daily run to Meco village, fewer to Lagoa de Albufeira.

By car

Follow the A2 motorway from the Ponte 25 de Abril, then the N378 to Sesimbra road. At a roundabout some 8kms (5 miles) on, the turning to Lagoa de Albufeira and Meco is signposted.

Around Lisbon

Royal haunts, postcard villages and Portugal's Eden.

West of Lisbon

Estoril

Estoril was once a grand resort for titled Europeans, although today its previous lustre has become a little faded. Portugal was neutral during World War II, and Estoril attracted both spies, including Graham Greene, and exiled royals such as Umberto of Italy and Juan Carlos of Spain. The **Casino** (21 466 7700) – which in its 1940s heyday attracted fur-clad society ladies and tux-wearing gents – was the inspiration for Ian Fleming's *Casino Royale*. Now owned by Macao-based tycoon Stanley Ho, it mainly draws slot-machine addicts but boasts the biggest weekly prizes in Europe. As well as over-the-top floorshows it has free shows by local groups. Over the road, a crafts fair operates every evening from June to September. Lovers of contemporary art will want to visit exhibitions at the new Ellipse Foundation gallery (*see p163* **Money talks... and walks**).

Where to eat

As well as the deluxe **Hotel Palacio Estoril** (*see p54*), there's a cheaper, Italian option opposite the Casino: **Al Fresco** (Galerías do Estoril, Rua de Lisboa, 21 467 6770, main courses €8-€21).

Tourist information

Turismo

Arcadas do Parque, Estoril (21 466 3813). **Open** *Sept-July* 9am-7pm Mon-Sat; 10am-6pm Sun. *Aug* 9am-8pm Mon-Sat; 10am-6pm Sun.

Getting there

By bus

Scotturb airport shuttle bus runs from the airport to Estoril and Cascais (hourly 7am to 9pm, then 10.30pm daily; 30mins). *See also p206.*

By train

From Lisbon, the train is the most scenic option: there are generally three trains per hour each weekday (5.30am to 1.30am) from Cais do Sodré station (about 30mins; fare €1.25), with a less frequent service at weekends.

Cascais

Cascais is an ancient fishing port (the day's catch is auctioned daily at around 5pm) but also a busy modern town and resort. On the seafront in the Baía (bay) de Cascais are lobster pots, gaily painted boats and old fishermen talking football. In the winding streets to the north you'll find the **Museu do Mar** (Rua Júlio Pereira de Mello, 21 482 5400, closed Mon) which pays tribute to fisherfolk and shipwrecks. Near the Cidadela, a 16th-century fort undergoing renovation, is the **Centro Cultural** (Avenida Rei Humberto II de Itália, 21 484 8900, closed Mon) which hosts varied free exhibitions and the **Casa de Santa Maria** (Rua do Farol, 21 481 5382, closed Mon) an early work by Portuguese architect Raúl Lino with a fine interior. Further on is **Museu Conde de Castro Guimarães**.

A 15-minute walk westwards is **Boca do Inferno** (Hell's Mouth) where great columns of water shoot up at high tide. It was here, in 1930, that Aleister Crowley faked his own death. En route is a palace where the Duke of Windsor and Mrs Simpson stayed after the abdication. By the Hot Dogs de Cascais stand, steps lead down to a rocky 'beach'. At the start of the road to Guincho is the **Casa da Guia** (21 484 32 15), a 19th-century *palacete*, now a chi-chi shopping centre, surrounded by esplanades with sea views.

Museu Condes de Castro Guimarães

Avenida Rei Humberto II de Itália, Cascais (21 482 5401). BusCas from Cascais rail station. **Open** 10am-5pm Tue-Fri; 10am-1pm, 2-5pm Sat, Sun. **Admission** €1.50; free under-15s, students, over-59s. Free for all Sun. **No credit cards.**

When the Count of Guimarães and his wife died childless in 1892, they left the town this lavishly decorated mansion and its contents: Indo-Portuguese furniture, oil paintings, porcelain and antique books. Visits are guided, on the hour.

Where to eat & drink

Beer, chips and live football are available at pubs around Largo de Camões. Nearby, **Dom Manolo** (Avenida Combatentes da Grande Guerra 11, 21 483 1126, main courses €6-€16) has good, cheap grilled chicken and **Eduardo's**

'Glorious Eden'

Lord Byron's phrase comparing **Sintra** with paradise is only a minor exaggeration. If you take one day trip from Lisbon, this should be it. Described by UNESCO, which made Sintra a World Heritage Site in 1995, as 'the first centre of European Romantic architecture', it is a magical (literally, early inhabitants believed) place of lush forests and turreted palaces, often shrouded in mist. Always several degrees cooler than Lisbon, it was once the royal family's summer retreat. That made it a magnet for Portuguese and foreign aristos and social climbers, who built fancy houses and laid out fine gardens mixing native and exotic plants, greatly influencing landscape architecture across Europe.

Few visitors are up to taking in all the sights on foot; a one-day ticket (€8.50) for Scotturb buses lets you roam the region (*see p206*), but if you're focusing on Sintra alone, a €3.80 special ticket for the 434 hop-on hop-off service should do. Alternatively, hire a horse-drawn carriage and head first for the Moorish castle ruins, with its dragontooth walls creeping over the Serra de Sintra (known to the Romans as the Mountains of the Moon). It's a lovely spot to sit in a turret and read a book.

On a clear day there are spectacular views to the sea and the pink and yellow **Palácio da Pena** (*pictured*) on the next hill. Built by German-born Dom Fernando II at the end of the 19th century around a ruined monastery, it is a pastiche of various styles. The exterior is covered with gargoyles and boasts an incredible bay window, held up by a huge stone Triton. The palace is entered through an impressive portcullis and set in acres of rolling gardens – a wonderful place to walk and picnic, particularly by the swan lake.

The town's other highlight is the **Palácio Nacional** – the building with two massive white chimneys. It was built in the 14th century by Dom João I, who lived here with his wife, Philippa of Lancaster, daughter of John of Gaunt. The tiled Arab room is striking, as is the Swan room. The hexagonal Sala dos Brasões ('coats of arms' room') is also lined with *azulejos*, while its domed ceilings are painted with the emblems of nobles of the court. One of the oldest parts of the palace is the Magpie room, painted with 136 of the birds, each bearing a rose and a scroll marked 'Por bem'. The story goes that Dom João I proffered a rose to a lady-in-waiting when Queen Philippa wasn't looking and a magpie snatched it. The king excused himself by saying 'Por bem' – 'all to the good'.

If you feel peckish after visiting the palace, pop over to **Periquita** (Rua das Padarias 1, 21 923 0626, closed Wed) or, at no.18, **Periquita Dois** (21 923 1595, closed Tue) for a *queijada* – a cheesecake with a secret recipe. Dotted around are pricey antique and lace shops. The nearby **Museu do Brinquedo** (21 924 2171, closed Mon & Tue), bursting with antique toys, will probably be more of interest to adults than children. Kids might prefer in-line skating in **Parque da Liberdade**, between Sintra station and the Palácio Nacional. You can hire the full kit for €1.50 per hr (11am-6pm Sat & Sun) and book lessons (91 240 3119).

Beyond the palace (and the 434 bus route) is **Lawrence's Hotel** (21 910 5500, www. portugalvirtual.pt/lawrences), where Byron

(Largo das Grutas 3, 21 483 1901, main courses €12.50-€17.50) Belgian cuisine. At **Enoteca de Cascais** (Rua Visconde da Luz 17, 21 482 2328, evenings only) you can try wines from around Portugal with tasty nibbles. Finish with fab ice-cream at the venerable **Santini** (Avenida Valbom 28, 21 483 3709, closed Mon). Near the Cidadela, **Mise en Scène** (Rua Luís Xavier Palmerim 14, 21 484 2313, closed Tue) is a cosy French café that serves tagines and mint tea. There's fancier fare on offer at **Rosa Maria** in the Farol Design Hotel (*see p54*), and lots of restaurants serving fresh fish along the coast road to Guincho, starting with **Furnas** (21 486 9243, main courses €15-€29).

Tourist information

Turismo

Rua Visconde da Luz, 14, Cascais (21 486 8204). **Open** *Sept-July* 9am-7pm Mon-Sat; 10am-6pm Sun. *Aug* 9am-8pm Mon-Sat; 10am-6pm Sun.

Getting there

By bus

See the Estoril section for details of buses from the airport. In town the cheapest option is the BusCas shuttle, which starts at the station and passes near Boca do Inferno. Fares are €0.50 (day passes are not valid). In summer Goose Travel (21 384 4250) runs a began writing *Childe Harold's Pilgrimage*. Said to be the oldest hotel in the Iberian peninsula, it has adept chefs and a copious wine list. Further on is **Quinta da Regaleira** (21 910 6650), a neo-Manueline fantasy with a garden full of grottos and a secret passage from a well. There are four guided tours a day; book well ahead as numbers are limited.

There are more grand houses up the hill, starting with the **Palácio de Seteais** (21 923 3200), a luxury hotel with a terrace overlooking the grounds. The **Palácio de Montserrate** (21 923 7300), which was once the Gothic home of English eccentric William Beckford, was later turned into a Moorish fantasy with subtropical gardens. It was renovated recently; book ahead to visit. The hilltop **Convento dos Capuchos** (21 928 9621, 21 923 7300) is an eerie place, where monks lived in tiny, cork-lined cells.

The only attraction in the new town centre (beyond the rail station) is the **Museu de Arte Moderna** (21 924 8170), whose contents are soon to be replaced by minerals and African art. Behind it is the **Centro Cultural Olga Cadaval** (21 910 7110, www.ccolgacadaval.pt), where **Festival de Sintra** (*see p151*) and other shows are staged.

At Odrinhas, 12 kilometres (8 miles) north of Sintra on the road to Ericeira, the **Museu Arqueológico** (21 961 3574, closed Mon & Tue) showcases artefacts of the many peoples who have inhabited this enchanted region.

Palácio da Pena

Estrada da Pena (21 910 5340). **Open** *Winter* 10am-5.30pm Tue-Sun (last entry 5pm). *Summer* 10am-7pm Tue-Sun (last entry 6.30pm). **Admission** *Palace* €4; €2 6-17s; €1.60 over-65s; free under-5s. *Park* €3.50. *Palace & park* €7; €5 concessions. Free to all Sun to 1pm. **No credit cards**.

Palácio Nacional

Largo da Rainha D Amélia (21 910 6840). **Open** 10am-5.30pm Thur-Tue (last entry 5pm). **Admission** €4; €2 concessions; free under-15s. Free to all Sun to 2pm. **No credit cards**.

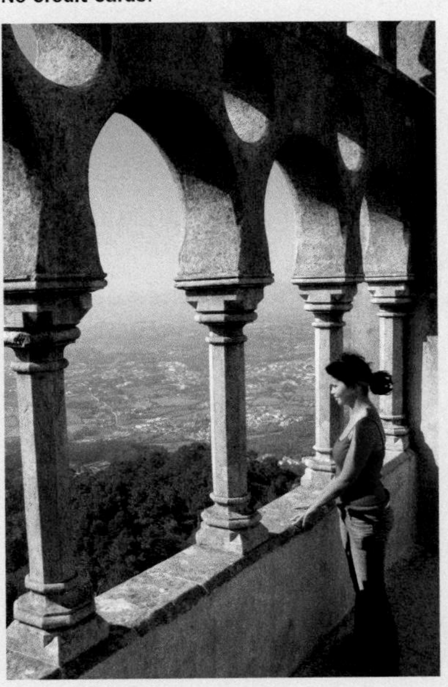

hop-on, hop-off open-top hourly guided tour (9.30am-6.30pm daily; ticket €12) along the seafront from Estoril to Guincho.

By train

From Lisbon's Cais do Sodré station. Cascais is 4mins on from Estoril by train (or a 20min walk along the seafront).

Cabo da Roca

The coast road west from Cascais rolls past rocky bays, wild dunes and windswept **Guincho beach** (*see p208*), then climbs up over a series of craggy cliffs, eventually reaching **Cabo da Roca**, continental Europe's westernmost point – Promontorium Magnum to the Romans.

Where to eat & drink

Just after the turning off the N247, a dirt track leads to the **Moinho Dom Quixote** (21 929 2523, closed Mon) an old windmill, now a cosy bar open till 2am that also serves snacks. Its *azulejo*-lined terrace offers views of Guincho.

Getting there

By bus

Scotturb bus 403 leaves Cascais (22mins) or Sintra (37mins) hourly. Fare €2.45.

Sintra

See p214 **'Glorious Eden'**.

Where to eat

Touristy cafés and restaurants abound in Sintra. **Orixás** (Avenida Adriano Júlio Coelho 7, 21 294 1673), near the Museu de Arte Moderna, is different: a Brazilian restaurant and gallery. Worth a detour if you're going to Praia das Maçãs (*see p209*) is **Colares Velho** (Largo Dr Carlos França, 21 929 2406, main courses €12.50-€16.50, closed Mon) next to Colares parish church (Igreja Matriz). It has inventive fish and vegetarian dishes, yummy desserts and tea and scones at weekends.

Tourist information

Turismo

Praça da República, Sintra (21 923 1157/www.cm-sintra.pt). **Open** *Oct-May* 9am-7pm daily. *June-Sept* 9am-8pm daily.
Other locations: Sintra station.

Getting there

By bus

From Estoril, take Scotturb bus 418; from Cascais, 403 (via Cabo da Roca) or 417. Journey time from Cascais 27mins; fare €3.15. You can buy discount tickets from Scotturb under the Cascaisvila shopping centre and opposite Sintra rail station. For Colares, catch the 403 from Sintra station. Within Sintra, the hop-on, hop-off 434 does the main sites for €3.85 (but passes and pre-bought tickets aren't valid).

By train

From Oriente, Roma-Areeiro, Entrecampos or Sete Rios stations. Trains leave Roma-Areeiro about every 20mins, 6am-1.30am Mon-Fri; 6.30am-1.15am Sat & Sun (42mins; fare €1.60).

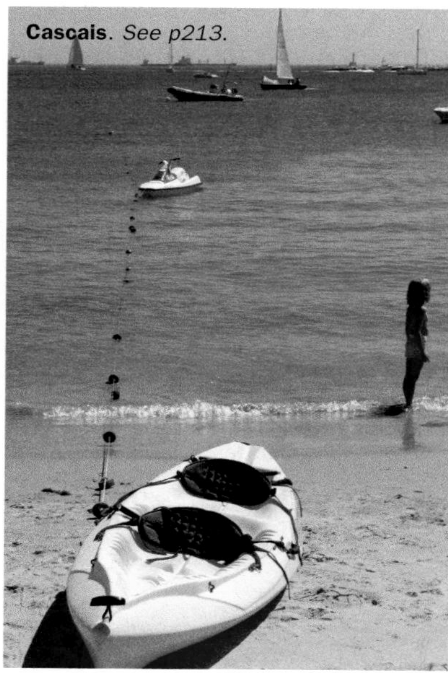
Cascais. *See p213.*

Queluz

This pink edifice started its life as a royal hunting lodge until, in 1747, Prince Dom Pedro decided he fancied it as a home and had it extended and converted into a rococo palace with delightful gardens. In 1760, when he married his niece, the future Queen Maria I, he organised operas and chamber concerts here for her. But in 1788, after the death of their son, she went mad, wandering the corridors tearing her hair and shrieking.

When the royal family fled to Brazil to escape the French invasion of 1807, they took most of the furniture with them, but the palace has been refurbished to give a fair picture of aristocratic life of the time. One wing accommodates visiting heads of state and the music room, with its superb acoustics, is used for concerts.

Palácio de Queluz

2745 Queluz (21 434 3860). **Open** *Palace* 9.30am-5pm Mon, Wed-Sun (last entry 4.30pm). *Gardens* May-Sept 10am-6pm Mon-Wed, Sun. Oct-Apr 10am-5pm Mon-Wed, Sun. **Admission** *Palace & gardens* €4; €2 concessions; free under-15s. Free to all Sun to 2pm. *Gardens* €1.50. **No credit cards**. **Photo** *p217*.

Where to eat

Cozinha Velha (21 435 6158, main courses €19-€30), situated in the old kitchens across the road, serves fine food (accompanied by a harp Tue, Thur). There's a basic café by the main entrance.

Getting there

By bus

Vimeca serves Queluz from Lisbon with the 107 from Marquês de Pombal to Queluz/Belas station (45mins; fare €2.45) and the 101 or 163 from Colégio Militar-Luz Metro to Quatro Caminhos (30mins, fare €1.65). Either way, it's then a 15min walk to the palace.

By train

As for Sintra, making sure you get off at Queluz/Belas and not Queluz/Massamá (13mins, then a 15min walk; fare €1.20).

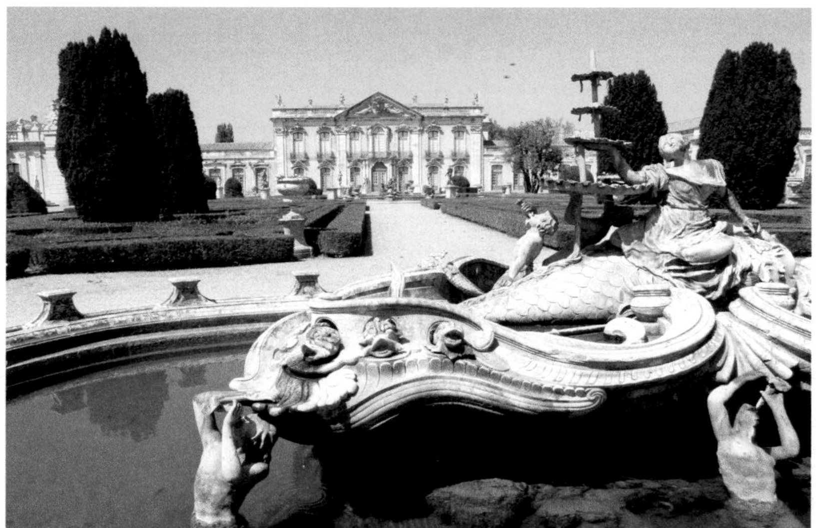

See how the other half used to live at the rococo **Palácio de Queluz**. *See p216.*

North of Lisbon

Mafra

The enormous pink marble **Palácio Nacional de Mafra** was begun in 1717 by Dom João V, and financed by gold from Brazil. The project – a combined palace and convent – became ever more elaborate, taking 38 years to finish and employing more than 50,000 builders.

The 880 rooms and 300 monks' cells have been fully restored. The dome is one of the world's largest, and the rococo library has a chequered marble floor and more than 38,000 leather-bound books. (Rats have feasted on some of them – in fact, stories of giant rats under the palace abound. But don't worry: they don't show up during the daytime.) The monks' pharmacy is quaint with its old jars and bizarre instruments.

Each of the chapel's belltowers has a carillon; the working one has 114 bells – the world's largest assemblage – used for concerts on summer Sundays. The chapel's six organs are being renovated and feature in Mafra's annual festival (*see p169*).

The monastery was abandoned after the 1834 dissolution, and the palace closed in 1910 after Portugal's last king, Dom Manuel II, escaped his republican persecutors from here. The adjoining hunting grounds, the **Tapada Nacional de Mafra** (261 817 050), have two guided walks daily (and at night when there's a full moon), mini-train tours at the weekends, and mountain-bike hire. There is an interesting wolf conservation project over near Malveira; book in advance (Centro de Recuperação do Lobo Ibérico, Vale da Guarda, Picão, 261 785 037, 91 753 2312).

Palácio Nacional de Mafra

Terreiro Dom João V, Mafra (261 817 550). **Open** 10am-5pm (last entry 4.30pm) Mon, Wed-Sun. **Admission** €4; €2 concessions; free under-15s. **Credit** AmEx, MC, V.

Where to eat

The town has eateries but if you're driving, consider a detour to the village of **Negrais** – 15 minutes south-east – which is famed for its *leitão* (suckling pig). Locals favour **O Caneira** (Avenida General Barnabe António Ferreira 171, Pêro Pinheiro, 21 967 0905, main courses €10-€15, closed Sun evenings & Mon). For fresh fish, visit **Ericeira** ten kilometres (six miles) from Mafra; the best restaurants are in side streets.

Tourist information

Turismo

Palácio Nacional de Mafra, Terreiro D João V, Mafra (261 817 170). **Open** 9.30am-1pm, 2.30-6pm daily.

Getting there

By bus

Mafrense serves Mafra from Campo Grande bus station in Lisbon (45mins; fare €3.35). From Sintra, its buses depart from Portela de Sintra station (40mins; fare €2.65).

By train

There's one direct train from Entrecampos (5.43am Mon-Sat, 6.43am Sun; 43mins; fare €2.23). Later in the day you must change at Mira Sintra-Meleças.

Óbidos

Picture-postcard perfect, this walled village on a hill was a wedding gift from Dom Dinis to his bride Isabel of Aragon in 1282. Its whitewashed houses have terracotta roofs and trademark ochre or blue bands painted around their base, and sport window boxes of geraniums.

Pick up a map at the booth in the parking lot at the entrance to town. Then enter the tiled main gate and search out the old pillory with the town's arms – a fishing net with a drowned person inside (Isabel and Dinis's son was drowned in the Tagus and fished out in a net) – and the **Igreja de Santa Maria**, where ten-year-old Dom Afonso V married his eight-year-old wife in 1444. The church has 17th-century tilework, wooden painted ceilings, and panels by **Josefa de Óbidos**, a Spanish-born artist (1634-84) who moved here, and whose dark still lifes are enjoying a revival. She is buried in the **Igreja de São Pedro**; there are works by her in the **Museu Municipal** (Rua Direita, 262 955 557, closed Mon). The castle is now a *pousada* but you can walk the walls and try to spot the sea – Óbidos was once a port.

Where to eat

The café by the main gate, **Porta da Vila**, serves local pastries. For first-rate Portuguese cuisine, search out **Alcaide** (Rua Direita, 262 959 220, closed Wed, main courses €10-€15); in summer, book ahead.

Tourist information

Turismo

2510-089 Óbidos (262 959 231). **Open** *May-Sept* 9.30am-7.30pm daily. *Oct-Apr* 9.30am-6pm Mon-Fri; 9.30am-12.30pm, 1.30-5.30pm Sat, Sun.

Getting there

By bus

Rede Expresso bus from Lisbon's Terminal Rodoviário to Caldas da Rainha (1hr 10mins; fare €6.60), then a local bus (10mins; fare €1.50).

By train

There is an early train from Entrecampos (see the Mafra section). Later on you must change at Bombarral, Caldas da Rainha or Mira Sintra-Meleças (2hrs 18mins; €7.30).

South of Lisbon

Sesimbra

Overlooked by a fairy-tale castle, Sesimbra is a busy fishing village-cum-resort with whitewashed streets leading up from the harbour. The town is reached by crossing the Ponte 25 de Abril and then traversing the **Serra da Arrábida**. This is a beautiful protected area of sandy coves and towering limestone cliffs covered with pines and thickets of green Mediterranean-style vegetation, which thrive thanks to Arrábida's microclimate.

From Sesimbra you can hire a boat to one of the beaches or drive to the sheltered **Praia do Portinho da Arrábida**, whose warm waters attract snorkellers. If you phone ahead, you can visit the **Convento da Arrábida** (21 218 0520, open 3-4pm Wed-Sun, admission €5), a 16th-century Franciscan monastery with fine views.

With a car, you can also head west to Cabo Espichel, where the **Santuário de Nossa Senhora do Cabo** (21 268 0565) stands on a windswept cliff, the approach lined with derelict pilgrims' cells. The 18th-century church contains candles lit by fishermen in front of their favourite saints. To add to the eeriness of the place, dinosaur footprints were found on the beach below.

Where to eat

Not surprisingly for a village that supplies fresh fish to plenty of posh Lisbon eateries, Sesimbra has some great seafood restaurants – try **O Farol** just off the main square (Largo da Marinha 4, 21 223 3356, closed Tue, main courses €10-€25).

Tourist information

Turismo

Largo da Marinha 25-7, Sesimbra (21 228 8540). **Open** *June-Sept* 9am-8pm daily. *Oct-May* 9am-12.30pm, 2-5.30pm daily.

Getting there

By bus

Transportes do Sul do Tejo buses leave Praça de Espanha about hourly (from 7.30am Mon-Fri, later Sat & Sun; 1hr; fare €3.10).

Directory

Features

Largo do Carmo. *See p77.*

Directory

Getting Around

Arriving & leaving

By air

Portela, Lisbon's main international airport, lies in the north-eastern corner of the city, within sight of the Ponte Vasco da Gama. A new, larger facility is being planned at Ota, some 20 miles north, but Portela will be in use for the next decade at least, and is in fact being expanded to cope with growing demand.

The **Aerobus shuttle** (bus 91) run by Lisbon's public transport company, Carris, departs every 20 minutes between 7.45am and 8.15pm daily, taking passengers via Rossio to Cais do Sodré for €3.10 – less if you have a TAP boarding pass or if you buy a Lisboa Card (*see p234*). A cheaper alternative (€1.20) is to take bus 5 or 22 to Areeiro, from where you can catch the Metro (€0.70); bus 83 to Marquês de Pombal/ Amoreiras; or bus 44 or 45 to Rossio. By car, it's a short drive into town down Avenida Almirante Gago Coutinho to Areeiro and then down Avenida Almirante Reis. A taxi downtown should not cost much more than €8.50 with a €1.60 additional charge for luggage. Some of the city's dodgiest operators work this route, so watch the meter.

You also have the option of paying in advance at the Turismo de Lisboa booth in the arrivals hall, in return for a voucher usable in taxis in this scheme (identifiable by a window sticker). There are a variety of options; for destinations in central Lisbon, you pay €14 during daytime, €16 between 10pm and 6am. You may end up paying slightly more than you would if you handled the transaction yourself (although the cost of the voucher does include tip and baggage fee) but it gives peace of mind.

For Estoril and Cascais, Scotturb shuttle 498 takes about 30mins (hourly 7am to 9pm, then 10.30pm, daily). The €12 ticket includes a day's unlimited travel on Scotturb buses, serving the whole Cascais-Sintra region, and trains between it and Lisbon.

The airport has a 24-hour telephone information service (21 841 3700), and there are both automated and staffed bureau de change services.

By rail

Trains from Spain, France or the north of Portugal end at Santa Apolónia. The station has its own tourist information booth and bureau de change. There is a taxi rank outside and a range of bus services. Trains also call at the showcase Gare do Oriente station at the Parque das Nações, the former Expo site. Unlike Santa Apolónia, it has a Metro station. It's about a 20-minute ride into town.

Trains from the Algarve no longer end south of the river; they use the rail link under the Ponte 25 de Abril, make a stop at Entrecampos, and end at Gare do Oriente.

By road

There are a variety of routes to Lisbon from Spain. From up north, there's the E8 European route from Salamanca, which turns into the Portuguese IP-5 at Vilar Formoso. The IP-5 continues on past Viseu eventually to meet the A1 Oporto-to-Lisbon motorway. However, the sharp twists and steep inclines of the IP-5 have resulted in an astronomic accident rate and the deathly nickname Estrada da Morte.

A safer option is the new direct motorway from Madrid via Badajoz, the E4 Euro-route. Once in Portugal, you'll be on the A6. This road forges through the Alentejo, past Évora and on to Palmela, about 35km (20 miles) south of Lisbon (by which time the motorway has metamorphosed into the A2). Just before Palmela, you have a choice of staying on the same road and entering Lisbon via the Ponte 25 de Abril, a suspension bridge, or taking the A12 and crossing the newer Ponte Vasco da Gama, a 17km (ten-mile) pontoon bridge. Both routes offer arriving traffic a fine introduction to the city's breathtaking topography.

Public transport

Lisbon is well served by a comprehensive network of trains, ferries, buses, trams and funiculars. The state-owned Metro has undergone a major expansion. The trams and funiculars are fun to use but are not the quickest way of getting around. These, and the bus service, are run by Carris, another state-owned company.

Information

Maps of both the bus and tram system are available at Carris booths and maps of the Metro are available at major Metro stations. The bus network was given a big overhaul in late 2006, so make sure your map is up to date. Carris's information line is 21 361 3000 (open 9am-5pm Mon-Fri); its website (www.carris.pt) is user-friendly. The Metro's call centre is at 21 350 0115 (open 9am-7pm Mon-Thur; 9am-6pm Fri) and its website at www.metrolisboa.pt. There are customer service desks at Marquês de Pombal and Alameda stations.

The Lisbon route-finder website www.transporlis.sapo.pt may also be of help.

Fares & tickets

Carris fares were also overhauled in 2006. There are no longer pre-bought double tickets; you either buy a ticket each time you enter the Metro or board a bus or tram, or get yourself a **7 Colinas** electronic card, chargeable at Carris booths and Metro vending machines and in post offices and PayShop agents. The card itself, which is valid for one year, costs €0.50; you then pay €3.30 for one day's unlimited travel on the Metro and Carris networks, or €13.20 for five days' travel. At Metro gates and on entering buses, hold rather than wave your card at the blue electronic pad to validate it.

Lisbon's tourist pass, the **Lisboa Card** (*see p234*), allows the bearer unlimited travel on metro, buses, trams and trains to Cascais and Sintra, as well as free entry to or reductions at sights and museums.

Finally, there are monthly passes (€26.50) offering unlimited Metro and bus travel within zone L (most of the city, including Belém). Unfortunately, first you need a **Lisboa Viva** smart card, available from Carris booths and the following Metro stations: Campo Grande, Entre Campos, Marquês de Pombal, Baixa-Chiado, Cais do Sodré, Arroios (northern atrium), Jardim Zoológico, Colégio Militar and Oriente. You provide ID and a photo, pay €6, and then wait up to ten days – or, to get it overnight, stump up €10 at the ticket offices at Campo Pequeno (southern atrium) or Alameda (the part on the red line).

Metro

The Metro is the speediest way to travel in Lisbon, though many of the main sights aren't covered by the network. Trains run from 6.30am to 1am daily – every two minutes during rush hour and every five minutes the rest of the day. Tickets are sold at station ticket offices (some of them with rather erratic hours) and vending machines. The fine for not having a valid ticket is €150 (plus fare).

All but three stations – Odivelas, Alfornelos and Amadoraa Este – are in zone L. A single ticket within this zone costs €0.70, a return €1.30, and a *caderneta* of ten tickets €6.65. There are also joint tickets (€1.10) that may be used once on the Metro and on as many buses as necessary for an hour after initial validation. Monthly passes just for the Metro cost €17.45 (zone L), but you need a Lisboa Viva card (*see above*).

The Metro has four lines, coloured coded on maps, with four interchanges. Work started years ago on extending the Blue Line along the river to Santa Apolónia but it has been bedevilled by problems (including the unexpected collapse of a tunnel). The official deadline for completion is July 2007 but that is unlikely. The extension of the red line from Alameda via Saldanha to São Sebastião (and ultimately to Campolide) is going more smoothly but probably won't open before 2009.

The lost property office for the network is at Marquês de Pombal.

Buses

Carris buses provide good services way out into the suburbs. Stops are indicated by a yellow sign. Many now also have screens telling you when each bus is due. At those that don't, if you have a Portuguese mobile you can send an SMS to Carris at 3599 (format 'C xxxx' where xxxx is the bus stop's number, printed on the sign); within seconds, you'll receive a reply giving you the low-down. The service is reliable but costs €0.25.

You get on at the front of the bus and off in the middle or at the back. The older orange buses are being replaced by more modern yellow ones, and there are now more than 200 buses in service that have ramps for wheelchair access. Evening services have recently been beefed up but night buses remain scarce and since taxis are relatively cheap they are a better bet.

Tickets can be bought from the driver at a cost of €1.20 per trip. Better-value multiple tickets and passes – loaded on to a 7 Colinas electronic card (*see above*) – can be bought from the Carris ticket booths dotted around the city: at Praça da Figueira, Areeiro, Alcântara, Cais do Sodré, Campo Pequeno, Santa Apolónia, Santa Justa, Alvalade and Campo Grande. Two rides within the city limits cost €1.50, five €3.55 and ten €6.65. For one-day and five-day combined Carris/Metro tickets, *see above*.

A monthly Carris pass costs €21.35 but, as for Metro passes, you need a Lisboa Viva card first.

Beyond the city other bus companies operate. *See p206.*

Trams

Today the more traditional *eléctricos*, or trams, that ply the 12, 15, 18, 25 and 28 routes have been joined on the 15 route by modern rapid transport models built by Siemens. All are run by Carris, fares are integrated with the bus system and, as for buses, stops are marked by a yellow sign – often hanging from the overhead wires. As with buses, you get on at the front and get off at the back.

You shouldn't leave Lisbon without riding the No.28, which passes through some of the city's most historically important and picturesque streets. It starts in the centre at Largo Martim Moniz, in Mouraria. From there it clanks up the narrow streets round Graça, Sé and Castelo, before crossing the Baixa and heading through Bairro Alto, down through São Bento and up to Estrela, where it stops outside the *basilica*. It's an excellent way of seeing the city, getting your bearings and enjoying the trip all at the same time. Beware of pickpockets, though, as they are all too common on this route.

The No.15 is also handy for tourists, as it connects Praça da Figueira with the many sights of

Belém. The No.18 starts at the bottom of Alfama, in Rua da Alfândega, and goes via Praça do Comércio and parallel to the river to Alcântara before climbing to Ajuda. The circular No.12 from Praça da Figueira heads uphill from Largo Martim Moniz before picking up the 28 route and following it as far as the Baixa. Finally, the No.25 runs from Rua da Alfândega to Campo Ourique via Praça do Comércio, Cais do Sodré, Lapa and Estrela.

Funiculars

Three funicular trams – known as *elevadores* or *ascensores* – negotiate the steeper slopes of the city; they and the Elevador de Santa Justa, which is a lift, are run by Carris and integrated with its fares system.

Elevador da Bica

From Bairro Alto (Calçada do Combro) to Santos (Rua de São Paulo). **Open** 7am-9pm Mon-Sat; 9am-9pm Sun.

Elevador da Glória

From Avenida da Liberdade (Restauradores) to Bairro Alto (São Pedro de Alcântara). **Open** 7am-midnight Mon-Thur; 7am-3am Fri, Sat; 8am-midnight Sun. Currently closed.

Elevador de Santa Justa

From Baixa (Rua do Ouro (Áurea) to Bairro Alto (Largo do Carmo). **Open** 7am-9pm daily.
The viaduct at its head was reopened in 2006.

Elevador do Lavra

From Avenida da Liberdade (Largo da Anunciada) to Campo de Santana (Rua Câmara Pestana). **Open** 7am-9pm Mon-Sat; 9am-9pm Sun.
Service suspended in late 2006.

Rail services

Local train services are run by branches of national railway CP-Caminhos de Ferro Portugueses (808 208 208, www.cp.pt). Trains run along the Estoril coast from Cais de Sodré station as far as Cascais (€1.05-€1.55) as often as every 20 minutes. There are also ten-trip passes for one, two or three zones (€9.45-€13.95). Escape to the beach is easy, thanks to Cais do Sodré Metro station.

The combined train and bus pass offered by Sintra-Cascais regional bus company Scotturb may be a good option. For more, *see p206*.

Rail services to Queluz and Sintra currently leave from Sete Rios, Entre Campos and Roma-Areeiro – all of which are on the Metro – so long as Rossio station, downtown, remains closed for major structural work. There are periodic scares among commuters about muggings on this line, but we've heard no reports of such incidents from foreign visitors, and there are transport police on every train.

Trains serving Almada suburbs and Setúbal cross the Tagus using the line beneath the Ponte 25 de Abril. For more, *see p206*.

Ferries

Ferries run by the Transtejo company (808 203 050, www.transtejo.pt) link various points of Lisbon with the south bank of the Tagus. They are usually packed during rush hour as people commute over the river, but offer unrivalled views of the city. Boats to Barreiro still leave from the Terreiro do Paço boat station, near Praça do Comércio, while all those to Cacilhas, Montijo and Seixal currently depart from the ugly new Cais do Sodré boat station, where car ferries also ply the Cacilhas route. At the Gare Marítima de Belém you can catch a ferry for Porto Brandão and Trafaria, at the mouth of the Tagus. Each station has an information office. Fares range from €0.72 to €2.15.

Taxis

Taxis in Lisbon are thick on the ground and inexpensive. There's a minimum charge of €2.35 (€2.50 at night) and the average journey will cost around €6, though fares go up after 10pm, and on weekends and holidays.

Tipping is optional and a moderate amount will be appreciated. You are rarely far from a taxi stand. Some of the most reliable are at Rossio, Largo do Chiado and Largo de Trindade Coelho (known as Largo da Misericórdia) in the Bairro Alto. There are 24-hour dial-a-cab services on 21 811 9000 (Radio Taxis de Lisboa), 21 793 2756 (Autocoope) and 21 811 1100 (Teletaxis). You pay an extra €0.80-€2 if you order one.

Driving

This is not the easiest city to negotiate by car. Traffic is chaotic and many of the streets are narrow, winding and one-way. Also, the Portuguese leave their fabled manners behind when they get behind the wheel. Outside Lisbon it is even worse. They often top the EU table for road deaths.

Note that police can also issue on-the-spot fines for minor driving offences. Don't argue. Speed limits are apparently 60 kilometres an hour in built-up areas, 90 elsewhere and 120 on the gleaming new EU-funded highways, but few people take any notice. Most of Portugal's motorways, or *auto-estradas*, are toll roads (*portagens*) – costing approximately €18 from Lisbon to Oporto – and are prefixed with the initial A on maps. Those prefixed with an E are cross-continental European routes. IP on maps stands for *itinerário principal*, or main road. IC stands for *itinerário complementar*, or subsidiary road. Other two-lane roads have the prefix N on some maps – but sometimes not. Confusingly, on some maps highways can also change prefixes.

Seat belts are obligatory in both front and back. The legal limit for alcohol in the blood is very low at 0.2mg/ml – so don't drink and drive.

Accidents & breakdowns

If you are involved in an accident on a motorway, use the orange SOS phone to call for help. In collisions, leave the car exactly where it is (regardless of the disruption) and wait for the police. In cases of breakdown drivers can call Automóvel Clube de Portugal for help (707 509 510, 24hrs). This is affiliated with organisations across Europe, and membership of a foreign automobile association is likely to result in entitlement to reimbursement of the service charges, provided this is within the conditions of your own membership.

Automóvel Clube de Portugal

Rua Rosa Araújo 24, Marquês de Pombal (21 318 0100/members' infoline 808 502 502/ww.acp.pt). Metro Marquês de Pombal. **Open** 9am-5.30pm daily. *Members' helpline* 8am-8pm daily. **Map** p246 L7.
Other locations: Loja ACP Centro Colombo, Lojas 74/75 (21 711 1158).

Portilavauto

Quinta São João das Areias, Lote 163, Camarate, Sacavém (21 949 7600). **Open** 24hrs daily. Large out-of-town company offering towing and repairs.

Socireb

Largo da Graça 66, Graça (21 882 0610). **Open** 24hrs daily. Tow trucks and repairs.

Fuel

There are plenty of petrol stations around Lisbon, most of which accept credit cards, but check first. Petrol (*gasolina*) comes as *com aditivo*, with additive to replace lead (although your hire car won't use that) and *sem chumbo*, unleaded, which comes in two grades – 95 and 98. Diesel is *gasóleo*.

To ask the pump attendant to fill the tank you say *cheio, por favor*; a small tip will be appreciated. There are various 24-hour filling stations, many of them close to main access roads into Lisbon (such as BP's on Avenida Almirante Gago Coutinho, near Areeiro, and at the roundabout facing the airport Arrivals hall). Otherwise hours are: Galp 7am-midnight, Repsol 24 hours, BP 7am-midnight (all daily).

Hitch-hiking

Hitch-hiking is not common and anyone sticking their thumb out will have to be very patient. Women should take great care.

Parking

Parking in Lisbon can be a trying task. Cars are often crammed nose to bumper, half on pavements, reflecting a lack of garages (tuck the mirror in on your rental car). Numerous underground car parks have been built in recent years and it is not hard to find space in these, but they are expensive. These are clearly signposted with a white P on a blue background.

Most of downtown Lisbon is covered by a meter system, for which you will need coins. Parking illegally will often result in a heavy fine or the vehicle being towed away. Even in metered areas, drivers may be met by *arrumadores* – roughly translatable as 'fixers' – who will guide you to a parking place. They will expect an advance tip of around €0.50 for this unsolicited service: refusing to pay may trigger unfriendly muttering. The *arrumadores* are there to watch your car and keep it from harm. Drivers not inclined to pay may worry about the consequences to their vehicle. However, local tales of damage to cars are exaggerated.

Car hire

To rent a car in Portugal you must be over 21 and have had a driving licence for more than one year. Several international rental companies have offices in Lisbon, although it often works out cheaper to arrange a deal through your travel agent or airline, or on the company's own website, from home. Some visitors find the UK websites more user-friendly when booking a car for pick-up.

Avis

Avenida Praia da Vitória 12-C L 11, Saldanha (21 351 4560/ freephone reservations 800 201 002/www.avis.com). **Credit** AmEx, DC, MC, V. **Map** p249 M5.
Other locations: Airport (21 843 5550); Hotel Tivoli (21 317 4231).

Budget

Rua Castilho 167B, Marquês de Pombal (21 386 0516/fax 21 383 0978/reservations 21 994 0443/ www.budget.com). **Credit** AmEx, DC, MC, V. **Map** p246 K7.
Other locations: Airport (21 849 5523).

Europcar

Aeroporto de Lisboa (Airport), Portela (21 840 1176/fax 21 847 3180/reservations 21 940 7790/ www.europcar.com). **Credit** AmEx, DC, MC, V. **Map** p249 03.

Hertz

Rua Castilho 72 A-B-C, Marquês de Pombal (21 381 2430/ reservations 21 942 6300/800 238 238/www.hertz.com). **Credit** AmEx, DC, MC, V. **Map** p246 K7.
Other locations: Airport (21 843 8660); Estoril (21 466 4528).

Iperrent

Avenida 5 de Outubro 54C, Saldanha (21 317 2160). **Credit** AmEx, DC, MC, V. **Map** p248 L5.

Cycling

Lisbon's streets are unfriendly to cyclists. Cobbles, tyre-trapping tram lines and bad driving makes it dangerous going. After 9.30pm and at weekends, bicycles may be taken on the Metro (up to two per carriage) and at weekends on suburban rail lines such as those to Cascais and Sintra, but in other circumstances rules for trains are rather complicated. It may be easiest to go out to Cascais and arrange bike hire there. The Estoril and Sintra areas offer the best in scenic cycling. Filipe Palma Aventura (91 227 2300, www.filipepalma.pt) is one of several companies that organise mountain bike tours and adventure trips in and around Lisbon and beyond.

Walking

Many tours include a free tram ride and at least you'll have someone to answer questions.

Inside Tours

96 841 2612/ www.insidelisbon.com.

Lisbon Walker

21 886 1840/96 357 5635/ www.lisbonwalker.com.

Walk Tours Lisbon

96 283 8261/ http://walk.impactus.pt.

Walking Around Lisbon

tel/fax 21 390 6149/mobile 96 908 6602/www.lisbonwalks.com.

Resources A-Z

Business

Doing business in Portugal is becoming easier all the time. Foreign companies don't need permission to invest (although they must register, for statistical purposes): to set up as a sole trader, general partnership, or limited company, procedures are the same as for locals. Your embassy's commercial section can advise you, as can the Centro da Formalidade de Empresas (*see p225*). If documents must be presented, take the original and two copies, and use the same signature as on your passport. Business people appear laid-back in their dealings but formal address, and dress, is the norm. For appointments, write and follow up with phone calls. Expect to be kept waiting by bigwigs.

Chambers of commerce

For a full list of bi-lateral Chambers of Commerce look in the *Páginas Amarelas* (Yellow Pages) under 'Câmaras de Comércio'.

British-Portuguese Chamber of Commerce

Rua da Estrela 8, Estrela (21 394 2020/fax 21 394 2029/www.bpcc.pt). Tram 25, 28. **Open** 9am-5pm Mon-Fri. **Map** p245 J8.

Câmara de Comércio Americana em Portugal

Rua da Dona Estefânia 155, 5°E, Estefânia (21 357 2561/fax 21 357 2580). Metro Saldanha. **Open** 9.30am-1pm, 2-5pm Mon-Fri. **Map** p246 M6.
This is the US Chamber of Commerce. The separate American Club of Lisbon, based at the Sheraton Hotel (*see p51*; 21 352 9308, www.americanclub oflisbon.com) is very active, with regular lunches and talks from major Portuguese figures.

Conventions & office hire

These business centres may be able to help with organising larger events, as will most major hotels.

Centro Luxor

Rua da Misericórdia 76, 4th floor, Chiado (21 321 0100/www.centroluxor.com). Metro Baixa-Chiado/tram 28. **Open** *Office staff* 9am-midnight Mon-Fri. *Reception* 9am-midnight Mon-Fri; 9am-6pm Sat. **No credit cards**. **Map** p250 L9.
Furnished offices with secretarial support. Also hire of meeting rooms.

Feira Internacional de Lisboa (FIL) – Centro de Reuniões

Parque das Nações, Rua do Bojador (21 892 1720/www.fil.pt). Metro Oriente. **Open** 9am-6pm Mon-Fri. **Credit** AmEx, MC, V.
The Lisbon International Exhibition Centre's conference facilities include three auditoria (including a 500-seater) plus four meeting rooms housing up to 50 people. Handy for the airport.

Forum Picoas

Avenida Fontes Pereira de Melo 38C, Saldanha (21 311 7000). Metro Picoas. **Open** 9am-6pm Mon-Fr. **No credit cards**. **Map** p246 L6.
An exhibition space, a 500-seater auditorium and meeting rooms.

Regus Business Centre

Avenida da Liberdade 110 (21 340 4500/www.regus.com). Metro Avenida. **Open** 9am-6.30pm Mon-Fri. **Credit** AmEx, MC, V. **Map** p246 L8.
Well-staffed serviced offices.

Couriers & shippers

EMS, the courier arm of the state postal service, offers a decent service, with delivery within 48 hours to major European capitals and between two and seven working days to other destinations. Sending a document up to 250g to the UK costs €24.10, to the US €31.

Chronopost

Avenida Infante Dom Henrique, Lote 10, Olivais (21 854 6000/fax 21 854 6010/www.chronopost.pt). **Open** 9am-12.30pm, 2-6pm Mon-Fri. **No credit cards**.
A package of 200g or less: €35 to London; €41.90 to New York.

DHL

Rua da Cidade de Liverpool 16, Anjos (707 505 606/fax 707 505 123/www.dhl.pt). **Open** 8.30am-7.30pm Mon-Fri; 9am-2.30pm Sat. *Client service* Avenida Marechal Gomes da Costa, 27AB. **Open**

Travel advice

For up-to-date information on travel to a specific country – including the latest news on safety and security, health issues, local laws and customs – contact your home country government's department of foreign affairs. Most have websites packed with useful advice for would-be travellers.

Australia
www.smartraveller.gov.au

Canada
www.voyage.gc.ca

New Zealand
www.safetravel.govt.nz

Republic of Ireland
foreignaffairs.gov.ie

UK
www.fco.gov.uk/travel

USA
www.state.gov/travel

9.30am-noon, 2pm-8pm Mon-Fri; 10am-2pm Sat. **No credit cards**. A package of 200g or less: €40 to London (24hr); €39 to US (48hr). **Other locations**: Airport, Rua C, Edifício 124 (phone as above).

TNT

Rua C, Edifício 77, Aeroporto de Lisboa (21 854 5050/fax 21 840 3080/www.tnt.com). **Open** 8am-7pm Mon-Fri. **No credit cards**. A package of 200g or less: €59.32 to London; €65.06 to New York.

UPS

Rua Francisco Sousa Tavares, Lote Quinta da Francelha de Baixo (707 232 323/www.ups.com/europe/pt). **Open** 8.30am-8pm daily. **No credit cards**. Express envelope (arrival by 10.30am the next day): €38.42 to London; €39.60 to New York.

Printing & copying

Simple photocopying jobs can be done by most small newsagents. For bulk, colour or anything more complex, try the following.

PostNet

Rua Braamcamp 9, Loja A, C/V, Marquês de Pombal (21 351 1050/www.postnet.pt). Metro Marquês de Pombal. **Open** 8.30am-8pm Mon-Fri; 9am-2pm Sat. **Credit** MC, V. **Map** p246 K7. Photocopying discounts for students and teachers as well as a wide range of services, including internet, design and printing of business cards and invitations, mailings, translations, secretarial support and key-cutting. **Other locations**: Largo Dona Estefânia 6-A, Estefânia (21 317 4967); Avenida Conde Valbom 40A, Saldanha (21 782 6630).

Secretarial services

Egor Portugal

Rua Castilho 75, 7th floor, Marquês de Pombal (21 370 3700/www.egor.pt). Metro Marquês de Pombal. **Open** 9am-6pm Mon-Fri. **Map** p246 K7.

Randstad

Rua Braamcamp 9, Loja C, Marquês de Pombal (21 319 4900/www.pt.randstad.com). Metro Marquês de Pombal. **Open** 9am-7pm Mon-Fri. **Map** p246 K7.

Other locations: Avenida João XXI 78E R/C (21 780 3440); Aeroporto, Rua C Edifício 124 (21 842 8590); Gare do Oriente, Espaço F1 (21 893 3050).

Translation & interpreters

The British Council (*see p229*) can provide a list of translators.

Traducta

Rua Rodrigo da Fonseca 127-1 Dto, Marquês de Pombal (21 388 3384/www.traducta.pt). Metro Marquês de Pombal. **Open** 9am-1pm, 2-6pm Mon-Fri. **No credit cards**. **Map** p246 K7. Established company offering translations and interpreter services.

Useful organisations

Centro da Formalidade de Empresas

Avenida Columbano Bordalo Pinheiro 86, Praça de Espanha (21 723 2300/fax 21 723 2323/www.cfe.iapmei.pt). Metro Praça de Espanha. **Open** 9am-6pm Mon-Fri. **Map** p248 K4. A one-stop shop for setting up a company (*sociedade*), with representatives from each official body. There's limited capacity for handling cases, so come early or make an appointment. **Other locations**: Rua da Junqueira 39, Santo Amaro (21 361 5400).

Banco de Portugal

Rua do Comércio 148, Baixa (21 313 0000/www.bportugal. pt). Metro Baixa-Chiado/28 tram. **Open** 8am-3pm Mon-Fri. **Map** p250 L10. The Portuguese central bank has departments dotted around town but the switchboard here is the best place to start.

ICEP Portugal

Avenida 5 de Outubro 101, Campo Pequeno (21 790 9500/fax 21 793 5028/www.icep.pt). Metro Campo Pequeno. **Open** 9am-5.30pm Mon-Fri. **Map** p248 L5. The Portuguese Investment and Trade Institute is the nearest thing to a one-stop shop for people wishing to do business in Portugal. Plenty of English speakers.

Loja do Cidadão

Praça dos Restauradores 17 (808 24 1107/www.lojadocidadao.pt). Metro Restauradores. **Open** 8.30am-7.30pm Mon-Fri; 9.30am-3pm Sat. **No credit cards**. **Map** p250 L10. This organisation brings together under one roof desks from a number of bureaucratic departments, dealing with things such as tax, social security and driving licences.

Ministério das Finanças

Rua da Alfândega 5, Baixa (21 881 6800/www.min-financas.pt). Metro Baixa-Chiado/28 tram. **Open** 9am-12.30pm, 2-5.30pm Mon-Fri. **Map** p251 M11.

Consumer

Consumer rights are not very well protected in Portugal. The most active campaigning organisation is Deco (21 841 0800, www.deco.proteste.pt), which can also offer advice.

Disabled

With cobbled streets and lots of hills, Lisbon is not the easiest city for disabled travellers. Indeed, the Portuguese word for disabled, *deficiente*, is indicative of local attitudes, although recent legislation has tightened up the rules for new buildings. In museums, hotels and shopping centres, facilities for the disabled are becoming more common, as are assigned parking spots.

Public transport company Carris has a special minibus service for the disabled (21 361 2141, 6.30am-10pm Mon-Fri, 8am-10pm Sat & Sun) but you need a special card: take a medical certificate proving disability, a photograph and passport to the Carris offices in Santo Amaro (Rua 1° de Maio 101, Alcântara). The service must be booked two days in advance and confirmed the next day; the cost is that of an ordinary bus ticket.

The website www.laterooms.com has a page listing hotels in Lisbon with disabled access, with prices – although full details are only in Portuguese and the list does not include cheaper accommodation. The tourism company Accessible Portugal (91 919 5680, 96 010 3034, www.accessibleportugal.com) can also hunt down the right accommodation for you, offers a range of tours and hires out equipment, from wheelchairs to grab rails.

Cooperativa Nacional de Apoio a Deficientes

Praça Dr Fernando Amado 566-E, Chelas (tel/fax 21 859 5332). Metro Chelas. **Open** 10am-1pm, 2.30-6pm Mon-Fri.
Has a department providing advice and information about tourism services for the disabled.

Drugs

Since July 2001 consumption and possession of drugs are no longer crimes punishable by imprisonment. Offenders are instead summoned before one of the administrative tribunals, which can impose a fine or compulsory counselling. Dealing is still taken very seriously, and is likely to result in imprisonment.

Addiction support

CAT Taipas

Rua das Taipas 20, Bairro Alto (21 324 0870/www.geocities.com/catdastaipas). Bus 58, 790. **Open** 9am-7pm Mon; 2-8pm Tue; 9am-8pm Wed; 9am-6pm Thur, Fri. **Map** p250/1 L8.
The most central of Lisbon's CATs, state-funded drug addiction support centres.

Instituto da Droga e da Toxicodependência

Praça de Alvalade 7, 5°-13°, Alvalade (21 111 2700/www.idt.pt). Metro Alvalade.
State institute overseeing drug policy implementation in Portugal; its website lists public and private treatment centres. It also has a special number for drug emergencies (1414, 10am-8pm Mon-Fri) and a helpline, SOS Droga (21 222 2700).

Electricity

Electricity in Portugal runs on 220V. Plugs have two round pins. To use UK appliances, simply change the plug or use an adaptor (available at UK electrical shops, but hard to find in Lisbon). American appliances run on 110V and require a converter, available at larger specialist electricity stores in Lisbon.

Embassies & consulates

For a complete list of embassies and consulates look in the *Páginas Amarelas* (Yellow Pages) under the headings 'Embaixadas, Consulados e Legações'.

Australian Embassy

Avenida da Liberdade 198, 2°E, 1300 (21 310 1500). Metro Avenida. **Open** 9am-5pm Mon-Fri. **Map** p248 L5.

British Embassy

Rua São Bernardo 33, Estrela, 1249 (21 392 9400/fax 21 392 4153/www.uk-embassy.pt). Tram 28. **Open** 9am-11.30am, 3-4.30pm Mon-Thur; 9.30am-12.30pm Fri. **Map** p246 K8.
Further information for Britons at www.bcclisbon.org.

Canadian Embassy

Edifício Vitória, Avenida da Liberdade 196/200-3, 1269 (21 316 4600/http://geo.international.gc.ca/canada-europa/portugal). Metro Avenida. **Open** 8.30am-12.30pm, 1.30-5pm Mon-Fri. **Map** p246 L8.

Irish Embassy

Rua da Imprensa à Estrela 1, Estrela, 1200 (21 392 9440). Tram 28. **Open** 9.30am-12.30pm Mon-Fri. **Map** p245 J8.

US Embassy

Avenida das Forças Armadas, Sete Rios, 1600 (21 727 3300/www.american-embassy.pt). Metro Jardim Zoológico. **Open** *Visas* 8-10am Mon-Fri. *Information* 11.30am-4pm Mon-Fri. *Commercial section* 2-5pm Mon-Fri. **Map** p248 J3.
The commercial section's library is generally open to the public at the same hours, but call first.

Emergencies

For emergency services dial **112**, and specify either *polícia* (police), *ambulância* (ambulance service) or *bombeiros* (fire brigade).

Gay & lesbian

Advice & information

Centro Comunitário Gay e Lesbico de Lisboa – ILGA

Rua de São Lazaro 88, Rossio (21 887 3918/www.ilga-portugal.pt). Metro Martim Moniz. **Open** *Community centre* 5-9pm Mon-Sat. *Helpline* 9pm-midnight Mon-Thur. **Map** p251 M8.
This friendly council-funded community centre offers advice, information and counselling (21 887 6116; Mon & Thur). The association rede ex aqueo (96 878 1841, http://ex-aequo.web.pt), a network of young (16 to 30) GLBTs 'and sympathisers', is also based here.

Clube Safo

Mailing address: Apartado 9973, 1911 (96 004 6617/www.clubesafo.com).
National lesbian rights defence association.

Opus Gay

Rua da Ilha Terceira 34, 2nd floor, Estefânia (96 655 4453/www.opusgay.org). Metro Saldanha. **Open** 10am-1pm, 4-8pm Mon-Fri. **Map** p246 M1
Opus Gay is one of the most active campaigning groups. It also offers counselling, advice and legal help.

Health

There are no special threats to health in Portugal, though, for children especially, strong sun cream and sun hats should be kept to hand and head.

Portugal's public health system is poor by EU standards. Once you reach the specialists, standards are reasonable, but GPs are underfunded, burdened with bureaucracy and inefficient. EU visitors who do not make social security payments in Portugal are entitled to reimbursement only on emergency treatment.

Those who have health insurance will be better off taking advantage of a strong private sector. A visit to a private doctor will cost around €60, but the service is good.

Complementary medicine

Portugal does not have a culture of alternative medicine, apart from the use of traditional herbal remedies.

Sociedade de Homeopatia

Rua Andrade Corvo 16, Picoas, 1050 (21 315 3355). Metro Picoas. **Open** 9am-7pm Mon-Fri. **Map** p246 L6.

Contraception & abortion

Condoms are easily available in pharmacies, supermarkets or dispensing machines. An attempt some years ago to change Portugal's abortion laws through a referendum failed to mobilise voters, and termination is legal only in strictly defined circumstances. A number of clinics quietly defy the law but there are also horror stories about botched backstreet abortions. Cases in which women faced criminal prosecution for having abortions have prompted the Socialist government to propose another referendum in early 2007. As well as the hospitals listed here, there are several state-funded helplines: Sexualidade em Linha (808 222 003), Linha SOS Grávida (808 201 139), Linha Verde de Medicamentos e Gravidez (freephone 800 202 844).

Hospital de Santa Maria

Avenida Professor Egas Moniz, Campo Grande (21 780 5000/ obstetrics ext 1422/information 21 780 5555/www.hsm.min-saude.pt). Metro Cidade Universitária/bus 701, 732, 738, 755, 768. **Open** *Obstetrics* 8am-4pm Mon-Fri. **Map** p248 K2.

Lisbon's largest general hospital, with comprehensive emergency services.

Maternidade Dr Alfredo da Costa

Rua Pedro Nunes, Saldanha (21 318 4077/21 318 4000/www.mac.min-saude.pt). Metro Picoas. **Open** *Family Planning* 2-6pm Tue-Thur; 8am-noon Fri. *Gynaecology* 8am-2pm Tue; 8am-1pm Wed-Fri. **Map** p248 L8.

Lisbon's main maternity unit: family planning and counselling. Book in advance.

Dentists

Public health dentists charge a nominal fee, but standards are patchy. We advise you to splash out on private treatment. Look under 'Dentistas' in the *Páginas Amarelas* (Yellow Pages).

Clínica Paris

Rua Cidade Nampoula, Lote 534, 1E, Olivais (21 853 6908). Bus 21, 31. **Open** 9am-7pm Mon-Fri. **Credit** MC, V.

Half-a-dozen dentists work at this large clinic near the airport. Dr Pimentel speaks English.

Thomas Schreiner

Rua Pascoal de Melo 60, Arroios (21 355 9424/ 8471). Metro Arroios. **Open** 9.30am-1pm, 3-6.30pm Mon, Tue, Thur. **No credit cards**. **Map** p247 N6.

Doctors

Clínica Médica Internacional de Lisboa

Avenida António Augusto de Aguiar 40 R/C E, Parque Eduardo VII (21 351 3310/www.cmil.pt). Metro Parque. **Open** 9am-7.30pm Mon-Fri. **No credit cards**. **Map** p246 L6.

Appointments with general practitioner Dr David Ernst.

International Health Centre

Rua do Regimento XIX 67, Cascais (21 484 5317). Train to Cascais from Cais do Sodré. **Open** 9am-1pm, 3-7pm Mon-Fri. **No credit cards**.

This centre offers a 24-hour service and home visits by English-speaking Portuguese doctors and nurses.

Helplines

Alcoólicos Anónimos

21 716 2969. **Open** 24hrs daily.

Centro SOS Voz Amiga

21 354 4545/freephone 800 202 669. **Open** 5pm-7am daily. *Freephone* 9pm-midnight daily.

Loneliness and depression.

Narcóticos Anónimos

Freephone 800 202 013. **Open** 8.30-10.30pm Mon, Wed, Fri.

Sociedade Anti-Alcoólica Portuguesa

21 357 1483. **Open** 9.30am-noon, 2-6pm Mon-Fri.

Hospitals: public

For a complete list of hospitals to be found in and around Lisbon, consult the *Páginas Amarelas* (Yellow Pages) under 'Hospitais'. Hospitals with emergency wards (*serviço de urgência*) that are open 24 hours daily include Hospital de Santa Maria (*see above*) and the following:

Hospital Curry Cabral

Rua da Beneficência 8, Praça de Espanha (21 792 4200/2). Metro Praça de Espanha. **Map** p248 L4.

Hospital Miguel Bombarda

Rua Dr Almeida Amaral, Campo de Santana (21 317 7400). Bus 30, 723, 790. **Open** 24 hours daily. **Map** p246 M7.

Hospitals: psychiatric

Hospital São Francisco Xavier

Estrada Forte Alto do Duque, Restelo (21 300 0300/21 301 7351). Bus 723, 732. **Map** p244 A8.

Hospitals: private

Anjos da Noite

Rua Francisco Franco 5-1E, Alvalade (21 792 1150/bookings 707 507 507/www.anjosda noite.pt). Bus 5, 21, 22, 91, 708. **Open** *Head office* 8am-10pm daily. **Map** p249 02.

Members of 'Night Angels' pay an €8.50 monthly fee for a range of medical services, with clinics and home visits included.

British Hospital/ Hospital Inglês

Rua Saraiva de Carvalho 49, Campo de Ourique (21 394 3100/www.gpsaude.pt). Tram 25, 28/bus 9, 720, 738. **Open** 8am-9pm Mon-Fri. **Map** p245 J8.

Portugal's oldest private health unit. The newer branch is open until midnight, every day.

Other locations: British Hospital Lisbon, XXI Rua Tomás da Fonseca, Edifícios B e F, Torres de Lisboa, Laranjeiras (21 721 3400).

Hospital Cuf

Travessa Castro 3, Avenida Infante Santo, Alcântara (21 392 6100/15/www.hospitalcuf.pt). Bus 60, 713, 720, 727, 738, 773. **Map** p243 G9.

Other locations: Hospital Cuf Descobertas, Rua Mário Botas, Parque das Nações (21 002 5200).

Hospital Particular de Lisboa

Avenida Luís Bívar 30, Saldanha (21 358 6200). Metro Saldanha. **Map** p248 L5.

Hospital São José

Rua José António Serrano, Campo de Santana (21 884 1000). Metro Martim Moniz/bus 790. **Map** p246 M8.

Opticians

See p148.

Pharmacies

Identified by a green cross. Many drugs are available without a prescription and you can get basic advice on the spot. Out of office hours there is at least one pharmacy open in each neighbourhood. The rota is posted in pharmacy windows.

STDs, HIV & AIDS

For most problems, see a GP, or use the emergency service of a hospital. Aids has been aggravated by high levels of needle sharing among heroin users, with exchange schemes slow to reach all users. English is spoken at the following HIV/Aids helplines:

Abraço

Freephone 800 225 115. **Open** 10am-7pm Mon-Fri.

Linha SOS Sida

Freephone 800 201 040. **Open** 5.30-9.30pm daily.

Information, orientation and support.

ID

Legally, you should carry ID with you at all times, which for Brits and non-EU nationals means a passport. In practice you won't be asked for it unless you get into trouble.

Insurance

The Departamento Legalização de Viaturas of the Automóvel Clube de Portugal (*see p223*) can help with the paperwork necessary for importing, registering and insuring a car in Portugal – but you have to join. *See also pp226-227.*

Internet

Internet access

For a full listing of wireless access points in Lisbon, see http://cnet.jiwire.com.

Blue Net Café

Rua da Rosa 165, Bairro Alto (no phone). Metro Baixa-Chiado. **Open** noon-midnight Mon-Fri; 3pm-midnight Sat, Sun. **Rates** €1/30mins. **No credit cards**.

Centro de Informação Urbana de Lisboa

Picoas Plaza, Rua do Viriato 13, Núcleo 6-E 1, Picoas (21 330 1920). Metro Picoas. **Open** 10am-8pm Mon-Fri; 2-8pm Sat. **Rates** free.

Ciber-Chiado

Rua Antónia Maria Cardoso 68, Chiado (21 346 6722/www.cnc.pt). Metro Baixa-Chiado/tram 28. **Open** 10.30am-6pm Mon-Fri. **Rates** free. **Map** p250 L9.

Cib@rcafé

Pavihão do Conhecimento, Praque das Nações (21 891 7138/www. pavconhecimento.pt). Metro Oriente. **Open** 10am-6pm Tue-Fri; 11am-7pm Sat, Sun. **Rates** free.

CiberOceanos

Avenida D. João II, Gare do Oriente, Loja G 109A, Parque das Nações (21 895 1995/www.ciber oceanos.com). Metro Oriente. **Rates** €1.15/15mins. **No credit cards**.

Internet Room

Rua da Adiça 18, Alfama (21 888 8046). Tram 12, 28/bus 37. **Open** 10am-11pm daily. **Rates** €0.80/20min. **No credit cards**. **Map** p250/1 N10.

Portugal Telecom

Praça Dom Pedro IV (Rossio) 58 (21 323 8700/808 202 048). Metro Rossio or Restauradores. **Open** 8am-11pm daily. **Rates** €1-€1.25/30mins. **Credit** MC, V. **Map** p250/1 L9/M9.

Other locations: Loja 0512 (21 716 8408); Picaos Plaza, Rua Viriato, Loja C.05, Saldanha (21 316 0257).

Web Café

Rua Diário Notícias 126, Bairro Alto (21 342 1181). Metro Baixa-Chiado/28 tram. **Open** 4pm-2am daily. **Rates** €4/hr; €2.50/half-hour; €1.50/15mins. **Credit** AmEx, MC, V. **Map** p246 L9.

Online services

If you don't have an internet account or you're not sure you'll be around for long, you can take advantage of a range of no-frills dial-up deals (from around €0.02/min). Some can be used with an ISDN (RDIS) line and then are more efficient. Cheap rate is weekdays 9pm-9am, plus weekends and holidays. The firms listed also offer ADSL packages similar to those of Telepac. In general, payment is made via ATM; you are given a code that allows you to recharge your account.

Clix

808 102 030/www.clix.pt.

IOL

808 226 744/www.iol.pt.

Oninet

Information 16509/technical help 16505/www.oninet.pt.

Sapo

707 227 276/www.sapo.pt (click on Sapo in 'Acesso à internet').

Telepac

Forum Picoas, Avenida Fontes Pereira de Melo 38, Picoas (808 207 070/www.telepac.pt). Metro Picoas. **Open** 9am-7pm Mon-Fri. **No credit cards**.

Left luggage

Airport

The Depósito de Bagagem (21 841 3500) is in the arrivals hall. Cost is according to weight: €2.50 per day for up to 10kg; €3.76 per day for 10-30kg; and €7.27 for 30-60kg. There is no limit on the number of days that you may leave luggage.

Legal help

If you get into legal difficulties, the British Embassy, or any other, can provide a list of English-speaking lawyers in Lisbon, or look on the US Embassy website. Also, look in the *Páginas Amarelas* (Yellow Pages) under 'Advogados'. Most big firms have English-speaking lawyers.

Centro Nacional de Apoio ao Imigrante

Rua Álvaro Coutinho, 14-16, Anjos (21 810 6100/www.acime.pt). Metro Anjos. **Open** 8.30am-4.30pm Mon-Fri; 8.30am-2.30pm Sat (appointments).
Help specifically for foreign residents, run by the Commission for Immigrants and Ethnic Minorities (ACIME).

Ordem dos Advogados

Largo de São Domingos 14, 1st floor, Restauradores (21 882 3550/www.oa.pt). Metro Restauradores. **Open** 9.30am-12.30pm, 2-6pm. Mon-Fri. **Map** p250 M9.
This professional body can find you an English-speaking lawyer.

Libraries

Specialist libraries are listed in *Agenda Cultural.*

British Council

Rua de São Marçal 174, Príncipe Real (21 321 4500/63/www.britishcouncil.org/portugal). Metro Rato/bus 58. **Open** 2-8pm Mon, Tue, Thur, Fri; 11am-8pm Wed; 9.30am-6.30pm Sat for language classes. **Map** p246 K8.
One of the oldest Council offices in the world. Its Information Centre has fewer books than it once did, but still boasts a decent collection of novels and poetry as well as DVDs and music. Access for reference purposes (and to use the internet PCs) is free; to borrow items you must join (€30/six months, €45/year; €25 and €40 concessions).

Biblioteca Municipal Central

Palácio Galveias, Campo Pequeno, 1000 (21 780 3020). Metro Campo Pequeno. **Open** 10am-7pm Mon-Fri; 11am-6pm Sat. **Map** p248M4.
This is the main municipal lending library. Present ID for access, and proof of residency for borrowing. Free internet access.

Biblioteca Nacional

Campo Grande 83, Campo Grande (21 798 2000). Metro Entre Campos. **Open** 9.30am-7.30pm Mon-Fri; 9.30am-5.30pm Sat. **Map** p248 L2.
Portugal's national library. Use is restricted to over-18s. Non-EU citizens must show a passport, EU citizens ID.

Lost property

For lost or stolen property, try the lost and found section of the Lisbon police (*see p231*). Theft should be reported at any police station, in person. For lost or stolen credit cards, contact your bank.

Airport

If your luggage has gone astray, go to the desk in arrivals set up for this purpose. Items found in the building and handed in go to the PSP police in the airport (21 849 6132).

Public transport

For buses and trams, contact the PSP police station in Olivais (21 853 5403). For the Metro, go to Marquês de Pombal station.

Taxis

If you leave something in a taxi, you will have to phone the company. If you have a receipt with the car's number on it, all the better. If you can't remember the name of the company, and your ride was in central Lisbon, there's a fair chance it will be Rádio Taxis de Lisboa, the largest (21 811 9000).

Media

Newspapers

A Bola/Record/O Jogo

These three football papers are the country's most popular daily read, respectively biased towards Benfica, Sporting and Porto.

Diário de Notícias/ Jornal de Notícias

Oporto-based *Jornal de Notícias* is the biggest selling daily. *DN* has good classifieds.

Diário Económico

A business daily. *Jornal de Negócios* is its rival.

Expresso

Political analysis.

Público

Comprehensive, quality coverage; good on international events.

Tal e Qual

Tongue-in-cheek tabloid.

English-language

The News

The English-language newspaper most easily found in the Lisbon area. Can be picked up free in pubs in the Cais do Sodré area, or online at www.the-news.net

People and Business

Slick property and business monthly for travellers and expats. Distributed free at many hotels.

The Resident

Another Algarve-based weekly which is also available online at http://portugalresident.com

Foreign newspapers

Delivery of British tabloids is regular, as the *Sun*, *Mirror*, *Mail* and *Express* print in Spain for expats, but quality dailies tend to turn up late in the afternoon or even the next day.

Radio

The airwaves are filled with music. Mainstream rock station **Rádio Comercial** (97.4FM) tends to beat the more varied state-run **Antena 3** (100.3FM) at the ratings game, while **Oxigénio** (102.6FM) is wall-to-wall dance music. Church-owned **Rádio Renascença** (103.4FM) has news and talk shows. It and its sister stations have the biggest combined audience. **TSF** (89.5FM) is news radio 24 hours a day. State-run **Antena 1** (95.7 FM) is also a good news and football source. French speakers can hear international news on **Rádio Paris Lisboa** (90.4FM), while the **BBC World Service** is on shortwave (frequencies and schedules are printed in local English-language newspapers) and online (at www.bbc.co.uk/radio).

Television

Privately owned **SIC** has a diet of *telenovelas* – Brazilian soaps – docudramas and absurd game shows. Its cable offshoot **SIC Notícias** leads in rolling news. **TVI**, the other private channel, is more downmarket. State flagship **RTP1** has sought to raise standards lately after a lengthy period of dumbing down. **RTP2** was modishly renamed '2' a couple of years ago and relaunched as a 'community' station.

Money

Portugal's currency is the Euro. The notes in public circulation are €5, €10, €20, €50, €100, €200, €500, while the coins come in €1, €2, 1 cent, 2 cents, 5 cents, 10 cents and 20 cents.

ATMs

You're never far from a Multibanco machine in Lisbon, and lisboetas conduct a vast amount of day-to-day transactions through them, from paying bills to making transfers. You can withdraw €200 per day from them – usually in the form of €20 notes – though you will probably be charged a handling fee. Terminals are also common in shops, and these and ATMs accept MasterCard, Visa and other major international cards, including Maestro and Cirrus, making this a good way to spend or transfer small sums.

Banks

Open from 8.30am to 3pm. Most have a small number of branches that stay open until 6pm. Watch out if changing travellers cheques, as banks can charge hefty commissions. You will get much better rates at a bureau de change (*see below*), or even at one of the larger hotels. All banks (except for Barclays) have retail branches throughout the city.

Banco Bilbao Vizcaya e Argentaria (BBVA)

Avenida da Liberdade 222 (21 311 7200/www.bbva.pt). Metro Avenida. **Open** 8am-3pm Mon-Fri. **Map** p246 L8.
Other locations: Rua Áurea (Rua do Ouro) 40-48, Baixa, 1100 (21 321 8500).

Banco BPI

Largo Jean Monnet 1-9º, Rua do Salitre, Avenida de Liberdade (21 310 1000/www.bancobpi.pt). Metro Avenida. **Open** 8.30am-3pm Mon-Fri. **Map** p246 L8.
Other locations: Avenida da Liberdade 9A (same phone).

Banco Espírito Santo

Avenida da Liberdade 195 (21 355 0410/www.bes.pt). Metro Avenida. **Open** 8.30am-3pm Mon-Fri. **Map** p246 L7.
The retail branch is next door.

Banco Santander

Praça Marquês de Pombal 2 (21 317 2560/www.santander.pt). Metro Marquês de Pombal. **Open** 8.30am-3pm Mon-Fri. **Map** p246 K7.

Barclays Bank

Avenida da República 50, 2nd floor, Campo Pequeno (21 791 1100/1222/www.barclays.pt). Metro Campo Pequeno. **Open** 8.30am-3pm Mon-Fri. **Map** 249 M4.

Caixa Geral de Depósitos

Avenida João XXI 63, Campo Pequeno (21 790 5000/www.cgd.pt). Metro Campo Pequeno. **Open** 8.30am-3pm Mon-Fri. **Map** p249 M4.
The Baixa branch has cash and money-changing machines open after hours.
Other locations: Rua Áurea (Rua do Ouro) 49, Baixa, 1100 (21 340 5000).

Millennium BCP

Avenida José Malhoa, Lote 1686, Praça de Espanha (21 721 8000/www.bcp.pt). Metro Praça de Espanha. **Open** 8.30am-3pm Mon-Fri. **Map** p248 J4.
Other locations: Rua Augusta 84, Baixa (21 321 1000).

Bureaux de change

There are clusters of these around Rossio and Praça da Figueira. They generally give a slightly better rate of exchange than the main banks and are also often faster. They are also generally able to change a wider range of currencies. The main Baixa branch of Caixa Geral (*see above*) has a money-changing machine, one of a handful dotted around the centre.

Credit cards

American Express, MasterCard and Visa are the most widespread, but use is far from universal.

Tax

Residents of EU member states may not claim back any value-added tax on purchases. US residents may do so if they buy goods at shops that adhere to the Tax-free scheme; they will have a sticker displayed in the window. Claims are made by filling in a form available at the Tax-free counter at the airport (21 840 8813, 24hrs), near Departures. There's also an information line (21 846 3025, 8am-7pm Mon-Fri).

Natural hazards

There hasn't been a big quake since the 1755 earthshaker. Unlike the Azores, where tremors are relatively common, the very occasional ones in Lisbon are tiny. Otherwise, aside from fierce Atlantic waves, Portugal is free of natural hazards.

Opening hours

Shops are normally open from 9am to 1pm and 3pm to 6pm or 7pm, although some high-street shops stay open during lunch. Most supermarkets stay open until about 8pm. In shopping centres, hours tend to be from 10am until 10pm. Banks usually open from 8.30am-3pm, weekdays only, and post offices (*correios*) from 9am-6pm, also weekdays only (smaller branches may close for lunch).

Police stations

Lisbon police have a relaxed air, but as is typical in former dictatorships, Portugal's law enforcers are only gradually regaining the trust of the population. Their training and image have improved, and you should find them polite and capable of helping out. But do not try to resist or argue if you get into bother. Quiet politeness is definitely the best way to deal with a policeman here. There is a police station for tourists in Palácio Foz on Praça dos Restauradores (21 342 1634).

Postal services

State postal service CTT (whose clunky site is at www.ctt.pt) has a monopoly on letter delivery. First class mail is *correio azul* (blue mail). Costing a minimum €1.80 it should get anywhere in Europe in under four days, and to the US in no more than six. Second class mail, *correio normal* to Europe (other than Spain) costs €0.60 for a standard-sized letter under 20 grams (7oz); to the rest of the world it costs €0.75.

Sending a 20-gram letter within Portugal costs €0.30, or €0.45 for *correio azul*.

Stamps are sold at all post office counters or from nearby machines. Mailing boxes offer two slots: one for regular post, one for *correio azul*.

Main post office

Praça dos Restauradores 58, Restauradores (21 323 8971). Metro Restauradores. **Open** 8am-10pm Mon-Fri; 9am-6pm Sat, Sun. **Map** p250 L8.

Poste restante

Mail can be addressed to 'Poste restante' and sent to a particular post office. It can be collected from the main post office.

Religion

Portugal is and remains a thoroughly Roman Catholic country, and thus you'll never be very far from a church. Check on the church doors for times of mass.

Anglican

St George's Church, Rua São Jorge, Estrela (21 390 6248/21 468 3570/www.lisbonanglicans.org). Tram 25, 28/bus 9, 720, 738. **Service** 11.30am Sun. **Map** p245 J8.

The parish itself dates from 1656 (*see p93* **The Brit pack**) while the church that now inhabits the site was consecrated in 1889, and has a fine organ. Buses stop right by the gates of the British cemetery through which you enter. Services are followed by sociable drinks in the Church Hall. The chaplaincy also covers Saint Paul's Estoril, which has a Sunday School.

Baptist

Igreja Evangélica Baptista da Graça, Rua Capitão Humberto Ataíde 28, Santa Apolónia (21 813 2889). Bus 35. **Services** 10am, 11.30am, 6pm Sun; 3pm Wed. **Map** p247 O8.

Average monthly climate

Month	Average max temp	Average min temp	Total rainfall (mm/in)
Jan	14.5°C (58.1°F)	8.2°C (46.8°F)	110/4.3
Feb	15.6°C (60.8°F)	9.0°C (48.2°F)	111/4.3
Mar	17.6°C (63.7°F)	9.9°C (49.8°F)	69/2.7
Apr	19.1°C (66.4°F)	11.1°C (52.0°F)	64/2.5
May	21.7°C (71.1°F)	13.0°C (55.4°F)	39/1.5
June	24.8°C (76.6°F)	15.6°C (60.1°F)	21/0.8
July	27.4°C (81.3°F)	17.4°C (63.3°F)	5/0.2
Aug	27.9°C (82.2°F)	17.7°C (63.9°F)	6/0.2
Sept	26.4°C (79.5°F)	17.0°C (62.6°F)	26/1.0
Oct	22.4°C (72.3°F)	14.6°C (58.1°F)	80/3.1
Nov	17.8°C (64.0°F)	11.2°C (52.2°F)	114/4.5
Dec	14.8°C (58.6°F)	8.9°C (48.0°F)	108/4.3

Buddhist

Budismo Tibetano Nyingma, Rua do Salitre 117, Avenida da Liberdade (21 314 2038). Metro Rato. **Open** Reception 10am-3pm, 4.30-7pm Mon-Fri. *Practice* 7.15am, 9.30pm Mon-Fri; 9am, 9.30pm Sat, Sun. **Map** p246 L8.

Catholic

Basílica da Estrela, Praça da Estrela, Estrela (21 396 0915). Tram 25, 28. **Open** 7.30am-1pm, 3-8pm daily. **Mass** 8am, 12.15pm, 7pm Mon-Fri; 7pm Sat; 9am, noon, 1.15pm (except July-Sept) Sun. **Map** p245 J8.

Sé Catedral, Largo da Sé (21 886 6752). Tram 12, 28. **Open** 9am-5pm daily. **Mass** 6.30pm Tue-Sat; 11.30am, 7pm Sun. **Map** p251 M10.

Hindu

Comunidade Hindú de Portugal, Alameda Mahatama Gandhi, Lumiar, 1600 (21 757 6524). Metro Campo Grande then bus 78. **Open** 9am-5pm Mon-Fri.

Ismaili

Centro Cultural Ismaelita, Rua Abranches Ferrão, Laranjeiras, 1600 (21 722 9000). Metro Laranjeiras. **Open** 9am-7pm daily. **Map** p248 J3.

Islamic

Mesquita Central de Lisboa, Avenida José Malhôa, Praça de Espanha (21 387 4142/2220). Metro Praça de Espanha. **Open** 9am-6pm daily. **Map** p248 K4.

Jewish

Comunidade Israelita de Lisboa, Rua Alexandre Herculano 59, Rato (21 393 1130). Metro Rato. **Open** 10am-1pm, 2-5pm Mon-Thur; 9am-1pm Fri. **Map** p246 K7.

Presbyterian

St Andrew's Church of Scotland, Rua da Arriaga 13, Lapa (21 468 0853/www.standrewslisbon.com.sapo.pt). Tram 25 then 5min walk/bus 60, 713, 727. **Worship** 11am Sun. **Map** p245 H10.

Founded in 1866, this is the only English-speaking Church of Scotland house of worship in Portugal. It is also used by Portuguese-speaking congregations – Angolan Methodists (early on Sunday) and members of the Apostolic Episcopal Church (weekdays).

Safety & security

Lisbon is a relatively safe town, but be aware of pickpockets among crowds, especially on trams. Lisbon's narrow streets and dimly lit alleys offer an ideal environment for street crime, but violent incidents are rare. Basic safety rules apply: do not carry too much cash; avoid dark and deserted places, and look after valuables. Be alert when visiting the Bairro Alto, Cais do Sodré and the lower Alfama. There is heavier drug-related crime in the poorest neighbourhoods and peripheral shanty towns, but visitors are unlikely to come into contact with this. Car crime is more common and the usual precautions should always be taken when leaving vehicles unattended.

Smoking

Smoking is not permitted on public transport or in museums. Elsewhere, there are relatively few restrictions and not many restaurants have no-smoking areas, although they are becoming more common.

Study

Language classes

There are several institutions that hold Portuguese language classes in Lisbon. We recommend the following: Cambridge School (21 312 4600/www.cambridge.pt); Cial (21 794 0448/ww.cial.pt) and International House (21 315 1493/4/6/www.ihlisbon.com). Português etcetera is a newcomer in the Baixa (21 886 0167/www.portuguesetcetera.com).

Universities

Universidade de Lisboa

Alameda da Universidade, Cidade Universitária, 1649 (21 796 7624/fax 21793 3624/www.ul.pt). Metro Campo Grande.

Portugal's first university was founded around 1288 by Dom Dinis and after a series of moves back and forth ended up in Coimbra. Only in the 19th century did higher education regain a foothold in the capital; in 1911 the Universidade de Lisboa was formed from the merger of the College of Languages and Literature (Curso Superior de Letras), the Medical College (Escola Médico-Cirúrgica), the Polytechnical College and the Pharmaceutical College. Other bodies were later integrated, including the Museu de História Natural, the Jardim Botânico, the Museu do Instituto Geológico e Mineiro and the Museu da Ciência. Today the university has eight Faculdades and four Institutos.

Information

CIREP

Avenida 5° de Outubro 107, Saldanha, 1050 (21 781 1690/www.sg.min-edu.pt/cirep_informacao.htm). Metro Saldanha. **Open** 9am-7pm Mon-Fri. **Map** p248 L5.

Education Ministry service providing information about all levels of the eduation system.

Telephones

Dialling & codes

To call Lisbon from overseas, first dial your international access code (0011 from Australia, 011 from Canada or the US, 00 from New Zealand and Europe) followed by 351 for Portugal. Lisbon numbers all start with 21, but this forms part of the number. (If you have an old seven-digit number you want to call, adding 21 at the front may work.)

Making a call

To dial another part of Portugal from Lisbon, simply dial the number, which invariably starts with 2. There are no longer any area codes. If you have an old number together with an area code starting with zero, replacing the zero with a 2 may do the trick. In some towns, however, an extra digit was added somewhere to bring it up to the full eight digits.

To make an international call from Portugal dial 00, followed by the country code, the area code and then the number. Useful country codes are: Australia 61, Canada and the US 1, New Zealand 64, the UK 44 (after which you drop the initial zero of the area code). Various calling cards are available but deals change constantly so look out for leaflets (invariably in English as well as Portuguese) at kiosks and in shops selling phone cards.

Operator services

For directory enquiries, dial 118. International directory enquiries is 177/9 but it's pricey; less well publicised is freephone 800 201520. To reverse charges call 120 for Europe; 179 for the rest of the world.

Public phones

Portugal Telecom (PT) has coin-operated booths and phone card kiosks, a handful of which are of the old red variety, dating back to the days when they were maintained by a British company. You can buy a phone card (*cartão telefónico*) from news kiosks, tobacconists or post offices, priced at either €5 or €10. The current model can be inserted into public cardphones or used as a calling card (you dial the access number followed by the card number and your PIN) on ordinary phones. This is a boon when phoning from hotels, from which international calls are usually extremely expensive. With these cards, the cheap rate applies on weekdays between 7pm and 9am, at weekends and on public holidays are cheaper. (In normal circumstances, PT's weekday cheap rate only kicks in at 9pm.) The older coin-operated booths are impractical for international calls. Portugal Telecom shops (*see p228*), the most central of which can be found in Rossio, have both payphones and booths from which pre-paid international calls can be made.

Telephone directories

The ordinary white-page directory for Lisbon covers the Greater Lisbon area, including Sintra and Cascais. It is online at www.118.pt, while the *Páginas Amarelas* (*Yellow Pages*) is at www.paginasamarelas.pt. The usefulness of these publications is undermined by the fact that shops and restaurants are often listed under the owner's name.

Mobile phones

The Portuguese love their telemóveis, and have more per head than any Europeans except the Scandinavians – in fact, they already outnumber the population. The main operators are Optimus, Vodafone and TMN. All have good coverage in the city, but it's worth checking out the deals of all three before subscribing. New users often buy phones or cards as part of a promotional pack at very competitive rates. All three offer a SIM card for €9.90 (incl €10 calls), sell products online, and have agents throughout the city. They also now have offshoots offering a no-frills service at low rates; one, Uzo, has a vending machine in the Bairro Alto (Rua do Norte 113) where you can get a SIM card for €5 (including €5 of calls) that you can then charge up with a minimum of €15 at post offices or ATMs and which offers ultra-cheap calls (from €0.06/min).

Óptimus

Mailing address: Apartado 52121, 1721-501 (shop 800 931 010//24hr customer support 1693/www.optimus.pt). **Open** 10am-7pm Mon-Sat. **Credit** V.
The company's shop in Colombo shopping centre (*see p132*) is **open** 10am-10pm.

TMN

Avenida Álvaro Pais 2, Entrecampos, 1649 (21 791 4400/24hr customer support 1696/www.tmn.pt). **Open** 8.30am-7.30pm Mon-Fri. **Credit** MC, V. **Map** p248 L3.
TMN's most central shop is in the Armazéns do Chiado (open 10am-11pm daily).

Vodafone

Avenida Dom João II, Lote 1.04.01, Parque das Nações, 1998-017 (21 091 5000/customer supoort 16912/www.vodafone.pt).
Has a shop in the Armazéns do Chiado (open 10am-10pm daily) and two at the airport.

Faxes

Faxes may be received and sent from all large hotels and some smaller ones (costs vary), and from post offices.

Time

Portuguese time is always the same as British time, in line with GMT in winter and an hour ahead in summer. The 24-hour clock is normally used, even in everyday speech.

Tipping

In restaurants and cafés a tip of anything between two and ten per cent is normal. Tipping in bars is less common, although meagre wages often warrant it. With taxi drivers it is less common and frankly few deserve it. We would encourage tipping those worthy few who actually manage to take you to your destination without griping or snapping.

Toilets

Lisbon is not particularly well blessed with public toilets (*sanitários* or *casas de banho*). Café owners are not too fussy about people wandering in off the street, but your senses may be abused by the state of some of the facilities. Museums, restaurants and shopping centres have the cleanest rest rooms. Men's are usually marked with an H for *homens*, women's with an S for *senhoras*.

Tourist information

The best one-stop shop is the Turismo in Praça dos Restauradores (*see below*). As well as this, the Welcome Centre, and desks at the airport and at Santa Apolónia, there are 'Ask Me' booths in Rua

Augusta and in front of the Mosteiro dos Jerónimos in Belém (both open 10am-1pm, 2-6pm Tue-Sat) that have helpful staff and lots of leaflets. Or call the Turismo de Lisboa's information line 808 781 212.

Lisboa Welcome Centre

Rua do Arsenal 15, Baixa 1100 (21 031 2700/fax 21 031 2899/ www.visitlisboa.com). Metro Baixa-Chiado/tram 12, 15, 18, 28. **Open** 9am-8pm daily. **Map** p250/1 L10.

A walk-in space opened by the public-private Lisbon tourist board, the ATL, in the building on the northwestern corner of Praça do Comércio that houses its headquarters. As well as an information desk where you can buy the Lisboa Card (*see below*), book a rental car or pricey sightseeing tour and arrange accommodation, there is an internet point (€1/15mins- €3/1 hr), a plethora of leaflets, a café and Artesanato do Tejo (21 031 2820; open 10am-6pm Mon-Fri; 10am-1pm, 2-6pm Sat & Sun), a shop selling Portuguese artefacts ranging fom olive oil to jewellery. The main entrance to the last of these is round the corner in Rua do Arsenal.

Other locations: Airport (21 845 0660; open 7am-midnight); Santa Apolónia station (21 882 1606; open 8am-1pm Tue-Sat); Cais da Rocha, Porto de Lisboa (cruise tours; 91 897 0217).

Turismo

Palácio Foz, Praça dos Restauradores 1250 (21 346 6307/www.visitportugal.com). Metro Restauradores. **Open** 9am-8pm daily. **Map** p250/1 L8.

Run by the national tourist institute, the ITP, this office can provide information about all of Portugal. City tourist officials also have a desk here (21 346 3314), and from them you can buy a Lisboa Card that offers up to three days unlimited travel on public transport, plus a range of discounts on cultural activities and entertainment. (Prices: 24hr card €13.50; 48hr €23; 72hr, €28; for 5-11s €6, €9.50 and €11.50.) You can also buy this or the Lisboa Restaurant Card (which offers discounts of up to 20% but only in 36 restaurants, and is not such good value) at the Welcome Center and at 'Ask Me' booths.

Other locations: Airport (21 849 3689).

Visas & immigration

Standard EU immigration law applies. That means that EU citizens planning to stay more than six months will need to apply for a residence permit, but are otherwise free to come and go. Nationals of Australia and New Zealand are entitled to stay up to 90 days without a visa, but US and Canadian citizens must apply for a 60-day visa before entering. Applications for extensions should be made at least a week before the expiry of the previous leave to stay.

When to go

At Easter Lisbon is overrun by visitors from Spain, who have enough days off over the holiday period to make a long weekend worthwhile. At New Year the Italians descend in force. The rest of the time Germans and Brits are most numerous at weekends and at half-terms, but with the weather mild (if at times unpredictable) foreign visitors are spread evenly throughout the year.

Climate

Lisbon has long, dry summers lasting from June to October and a mild winter, limited to a period of wetter and cooler weather between December to February. Autumn (October and November) and spring (March to May) are mild, but sometimes very wet. May is a particularly beautiful month. August is generally the hottest month but temperatures rarely rise to the levels of, say, Madrid. Outside the July-August period the nights can be cool. On sunny days a protective cream is a must for most skin types.

Public holidays

Most shops close on public holidays, except for shopping malls and big supermarkets. Restaurants, cafés and cinemas tend not to close either, but museums do. Public holidays are: **New Year's Day** (1 Jan); **Good Friday**; **Revolution Day** (25 Apr); **Labour Day** (1 May); **Corpus Christi** (6 June); **Camões Day** (10 June); **Assumption** (15 Aug); **Republic Day** (5 Oct); **All Saints Day** (1 Nov); **Independence Day** (1 Dec); **Immaculate Conception** (8 Dec); **Christmas** (25 Dec). Most lisboetas also take June 13, Santo António's Day, off.

Women

Lisbon is fairly safe, but it's best not to walk alone late at night in some dingier districts.

Working in Lisbon

EU citizens are free to work in Portugal, although if they intend to stay for more than six months they will need a residence permit. Permits are issued occasionally, but are not easily arranged. For more information, contact the Portuguese embassy or the consulate in your home country.

Useful addresses

Serviço de Estrangeiros e Fronteiras

Avenida António Augusto de Aguiar 20, Marquês de Pombal, 1050-017 (21 358 5500/www. sef.pt). Metro Parque. **Open** 9am-3pm Mon-Fri. **Map** p246 L6.

Either you or your *despachante* (agent) must queue here if you intend to get a residence permit.

Bureaucratic Help Service

Centro Comercial Charneca, Loja 13, Rua das Lapas, Cascais, 2750-772 (21 485 8233/fax 21 485 8238/). Train from Cais do Sodré. **Open** 9am-6pm Mon-Fri.

Handles work-related problems.

Vocabulary

Although Portuguese can sound indecipherable even to Brazilians, speakers of other Romance languages are in better shape than they might think, as reading it is a lot easier. The Portuguese are excellent linguists. For decades millions have packed their bags to try their luck elsewhere; of those who return, most speak another language.

Pronunciation

Pronunciation follows some clear rules. The s always takes the sh sound at the end of words. Elsewhere, it becomes sshh only when followed by t or c. Watch the latter: Cascais is 'Kashkaish', whereas *piscina* is 'pisheena'. Another feature is the nh and lh consonants, which are similar to the Spanish ñ and ll. Thus Saldanha is 'Saldanya', and *bacalhau* is 'bakalyow'.

The c is soft before e and i, but hard elsewhere. Note also that m takes on a nasal tone at the end of words. Thus *sim*, for yes, sounds like the Spanish *sí*.

Vowels are tricky. Accents usually denote a stressed syllable, although the tilde (~) and the ^ also give the vowel a more elongated sound. The ão is unique to Portuguese. A nasal, truncated 'ow' is the best description. Thus *informação* is 'informasow', with a nasal yelp on the last syllable.

The e is silent at the end of the word, unless it has an accent. So *saudade* is 'sowdad', whereas *café* is 'kaffay'. Also:

ç – like the 's' in song
sh – like the sh in ship
j – like the s in treasure
g – is like j, except when it comes before an a, o or u when it is hard
q – is like k in English
x – is like the sh in Welsh
ei – like the ay in hay
ou – like the or in sorted

Useful phrases

Yes *Sim*
No *Não*
Maybe *Talvéz/Se calhar*
Hello *Olá*
Good day/evening/night *Bom dia/boa tarde/boa noite*
Goodbye *Adeus* (formal) *ciao* (informal)
See you later *Até logo*
How are you? *Como está?* (formal) *Como estás?* (informal) *Tudo bem?* (more informal)
I'm fine *Estou bem*
Thanks *Obrigado* (masc) *Obrigada* (fem)
You're welcome *De nada/Não tem de qué*
Please *Por favor/Se faz favor*
Excuse me *Com licença*
Sorry *Desculpe* (formal) *Desculpa* (informal)
That's/It's okay *Está bem/Não faz mal*
Today *Hoje*
Tomorrow *Amanhã*
I'd like *Queria*
Where is (a fixed thing) *Onde fica?*
Where is (a movable thing or person) *Onde está?*
Where is the toilet? *Onde fica a casa de banho?*
Men's *Homens/Senhores*
Women's *Mulheres/Senhoras*
There is/There are *Há*
There isn't/aren't *Não há*
Why *Porquê*
When *Quando*
Who is it? *Quem é?*
Very *Muito*
Near *Perto*
Far *Longe*
Big *Grande*
Hot *Quente*
Cold *Frio*
Small *Pequeno*
Now *Agora*
Later *Mais tarde*
Before *Antes*
With/Without *Com/Sem*
Is it cheap/expensive? *É barato/caro?*
How much is it/are they? *Quanto é/quanto são?*
Buy *Comprar*
Rent *Alugar*
Open *Aberto*
Closed *Fechado*
Entrance *Entrada*
Exit *Saida*
Good *Bom* (masc) *Boa* (fem)
Bad *Mau* (masc) *Má* (fem)
I like... *Gosto de...*
I don't like... *Não gosto de...*
I don't speak Portuguese *Não falo Português*
Do you speak English? *Fala inglês?* (formal) *Falas inglês?* (informal)
I don't understand *Não entendo*
Speak more slowly please *Fale mais devagar, por favor*
What is your name? *Como se chama?* (formal) *Como te chamas?* (informal)
My name is *Chamo-me*
I am English/American *Sou inglês/norte-americano* (masc) *Sou inglesa/norte-americana* (fem)
Train station *Estacão de comboios*
Bus station *Rodoviário*
Do you know the way to... *Sabe o caminho para…*
Left *Esquerda*
Right *Direita*
Straight on *Sempre em frente*
Bus stop *Paragem de autocarros*
Petrol *Gasolina*
Diesel *Gasóeo*
Ticket office *Bilheteira*
Single *Ida*
Return *Ida e volta*
I'd like to go to... *Queria ir á...*
One/two/three o'clock *Uma/duas/tres horas*
Do you have a single/double room for tonight? *Tem um quarto individuo/duplo para hoje?*
Bathroom *Casa de banho*
Bed *Cama*
Bath *Banheira*
Shower *Chuveiro/Ducha*
I feel ill *Sinto-me mal*
Doctor *Médico*
Pharmacy *Farmácia*
Sunday *domingo*
Monday *segunda-feira*
Tuesday *terça-feira*
Wednesday *quarta-feira*
Thursday *quinta-feira*
Friday *sexta-feira*
Saturday *sábado*
one *um/uma*
two *dois/duas*
three *três*
four *quatro*
five *cinco*
six *seis*
seven *sete*
eight *oito*
nine *nove*
ten *dez*

Index

Note: page numbers in **bold** indicate section(s) giving key information on a topic, *italics* indicate photos.

Accommodation index

Advertisers' Index

Please refer to the relevant sections for addresses/telephone numbers

Place of interest and/or entertainment	
Railway stations	
Tube stations	M
Parks	
Hospitals	
Steps	
Churches	✚
Area	CHIADO

Maps

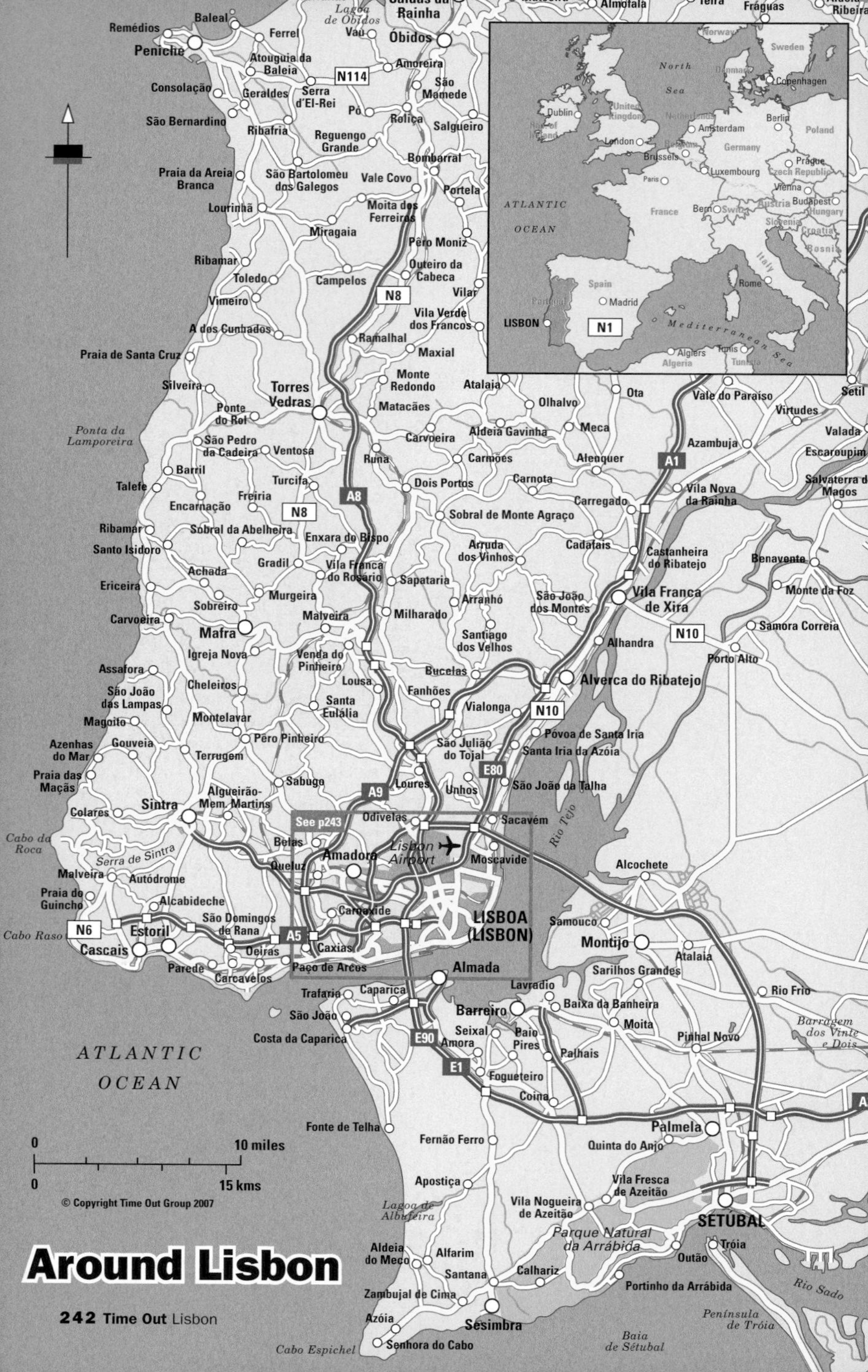

Around Lisbon

Greater Lisbon

Belém

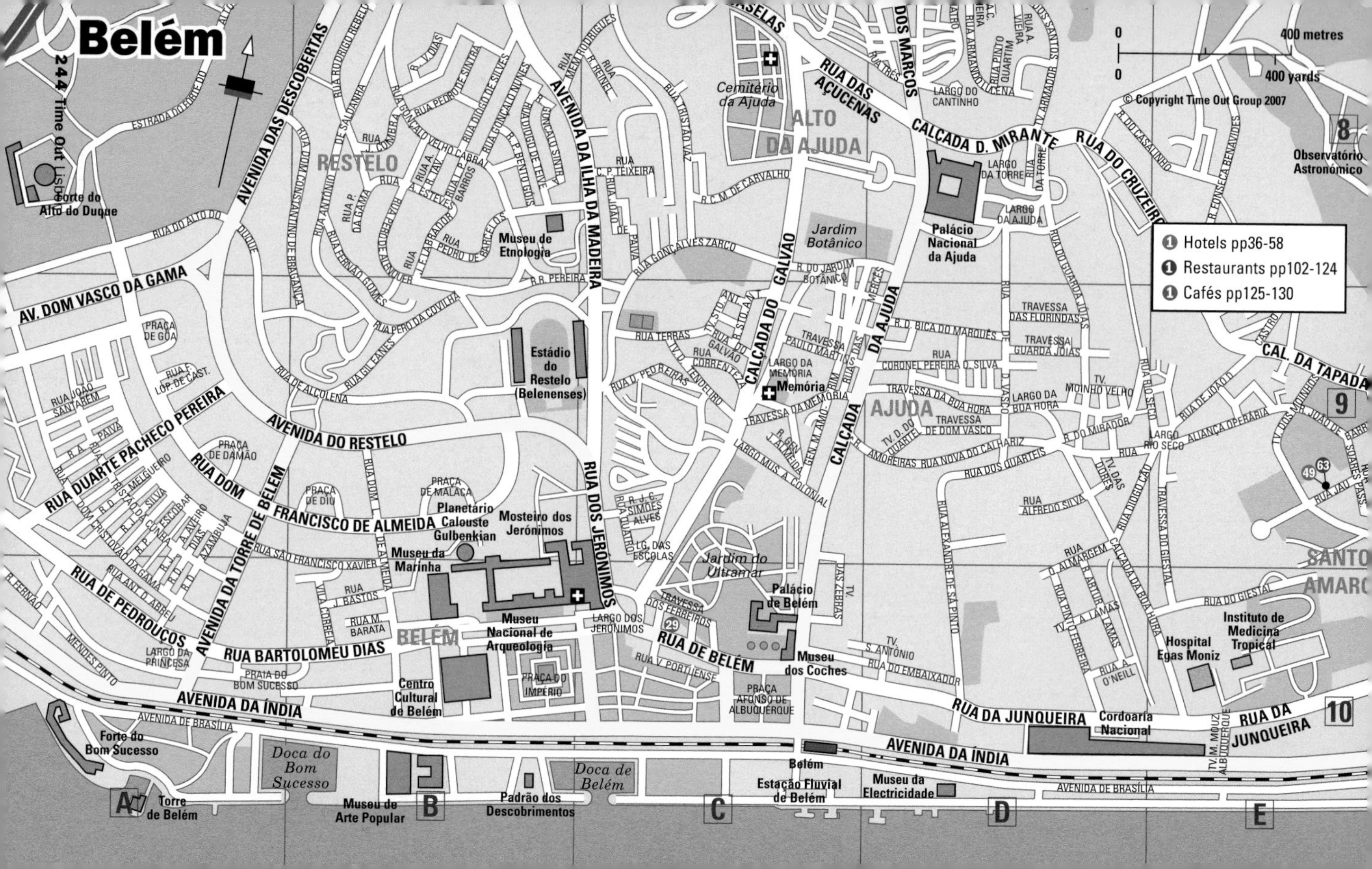

400 metres
400 yards
Hotels pp36-58
Restaurants pp102-124
Cafés pp125-130
Avenida das Descobertas
Avenida da Ilha da Madeira
Av. Dom Vasco da Gama
Avenida do Restelo
Rua Duarte Pacheco Pereira
Rua Dom Francisco de Almeida
Avenida da Torre de Belém
Rua de Pedrouços
Rua Bartolomeu Dias
Avenida da Índia
Avenida de Brasília
Rua dos Jerónimos
Rua de Belém
Rua da Junqueira
Calçada do Galvão
Calçada da Ajuda
Calçada D. Mirante
Rua do Cruzeiro
Rua das Açucenas
Cal. da Tapada
Restelo
Alto da Ajuda
Ajuda
Belém
Santo Amaro
Forte do Alto do Duque
Museu de Etnologia
Estádio do Restelo (Belenenses)
Cemitério da Ajuda
Jardim Botânico
Palácio Nacional da Ajuda
Observatório Astronómico
Memória
Planetário Calouste Gulbenkian
Mosteiro dos Jerónimos
Museu da Marinha
Museu Nacional de Arqueologia
Centro Cultural de Belém
Jardim do Ultramar
Palácio de Belém
Museu dos Coches
Praça Afonso de Albuquerque
Praça do Império
Hospital Egas Moniz
Instituto de Medicina Tropical
Cordoaria Nacional
Forte do Bom Sucesso
Torre de Belém
Doca do Bom Sucesso
Museu de Arte Popular
Padrão dos Descobrimentos
Doca de Belém
Belém
Estação Fluvial de Belém
Museu da Electricidade
A
B
C
D
E
8
9
10

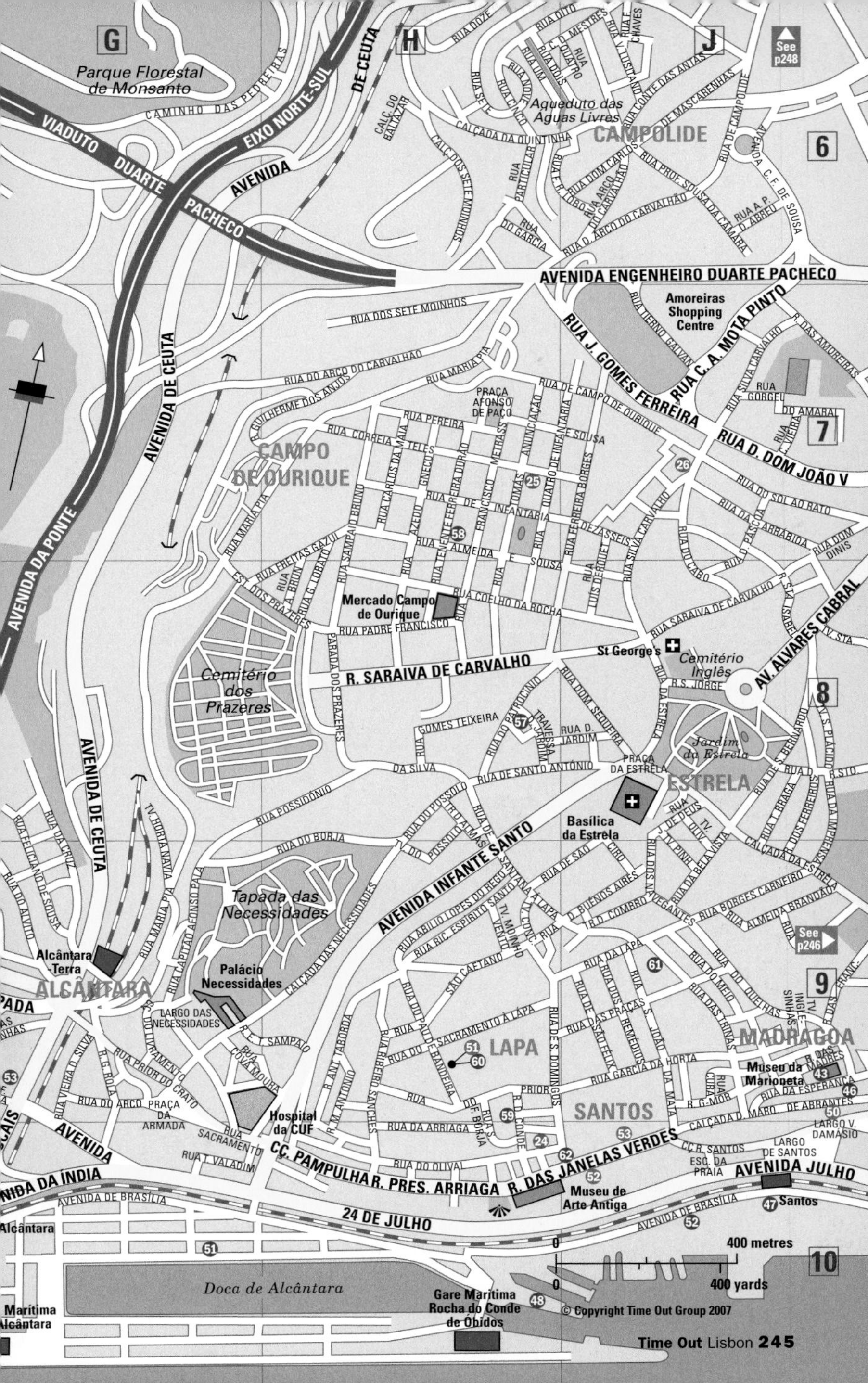

See p248
See p246

K
L
M
6
7
8
9
10
See p248
See p245
R. Marquês de Fronteira
Alameda Cardeal Cerejeira
Estufa Fria
Pavilhão Carlos Lopes
Parque Eduardo VII
Avenida Sidónio Pais
Av. António Augusto de Aguiar
Parque
Rua Castilho
Rua Rodrigo
Rua Artilharia Um
R. Joaquim António Aguiar
Praça Marquês de Pombal
Marquês de Pombal
Avenida Fontes Pereira de Melo
Avenida Duque de Loulé
Rua Conde de Redondo
Picoas
Praça José Fontana
Liceu de Camões
E
Estefânia
Hospital Dona Estefânia
Rua de Dona Estefânia
Rua Joaquim Bonifacio
Rua Pascoal de Melo
Avda. Casal Ribeiro
Largo Dona Estefânia
Rua Alexandre Braga
Rua de Gomes Freire
Amoreiras
Jardim das Amoreiras
Mãe de Água
Rua da Fonseca
Rua Braamcamp
Rua Castilho
Rua Alexandre Herculano
Rua Luciano Cordeiro
Avenida da Liberdade
Rato
Rua da Escola Politecnica
Rua do Salitre
Museu da História Natural
Jardim Botânico
Parque Mayer
Avenida
Hospital dos Capuchos
Largo do Mitelo
Largo do Mastro
Faculdade de Medicina
Torel
Campo de Santana
Rua da Palma
Largo S. Barbara
Largo C. Pombeiro
Av. Almirante Reis
Intendente
Rua de S. Bento
Praça de S. Bento
Assembleia Nacional
Praça do Principe Real
R. Dom Pedro V
R. S. Pedro Alcantara
Praça das Flores
Praça da Alegria
Largo Anunciada
Palácio Foz
Correios
Coliseu
Hospital de São José
Martim Moniz
Praça dos Restauradores
Restauradores
Teatro Nacional
São Roque
Estação do Rossio
Praça Dom Pedro IV (Rossio)
Rossio
S. Domingos
Praça da Figueira
Mouraria
Academia das Ciências
Largo D. Jesus
Santa Catarina
Bairro Alto
Convento do Carmo
Largo do Carmo
Rua Áurea (Rua do Ouro)
Rua Augusta
Rua da Prata
Rua dos Fanqueiros
Baixa
S. Cristovão
Castelo de São Jorge
Avenida de Dom Carlos I.
Museu da Farmácia
Bica
Praça Luís Camões
Lg. Chiado
Rua Garrett
Baixa-Chiado
Chiado
Rua do Alecrim
Museo das Comunicações
Museu do Chiado
Câmara Municipal de Lisboa
Sto. António
Sé
Teatro Romano
Casa dos Bicos
24 de Julho
Mercado da Ribeira
Praça Luís I
Cais do Sodré
Praça D. da Terceira
Correios
Praça do Comércio
Campo das Cebolas
Avenida da Ribeira das Naus
Estação Fluvial
Estação Fluvial Terreiro do Paço
Doca da Marinha

N
O
P
See p249
6
7
8
9
10
PENHA DE FRANÇA
SAPADORES
GRAÇA
ALFAMA
Arroios
Praça do Chile
Largo Penha França
Praça Paiva Couceiro
Rua Morais Soares
Avenida Mouzinho de Albuquerque
Av. Mouzinho de Albuquerque
Avenida Afonso III
Avenida General Roçadas
Avenida Almirante Reis
Rua Pascoal de Melo
Estrada de Chelas
Rua Gualdim Pais
Rua N. Barros
R. Madre de Deus
Cemitério do Alto de São João
Parada do Alto de São João
Praça S. da Costa
Calçada do Carrascal
Rua do Sol a Chelas
Museu Nac. do Azulejos
Madre de Deus
Praça N. Nações
Praça A. Sardinha
Rua dos Sapadores
Rua do Vale de S. António
Rua da Senhora da Glória
Rua Leite de Vasconcelos
Rua Washington
Rua Cruz S. Apolónia
Rua Barão Monte Pedral
Calçada da Cruz da Pedra
Museu de Água
See pp250-251
Largo da Graça
Graça
S. Vicente de Fora
Campo de Santa Clara
Santa Engrácia (Panteão Nacional)
Largo Sta. Marinha
Portas do Sol
Sto. Estevão
Museu de Artes Decorativas
S. Miguel
Largo Chafariz de Dentro
Rua dos Remédios
Rua do Paraíso
R. Caminhos de Ferro
R. Bica do Sapato
Santa Apolónia
Museu Militar
Avenida Infante Dom Henrique
Doca do Terreiro do Trigo
Rio Tejo
41
70
71
1 Hotels pp36-58
1 Restaurants pp102-124
1 Cafés pp125-130
0
600 metres
0
600 yards

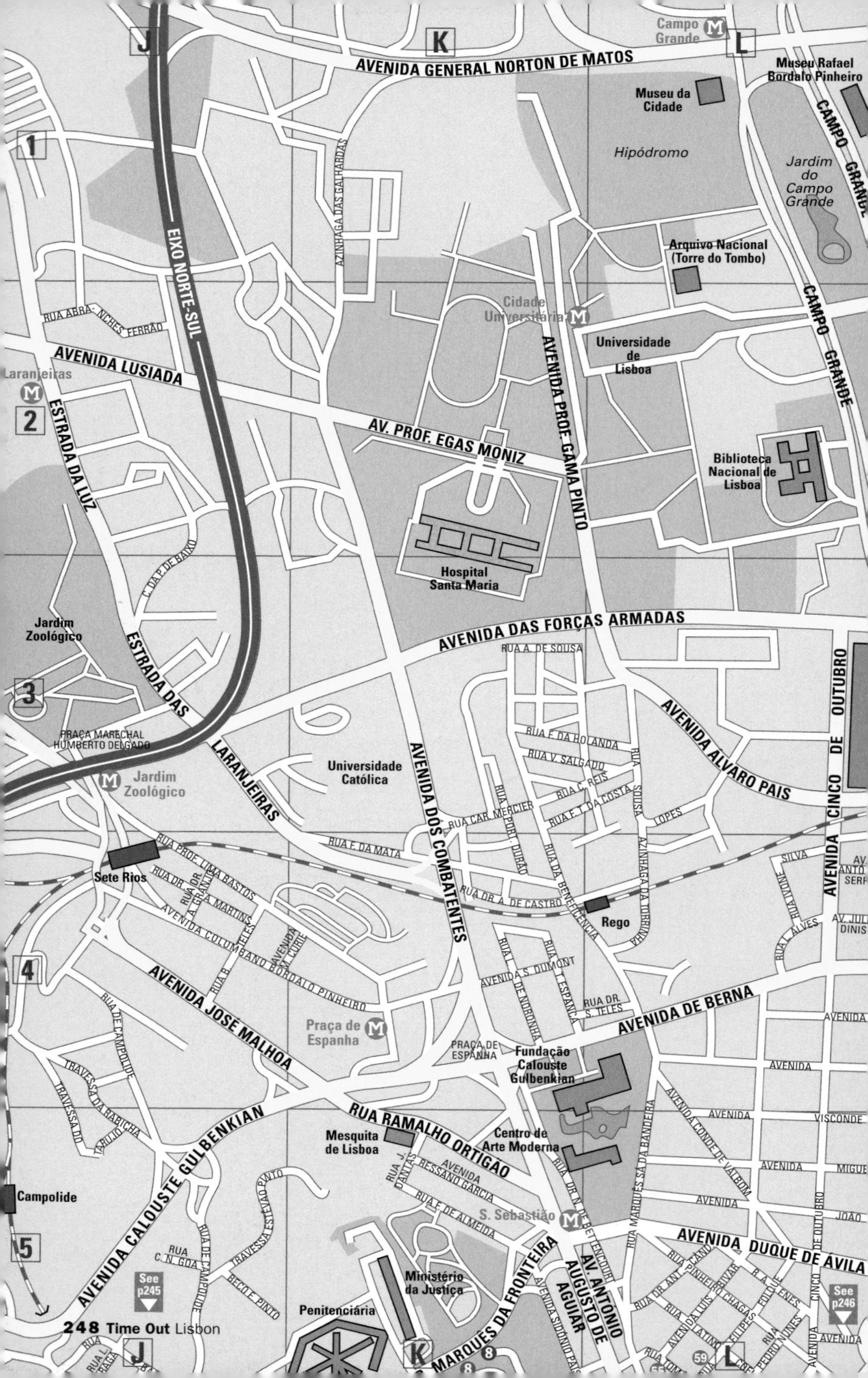
AVENIDA GENERAL NORTON DE MATOS
Campo Grande
Museu Rafael Bordalo Pinheiro
Museu da Cidade
Hipódromo
CAMPO GRANDE
Jardim do Campo Grande
EIXO NORTE-SUL
AZINHAGA DAS GALHARDAS
Arquivo Nacional (Torre do Tombo)
Cidade Universitária
Universidade de Lisboa
AVENIDA LUSIADA
Laranjeiras
ESTRADA DA LUZ
AV. PROF. EGAS MONIZ
AVENIDA PROF. GAMA PINTO
Biblioteca Nacional de Lisboa
Hospital Santa Maria
Jardim Zoológico
ESTRADA DAS LARANJEIRAS
AVENIDA DAS FORÇAS ARMADAS
AVENIDA ALVARO PAIS
AVENIDA CINCO DE OUTUBRO
PRAÇA MARECHAL HUMBERTO DELGADO
Universidade Católica
AVENIDA DOS COMBATENTES
Sete Rios
Rego
AVENIDA COLUMBANO BORDALO PINHEIRO
AVENIDA JOSE MALHOA
AVENIDA DE BERNA
Praça de Espanha
Fundação Calouste Gulbenkian
RUA RAMALHO ORTIGÃO
Mesquita de Lisboa
Centro de Arte Moderna
AVENIDA CALOUSTE GULBENKIAN
Campolide
S. Sebastião
AVENIDA DUQUE DE AVILA
Ministério da Justiça
Penitenciária
MARQUES DA FRONTEIRA
AV. ANTONIO AUGUSTO DE AGUIAR
See p245
See p246

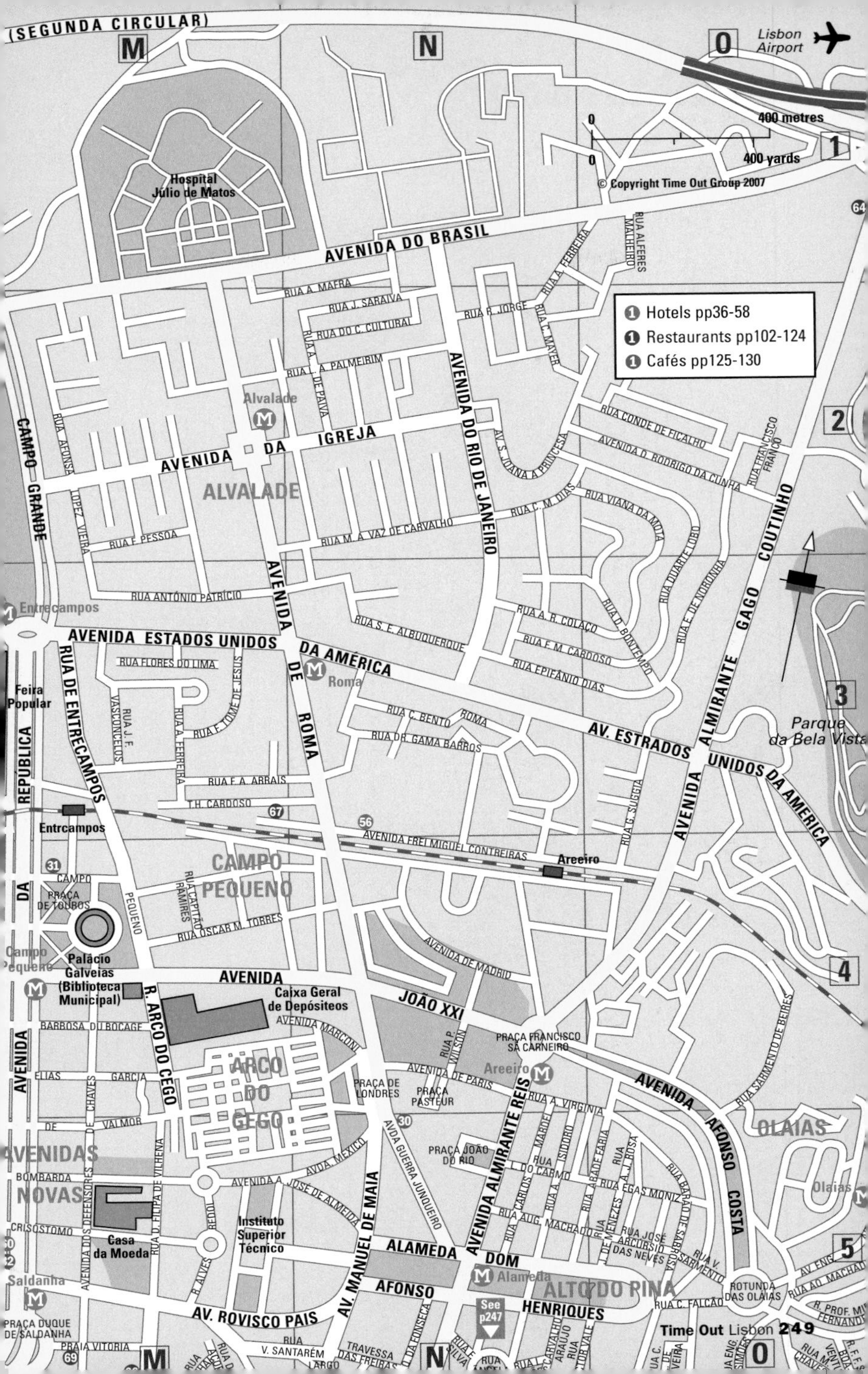
(SEGUNDA CIRCULAR)
M
N
O
Lisbon Airport
1
2
3
4
5
0
400 metres
0
400 yards
© Copyright Time Out Group 2007
Hospital Júlio de Matos
AVENIDA DO BRASIL
Hotels pp36-58
Restaurants pp102-124
Cafés pp125-130
Alvalade
AVENIDA DA IGREJA
ALVALADE
AVENIDA DO RIO DE JANEIRO
CAMPO GRANDE
Entrecampos
AVENIDA ESTADOS UNIDOS DA AMÉRICA
AVENIDA DE ROMA
Roma
AVENIDA ALMIRANTE GAGO COUTINHO
Parque da Bela Vista
AV. ESTRADOS UNIDOS DA AMERICA
Feira Popular
AVENIDA DA REPÚBLICA
RUA DE ENTRECAMPOS
Entrcampos
AVENIDA FREI MIGUEL CONTREIRAS
Areeiro
CAMPO PEQUENO
Praça de Touros
Campo Pequeno
Palácio Galveias (Biblioteca Municipal)
AVENIDA JOÃO XXI
Caixa Geral de Depósiteos
R. ARCO DO CEGO
ARCO DO CEGO
AVENIDA DE MADRID
PRAÇA FRANCISCO SÁ CARNEIRO
AVENIDA AFONSO COSTA
OLAIAS
AVENIDAS NOVAS
Casa da Moeda
Instituto Superior Técnico
AV. MANUEL DE MAIA
AVENIDA ALMIRANTE REIS
ALAMEDA DOM AFONSO HENRIQUES
Alameda
ALTO DO PINA
ROTUNDA DAS OLAIAS
Olaias
Saldanha
PRAÇA DUQUE DE SALDANHA
AV. ROVISCO PAIS
See p247

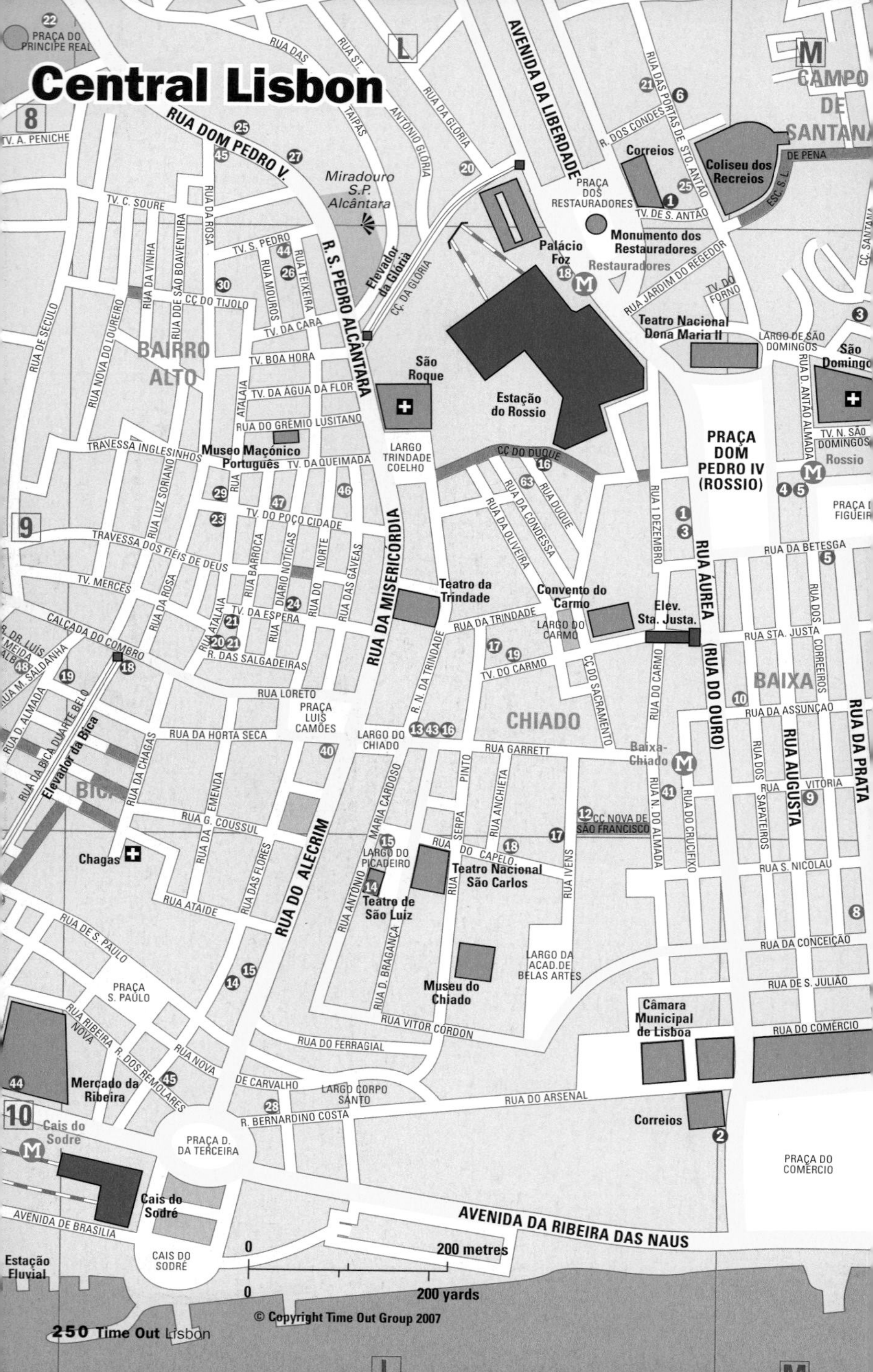
Central Lisbon
8
9
10
L
M
PRAÇA DO PRINCIPE REAL
TV. A. PENICHE
RUA DOM PEDRO V.
RUA DAS TAIPAS
RUA ST. ANTÓNIO GLÓRIA
RUA DA GLÓRIA
AVENIDA DA LIBERDADE
RUA DAS PORTAS DE STO. ANTÃO
R. DOS CONDES
Correios
Coliseu dos Recreios
CAMPO DE SANTANA
DE PENA
ESC. S. L.
CC. SANTANA
Miradouro S.P. Alcântara
PRAÇA DOS RESTAURADORES
TV. DE S. ANTÃO
Monumento dos Restauradores
Palácio Foz
Restauradores
RUA JARDIM DO REGEDOR
TV. DO FORNO
Teatro Nacional Dona Maria II
LARGO DE SÃO DOMINGOS
São Domingos
TV. C. SOURE
RUA DA ROSA
TV. S. PEDRO
RUA DA VINHA
RUA DDE SÃO BOAVENTURA
RUA MOUROS
RUA TEIXEIRA
R. S. PEDRO ALCÂNTARA
Elevador da Glória
CÇ. DA GLÓRIA
CÇ DO TIJOLO
RUA DE SÉCULO
RUA NOVA DO LOUREIRO
BAIRRO ALTO
TV. DA CARA
TV. BOA HORA
ATALAIA
TV. DA ÁGUA DA FLOR
RUA DO GRÉMIO LUSITANO
São Roque
Estação do Rossio
PRAÇA DOM PEDRO IV (ROSSIO)
RUA D. ANTÃO ALMADA
TV. N. SÃO DOMINGOS
Rossio
TRAVESSA INGLESINHOS
Museo Maçónico Português
TV. DA QUEIMADA
LARGO TRINDADE COELHO
CÇ DO DUQUE
RUA DA CONDESSA
RUA DUQUE
RUA DA OLIVEIRA
RUA 1 DEZEMBRO
PRAÇA DA FIGUEIRA
RUA LUZ SORIANO
TV. DO POÇO CIDADE
TRAVESSA DOS FIÉIS DE DEUS
RUA BARROCA
DIARIO NOTICIAS
RUA DO NORTE
RUA DAS GÁVEAS
RUA DA MISERICÓRDIA
RUA DA BETESGA
RUA ÁUREA (RUA DO OURO)
TV. MERCÊS
RUA DA ROSA
TV. DA ESPERA
Teatro da Trindade
Convento do Carmo
Elev. Sta. Justa
RUA DOS CORREEIROS
CALÇADA DO COMBRO
RUA ATALAIA
R. DAS SALGADEIRAS
RUA DA TRINDADE
LARGO DO CARMO
RUA STA. JUSTA
R. DR. LUÍS ALMEIDA ALBUQUERQUE
RUA M. SALDANHA
TV. DO CARMO
RUA LORETO
R. N. DA TRINDADE
CÇ DO SACRAMENTO
RUA DO CARMO
BAIXA
RUA DA ASSUNÇÃO
RUA DA PRATA
RUA D. ALMADA
RUA DA BICA DUARTE BELO
Elevador da Bica
BICA
PRAÇA LUIS CAMÕES
CHIADO
RUA DA HORTA SECA
LARGO DO CHIADO
RUA GARRETT
Baixa-Chiado
RUA DA CHAGAS
RUA DA EMENDA
MARIA CARDOSO
PINTO
RUA SERPA
RUA ANCHIETA
RUA N. DO ALMADA
RUA DO CRUCIFIXO
RUA DOS SAPATEIROS
RUA AUGUSTA
RUA VITÓRIA
RUA G. COUSSUL
CÇ NOVA DE SÃO FRANCISCO
Chagas
LARGO DO PICADEIRO
RUA DO CAPELO
Teatro Nacional São Carlos
RUA IVENS
RUA S. NICOLAU
RUA DAS FLORES
RUA DO ALECRIM
RUA ANTONIO
Teatro de São Luiz
RUA ATAIDE
RUA DE S. PAULO
RUA D. BRAGANÇA
LARGO DA ACAD. DE BELAS ARTES
Museu do Chiado
RUA DA CONCEIÇÃO
RUA DE S. JULIÃO
PRAÇA S. PAULO
RUA RIBEIRA NOVA
R. DOS REMOLARES
RUA NOVA DE CARVALHO
RUA VITOR CORDON
RUA DO FERRAGIAL
Câmara Municipal de Lisboa
RUA DO COMÉRCIO
Mercado da Ribeira
LARGO CORPO SANTO
RUA DO ARSENAL
R. BERNARDINO COSTA
Correios
Cais do Sodré
PRAÇA D. DA TERCEIRA
PRAÇA DO COMÉRCIO
Cais do Sodré
AVENIDA DE BRASILIA
AVENIDA DA RIBEIRA DAS NAUS
CAIS DO SODRÉ
Estação Fluvial
0
200 metres
0
200 yards
© Copyright Time Out Group 2007

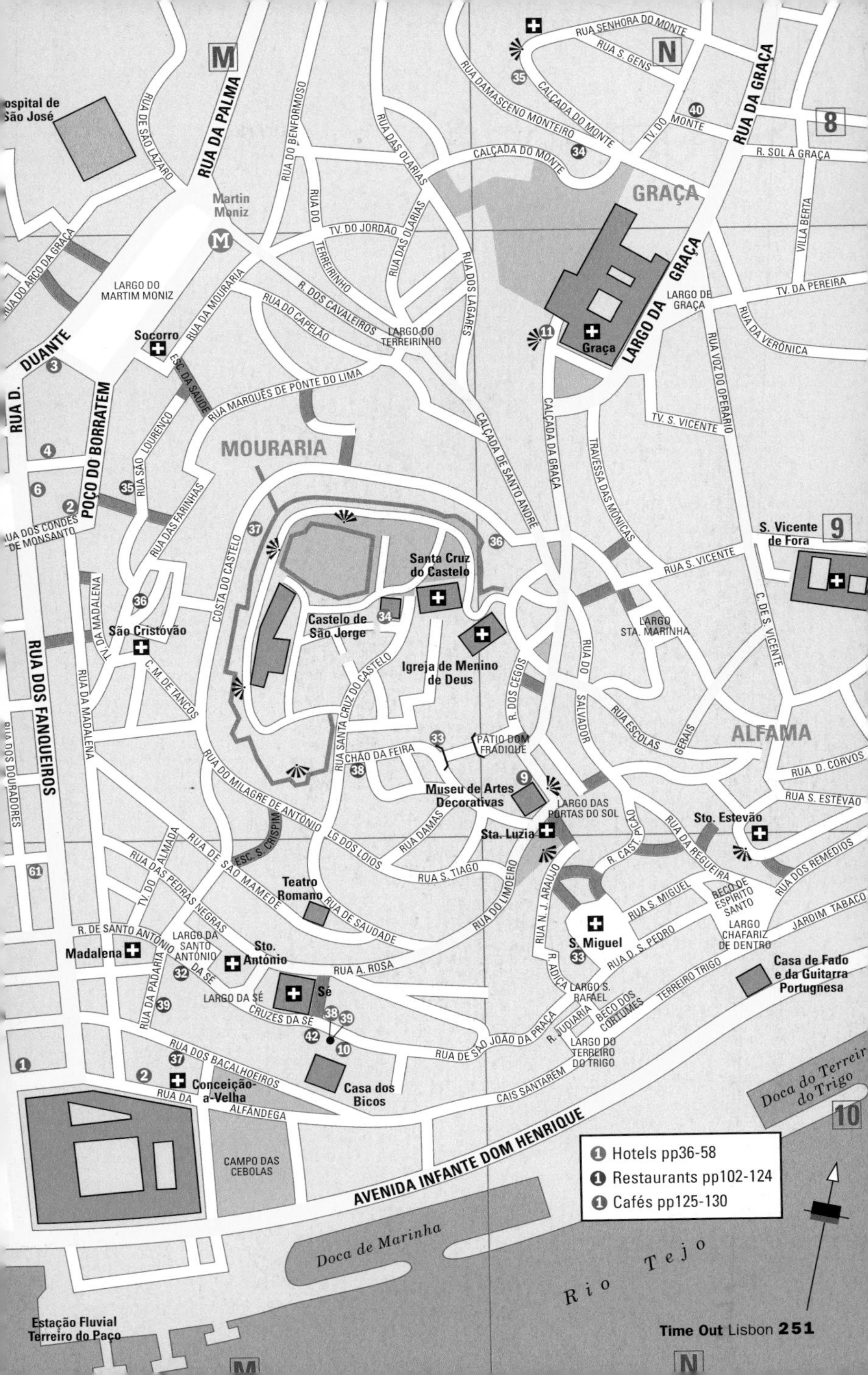

M
N
8
9
10
ospital de
São José
RUA DE SÃO LÁZARO
RUA DA PALMA
RUA DO BENFORMOSO
RUA DAS OLARIAS
RUA DO
TERREIRINHO
RUA SENHORA DO MONTE
RUA S. GENS
RUA DAMASCENO MONTEIRO
CALÇADA DO MONTE
TV. DO MONTE
RUA DA GRAÇA
R. SOL À GRAÇA
CALÇADA DO MONTE
GRAÇA
Martin
Moniz
TV. DO JORDÃO
RUA DOS LAGARES
VILLA BERTA
RUA DO ARCO DA GRAÇA
LARGO DO
MARTIM MONIZ
RUA DA MOURARIA
R. DOS CAVALEIROS
RUA DO CAPELÃO
LARGO DO
TERREIRINHO
LARGO DA GRAÇA
LARGO DE
GRAÇA
TV. DA PEREIRA
RUA DA VERÓNICA
Graça
Socorro
DUANTE
RUA D.
ESC. DA SAÚDE
RUA MARQUÊS DE PONTE DO LIMA
POÇO DO BORRATEM
RUA VOZ DO OPERÁRIO
TV. S. VICENTE
MOURARIA
CALÇADA DE SANTO ANDRÉ
CALÇADA DA GRAÇA
TRAVESSA DAS MONICAS
RUA SÃO LOURENÇO
RUA DAS FARINHAS
RUA DOS CONDES
DE MONSANTO
COSTA DO CASTELO
S. Vicente
de Fora
Santa Cruz
do Castelo
RUA S. VICENTE
Castelo de
São Jorge
São Cristóvão
TV. DA MADALENA
RUA DOS FANQUEIROS
RUA DOS DOURADORES
C. M. DE TANCOS
RUA DA MADALENA
Igreja de Menino
de Deus
LARGO
STA. MARINHA
RUA DO
SALVADOR
C. DE S. VICENTE
R. DOS CEGOS
RUA ESCOLAS
GERAIS
ALFAMA
PÁTIO DOM
FRADIQUE
CHÃO DA FEIRA
RUA SANTA CRUZ DO CASTELO
RUA DO MILAGRE DE ANTÓNIO
Museu de Artes
Decorativas
LARGO DAS
PORTAS DO SOL
RUA D. CORVOS
RUA S. ESTEVÃO
Sto. Estevão
ESC. S. CRISPIM
LG DOS LOIOS
RUA DAMAS
Sta. Luzia
RUA DA REGUEIRA
R. CAST. PICÃO
RUA DOS REMÉDIOS
RUA DE SÃO MAMEDE
RUA DAS PEDRAS NEGRAS
TV. DO ALMADA
RUA S. TIAGO
RUA DO LIMOEIRO
Teatro
Romano
RUA DE SAUDADE
RUA N. J. ARAÚJO
RUA S. MIGUEL
BECO DE
ESPÍRITO
SANTO
R. DE SANTO ANTÓNIO
LARGO DA
SANTO
ANTÓNIO
DA SÉ
Sto.
António
Madalena
S. Miguel
LARGO
CHAFARIZ
DE DENTRO
JARDIM TABACO
RUA D. S. PEDRO
RUA A. ROSA
Casa de Fado
e da Guitarra
Portugnesa
RUA DA PADARIA
Sé
LARGO DA SÉ
R. ADIÇA
LARGO S.
RAFAEL
TERREIRO TRIGO
CRUZES DA SÉ
BECO DOS
CORTUMES
R. JUDIARIA
RUA DE SÃO JOÃO DA PRAÇA
LARGO DO
TERREIRO
DO TRIGO
RUA DOS BACALHOEIROS
Conceição-
a-Velha
Casa dos
Bicos
RUA DA
ALFÂNDEGA
CAIS SANTARÉM
Doca do Terreiro
do Trigo
AVENIDA INFANTE DOM HENRIQUE
CAMPO DAS
CEBOLAS
1 Hotels pp36-58
1 Restaurants pp102-124
1 Cafés pp125-130
Doca de Marinha
Rio Tejo
Estação Fluvial
Terreiro do Paço

Street Index

Metro System

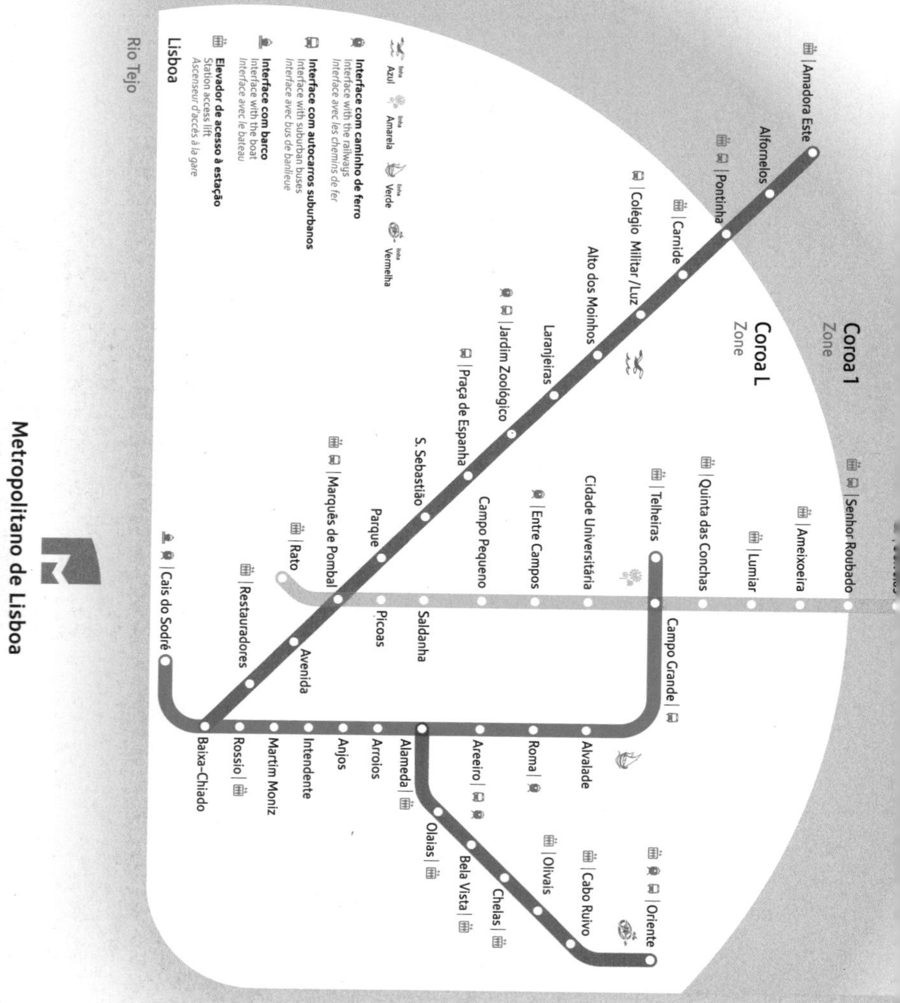

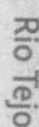

Metropolitano de Lisboa

Coroa 1
Zone

Coroa L
Zone

Amadora Este
Alfornelos
Pontinha
Carnide
Colégio Militar /Luz
Alto dos Moinhos
Laranjeiras
Jardim Zoológico
Praça de Espanha
S. Sebastião
Parque
Marquês de Pombal
Avenida
Restauradores
Baixa-Chiado

Senhor Roubado
Ameixoeira
Lumiar
Quinta das Conchas
Telheiras
Campo Grande
Cidade Universitária
Entre Campos
Campo Pequeno
Saldanha
Picoas
Rato

Alvalade
Roma
Areeiro
Alameda
Arroios
Anjos
Intendente
Martim Moniz
Rossio
Cais do Sodré

Oriente
Cabo Ruivo
Olivais
Chelas
Bela Vista
Olaias

Linha Azul · Linha Amarela · Linha Verde · Linha Vermelha

Interface com caminho de ferro
Interface with the railways
Interface avec les chemins de fer

Interface com autocarros suburbanos
Interface with suburban buses
Interface avec bus de banlieue

Interface com barco
Interface with the boat
Interface avec le bateau

Elevador de acesso à estação
Station access lift
Ascenseur d'accès à la gare

Lisboa

Rio Tejo